Second Edition

The Wing-T from A to Z

Volume 1: The Base Plan

Dennis Creehan

ISBN: 1-58518-921-9
Library of Congress Control Number: 2004115571
Cover design: Jeanne Hamilton
Book layout: Jeanne Hamilton
Front cover photo: University of South Dakota Sports Information Department

Coaches Choice
P.O. Box 1828
Monterey, CA 93942
www.coacheschoice.com

Dedication

I would like to dedicate this book to everyone in my family. They have all been very patient and understanding over the years as we have moved all around the country so that I could pursue my dream of coaching football.

To my loving wife, Linda, who is the best dance teacher in the country and has given up four different successful dance studios as we have moved. To my sons, Kevin and Casey, who attended four different schools while I chased my coaching dream. To Kevin, the older of my two sons, who is so intelligent that he has decided to use his brain power in the world of industrial engineering rather than in the arena of coaching – even though he could be a great coach, as evidenced by the American Legion state baseball championship his team won in his first and only coaching opportunity. To my younger son, Casey, who actually wants to go into the field of coaching, and is just hardheaded enough to be a great coach.

Finally, I would also like to dedicate this book to my mother and late father, Peggy and Jerry Creehan, who have been big supporters of mine, no matter where I have coached, and to my brothers and sisters, Jerry Jr., Rick, Karen, Kathy, and Kenny. Rick and Kenny have already been quite successful as baseball coaches.

Acknowledgments

Many great coaches have touched my life, and I would like to thank all of them for their leadership and guidance. My high school coaches, Dan Galbraith and Joe Nicoletti, who instilled in me the desire to play the game and taught me the fundamentals at Bethel Park (PA) High School. My college head coach, Bill McDonald, who turned Edinboro University of Pennsylvania from a 40-year loser into a champion. My college position coaches, Sam Ruvolo, Jack Hyland, and Bill Straub, who helped me to achieve more personal success than I ever thought possible for myself.

Upon graduation from college, I had no idea that I would ever coach, but Jerry Mancini brought me into the profession at Keystone Oaks (PA) High School. Johnny Majors and Jackie Sherrill gave me my first taste of college football as a graduate assistant at the University of Pittsburgh. Joe Gasparella and Chuck Klausing gave me my first real college coaching position at Carnegie-Mellon University. My first full-time position in college football came from Bill McDonald, my college coach at Edinboro. Three years later, I got a lucky break and succeeded Bill when he retired. During my 12 years as a head coach, I was very fortunate to have many great assistant coaches who have gone on to become college or pro head coaches themselves: John D'Ottavio, Utah Pioneers of the PSFL; Gerry Gallagher, St. Francis (PA) and William Patterson (NJ); Budgie Hamilton, San Francisco State; Tom Herman, Gannon University (PA); Mike Kelly, Valdosta State University; Malen Luke, Defiance (OH) and Clarion University (PA); Tom Menage, Westmar University (IA); Dave Lyon, Thiel College (PA); Ron Rankin, University of South Dakota; and Blair Hrovat, Allegheny College in Pennsylvania.

Finally, I would like to thank the coaches who taught me the wing-T offense: Ted Kempski of the University of Delaware and, most of all, John D'Ottavio, who is out of coaching, but who is, in my opinion, the most knowledgeable wing-T coach I have ever met.

Contents

Preface

This two-volume set of books on *The Wing-T from A to Z* was written in order to provide coaches and players at all competitive levels with a useful tool that can enable them to better understand the intricacies of the wing-T offense. In this comprehensive overview of one of the game's most popular offensive schemes, the fundamentals and nuances of the wing-T offense are presented in great detail.

The first volume in the set provides an excellent guide to understanding and developing a sound *base plan* for the wing-T offense. This volume features chapters on philosophy and organization, goal line attack, and movements (20 series, 30 series, 60 series, and 80 series).

The second volume in the set explains how to install and implement this innovative offensive package. The responsibilities and techniques essential to each offensive player position are identified and reviewed in a step-by step manner. This volume also includes detailed chapters on establishing an efficient and effective plan for practicing the wing-T and developing a successful offensive game-day plan.

Hopefully, the insights and the information presented in these books will also enhance the reader's sense of appreciation for the wing-T. In my opinion, the more that an individual knows about this offensive scheme, the greater the level of appreciation. I can only hope that every coach and player who reads these books will enjoy them as much as I enjoyed writing them.

— Dennis Creehan

1

Philosophy and Organization

Philosophy

This chapter is designed to introduce the reader to my philosophy on the wing-T: what my view of the offense is and how this offense is organized. It provides you with a thorough understanding of how our plays are called and what our communication system is, including our cadences, formations, series, and hole numbers, as well as all the things you need to understand as you start running your offense.

Many people ask me questions at clinics. They tell me, "We run wing-T." Then, when I watch their film, I see an I formation, four wideouts, pro, or all of those things. Only once in a while, do I see a wing formation, a sweep, or a trap play. In reality, the wing-T is much more than a formation and much more than one play or one series of plays.

The wing-T is an entire system of offense. When I was a player in college, the "Houston veer," or the "splitback veer," was a huge offense. The reason so many coaches liked it was that it had answers for the defense. If the defense did this, then you did that! You took advantage of defensive reactions and put defensive players in "assignment conflicts." The wing-T does exactly that and more. It creates flanking angles, where you can block people at angles. In these circumstances, you do not necessarily have to have the biggest, strongest guys in the world to block defenders and move the ball. Deception exists in this offense. Even if you don't have dominating personnel, you can still move the ball. You can score points, and you can have a lot of fun running this offense, as long as you run the system so that you have packages of plays that can take advantage of defensive reactions.

Assignment Conflict

The term "defensive conflict," or "assignment conflict," is really important. When you set up your game plan, you should look at the defenders and their responsibilities in the opponent's defense, and attempt to put each defender in an assignment conflict. In other words, regardless of the reaction by the defender, you will have a play that takes advantage of that reaction. Each reaction offers you a new play, and the entire package accounts for every defensive reaction possible.

For example, if you line up in a basic wing formation (Diagram 1.1) and run a play at the third defender to the tight end wingback-side, then, in this case, the defense is in a traditional 50 alignment. As a result, the third defender playside is the defensive end. Your goal should be to find the third defender and put him in an assignment conflict. You should draw an imaginary line through the attack-side A gap, since the play is going in that direction. The right A gap, or the right center-guard gap, would be the attack-side A gap. The defenders should be numbered from inside out. The first defender is #1, then #2, then #3. The defender who has force versus the run, pitch versus the option, and also has the flat coverage is #4. The defender who is covering deep is #5. That numbering system for the defense should be used to teach your players each play. On the backside, since the system does not employ an "O", you have #1, #2, #3, #4, and #5, all on the backside.

You might motivate your game plan by deciding to put #3 in an assignment conflict. You will then block the tight end down and observe what the defensive end, the outside linebacker, or the #3 defender's reaction is. If he is a man who seals and tries to close the off-tackle area, you will then know that you would like to continue outside of him. Therefore, if he seals, you will either block down on him with the wing, log him with a guard, or log him with a tackle, depending on your scheme and your game plan. In other words, you will do anything you can to take advantage of the fact that he has sealed inside.

At this point, the point of attack moves outside to the fourth defender. How are you going to attack the fourth defender? Basically, you should run a play right at him and see how he reacts. If you run a play directly at him and find that he is extremely aggressive coming up to force the run, then you know that the play-action pass behind him should be a good call. If he is soft and is playing for pass, you could continue to run the ball at him.

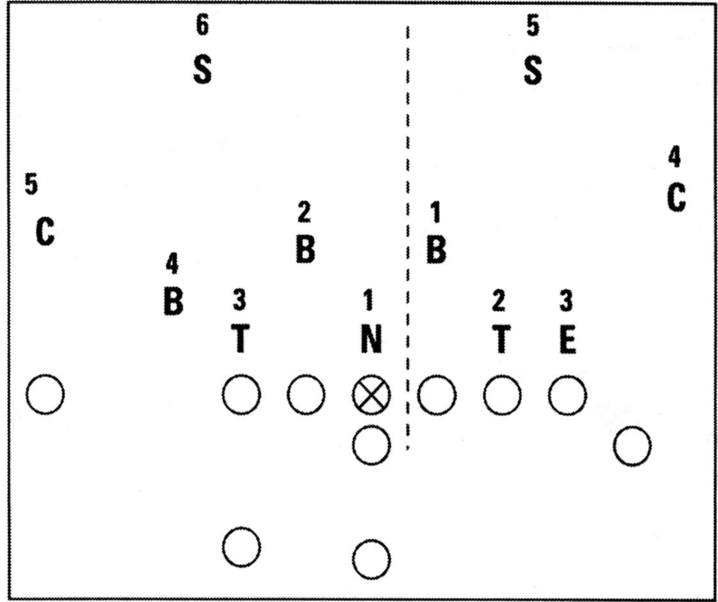

Diagram 1.1

The #3 defender could be an upfield penetrator, or he could work out into the wingback's block and not allow the wingback to block down on him. In either of those cases, since he is not sealing, you can run off tackle. You then put the second defender in a conflict by doing the same thing. You should block the tackle down to the inside linebacker (#1) and see what the second man's reaction is. If he seals, you know that you need to run outside of him, making #3's reaction the key. If #3 penetrates, you are going to stay off tackle, because #2 sealed, thus creating a nice off-tackle lane to run through. If the second defender seals, and the third defender also seals, you know to go outside and attack #4. On the other hand, if the second defender penetrates upfield as you block down with the tackle, you need to use your internal running game inside #2.

Just as the "splitback veer" created conflicts in the 1970's, the wing-T currently provides coaches with those same assignment conflicts. As such, the wing-T is a smart way to attack a defense. Since a defensive coach may change up reactions, an offensive coach, in order to be successful, needs to call a play that has a chance to work. If you watch the defensive reactions, and you have an entire package of plays that attack the second, third, and fourth defenders, you are going to have a chance to take advantage of each of their reactions by running the complementary play.

By the same token, if your offensive line can get at least stalemates on the line of scrimmage, you can move the football, and you can score points. The wing-T is an offense that can move the ball without the benefit of dominant linemen, but if you have the linemen to dominate, you are going to do even better. Most coaches firmly believe that the basic formula for winning involves three factors, beginning with the ability to run the ball and stop the run. Next, you need a sound kicking game. Finally, you must do a good job in the turnover department. If you can do those things successfully, you are going to win a lot of football games.

For the reasons detailed in this chapter, you should look at the offense as a "system." The wing-T offense offers innumerable benefits, particularly its ability to create assignment conflicts for each of the defenders. Furthermore, a coach does not have to be some kind of football genius to call the plays. The plays work over and over again, year in and year out.

As a wing-T coach, your offensive philosophy should adhere to at least two key elements. First, if you are going to put in a play, then have the necessary companion plays ready to go with it. Second, you should be able to run each of those plays both strong and weak.

It is necessary that you do not get caught up running just to the tight end and wing. In that regard, you may decide that your offense should be more split-end oriented than it is tight-end oriented, because people see the tight end and wing and want to overload that side defensively. In all formations, you need to be able to run your offense both strongside and weakside, regardless of what formation you decide to use. In reality, a number of great coaches exist who have a lot of great philosophies. In terms of the wing-T, however, the system and the systematic method it uses for play calling, as well as its run-pass balance and formation integrity, that are detailed in this book have proven to be very effective.

Organization

A three-digit call system can be used to organize the offense. Each of the three digits in the call system gives the *formation*, the series (meaning the backfield series), and the *hole numbering* or point of attack. A complete play call is contained in the three-digit call, plus modifying words or phrases.

In addition to explaining how play calls are made, subsequent sections in this chapter discuss how to modify formations, how to modify the spread of the ends, and how you can shift formations and change them up to improve blocking or flanking angles, in order to give the offense a chance to outnumber the defense, or to take advantage of coverage situations. Keep in mind that while shifting may not win you a game, it certainly can help you in terms of making the defense play more basic, or at least give your team a numbers advantage and a chance to attack the defense's weakness. For instance, if you shift your tight end, will their best defensive end line up on your tight end, or will he stay to one side, while you shift the tight end and attack a defensive end who is not as good? As such, this chapter also addresses the types of motion that you can utilize.

Subsequent sections in this book also go over the numbering of the defense again, using more defenses than simply the one shown earlier. It is extremely important that you understand exactly how those defenders are numbered and what you should be looking for when you try to set up assignment conflicts. I will review our huddle, our cadence, our offensive line calls, and how we term our option blocking. As a rule, this information should be in the beginning of your playbook and should explain exactly how you organize and teach your offense.

Three-Digit Call System

Diagram 1.2 illustrates a sample 121 play call. It shows 100 formation, 20 series, and the point of attack (or the hole number) is wide to the right, which is your 1 hole. The 121 call, therefore, communicates the three necessary elements of a play call: the formation, the series, and the point of attack. The first digit represents the formation. In this package, the 100 formation places the tight end-wing combination to the right, the split end to the left, and the backs offset away from the tight end-wing. The second digit is the series, which is the backfield action. The 20 series is shown with the buck action. Buck action has the fullback driving for the backside foot of the center. The halfback crosses over and runs through the backfield, through the fullback's heels. The quarterback can fake a sweep to the halfback, can give the ball to the fullback, or can come out and attack the flank on a play-action bootleg, which is called waggle. If you are running the sweep, the left halfback is the ballcarrier to the right flank, or 1 hole. If you take these three concepts together and say, "100 formation, 20 series, and the 1 hole," you are basically adding these three numbers together to get 121. You are adding the 100 formation, the 20 series, and the 1 hole. It's simple math, and 121 is the resulting play.

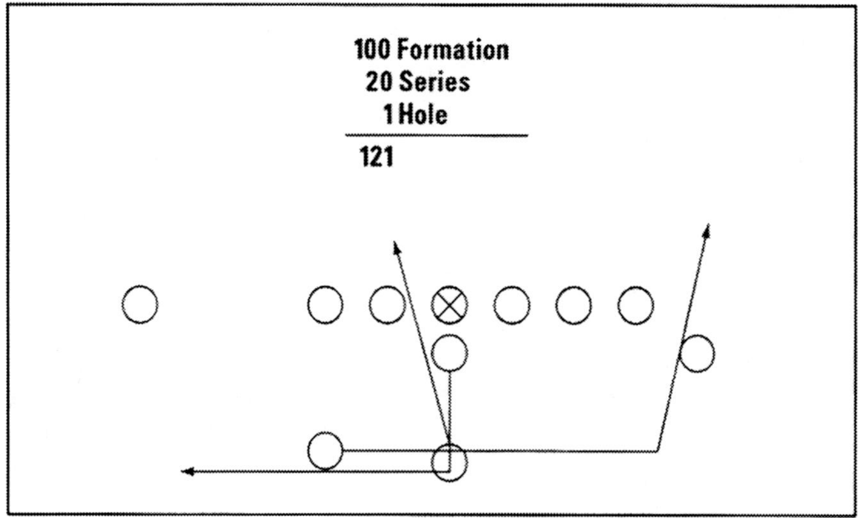

Diagram 1.2

All of your plays can be called that way. In the three-digit call system, the first number is the formation. If you say, "100," then that is your wing right formation. You can put a prefix in front of the 100 formation. A prefix will modify (alter or change) the formation. If you call, "Split 121," the word split brings your split end down to a position where he is four to six yards from the offensive tackle. In other words, he is in a nasty split. That prefix, split, now has modified the formation slightly. When you say, "Split 121," you have the same play from a modified formation. If you add a suffix on the end of the play after the final digit, the suffix will alter the blocking for the play, as in the example, "Split 121 tackles." Tackles is a call that means the guard and the tackle will exchange assignments. On 121, the tackle would then pull and kick out the force man and the guard would block #1.

The offense is communicated in this way. You call a formation, a series, and a point of attack. Any word before the formation can modify that formation; any word after the point of attack can modify blocking or pass patterns. You can modify whatever you want to be changed in the plays—most of the time, the blocking, but many times, the pass patterns as well. For instance, if you called, "Split 121 waggle out," you are modifying a pass pattern as opposed to modifying blocking. Suffixes will modify the play by either changing the blocking or the pass patterns.

Hole Numbering

Diagram 1.3 illustrates your hole numbering, or what many people call the points of attack. Notice that they also relate to your formations, since the wingback is in 100 formation and is also in the 1 hole. If you look at this diagram, you see your center, your two guards, your two tackles, and your two ends (if both ends were tight). The holes are numbered from your right to your left, and formation numbers relate to the hole numbers. This system was learned from other coaches, and it is easier to communicate with those coaches if you use the same terminology they use. It really does not matter what hole numbers you use. Many people use 2, 4, 6, 8; some people go 8, 6, 4, 2; some use odd on the right, even on the left; some use even on the right, odd on the left. It doesn't make any difference, as long as your players understand the concept that three-digit calls translate as formations-series-holes. By numbering the same way as others who run the same offense do and using the same numbering system, you are able to communicate with other coaches. As a result, everyone talks the same language. It is a lot easier to learn new ideas when you don't have to bridge the terminology gap all the time. The 1 hole corresponds with 100 formation; 100 formation is wing-T to the right, just as the 1 hole is to the right. The 9 hole is to the left, and 900, which is opposite of 100, would be your wing left formation. In this system, the hole numbers also correspond to the formation numbers.

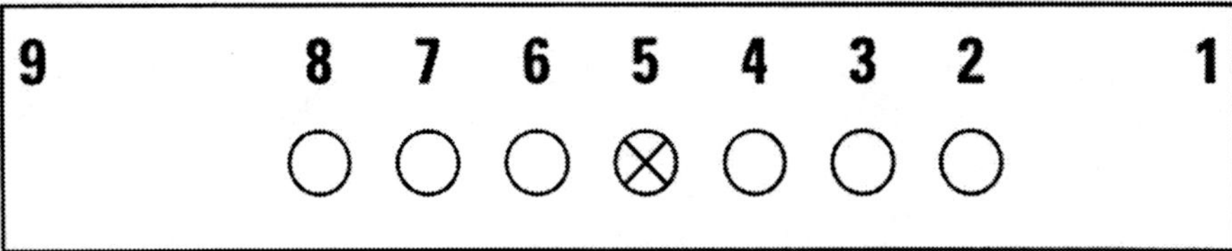

Diagram 1.3

Another helpful concept built into this system is that when you call a 2 hole play, you attack the 2 hole, and your tight end is the lead blocker with the play call at his hole or over him. He establishes the hole by blocking down. Additionally, if the tight end blocks down, his assignment is to block down on a 2 hole play, and if nobody is over the 3 man (tackle), then the play moves in one hole shorter. Next, the tackle would establish the hole by blocking down, and the hole is one hole closer to the ball. You make the cut one hole shorter and move everything in one. Even though it is called a 2 hole play, the ball will hit inside the original point of attack.

When the 2 man (end) comes down, he establishes the lead block. Most of your offense is set up so that you have a block down or in at the hole, a block out at the hole, and a block through the hole. This set-up is the essence of wing-T football. Most plays in the traditional wing-T offense are set up like that.

Formations

100/900

The basic formations in the wing-T have carryover between the formation numbers and the hole numbering. The wing-T formation known best is the tight end and wing on one side, with the diveback and split end on the other side. This formation is called 100 and 900. Diagram 1.4 shows 100 formation, which tells your players that the right halfback is in the wingback position and the tight end is to the right. The 1 hole is also to the right. Away from the 1 hole, to your left, you align your split end and your left halfback, who is in a diveback position. The opposite of this formation would be called 900. This formation places the tight end to the left, to the 9 hole side. Your left halfback is now the wing, your split end is to the right, and your right halfback is now in a diveback position.

Split Call

A prefix can modify this formation. If you call "split 100" (Diagram 1.5), you now take the split end and align him in a position four to six yards from the tackle, instead of split out in his usual position, past the hash mark. Your normal split is to align in what is called the alley, which is halfway between the hash and the numbers.

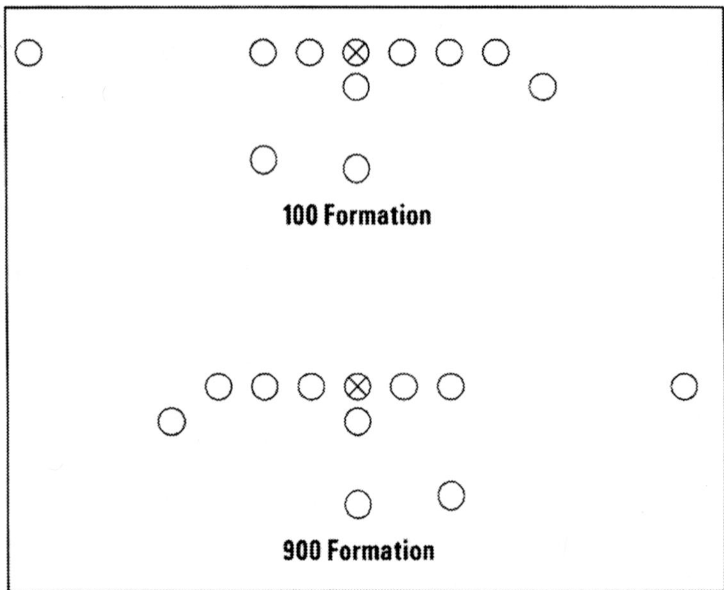

Diagram 1.4

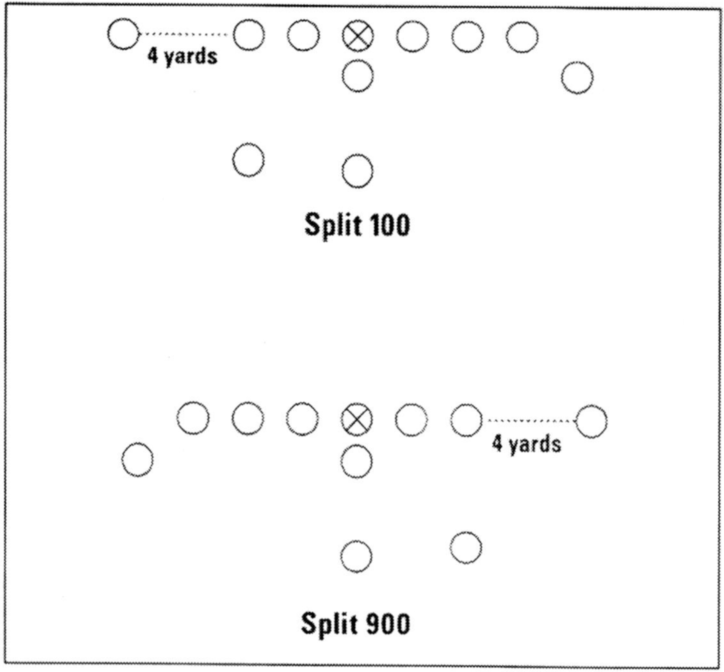

Diagram 1.5

200/800

You can also change the backfield sets. In your system, 200 formation is split backs with tight end and wing set to the right. The right halfback is the wing, and the tight end is to the right, similar to 100. The left halfback is the left diveback, and the split end aligns on the left. The only difference is your fullback, who now moves to the right in the right diveback position. Other ways to create the 200 formation include putting the fullback behind the tackle or the guard or simply having him make a small movement by putting his left foot on the ball. It is based entirely on what you are trying to accomplish by going to splitbacks. The opposite of 200 formation is called 800 formation. The 8 hole is to the left, serving to remind the tight end and wing to align to the left. The split end is right, the right halfback is in a diveback position, and the fullback has moved to the left as a diveback.

300/700

Another backfield set you can use is 300 and 700 (Diagram 1.6). The 300/700 are used a lot in the wing-T. From these formations, a good package of plays can be created to complement each other. In 300 formation, you align the left halfback in the wingback position to the right and the right halfback in his diveback position on the right, with the fullback behind the quarterback, thus creating a strong backfield set to the wingside. The opposite of 300 would be 700 formation. Your right halfback aligns as the left wing, your left halfback is in his left diveback position, and your fullback is in the fullback position. The tight end is left, and the split end is right. These formation numbers — 100/900, 200/800, and 300/700 — are used for the first digit of the three-digit play call. Both halfbacks have also been aligned in double-wing positions, and those formations are named with colors.

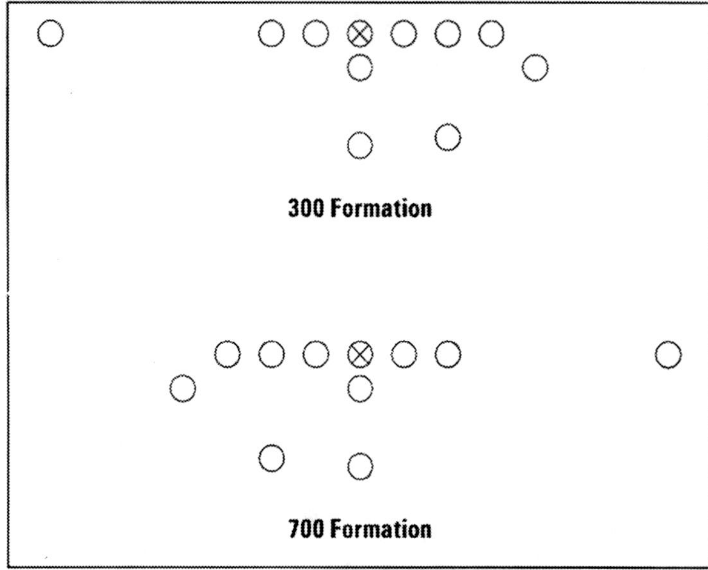

Diagram 1.6

Spread Call

Remember, prefixes are used to alter the alignments within a particular formation call. Split 100 adjusted the alignment of the split end closer to the tackle. Another common formation used is called spread 100 (Diagram 1.7). In 100 formation, the right halfback is aligned as the wing on the right, with the left halfback in a left diveback position. By prefixing the word spread, the spread end is moved to the same side as the wingback, with the tight end opposite the split end. Spread 100 puts both halfbacks in their 100 alignment, but flips the ends, putting the split end to the call. Spread 100 creates a wide receiver and wing to the same side, with the tight end opposite and with the backs offset to the tight end. The opposite would be spread 900. In spread 900 formation, the spread end goes with the wing to the call (900 left), and the tight end goes opposite. The 900 tells your left halfback to align as the wing to the left and the right halfback to be in the diveback position to the right.

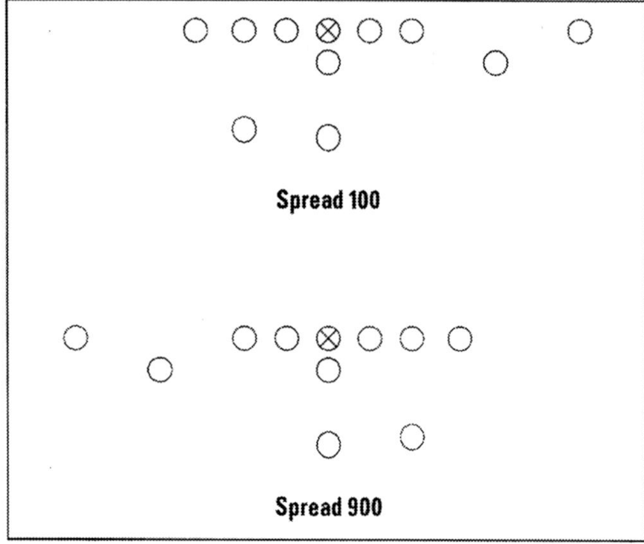

Diagram 1.7

Tight/Closed Calls

Many different ways exist to modify 100 and 900 formations. Another very common formation is two tight ends (Diagram 1.8), also called, "Tight 100." All players align in 100 formation except the split end, who has moved to a tight end position on the left, usually done through substitution of a second tight end. The right halfback would be the right wing, the left halfback would be the left diveback, and the fullback is in the normal fullback position. By simply adding the word "tight," the formation is changed to two tight ends. This formation is used in the goal line offense extensively. Tight formations have two different styles: one formation is called closed 100, and the other is called tight 100. The difference is that, if closed is called, two tight ends are in the tight end positions and everybody has normal splits. If tight is called, then two tight ends are in tight end positions, but everybody cuts their splits down and crowds the ball in short-yardage and goal line offenses. The opposite of tight 100 would be tight 900 formation. The left halfback aligns as the wing to the left, while the right halfback is in a right diveback position, and both ends are tight.

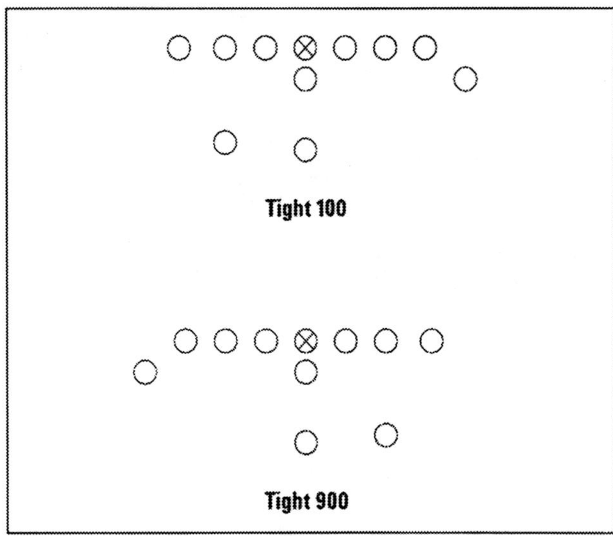

Diagram 1.8

Loose Call

The opposite of tight is a loose call (Diagram 1.9). Loose is a prefix that tells both ends to split out, creating a set with wide receivers on both sides. To get to loose formations, another split end can be put in the game, replacing the tight end, or if you have an athletic tight end, you can spread him out. If you do not want to alert the defense that you are going to loose, do it with the regular personnel without substitution. Loose 100 means two spread ends, the right halfback in the right wingback position, the left halfback in a left diveback position, and the fullback behind the center. The opposite formation would be loose 900. Both ends spread wide, the left halfback is in a left wingback position, and the right halfback is in a right diveback position.

Right/Left Calls

The next prefix is very simple, but can really give a defense headaches. The simple call of right or left (Diagram 1.10) creates unbalanced formations. Visualize a normal 100 formation, with the tight end aligned right, the wingback right, and the left halfback in a left diveback position. The addition of the word rightsimply tells both ends to go to the right. The split end now flips over to the right side in his normal split alignment, but outside of the tight end and the wing, who are already aligned to the right. You now

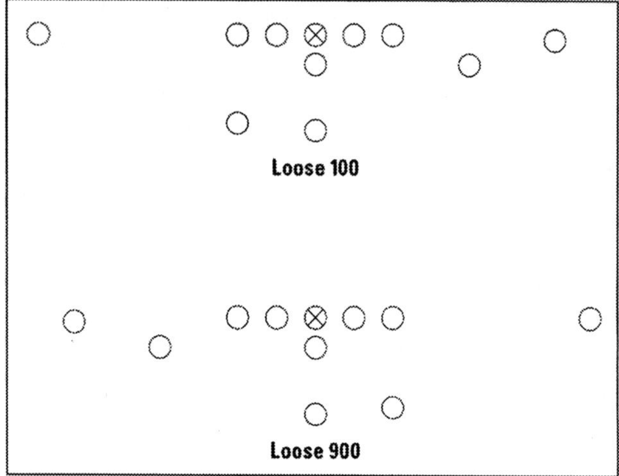

Diagram 1.9

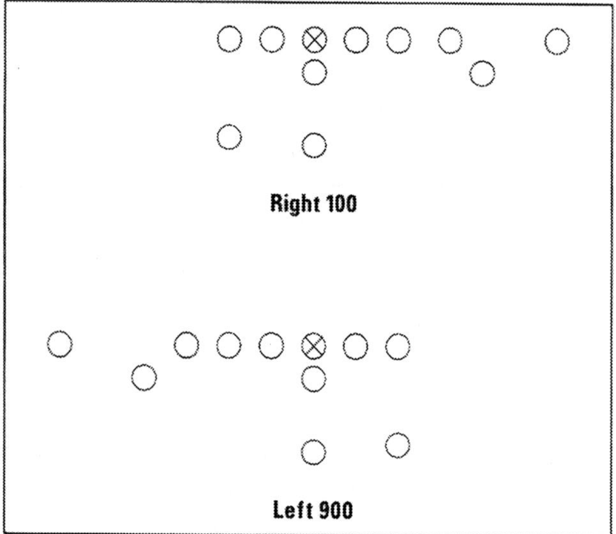

Diagram 1.10

have an unbalanced formation. This type of formation does many things for the offense. First of all, if the defense doesn't adjust, they can be outnumbered. Second, you could widen a coverage man normally used to force the run. Also, many things can be done with this unbalanced set if the defense adjusts too heavily to the unbalanced side. You still have a four-back attack and a great weakside attack for teams that overcompensate. This formation is used quite a bit. Unbalanced formations are used on about 33 to 40 percent of the snaps. With a 900 call, the left halfback can align in a left wingback position and the right halfback in a right diveback position, and the ends can be unbalanced away from the wing with the right 900 call. At this point, both ends go to the right, creating a different type of unbalanced formation: one away from the wing and to the diveback. A simple call of right or left does that much. You can unbalance to the wing, right 100 or left 900, or away from the wing, right 900 or left 100, simply by placing the right or leftcall either to the numbered formational call or away from it, depending on what you think helps the most.

Red/Blue Calls

One more formation variable is used to place both backs in wing formation (Diagram 1.11). If you want both the right halfback and the left halfback to align as wings, many names could be used. Using colors, if the tight end is to the right, the call is red, and, if the tight end is to the left, the call is blue. Red is exactly the same as the 100 formation, but now the left halfback is in a left wingback position as well. You have two wingbacks and a four-quick receiver offense, with the fullback as the single back in the backfield. If you watch pro football, you see this offense all the time. If you take red formation, you can have two tight ends and call, "Tight red," or you can have two spread ends and call, "Loose red." Rather than calling this formation wing 100 or slot 100, go with the least amount of verbiage and just call it red. This practice is not something revolutionary, but red is very simple. The opposite of red is when you have the tight end to the left and both halfbacks in a wing alignment, so this formation is called blue. The "r" in red tells the tight end that both halfbacks are in wingback positions and to align tight to the right. The "l" in blue does the same thing for the tight end by telling him to align to the left. By using simple names like red and blue, the call can easily be, "Tight red," "Tight blue," "Loose red," "Loose blue," "Right red," or "Left blue." You can get many different formations variables, still keep both halfbacks in a wing, and not have a lot of verbiage.

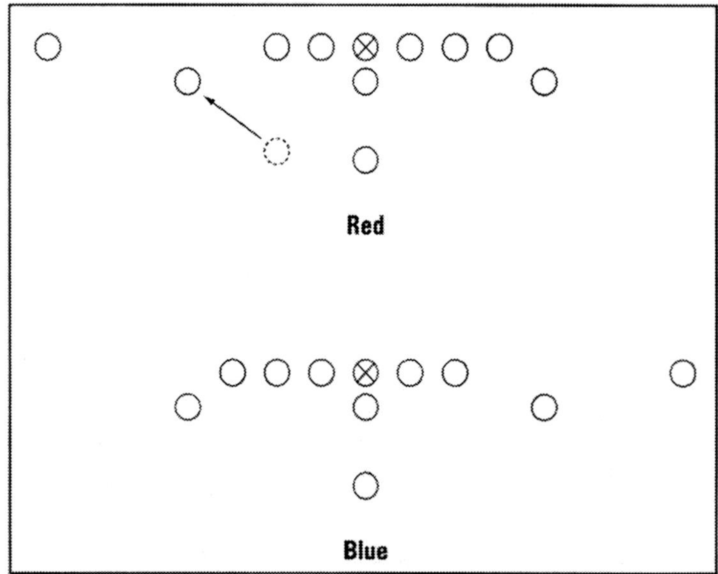

Diagram 1.11

Game Planning

Every week's game plan should include three basic formation concepts (Diagram 1.12). The first one is referred to as some form of wing (100). The second formation in every game plan is a form of slot (spread 900). The final formation in every game plan is some type of double wing (red). So, a wing, slot, and double wing formation are in every game plan each week. Start with those three formations, and talk about them as a staff: "What does each do for us?" "How can we gain an advantage by using each of those formations?" When first putting the offense in during summer camp or in spring ball, you can also begin by putting in the basic forms of the wing, slot, and double wing formations. Each opponent you play will have to have answers for those three formational concepts. Since you use those formations each week, you will know exactly what to look for from the defense and what types of adjustments to expect.

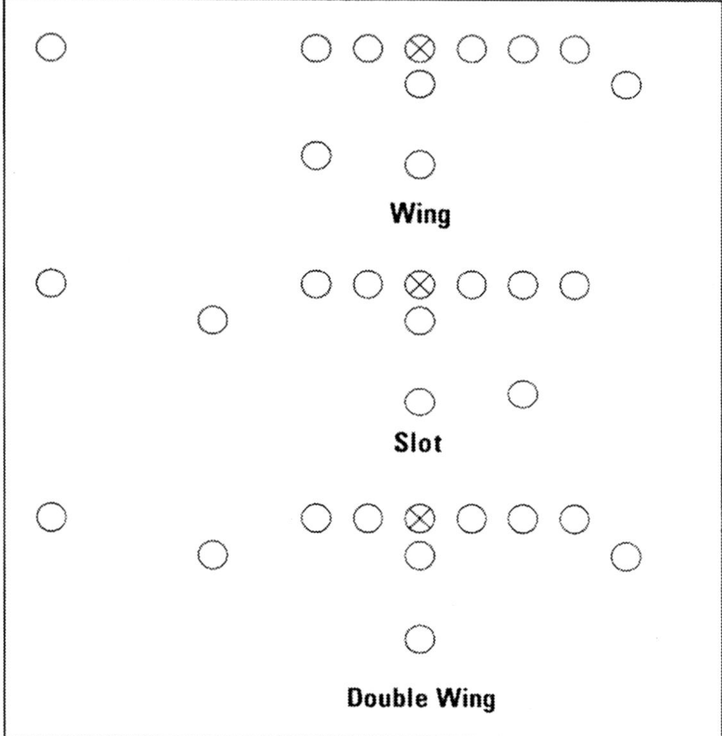

Diagram 1.12

The next formations put in the game plan are any adjustments to those very same formations already in use. Some common adjustments used would be loose, where both ends are spread; tight, with both ends in tight end positions; and forms of unbalanced, with both ends to the right or both ends to the left. Using loose unbalanced means either both ends are spread and to the right or both ends are spread and to the left. You can have formations with loose unbalanced and have an ineligible receiver or can shift the halfbacks and the ends to allow each receiver to become eligible. Simply having one step on the line and another one step off the line makes everybody eligible. This maneuver allows you to create a four-back attack with trips receivers. Very few offenses have that, but the wing-T does. This offense is virtually limitless in terms of all the variables you can create. Correspondingly, multiplicity is one of the wing-T's weaknesses. You must guard against getting caught up in trying to do too much and, therefore, executing nothing. To avoid this mistake, you should take a smaller package of plays and be able to run each of those plays from all of your formations. You can make a little bit look like a lot by doing a select number of plays from a wide variety of formations. After using this practice, you will really believe in that concept.

Series

The series are packaged together by backfield actions and denoted with two-digit numbers. The first number of each series corresponds to the second number in our three-digit play call, including teens, 20s, 30s, 40s, right on through the 90s. Every series has a style of backfield action that corresponds to it. Will you use every series every year? No. In this book, the focus is primarily on the 20s, 60s, 30s, and 80s. Those series are primary each year. The other series can be in the players' playbooks, but, some years, certain plays are used, and, other years, because of your selection of personnel, you will chose to not feature them. These other series should be kept in the playbook because during some years different series can be taken out of the closet, because football is cyclical, and sometimes those series come back and do well. Diagrams 1.13 and 1.14 illustrate the entire package of series actions. The first illustration (Diagram 1.13) focuses on the four series highlighted in this book, while Diagram 1.14 shows the completed set of all the series to be included in the playbook.

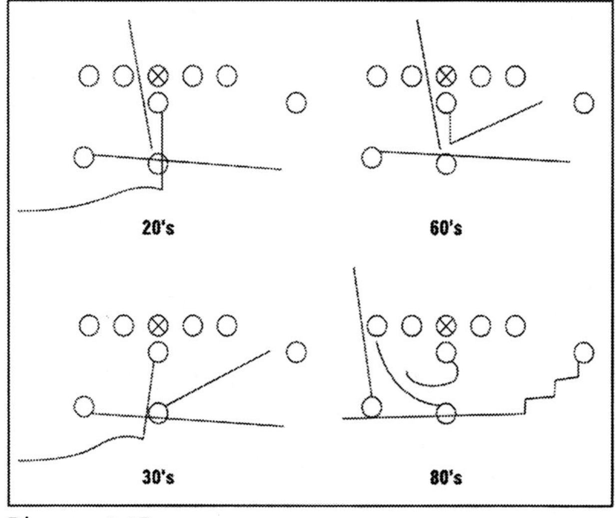

Diagram 1.13

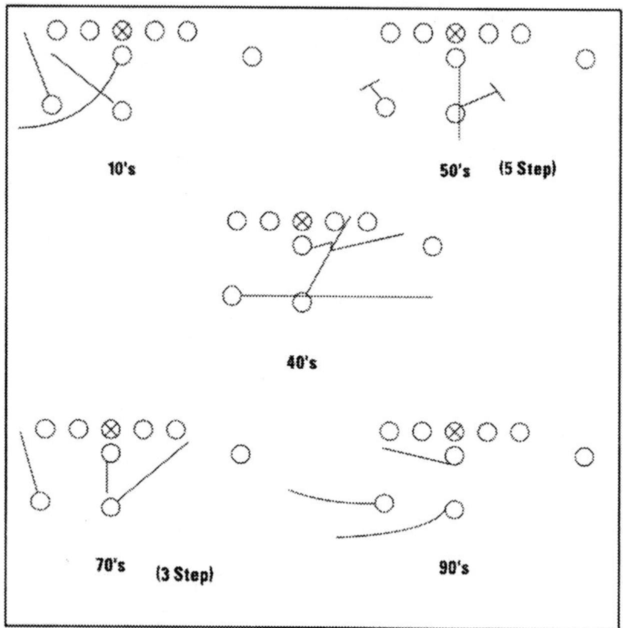

Diagram 1.14

The first series, in numerical order, is the 10s or teens. Looking at teens in the diagram, you can see that the teens series is full-flow, sprint-out action for the quarterback. If any teens is called, the quarterback is going to take the snap, attack the flank as fast as he can, and execute a run-pass option at the flank. He will be led to the flank by both of the backs. The 11 sprint is sprinted all the way to the flank. Whereas, 14 roll and 16 roll use a half-sprint type of play-action. The sprint draw plays are called 14 and 16, or 13 and 17 sprint draw. The teens series features sprint draw plays and sprint action. When you have real mobile quarterbacks, guys who can get to the flank with the speed to get outside, you will like the sprint package and will let the quarterback keep the ball. You can half-sprint the quarterback to throw the ball and complement it with some kind of draw or sprint draw off the same action. This series has been very productive over the years for us, although we are not featuring it currently, but it is in our playbook.

As you can see, the 20 series is the first series where the fullback dives to the backside of the center and the halfback crosses the backfield. The quarterback will then hand the ball off to either back, or keep the ball at the flank on a bootleg, or waggle play. With this buck action, you have flank-to-flank offense. You can run wide with 21, off-tackle with 22 or 23 guard trap, or inside with 24 guard trap. You can come backside with 27 counter, 29 waggle, and waggle shovel. A lot of different plays that counter back to the weakside flank, thus giving you flank-to-flank offense from one formation and using one backfield action.

The next series is the 30 series. The 30s are full-flow, double-team down, and kick-out power plays. The 30s are best in short-yardage situations or when you are getting a lot of internal stunting from defenses that are not reading guards, flow, or backfield action. In this series, the quarterback is still going to be faking waggle, but both of the backs will be attacking in the direction of the flow. This full-flow package, effective in short yardage, is effective also because, in 30s, the blocking is fire-on-backer, which enables you to pick up all kinds of internal stunting with good zone blocking.

The 40 series is a package to run with very mobile quarterbacks. If you look at the 40 series and say that it is nothing more than the wishbone, you are exactly right. You use an open pivot by the quarterback, a direct dive action by the fullback, and a pitch relationship maintained by the halfback to give the wing-T some additional versatility that takes advantage of the types of personnel recruited.

As you can see, 50 action with the quarterback gives five-step, drop-back passing action. The backs are going to be pass blockers first, and then after they check a blocking assignment, they will release into the pass pattern.

The next backfield action is the 60 series, which looks similar to the 20 series. The fullback is diving for the backside foot of the center and the left halfback is crossing over and then running through the heels of the fullback. The quarterback takes two steps on the midline, and, to that point, everything looks like 20s. Then the quarterback will plant on his second step, turn, and come downhill to the playside with the action of trap option. As you go through the series, you will see the different plays you can run with the same backfield action. The ball can be handed to the fullback or pitched to the halfback. You can throw the ball to the spread end or pitch it to him on a reverse. Several counter plays exist. From one backfield action, you have a complete series of plays that attack flank to flank and take advantage of the defense in different ways. The 20 series and the 60 series intermingle very well and can be used to complement each other.

The 70s series is a form of three-step drop passing. The backs are blockers, and the action is a pure pass action, not play action. Both of the backs are aggressive blockers. They are going to block the first thing that shows outside the tackles, while the quarterback takes a short three-step drop. The footwork is right, left, right for the quarterback, and then he sets and throws the ball. You can back him out, or you can drop him back with his shoulders turned – whatever you feel is the best.

The next series is the 80 series, a belly series, and it consists of the plays used most frequently. It is direct full-flow action and is power oriented, but also includes the sprint-draw type of play (belly) in the wing-T. This play can hit almost anywhere. The halfback is the lead blocker, the fullback is the ball carrier, and the quarterback is reverse pivoting, with a full-flow type of action. The halfback is leading through the hole, and the fullback has the ball on the belly play. Then, you can run the counter, the keep pass, the counter bootleg, and all those plays that relate to belly. The 80s are power oriented, but have inside plays, outside plays, counters, reverses, and action passes. Anything a coach might need in order to take advantage of defense conflicts is included in this package.

The last series is the 90 series. The 90 series begins with a lead-option, or speed-option, type of play. Although you may not always use the 90s, a place can always be made for this series. It is especially effective in goal line situations. If you can get a quick read off the pitch key, or if you have a mobile quarterback or a fast fullback, then this play is exceptional. Looking at Diagram 1.14, you can see that the 90s are also full-flow plays, with the quarterback coming downhill immediately, attacking the option key, and with the fullback used as the pitchback. This way gets the ball quickly to your fullback outside. You can toss it to him – called 91 and 99 sweep – or you can run option and give the quarterback a chance to pitch the ball or keep it.

These are the series, 10 through 90. Nine different backfield actions can be incorporated into the offense, and, probably, two or three of those actions will not be used much at this time. You are going to feature certain things in your offense, and you know everything cannot be featured every year. Usually you don't have enough time to practice that much.

Hole Numbering

The final phase of the communication and call system is hole numbering. As explained earlier, the hole numbering goes from right to left, from 1 through 9. The numbers get larger as you go to the left. Diagram 1.15 illustrates hole numbers: 1 and 9 are wide and correspond to flank plays; 2 and 8 are corner game plays, which are off-tackle type plays; 3 and 7 are also off-tackle hole plays; and 4 and 6 are internal plays.

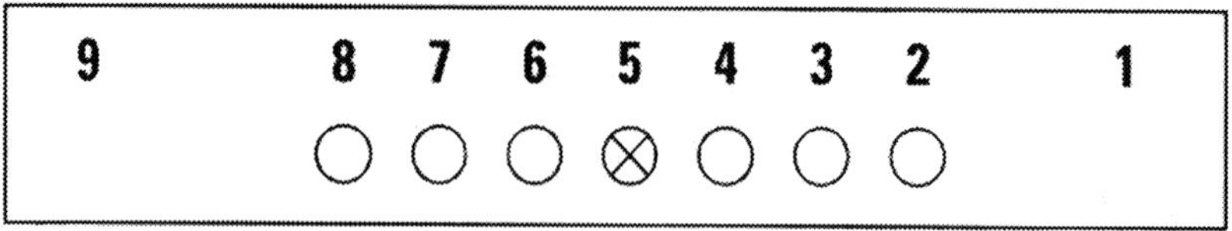

Diagram 1.15

No matter what offense you use – the I, the splitback veer, or a one-back passing attack – this form of communication is the best system because it is so simple and quick. The three-digit number system with prefixes and suffixes is so versatile. The number of variables available for something so easy for players to learn and communicate is unbelievable. You can be in and out of your huddle fast, without fighting the 25-second clock. If you are going to utilize shifting, time becomes a concern, and it is essential that your players quickly communicate the information. It is also easy to use in a no-huddle situation.

The Spread of Ends

Basic Split Rules

The split rules for the spread ends or the wide receivers are referred to as minimum, maximum, and normal split rules, as shown in Diagram 1.16. If the ball is on the hash, and you are the wide receiver to the wideside of the field, your normal split is between the hash mark and the numbers. When teaching players a particular play, tell them which split they should be using. If you want a player to be in what is called a minimum split, he would be out on the hash mark. If you want him in a maximum split, he would be out on the numbers. Minimum is on the hash; normal is in the alley; and maximum is on the numbers. If the ball is snapped from the middle, then the split of the wide receiver to either side would be on the numbers to both sides of the formation. If the ball is on the closest hash and the split end is to the shortside of the field, you want him five to seven yards from the sideline, depending on the play. Five yards is the normal split used into the boundary. Whether the end is on the frontside of the formation or the backside of the formation, whether it is wing, slot, double wing, or loose, the split rules are the same. In summary, minimum, normal, and maximum split rules are for when the end is to the wideside of the field. When the ball is in the middle, the receiver is on the numbers, unless adding the word split or slot. When he is into the boundary, he is five to seven yards from the sideline.

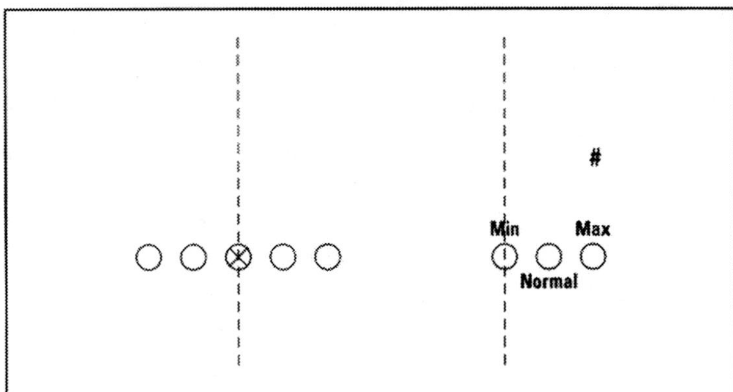

Diagram 1.16

Prefixes to the Formation

The split rules can be modified by prefixes to the formation, which alter the splits. Anytime you add a word prefix to the call (e.g., split or slot), the spread of the ends gets modified. If using split 100, then the players align in a 100 formation with the tight end to the right, the right half in a wingback position, the left half in a diveback position, and the split end on the left (Diagram 1.17). If you do not use the word split, the wide receiver uses normal rules. If you use split, he comes down to a position four to six yards from the tackle, depending on what kind of play is called, what his assignment is, and what his best split to execute on that particular play would be.

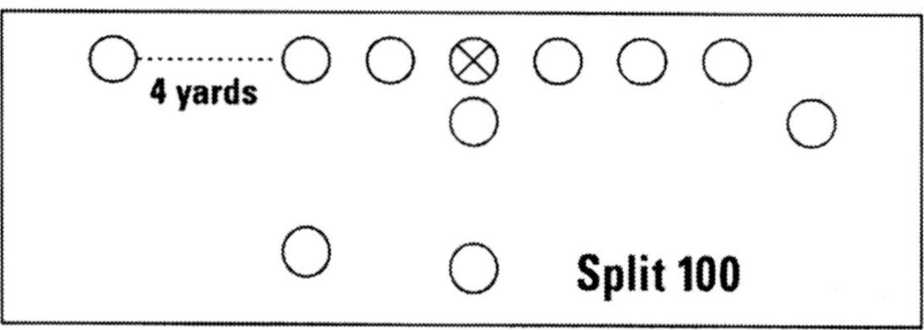

Diagram 1.17

The same holds true for a spread end to the side of the wingback. You would normally call this spread 100 or spread 900. On spread 100, the spread end is to the wingside of the call (100 right) with his normal split rules. If calling spread, you use the same split rules: the minimum, normal, and maximum split. If saying, "Slot 100," then the receiver reduces this split to six to eight yards from the tackle. He is now six to eight yards from the tackle, depending on what his assignment is, what he has to do on that particular play, and what his best alignment would be to execute that assignment. Changing the spread of the ends is a way to modify your formations.

Formation Adjustments

The next concept to consider is the formation adjustments and how to execute them. If looking at Diagram 1.12, you can review the fact that you would like to have three concepts – the wing formation, the slot formation, and the double wing formation – built into the game plan. Diagram 1.18 illustrates a regular 900 formation, which is an example of a tight end/wing concept. You also want to have in the game plan what is called slot, which aligns the wingback on the spread end side and the diveback on the tight end side. An example of a slot type of formation is the call, "Slot 100," or, "Spread 100." Whenever you have a wingback to the spread end side and the other halfback in a diveback position, this alignment is commonly referred to as a slot alignment. You also want to include the double wing formations. Both halfbacks are in a wing position, with the tight end to one side, the split end to the other side, and both designated by colors. With these three formation variables (wing, slot, and double wing), the tight ends may be aligned tight, loose, unbalanced, or loose unbalanced.

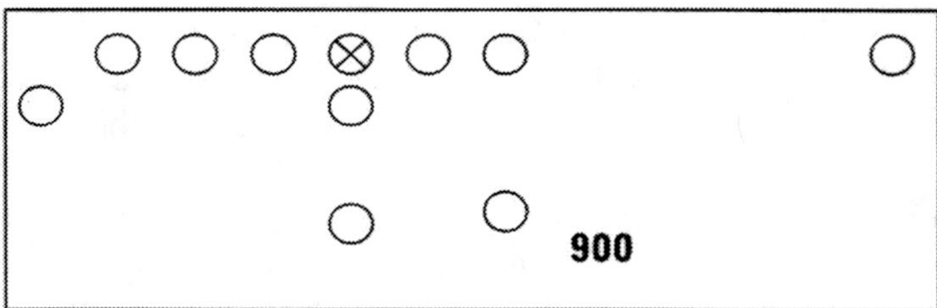

Diagram 1.18

Using one formation (Diagram 1.19) you can see the evolution of the formation and how it can change with prefixes. Recall that the tight end aligns to the right, the right halfback in a wing position, the split end to the left away from the tight end/wing combination, and the left halfback in a diveback position. The opposite formation is 900. This formation is very common to the wing-T and often considered the primary wing-T formation.

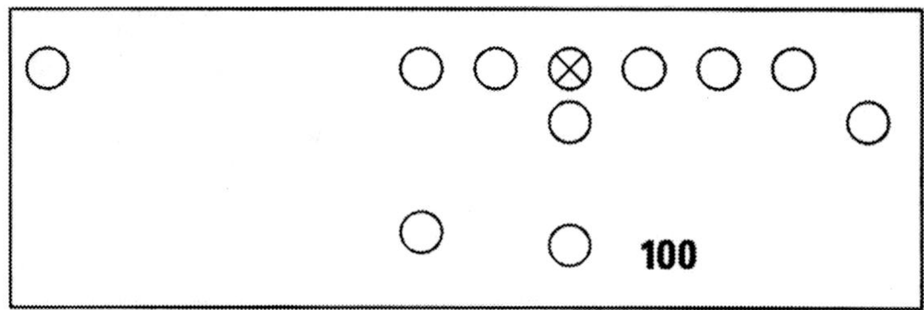

Diagram 1.19

If you call, "Tight 100," both ends will align tight. The basic 100 formation is with a tight end wing to the right, the left halfback in a diveback position, and the other end also tight.

The opposite of tight is loose. Instead of both ends being tight ends, both ends are spread (Diagram 1.20). Loose 100 now has a basic 100 formation with both ends aligned wide. If, as a coach, you want a pro-style passing game, you can take loose 100 and basically have what the pro offenses have. The difference between a pro attack and the loose 100 is #2 on the line and #2 off. This difference is no big deal, because

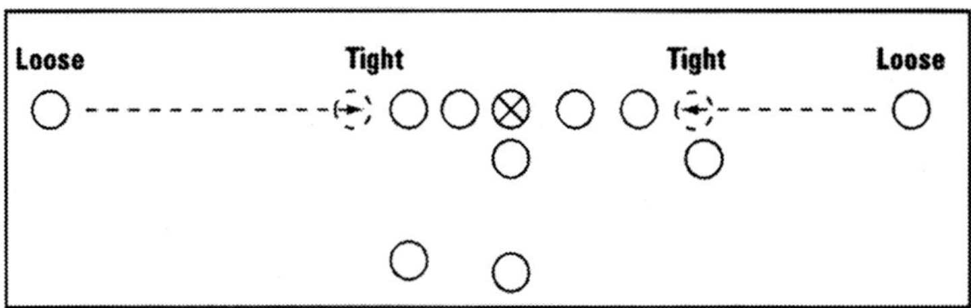

Diagram 1.20

#2 can release better into a pass pattern than a tight end can, anyway. You can keep the integrity of the four-back attack by just modifying formations and get what you need in order to do other things. If you want to throw the ball a lot, this formation is great.

If you add right 100 (Diagram 1.21), both ends go to the right. You still have the 100 formation, but both ends are to the right, so you have an unbalanced attack to the wing. The next variable uses the same philosophy, but keeps the 100 formation intact and is called, "Left." As you look at the diagram, you can see that both ends are now to the left with 100 formation. The right halfback is still a wingback, and the left halfback is still a diveback (Diagram 1.22). You have created an unbalanced away from the wing, which is fine, because you can have either unbalanced to the wing or unbalanced away from the wing. Often, a better way to unbalance is away from the wing, especially if the strong safety will stay to the wingback side, as opposed to coming with the ends. At times, you can go tackles right or tackles left to keep the tight end at home on the backside and bring both tackles to the right or left. Now you have eligible receivers on the backside of the formation, and then the secondary of any defense must play honest. If you bring both ends over on the same side and cover one of them up, you lose an eligible receiver.

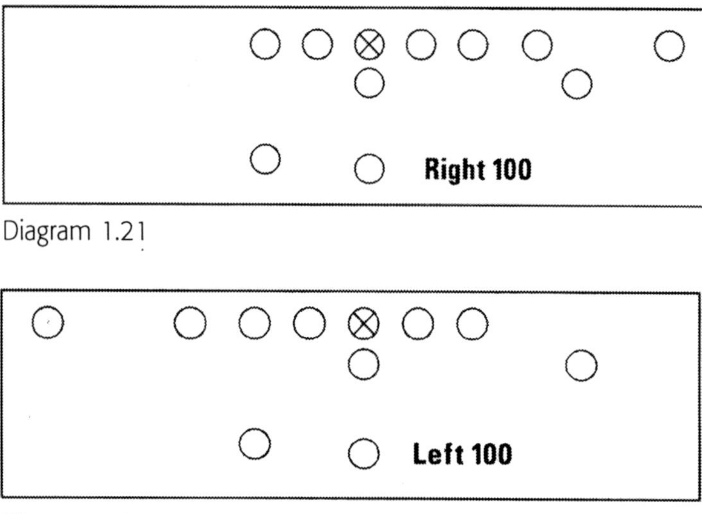

Diagram 1.21

Diagram 1.22

Another way to solve the eligibility problem is with the formation called either port 100 or star 900. With port 100, both ends are brought to the left, and, with star 900, both ends align to the right (Diagram 1.23). Both ends are to the left (port), and you have a 100 type of setup with the left halfback in a diveback position and the right halfback in a wingback position. The difference is the right halfback will step onto the line and the spread end will step off the line. Port 100 gives you unbalanced to the left with everybody eligible. If you shift to port formation or to left 100 and are shifting or lining up and snapping the ball quickly, it will be very difficult for the defense to know if you are balanced or unbalanced. When shifting to these formations, you find that defenses play very basic and will not really overload much to the unbalanced side. You have created a numbers advantage that you can use when attacking the defense.

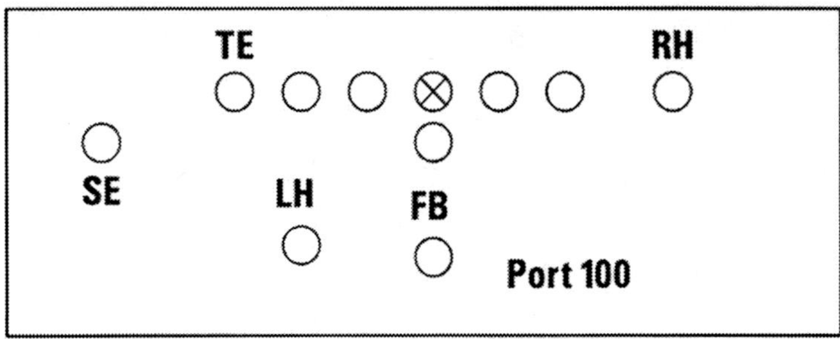

Diagram 1.23

Diagram 1.24 is a loose right 100 formation. This formation is with both ends to the right, but they are both loose. With a right halfback in a wingback set, you can have a trips formation. One of these receivers is covered up and, therefore, ineligible. This fact doesn't mean the ball can't be thrown. A couple of things can be done with the end, even though he's ineligible. One of the things is to belly him back on a pass pattern and have him stay behind the line of scrimmage, which is perfectly legal. Everybody else can run their pass patterns, and you'll be amazed at how many times the strong safety will run to cover this ineligible receiver. Another thing to do is fake him on a reverse through the backfield. Either alternative is good, and, before the game, you should try to alert the officials that you might be doing something like this.

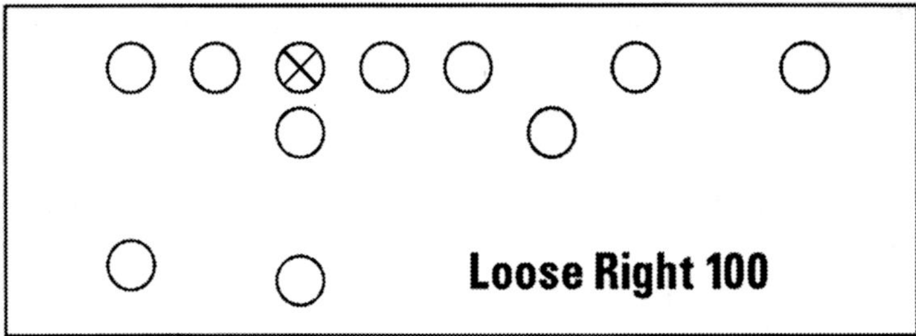

Diagram 1.24

Using prefixes can create as many offenses as you want. You can run the loose 100 formation, call 24 guard trap, or any play where the tight end is not the lead blocker at the point of attack. Also, you can run most of the same offense, only with two split ends. This method uses the threat of pro passing while still running wing-T. You can run a few plays from multiple sets, and you haven't taught anybody anything new, except the ends line up in different places. The ends are taught that, if they are to the play, they do this, and, if they are away from the play, they do that, learning very simple rules. The ends will find this offense relatively easy to execute. Little practice time is required, and you are showing multiple offenses requiring a multitude of adjustments, yet running very few plays. These formation variables have been used often and will continue to be used. You should like to be as multiple as possible with our formations, run a few plays out of many formations, and make a little bit look like a lot.

Backfield Positioning

The backs are going to align with precision. If the football is out in front of the center, and he is reaching out with the ball just the way he is taught, then the back tip of the football will be somewhere out in front of the center's nose. The fullback is going to line up with his heels four yards from the back tip of the football (Diagram 1.25). Some coaches think it is too tight. I do not. Having been a wing-T coach for many years, I will tell you that the fullback should be a quick threat up the middle. He should pop up the middle as fast as he can on 24 and 26. If you run any kind of option play, the fullback should be up in the line of scrimmage and really forcing the defense to collapse quickly. He is going to be quick, even if he is not quick. He will be quick by moving up a little closer. The fullback is taught to put his heels at four yards, and it works out just fine. Coaches who put the fullback's heels at five or five and a half yards deepen the motion of the wingback. This method destroys the deception of the first three steps of motion, making it look so deep that the defense can see the difference. The backs will have their heels at four yards in order to make it difficult for the defense to distinguish between the motions by looking at the depth. This depth works out fine for the wing-T offense. The fullback is directly behind the center, and the quarterback is on the midline. If the halfbacks are in a diveback alignment, then they line up the same as the fullback, with their heels four yards from the back tip of the football and even with the fullback. As they align, they split the outside leg of the tackle. Some people call it thatching the outside leg of the tackle. If the diveback puts the tackle's outside leg right through the center of his body, then he is exactly where he should stand. The halfback is in a parallel stance, heels at four yards, and thatching the outside leg of the tackle. If

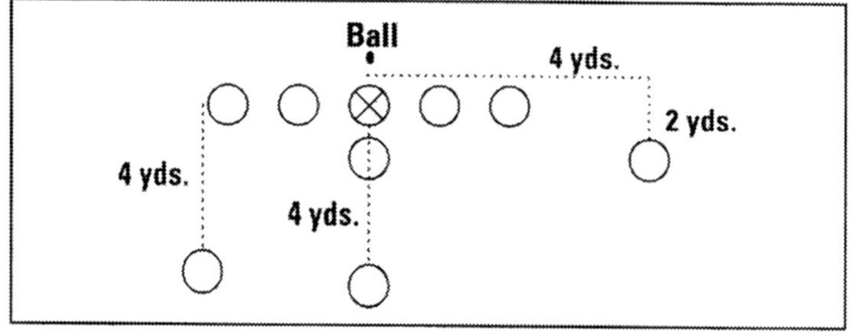

Diagram 1.25

the halfback is a wingback, then his shoulders should be parallel to the line of scrimmage. He should not turn and angle his shoulders in. With the shoulders parallel to the line of scrimmage, he can block down, go in motion, flare, or release vertically for a pass. He can do any of the things needed in this offense, with equal facility.

The wingback's toes are two yards from the back tip of the ball. His shoulders are square, and his feet are in a position where the outside foot is in its normal position and the inside foot is back, with the toes of the inside foot even with the heels of the outside foot. He should have very little stagger with his feet. This stance facilitates two things: the pull release, or pull step, that he might have to take in order to block down on a sweep or any other load-blocking scheme; or the halfback leaving in the three-step motion. You tell the back to take an open step, or a depth step, on his first step of motion. Step two and step three should put him back to the outside foot of the tackle after just the three-step motion. When backs go in motion, they run at full speed. The wingback stance facilitates these types of movements. If the halfback goes in the three-step motion and is going to be a ballcarrier, then he aims for the heels of the outside foot of his diveback position. If he is going to be a blocker or a pitchback at the opposite flank, he aims for the toes of the inside foot of his diveback position. The maneuver gets him across the formation faster, with more speed, and enables him to be in better pitch relationship on the option. It also enables him to be in position to block at the flank quicker.

The base rules for the offensive line splits between the center and the guard and the tackle should be two-foot splits. The tight end should have a three-foot split. These splits are modified at times. Normally, the guards will be at two feet. Tackles will adjust if the guards are uncovered. A head-up nose and both guards uncovered would put the tackles out to three feet. If the tackle is uncovered and the defense is in some type of even spacing, then the tight end moves his alignment out to five, or even six, feet, depending on how far that defensive end will come out with him. If the tight end can stretch the defensive end and he will come out to six feet, that's good, because that widens the off-tackle hole. It makes it much tougher for him to seal down inside and stop the off-tackle area.

The next concept for the offensive linemen is their vertical split — in other words, how far off the ball they align. The answer is to be back off the ball as far as legally allowed. The blocking footwork is coached so that contact occurs on the second step. They should take a short, six-inch power step and then explode through the block as the second step comes in contact with the ground. That first step is a quick, replace-the-toes-with-the-heels type of step, and then, on the second step, contact occurs. At that point, they are making contact with the same foot and the same shoulder and then finishing the block with some power in it. The vertical split needed for executing blocks this way is achieved by telling your guards to put their hand down even with the center's toes. The offensive tackles will do the same, as will the tight end.

Shifting

Advantages of Shifting

Several shifts are used all the time. Shifting is used in order to try to destroy offensive recognition from the defense and to gain a personnel or numbers advantage at the point of attack. Even if the defense stays exactly the same and does no adjusting at all, shifting destroys their offensive recognition, or at least hinders it. This lack of recognition is a plus, because if you just line up and run the play, the defense can say, "They are in this formation, and they are going to run this play." Recognition always gives the defense an advantage. If you shift, even if they don't adjust, you are going from wing right to slot left or from unbalanced left to wing right, etc. The defense now must refocus and try to re-identify the formation and what the tendencies might be in a much shorter time frame. If defensive reaction can be slowed down, you have gained an edge. Another reason to shift is to outnumber the defense at the point of attack. By shifting, you can possibly get a numbers advantage. Extra numbers are big in football. If you can get a numbers advantage and outnumber the defense, you have a huge edge in offensive football.

Another reason for using shifting is to attack a weaker defensive person or maybe even a stronger defensive person. Sometimes, you want to run a certain play right at the best defender – either you want to double-team him or to intimidate him, to defeat strength, and then attack weakness. You can do that with shifting. If the defense is consistently putting their best defensive player away from the tight end, and you want the tight end on him in order to neutralize him, then you can trade the tight end and attack him. You have thus created a dilemma for the defense. Are they going to shift all 11 defenders? You shouldn't think so. Are they even going to shift the defensive ends? They probably wont. If they do, you can use a wrinkle called trade-back. The tight end starts across, then trades back to his original position; or you can just keep shifting all day long and wear them out.

Shift to

Although several types of shifts are used, the simpler ones will be illustrated first. Looking at Diagram 1.26, you see one of the easiest shifts used, which is called shift to. For example, when you execute shift to 900, you are trying to get the defense to line up with their personnel on the wrong side. The split end is in a tight end position, and the tight end is in a split end position. The left half aligns in a diveback position, and the right half in a wing position. Both of the ends and the halfbacks are in the opposite alignment, but on the correct side, from their final positions in 900 formation. On command, the spread end sprints out wide, the tight end sprints in tight, and both backs change positions. Also, you can do this with a spread end lining up on the right, the tight end lining on the left, and both ends trading all the way across to the other side. This variation just takes a little longer.

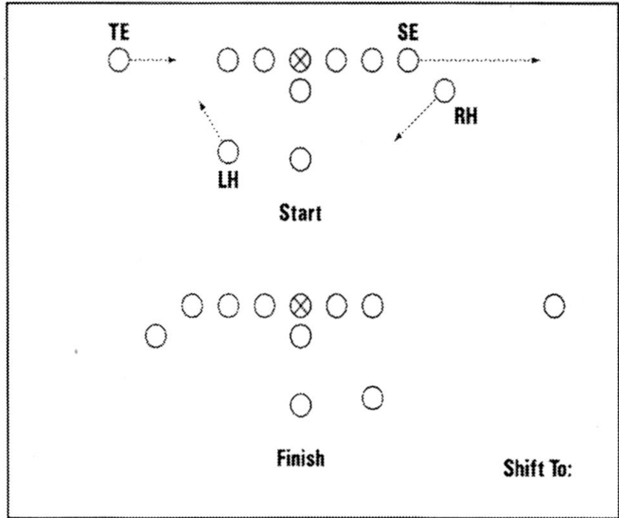

Diagram 1.26

Two different timings to shifting are used. One timing is for everyone to shift at the same time. Another is to shift in sequence, with a typewriter effect. The ends shift first, then the halfback, who is going to end up as a diveback second, and finally the halfback, who ends up as the wingback last.

Slide to

The next shift involves only the tight end and the two halfbacks. This shift is called slide to (Diagram 1.27). If you call, "Slide to 929," then you are going to run the sweep to the left, to the 9 hole. The offense lines up with the tight end and the halfbacks in the opposite positions. If you look at this formation before the shift, you have an unbalanced wing formation to the right. The shift is made, and now the strength is on the other side. You can see how you can attack strength or attack weakness simply by shifting. You can be strong to the left, where, earlier, you were unbalanced strength to the right. Slide to simply combines the tight end trading sides with the halfbacks shifting to the opposite alignments. In the huddle, you just say, "Slide to 929." The halfbacks and ends know to align opposite their final position and then shift. The split end aligns in his final position and does not shift. This shift is easily communicated.

Trade to

If you wish to shift just the tight end, you call trade to (Diagram 1.28). In this particular case, only the tight end trades. The backs and the other end align in their final position

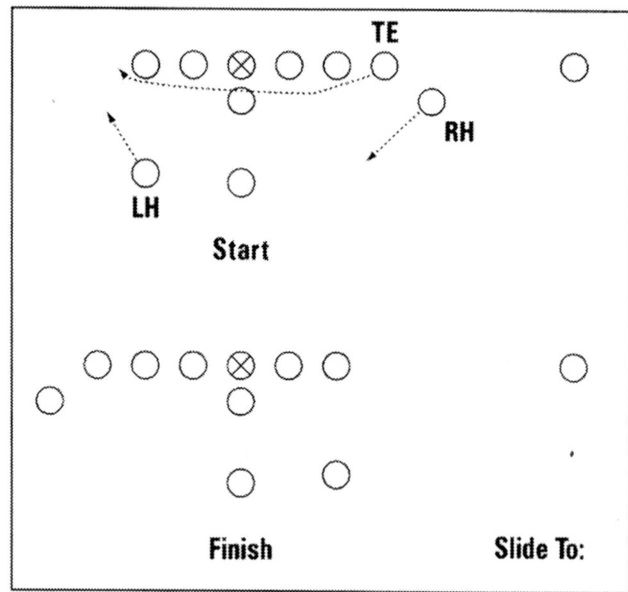

Diagram 1.27

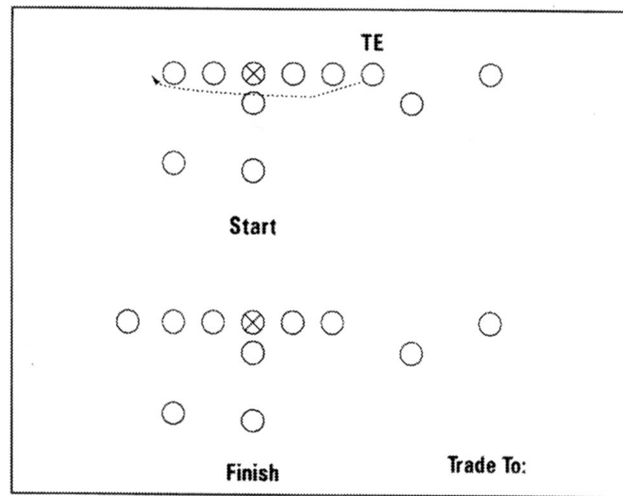

Diagram 1.28

and remain the same. Again, this shift offers the ability to start out with unbalanced wingback strength to one side and end up in a spread formation. In this illustration, you simply call, "Trade to spread 100," and then call whatever the play is.

Flip to

The next shift is one as old as the hills, but has been brought out of retirement. This shift is called flip to (Diagram 1.29). As you look at the diagram, you can see that in flip to the tight end lines up as the fullback. The fullback lines up as a wing, and one of the wingbacks lines up as a wide receiver. If you run a lot of loose red and blue, with two wide receivers and four backs, or actually four quick receivers, as in the run-and–shoot, you want a good shift out of it. This shift can be very meaningful. If the defense recognizes that the tight end is in the backfield and just stands there and waits for the shift, then put in one play out of pre-flip, which means you run the play before the shift. You just call, "Pre-flip," and whatever play you want to run. Something where the tight end can run a simple pass pattern or block a certain defender is easy to do. Again, in flip to, you start out in loose red or loose blue. You flip, meaning the tight end goes to the side he wants to end up on and the fullback jumps back to his position. The left half comes back to his position, and you have flip to 100. To call a play is simple: you say, "Flip to 121." Now you have all kinds of shifting and deception on the field, and all you said was, "Flip to 121." This method is very simple, but also very effective.

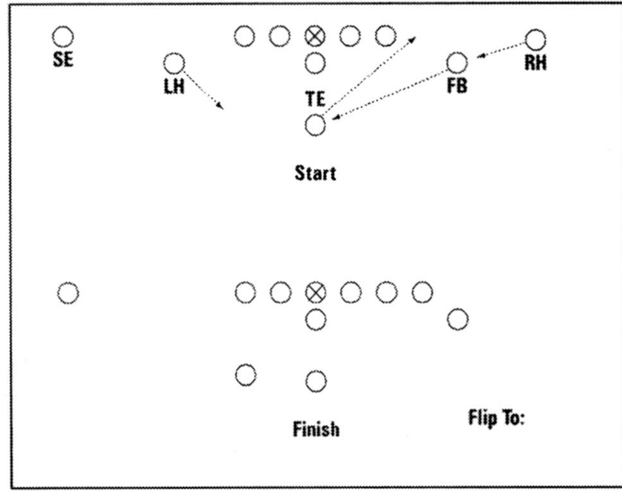

Diagram 1.29

Step to

Two more shifts exist. The first one is in conjunction with the loose unbalanced plays, which are the trips package. This shift is called step to (Diagram 1.30). You put all the halfbacks and ends on the line of scrimmage in a two-point stance and step two of them back off the line of scrimmage. This formation is similar to loose right formation, but here you have one of the ends off the line of scrimmage and one of the halfbacks on the line of scrimmage, which makes everybody eligible. Now you have a formation that is trips oriented, but still has the potential of a four-back attack, if you want to use it. This formation is very effective. If you like trips, doubles, loose red, and loose blue, the trips package gives you a wide-open style of attack, but is still wing-T offense. By stepping two people back, you can create all kinds of formation variables. In this diagram, you see that the right half and the split end step back, which gives you a tight end, a split end, and a right halfback who are eligible. Often, you can substitute a second spread end for the tight end.

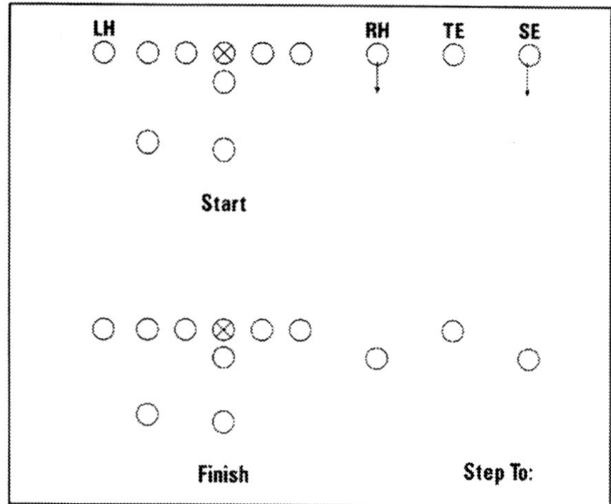

Diagram 1.30

Jump to

The last shift is the simplest of all and is called jump to (Diagram 1.31). One of the halfbacks jumps up into a double wing position, or starting in double wing and jumping back. If you say, "Jump to blue," the left half and a tight end line up just as they always do when you say, "Blue," except the right halfback will shift from a diveback position up to a wingback position. If you are attacking a team that puts the strong safety to the tight end and wing, you can jump the right halfback up on the other side, away from the strong safety, bring the left half in motion, and attack the weakside by creating a numbers advantage. Jump to is simply the halfback shifting and nothing else.

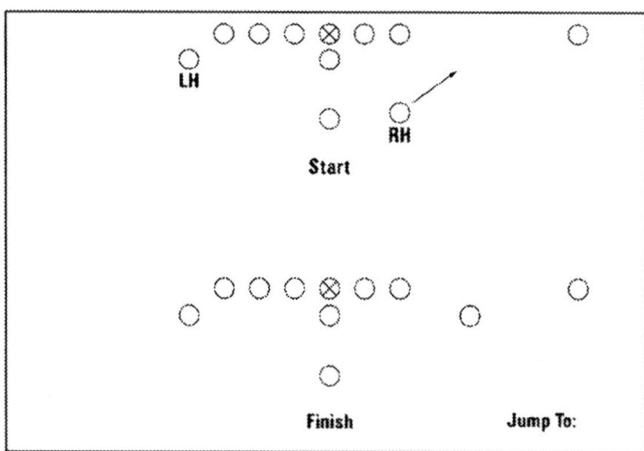

Diagram 1.31

Motions

You can use four kinds of motion: first, one step from the diveback, second, three step from the wingback, three, return motion from the wingback, and, four, extended or long motion from either a wingback or a diveback (Diagram 1.32). You should practice these on your spacing boards as part of the routine period.

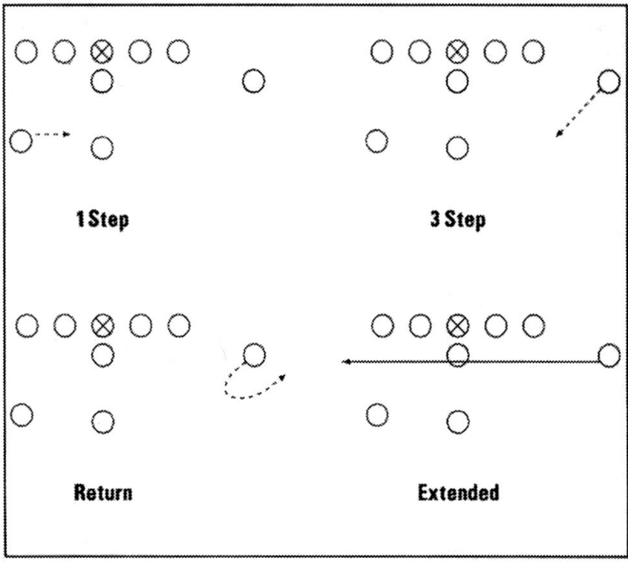

Diagram 1.32

One-Step Motion

If you are practicing one-step motion, put the halfbacks in the diveback position on the outside leg of the tackle and work in one-step motion. It means to take one step, with the second step occurring when the quarterback snaps the ball. One-step motion comes only from the diveback spot and is a way you can get the halfbacks out in front of the quarterback whenever they have to be either a blocker or a pitchback. You can do this with all the left halfbacks going to the right on one side of the field and with all the right halfbacks going to the left on the other side. The fullbacks practice both sides, which cross trains them to play all positions.

Three-Step Motion

The second kind of motion is three-step motion, which is done only from the wingback position. When you go in motion, you aim for the feet of the diveback position using different points for landmarks. When motioning to be a ballcarrier, the inside foot is back, and you take a slight depth step, aiming for the heels of the outside foot. Take one step, two steps, and on the third step be right back in the diveback alignment. If you have to go in three-step motion to be a blocker or a pitchback at the opposite flank, you are going to aim for the toes of the inside foot of the diveback potion. This path will be flatter. Again, you will be back at our diveback spot after three steps. One path is slightly deeper than the other.

Return Motion

You can also use return motion. Here, the halfback is in a wingback position, and he begins three-step motion to his diveback spot. At the snap, he reverses his field and comes back out in the direction he started from. This change-up is great to use if the secondary or defense is adjusting with motion. If the secondary rotates with motion or the defensive line shifts with motion, you can attack any weakness they create by using return motion.

Extended Motion

Finally, the last motion used is called extended, or long, motion. The halfback is in the wingback position, and when the quarterback reaches a certain part of the cadence, he takes off and sprints. All of these motions are done at full speed, as fast as you can possibly run. You do not teach your people to go in motion with a slow jog type of technique. You want this to be fast, so as not to give the defense time to recognize what you plan to do. When you go in extended motion 7, you go across the formation and snap the ball when the motion back gets to a certain landmark on the field.

Numbering the Defense

Numbering the 50 Defense

Numbering the defenders is very important because most of the blocking rules are communicated with respect to the numbers of key players in the defensive scheme. This system of numbering the defense is taught to players on the first day of training camp, as well as on the first day of spring practice. Diagram 1.33 shows a 50 defense. If you are going to run a play to the right, you draw an imaginary line through the attackside A gap and number the defensive team from inside out. The inside linebacker is #1, the defensive end is #2, the outside backer is #3, and the defensive back is #4. If the coverage is sky support or safety support, the flat defender is #4. If the coverage is using corner support, that corner in the flat is numbered #4. The man covering deep would be #5. In this diagram, the corner is up close, and the safety is back, making the corner the fourth man. You call him #4 and call the safety covering deep #5.

On the backside, you do not use 0, so the nose would be #1, the inside backer #2, the defensive end #3, and the outside linebacker #4. The backside corner, then, would be #5. The safety on the backside would be the 6 run defender to either side. The game plans are set up to attack #3 in most defenses, find out what his reaction is, and then go to the companion plays that attack #2 or that attack #4. Since plays are called this way, it is important that all of the team and coaches know how to number defenders.

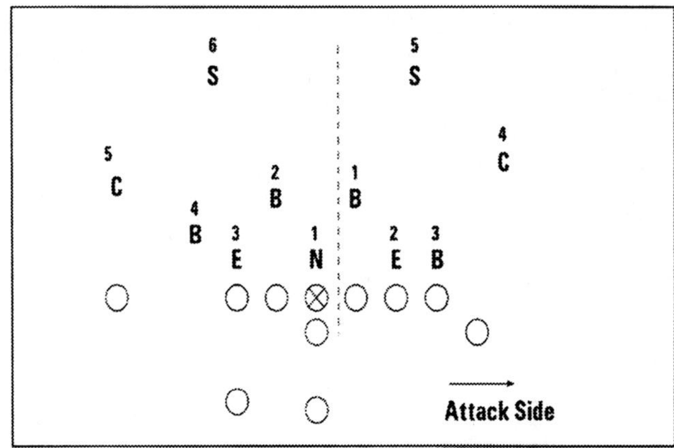

Diagram 1.33

Numbering the 43 Defense

Option blocking is dependent on knowing who is #2, #3, and #4. If you look at the 4-3 defense illustrated in Diagram 1.34, you see another seven-man front. In order to run a play to the right, you draw the imaginary line through the attackside A gap and again number defenders from inside out. The defensive tackle is #1; the outside backer over the tackle is #2; the defensive end is #3; the force player, or flat defender, is #4; and the deep cover guy is #5. To the backside away from the direction of the play, the middle backer is #1, the defensive tackle is #2, the defensive end is #3, the outside backer is #4, the corner is #5, and the weak safety is #6. It is very important that everyone understands this numbering and are on the same page.

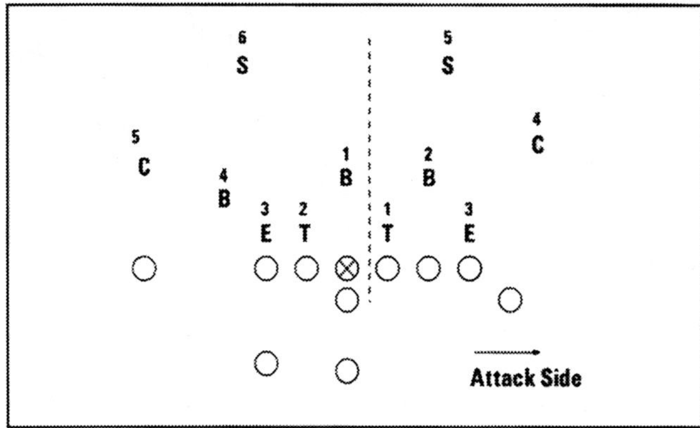

Diagram 1.34

Numbering the Eight-Man Front

The eight-man front defense is shown in Diagram 1.35. In this defense, to run a play to the right, you draw the imaginary line through either the attackside A gap or the right A gap and number inside out. The defensive tackle and the inside linebacker are going to be #1 and #2. If the inside backer is on an inside shade and the tackle is on an outside shade, then the backer is #1 and the tackle is #2. If the tackle is inside and the backer is outside, then reverse the count. The defensive end is #3, the outside linebacker is #4, the corner is #5, and the safety is #6. To the backside, the defensive tackle and the inside linebacker are again #1 and #2, the end is #3, the backer is #4, and corner on the other side is #5. The eight-man front is a balanced defense.

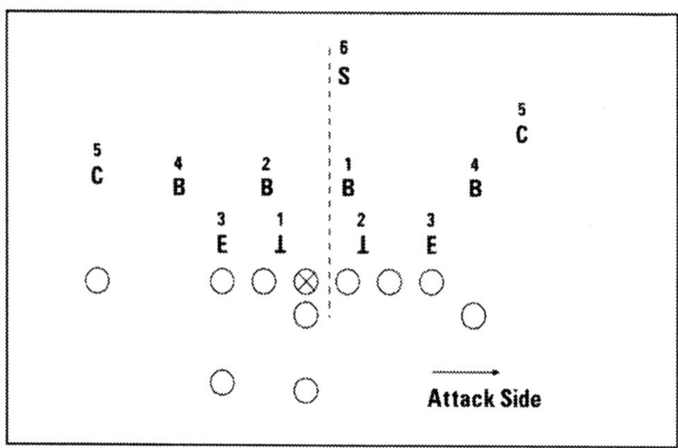

Diagram 1.35

Huddle Procedure

Coaching huddles should not be a big deal. You tell your players what you want them to do and expect them to do it. Here, several things about the huddle that are important are mentioned. The huddle is illustrated in Diagram 1.36. The center sets the huddle seven yards from the football, with his shoulders square, facing the quarterback. In the huddle, all players stand in a two-point stance with their hands on their knees and their eyes on the quarterback. The split end (X receiver) is also next to the center. The center is here because he has to get to the ball and get ready to snap, and the spread end usually has the farthest to run to get lined up. You want the split end as far up in the huddle as you can get him. The two guards (#4 and #6 men) are next to those two on a 45-degree angle. They are also in a two-point stance, their shoulders are 45 degrees, but they are looking at the quarterback. The tackles, the #3 man and the #7 man, align next and are now perpendicular to the line of scrimmage and facing each other. The tight end and the fullback are next in the huddle and are facing each other. The right half and the left half are last in the huddle and face each other. The quarterback steps into the huddle and is also standing. The play is called in the huddle only once. Some teams call the play twice, but when the quarterback steps into that huddle and says, "Ready," everybody has his eyes up and on the quarterback. He is going to call the play one time. Time does not exist for guys to be arguing about who's open, who can block some guy, etc. All the huddle chatter must be stopped. The leadership capabilities of the quarterback must take over in the huddle, and stopping chatter is where it starts. If chatter is going on in the huddle, then it's going to be disruptive, and players will miss cadences and miss plays. They are not going to stand in huddles, repeat the play two or three times, and waste time. The play is said once. Players are expected to listen, pay attention, concentrate, say, "Ready, break," clap their hands, and sprint to the line of scrimmage as fast as they can. These simple rules are all you coach in huddle procedure. You don't overcoach it. You expect the quarterback to take control in the huddle, and he is only going to call each play one time. The players are expected to listen and concentrate.

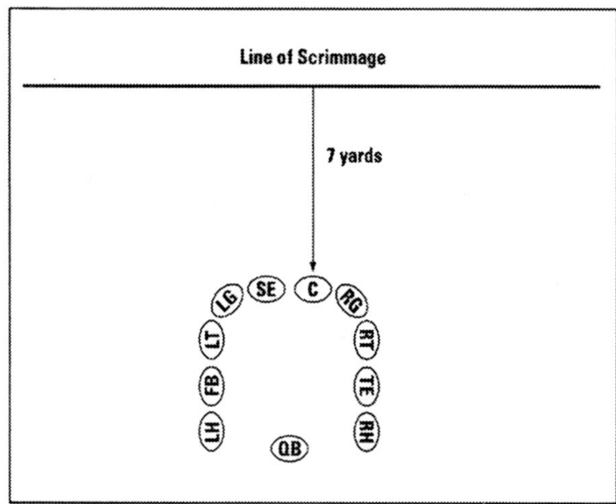

Diagram 1.36

Cadence

Many people ask how the team does all the shifting and motioning and gets it timed up properly. The answer is to time it up with a lot repetitions and also time it up with cadence. Three basic cadences exist. The first one is on sound – the quarterback says, "On sound." The second cadence is on go, and the third is on short go.

Each of these three cadences has a delayed version. Three simple cadences can blossom into a number of different cadences. The first one is the first sound cadence, and in the huddle, the quarterback says, "On sound." After leaving the huddle, the players sprint to the line of scrimmage and run the play on the first sound they hear. The quarterback checks to make sure everybody is positioned properly and ready to go, and then he says, "Set." When he says does, the ball should be snapped on the "s" in set. You do not want the ball coming up late. You want it coming up quickly so the whole team takes off on the "s."

The second cadence is on go. The quarterback, in the huddle, will say, "On go." At the line of scrimmage, the quarterback will say, "Set," which corresponds to on sound.

If the defense jumps on the "s" in set, they are offside. The quarterback says, "Set," pauses, and then calls two numbers, "21," pauses, "21," pauses, "Red," pauses, "Set go." You can also enable an audible system. The quarterback can come to the line, look the defense over, select the play he needs, and then start the cadence and call the two-digit number that corresponds to the play to run. He can call a definite play in the huddle, sprint up to the line of scrimmage, and call any number, which means nothing because the play has already been called in the huddle. The ball will be snapped on the "g" in go. As soon as the quarterback says, "Set go," the players fire off on the "g" as they explode off the ball and run the play. Cadences are used sometimes to time up motion. When your backs are going in three-step motion, if they leave on the "r" in red, it will time up well. If they leave in one-step motion, you tell them to leave just about the time the "s" in set is being uttered. Not a lot of time is between set and go. You tell the backs to anticipate the "s" in set and leave just a little ahead of the "s." The players get used to that timing through repetition. With time, they can work the timing out on their own. You don't have to do this, though. Many coaches just give a nod, or lift a heel, and the back takes off, and they snap the ball.

The third cadence is on short go. This phrase means the quarterback comes out over the ball and simply says, "Red," pauses, "Set go." Again, the ball will be snapped on the "g" in go. Three-step motion starts on the "r" in red. One-step motion starts on the "s" in set. The ball is snapped on go.

In practice, you should use on sound for every drill you do in order to save time. The other cadence used in drills occurs when the backs are timing plays with three-step motion or one-step motion, where you should use short go. You should not waste time with a lot of different cadences in practice. Use set all the time so you don't waste time and, in the process, get more reps. The more reps you get, the better. Use the cadence, "Red, set go," for timing plays and set for doing drills. During team period, when practicing 11 on 11, the quarterbacks should never call the same cadence twice. They should keep mixing it up.

To create other cadence variables, look at these three basic cadences and create a delayed version of each one. If the quarterback says, "On delayed sound," then the players will sprint-out over the ball, and the quarterback will yell, "Set." Everybody then pauses, and when he's ready, the quarterback will say, "Set," again. The ball will be snapped on the "s" in set, the second time the quarterback says, "Set."

If the quarterback says, "On delayed go," then he goes through all the numbers and says, "Set," pauses, "83," pauses, "83," pauses, "Red," pauses, "Set go." If the defense thinks that, once they hear numbers, they're going to get off as soon as the quarterback says, "Go," then you get them with this cadence, because the ball is not going to be snapped on go. A second set of, "Red, set go," will be called. The ball will be snapped on the second go, three-step motion will start on the second red, and one-step motion will start on the second set go. The quarterback is going to say, "On delayed go," come up over the ball, and say, "Set, 83, 83, red, set go, red, set go." The quarterback can snap the ball on the second sequence, and the defense has no idea when the ball is going to be snapped.

The last one is on delayed short go. That cadence simply means that the quarterback says, "Red, se, go," as he did short go, except he says it twice. The quarterback says, "Red," pauses, "Set go," (nothing happens) pauses, "Red," "Set go." The ball is snapped on the "g" in go, three-step motion starts on the second red, and one-step motion starts on the second set.

You can have a multiple cadence system. You don't want to get locked in so that the defense knows when the ball is snapped. One of the things that can happen is that, if you have, "Red, set go," and another, "Red, set go," when you say it the second time, your backs start in motion. Once the defense sees your backs going in motion, then they know that the next, "Red, set go," is the live count. However, you can do a couple of things to create some doubt for the defense. One is to say, "Red, set go," but have your backs shift on the first set of, "Red, set go," then snap the ball on the second set of, "Red, set go." The backs have reset themselves, and you say, "Red, set go," again, and now the ball is snapped, and you take off.

The other cadence you can use is sight, motion, sound. That cadence means the quarterback turns and makes eye contact with the running back to set him in motion, and you snap the ball on sound. Now the defense has no way of knowing what you are doing, so you have them in a rocking chair, guessing.

Line Calls

As you look at your offensive line, the first man over the ball is the center; he is going to be the first guy who makes a call. His call is odd, even, gap, or shade. He will make one of those four calls. If a head-up noseguard is on him, he calls, "Odd." If the guards are covered and the center is not, he calls, "Even." If two players are in each A gap, then he calls, "Gap." If one is in the gap, or shaded, and nobody is in the other gap, then he calls, "Shade."

The guards will also call one of four calls. They will say, "Uncovered," which means the center and the tackle are covered and the guards are not. They can say either, "Covered inside," or "Covered outside." If they say, "Covered," and do not say, "Inside," or "Outside," then the defender is directly in a head-up 2 technique. As the center finished his calls, then both guards make the call on their side.

The tackles call technique numbers. If a nose is on the center and nobody is on the guards except linebackers off the ball, plus two defensive tackles that are head-up in 4 techniques, then the tackles say, "0-4." Those numbers are the first two defensive line techniques (0 and 4) on their side. If the defense has a nose in a 2 technique and a defensive tackle in a 5, then the call is 25. If you have a 3 technique and a 5 technique, then it's 35. A 3 technique and a 7 technique is 37. Tackles simply call a two-digit number for whatever techniques they see the defensive linemen in. They call the first two techniques from the nose of the center to their side, and they just call the numbers. This method helps greatly during games.

Oftentimes, your press box coach will have a great deal of difficulty identifying the defensive techniques and alignments of the defense. Your coordinators can get the players on the sideline after the first series of the game, sit them down, and ask their line calls. The center might say, "I called odd." The guards might have called, "Uncovered." The tackles may have called, "0-5." By doing this on the sideline, you can reconstruct whatever the defensive spacing was, even if you as the coach on the sideline can't see it very well. If the press box coach can't see it very well, you can reconstruct the defense on the sideline just by having the players call out those techniques. The other advantage of reconstructing the defense is that the linemen can listen to those line calls and learn how to interpret their blocking rules. If an end is supposed to block down, and he is hearing a 35 call, he knows a man is on the guard and the tackle, and he knows he has someone for him to block down to. As an offensive coach, you have your players make those calls every snap, and the defense never knows if a call means you're adjusting your blocking scheme or just calling their alignments in front of them. These calls mean nothing to a defensive coach, but it means everything to an offensive coach.

Option Blocking

The last item covered in this chapter concerns the option blocking rules, which are also covered in the receiver chapter. The fact that you must know how to number the defense must be reemphasized. If you are playing against the 50 defense, for example, the inside backer is #1, the defensive end is #2, and the outside backer is #3. The strong safety is the fourth player and is #4. The comer is the deep player, so he is #5. If you say, "Option," the halfback and the end are going to block #4 and #5. Whoever aligns widest blocks #5. The spread end's rule is to release and stalk #5. The word option tells the widest man to release and stalk #5; therefore, the halfback inside the end will flare and block #4. The rules are release and stalk #5, flare and block #4. This rule also tells the quarterback that his pitch key is the third defender.

A change-up to option is what is called option load. If you call option load against the same defense, the widest man will again release and stalk #5. He can run him off to the goal line if he is in man coverage. The inside man will load #3. Load tells the quarterback that his pitch key is #4. It also tells the inside back to load block #3 because the quarterback is going to #4.

If you add option crack against the 50 defense, the widest man will crack #4. If #4 is in a crackable position, you crack him. You come down and crack #4 by putting your head across the front and above the waist (this scenario will be explained in Volume 2). The inside man will flare and block #5. Option crack also tells the quarterback his pitch key is still #3.

You can use two other adjustments. The first is option gut. If you go back to the 50 defense, option gut means the flank would still be blocked like option – the widest man releases and stalks #5, while the inside man flares and blocks #4. The quarterback is still going to option #3. Option gut means that you are going to exchange the assignments of the guard and the tackle. You bring the tackle inside and pull the guard around for the backer. The defensive end is unblocked, and you take care of him with either a backside pulling guard or the fullback, depending on what style of option you run. If the defense is going to squeeze down to your tackle all day and scrape the linebacker over the top, this scheme will be effective at picking up the linebacker.

The other – and final – adjustment is called option pitch. Using that same 50 defense, what happens is that the halfback and the guard switch assignments. You are still going to block #2, option #3, and block #4 and #5. What happens is that the spread end will release and stalk #5 or run him off if he is man-to-man. The tackle blocks on, but now the halfback is going to block the inside linebacker, and the guard is going to pull and then block #4. You have the fullback fill for the pulling guard in case the backer plugs. Option pitch is the switch in assignments between the guard and the halfback. You could include the tackle with the option pitch, bring the tackle down, and let the fullback load #2, or you can keep it between the guard and the halfback and have those two switch assignments.

Summary

The basic organization for the offense described in this chapter is a wonderful system. It has the chance to be multiple, yet quite simple, and facilitates easy and quick communication.

2

20 Series

This chapter is about the 20 series. The 20 series is a series of plays – not just the sweep play. The 20 series includes the waggle, the trap up the middle to the fullback, the sweep play outside, off tackle plays, and counter plays. When putting your play packages together, you should have, at the least, an inside play, an outside play, a counter, and a pass. Having a complementary set of plays will help you complete the package. In the 20 series, the basic action in the backfield is the fullback diving for one side of the offensive center, with the halfback crossing the backfield and attacking the flank to the other side. The quarterback attacks the flank away from the direction that the halfback is attacking. You can see that at the same time you get at least three different points of attack threatened against the defense.

The 20 series is known to some people as the buck series. If the series is executed correctly, the offense should have great misdirection, and you should freeze the defense, especially the linebackers. The defense should not have any idea where the ball is or should at least be slowed down in terms of their pursuit, which allows your blockers to get to them. You want to be able to have your blockers get to those linebackers and those defensive people. And, if you can do that, you can force the defense to tackle your ballcarrier 1-on-1, which is another important thing the wing-T offense can do for you. If your backs are able to gain YAC (yards after contact) or break tackles, then you have a chance for some big plays.

121-129 Sweep vs. the 50 Defense

Starting with the easiest and most common 20 series play, the buck sweep play is also known as the 21 and 29 or sweep right and sweep left – you can give this play whatever name. Each play will be explained against three different defenses and will also be illustrated against the three most common defenses:

- The seven-man-front 50 defense
- The seven-man-front 4-3 defense
- The eight-man-front 4-4 defense

If you refer to the rules as each play is discussed, you will see you can basically block any defense with a simple set of blocking rules.

Diagram 2.1 illustrates the sweep right, which is also called 21, from the 100 formation. The series is the 20 series, indicated by the 2, and the point of attack for this play is the 1 hole on the right flank. When you put all these things together, you have a play call of 121.

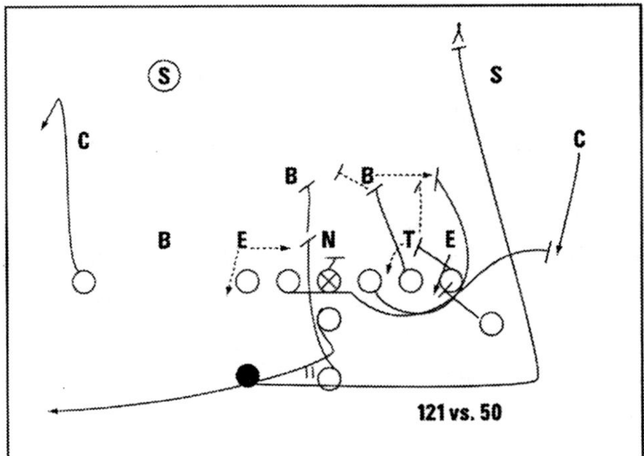

Diagram 2.1

In the playbook, the rule for the tight end, when aligned to the call, is gap-read-down. That rule means if a man is in the gap between the tight end and the tackle, then the tight end would block down on that man in the gap. He can use either a gap technique, with his head in front, or a down technique, with his head behind. He must use the gap technique if any threat exists of that defensive man penetrating the line of scrimmage. You say, "Gap-read-down," because if, for some reason, this defensive tackle would pinch inside and cross the offensive tackle's face, then the tight end would read that and go to the next level to help block the linebacker.

The offensive playside tackle's rule is also gap-read-down. When you start blocking even defenses, you will see how the tackle can also incorporate the read-down aspect into his technique. A couple of different things can happen against the 50 defense. You can interpret the tackle's rule to mean that he can come down on the first down man inside of him. If he does that, the tackle would come all the way down to the noseguard and help the center with his block. That assistance is one thing the tackle can do if you are playing against a great noseguard and you want to intimidate that guy a little bit. Bring the tackle down on him a few times, and he will be shaken up a bit. It will certainly get his attention and maybe even slow him down. The other thing that you can do is, if you feel that your center can handle the noseguard well, then give the center the noseguard by himself. Tell the tackle to interpret his rule as blocking the linebacker. His down block would be the first man to his inside, whether he's on the line or off the line. Therefore, he would be blocking the inside linebacker. When doing that, the tackle is going to rip through the inside number, or inside armpit, of the defensive tackle, and try to climb for the inside linebacker inside him. You always try to block these linebackers with your head across the front, so that the block is executed with the proper shoulder. The reason is that, in case the linebacker steps up hard, you can cut off any penetration that he might have.

The right guard's rule is to pull and kick out force, or kick out the first man outside the wingback's block. You pull with depth. The guard is coached to take two good depth steps and then flatten out and start working downhill. He is going to come tight, right off the wingback's block.

The center's rule is reach-area-away. You can interpret his rule however you want, or however you need to. If the guard has a head-up noseguard and wants to use a fire technique, that would be fine. If the noseguard is shaded a little bit and the center wants to use a reach technique, that would be fine also. Initially, you will execute a fire block, so the center would fire right, block with his left shoulder, and have his head to the right of the noseguard.

The backside guard will also pull. He will pull flat to the other guard's position, and from there he will get about a yard of depth. While he's pulling, he is looking at the playside inside linebacker.

The backside tackle is sent straight across the field to the cutoff. The cutoff is a point defined to be about four yards vertically up the field from the point of attack, which is the 1 hole. You're going to try to get the left tackle all the way across the field to the wide right side, four yards above the 2 hole. He is going to take the easiest release off, around, inside, or under the inside linebackers and get to this point to block at the cutoff. He's going to block the filling free safety or anybody who is filling at the point of attack. The corner is going to come and force the play, once he sees all the action. You need the frontside guard to kick out one of the players filling, corner or safety, whoever arrives first. Then you need the backside tackle to try to cut off the other one.

The halfback in the wing position is going to step for the inside foot of the tight end. The wing is going to block the first free man to his inside, which in a 50 defense would be the defensive end. If that defensive end wants to penetrate upfield, the wing must be on course to cut off that penetration. You want the wing to get his head across the front and make this block with his right shoulder, executing what is called gap technique. If the defensive end would be a reading type defensive end, and not a threat to penetrate, the wing would use down technique, putting his head behind and finishing the block down the line of scrimmage.

The frontside guard gets two good steps of depth and begins to flatten out on his third step. While he is pulling, he is looking at the corner. He is going to feel the wingback, come tight off the wingback's tail, and come on out to kick the corner out. As depicted in Diagram 2.1, pulling right will use a right shoulder block. The frontside guard is blocking the fourth player, who is the first man who shows outside the wingback's block. If a scraping linebacker were coming out and becoming the next guy closest to the wingback's down block, then the guard would kick out the scraping linebacker.

As the backside guard pulls, he's looking for the frontside inside linebacker. He gets to about a yard of depth to help him step around any of the trash around the line of scrimmage. As he comes around, he's going to wall off on the frontside inside linebacker as he scrapes. If that inside linebacker scrapes quickly, then the frontside guard should be in good position to wall him off. If that positioning happens and the right tackle – as he comes to the scraping linebacker – cannot get to him, the tackle will then look for the backside linebacker. You should get a block on both of the linebackers by doing this. If the frontside linebacker steps up, the tackle blocks him, and the backside linebacker scrapes, then the left guard would look for him to pick him up.

The fullback on the sweep is part of the blocking and is responsible for blocking the left backside A gap. The fullback takes a crossover step with his right foot and dives for the left foot of the center. Between the first and second step, he's going to be faking over an imaginary ball on his way to block his area. A couple of things can happen. The defensive end can squeeze down inside, and the fullback might end up blocking him. The defensive end may react vertically up the field. In that case, the fullback would continue on and block the backside A gap area for any pursuit, regardless of who shows.

The left halfback is the ballcarrier. The quarterback is going to come back two steps on the midline, begin to cross over on his third step, and the handoff will occur at this time. The halfback takes a crossover step on his first step, runs right through the heels of the fullback, and receives the football. As soon as he gets width outside the down block of the wingback, you want the halfback to make a north and south cut and get in the alley formed by the blocking of the pulling guards and the cutoff tackle.

The quarterback will continue to the flank and fake waggle. What he should be doing every time is keying the free safety to find out what kind of reaction the safety gives when you show the sweep play. You are going to come back and run the waggle play off the action of the free safety.

You can do a lot of things with the split end. You can send him to attempt to cut off the safety or can set up the waggle play by having him run a pass route. A lot of times, you can work on a waggle-out concept and hope that the corner covers the out. Then, one less body will be in the way of the sweep. Diagram 2.1 illustrates all of the blocking rules discussed.

121-129 vs. the 4-3 Defense

Another very popular seven-man front is the 4-3 (Diagram 2.2). This defense is extremely popular with the Miami Hurricanes and the Dallas Cowboys and has spread all over the country. Everyone seems to be running this defense. If you follow your rules, you should be able to block any defense, regardless of the defensive spacing.

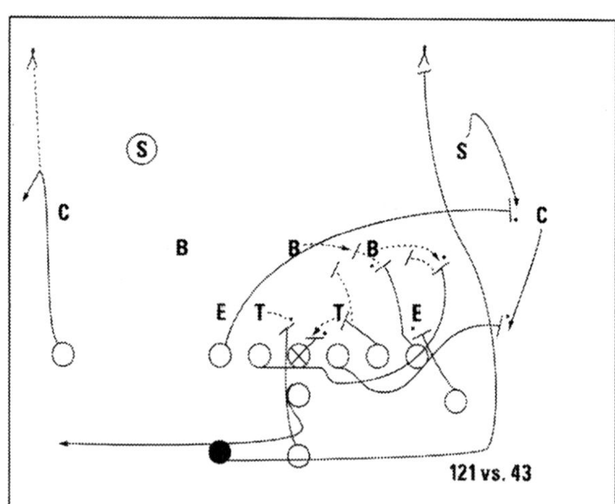

Diagram 2.2

The tight end is going to block gap-read-down. He's going to block the first free man to his inside on or off the line of scrimmage. In the 4-3 defense, the tight end would release inside and try to block the frontside strong linebacker. Release technique becomes important at this point. The tight end is told to use a down release. He will take a fire step inside, take his outside shoulder and forearm and rip through to get vertical on his linebacker. He would block with his head across the front (in Diagram 2.2, this block would be with the right shoulder). What can happen very quickly in this defense is for the strong linebacker, who is playside, to be scraping over the top and to the outside. If he does that, then the middle linebacker is probably a fast-flow guy. If the tight end stays on course and cannot get the frontside linebacker, he would then adjust his course and go block the middle linebacker.

As mentioned earlier, the right tackle's rule is also gap-read-down. In this defense, he has a man to block down. A defensive tackle is covering the guard, so he would interpret his rule and down block. He also knows he can read down, because the tackle can pinch inside. If he would pinch inside, the center's reach assignment would take care of him, and, at this time, the right tackle would also be a blocker at the linebacker level.

The right guard is going to pull with two good steps of depth, as described earlier. He will come tight off the wingback's block. The center takes a reach step and prepares to execute a fire technique against a potentially pinching defensive tackle. If the man is not pinching inside, then, as the right tackle comes down, he will finish this block off. In this case, the center has no one to block, so he drops his left foot back and holds in the frontside A gap area to protect against any penetration knocking off the pulling guards. It is basically an area assignment. You do not want any backside linebackers or any backside defensive linemen to run through that strong A gap and stop the sweep in the backfield. That coaching point is very important.

The backside guard pulls and, when he gets to the opposite guard's position, starts to get a little depth. The backside tackle goes for the cutoff four yards in front of the point of attack. The wingback is going to block the first free man to his inside. He's going to come down on the defensive end using either gap technique or down technique. The right guard pulls two good steps of depth, flattens out on the third step, and comes tight off the wingback's tail to block any force player who's coming to force the sweep. If you get the safety coming also, then the backside tackle is responsible for getting there and blocking him.

As the backside guard pulls, he gets a little depth so he can step around any penetration and wall off the frontside linebacker. If the guard is in position to wall him off, then he will have his head upfield. He will block with the left shoulder and wall the linebacker off. What often happens is this linebacker scrapes so fast that he's over in the kick-out area. The frontside guard would then kick him out, which means the backside guard can turn back and look for a middle linebacker. You really have two players assigned to every one of those linebackers and should have a great chance to get those linebackers blocked.

The fullback is going to dive with his right foot for the left foot of the center and block the defensive tackle if he closes in the A gap. If the A gap is not being threatened with pinch, it will definitely be threatened on the snap when the defensive tackle reads the guard pulling and starts to chase off his tail. The left halfback, again, is the ballcarrier and will receive the handoff from the quarterback, who takes two steps on the midline, crosses over, and then begins to attack the flank. The quarterback fakes waggle, and the halfback gets outside the tight end and the wingback's down blocks and makes a north-south cut. The spread end will work on his out route concept. Anytime you have an out route and the corner squats on you, the route turns into a fly. The receiver can get a pretty good feel for how the corner's going to play the out route. If the quarterback attacks the flank, he should read the weak safety and find out what his reaction is every time the ball is handed off.

121-129 Sweep vs. the Eight-Man Front

Diagram 2.3 illustrates the most common eight-man front. You can call this defense a 4-4, an eight-man front, a wide-tackle 6, or whatever type of nomenclature you want to give to this defense. The defense is going to be in positions somewhat similar to those illustrated.

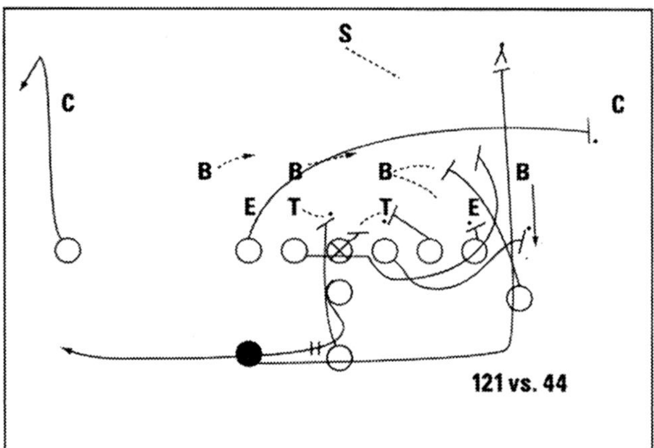

Diagram 2.3

Interpreting the rules again, this time the position to start with is the wingback. The wingback is going to block the first free man to hit his inside. The wing and the tight end need to communicate in this defense, because if the defensive end is playing an inside shade or is pinching inside, then the tight end is going to make a call and take the defensive end by himself. These two work together and are basically going to say, "You and me." They can call out numbers reflecting the technique of the defenders. These calls tell them who they are blocking and who they're not blocking. If the defender is inside the tight end, then the tight end should be able to take him, and the halfback will take the first free man inside, which would be the inside linebacker. Remember that the halfback's rule is the first free man to the inside. If the defender on the tight end is shaded a little bit outside or is head up but he's not jamming the tight end, you can get inside that defensive end to the linebacker and make that block successfully. The tight end goes to the inside linebacker, and the halfback takes the defensive end. The most common way to see this defense is with inside 7 techniques. The tight end will then block down on the 7-technique defensive end, since he's lined up a little bit inside of him and the wingback is blocking the first free man inside. The first free man would be the linebacker, who should be scraping directly to the play.

If the defense tries to run the linebacker through the C gap, they're probably not going to put the defensive end also in the C gap. In this case, the tight end would make the block on the C gap linebacker and the wingback would block the defensive end. The wing and the tight end, however, are 2-for-2 on the defensive end and the playside inside linebacker.

The right tackle is gap-read-down. He is going to come down on the man who is inside and use either a down technique or a gap technique, depending on the defensive tackle's reaction. If you don't know for sure, you always use the gap technique and put the head across the front. You block with the right shoulder, execute gap assignment, and keep that man between the blocker's legs.

The #4 player in this defense, the outside linebacker, is a little bit tighter. He's going to be the one who comes to force the sweep. The right guard, as he pulls and takes the good depth steps, better be ready. He's got to have his eyes on his target as soon as he takes his first step, and he ought to be ready for a fast kick-out block. The center will reach and hold the A gap area. He's looking, basically, for anything coming to the frontside A gap, which could be the tackle pinching, the linebacker blitzing, a linebacker taking a run through, or a backside tackle chasing. The center must hold in the A gap and not run upfield too fast, creating a run-through seam for linebackers or defensive linemen to stop the play in the backfield.

The fullback is an essential part of this blocking. He dives right foot for the left foot of center and is going to block the backside A-gap area. The backside guard will pull and get as far as the frontside guard position and then get some depth so he can step around all the trash. He gets a good yard of depth and then walls off tight to the down block. He's looking for the first backer to the inside. If that backer is already blocked, then he blocks the first man inside. It could be the outside linebacker going over the top. It could even be the backside linebacker going over the top. It also could be the free safety going through the alley. He must have his eyes up and on his target, which is the frontside linebacker, as soon as he pulls.

The left tackle, again, needs to go to cutoff as fast as he can. This time he'll probably have to cut the corner off. Against this defense, you have to recognize the reactions that you're seeing up front and also what kind of secondary rotation you're getting. A three-deep secondary can easily rotate to two deep, yet this offense has answers for it. More details about recognizing reactions will be discussed in the game planning section.

The spread end will work on his out route. The left halfback is the ballcarrier, and the quarterback's technique is the same. The quarterback hands the ball off to the left halfback and attacks the flank. The left halfback is nice and tight off the wingback's down block. Being tight to the wingback's block is important at this point. If the ballcarrier runs too wide, you give the outside linebacker or force player a chance to come into the backfield, beat your guard, and stop this play for a big loss. You do want to stretch the play, but as soon as you get outside the wingback's block, you want to turn north and south and make a good 90-degree cut. Even though the kick-out block might not be real wide in this defense, you can still make this sweep work.

124-126 Guard Trap vs. 50 Defense

The next play is 24 and 26, which is the handoff to the fullback up the middle. In this play, a lot of different blocking schemes can be used. The first one to discuss is 24 guard trap. Using 100 formation, with the play 24 guard trap, you get a play call of 124 guard trap (Diagram 2.4). This play will probably be the best that you can run against all the defenses, although really good alternatives exist for all the defenses. By following the blocking rules, you can block any type of play against any type of defense.

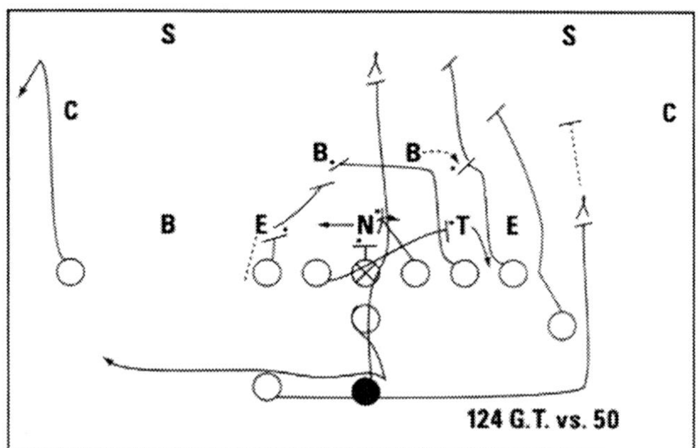

Diagram 2.4

The tight end's rule on 124 guard trap, when he is playside, is to go linebacker to cutoff. The tight end will step down inside, giving the picture of a sweep. After the first step, he is going to block the linebacker first and, if that man is taken care of, then will go to the cutoff.

The right tackle's rule is first backer from five, which means to block the first linebacker from the 5 man, the center. In the past, the tackle has gone immediately to the frontside linebacker, and the backside linebacker comes over the top and makes the play all the time. Instructing the frontside tackle to go immediately all the way to the backside linebacker allows the tight end to take the frontside linebacker. The guard trap now has one blocker, at least, assigned to each of the linebackers, giving the play a little bit of a chance. The right tackle uses evasive technique and tries to get away from the defensive tackle. Normally, the frontside linebacker is going to scrape. If he scrapes for the sweep, then the tight end will block him, while the right tackle goes for the backside linebacker.

The right guard's rule is gap, lead, backer, or influence. That rule is made up of a lot of words. Gap means, if somebody is in his inside gap, he's got to block down. Lead means, if nobody is in his inside gap, but a man is on the center, he's going to be the lead blocker on that defender. The lead blocker is, basically, the double-team blocker. The center's rule is going to be post left. Therefore, against a 50 defense, these two guys would post and lead on the noseguard. The center is going to post. He steps with the left foot and blocks with his right shoulder. He elevates his aiming point a little bit higher up in the numbers and tries to get the noseguard up so his hip is exposed. This maneuver enables the lead blocker to block him at the hip, which gives great line movement. The backer and influence part of the right guard's rules applies to even defenses. In this case, against a 50 defense, he does have somebody to lead on, so he comes down. The guard and the center should work their tails together, swing their tails, and finish the block down the line. You want the noseguard to be driven to the left.

The left guard's rule is to pull and trap. He is going to pull inside out and trap. He will pull and adjust to the post lead. The left guard adjusts tightly and comes inside out, trapping the first player who shows beyond the right guard. As he finishes his block, he should swing his tail and finish the defender back into the backfield, creating a nice lateral opening in the defense.

The left tackle's rule is to block the second man. When you count the backside of the defense, he is going to block the second man on the backside. you want him to cut off the defensive end. If the end is an upfield player, he will not stop this play, and, therefore, you can continue on to cut off the linebacker.

The right halfback's rule is to fake his sweep block and then go to cut off. The other thing you can do is, if the frontside defensive end is a real pain for the offense, you can continue to block down on him with the wingback or the tight end. If you know you can get the linebackers blocked without using the tight end, you could block the tight end on to help with the defensive end. In most cases, the defensive end should be frozen by the sweep action coming to him.

The fullback gets the ball going up the middle. His footwork against the odd defense is to run straight up the midline. He takes his first step with his right foot and runs right down the midline. The quarterback will reverse pivot for two steps but give the fullback the midline in odd defense. If the noseguard fights the center-guard double-team, then the ballcarrier can actually cut behind the double-team. Sometimes, that move gives you a great play. Normally, you would like to have the double-team be successful and move the nose to the left. The fullback, as he comes through on the midline, can break tightly off the double-team toward the 4 hole. You want to stay tight to the lead blocker when you run through a hole and stay away from the trapper. The ballcarrier is told not to trip on the trapper's feet.

The left halfback crosses over and makes a great sweep fake with the quarterback. As the quarterback attacks the flank, he fakes waggle. The halfback attacks the flank, makes the north-south 90-degree cut, and practices his sweep cut. He can also become a downfield blocker. You can do a number of things with the split end. You can send him to cutoff or can continue to work the waggle-out concept and find out how those corners are going to play.

124-126 Guard Trap vs. 4-3 Defense

Diagram 2.5 illustrates how the rules are going to be interpreted for the 4-3 defense. The play shown is 124 guard trap. The tight end is backer cutoff. He is going to try to release inside and get the linebacker blocked. If the linebacker is scraping quickly to the outside, the end can turn with him and try to chase and block him, or the end can let him go and move on to the cutoff area and try to block one of the safeties. If the linebacker is scraping quickly toward the line of scrimmage, he is probably not going to make the play on 24 guard trap, because he is trying to scrape out and make the tackle on the sweep. You can also have the tight end block on, if the defensive end has become a real problem.

The right guard's role is gap, lead, backer or influence. The defensive tackle is usually a two or three technique, therefore, the guard doesn't have anybody in his gap. The center is not covered, therefore, the guard would not use his lead assignment and would double-team. The third part of the guard's rule is to go to backer. The guard goes to the linebacker, if he can get there. He must go using his good release technique. He will try to block the middle linebacker with his head across the front using a right-shoulder block. If the defensive tackle is lined up in a very tight head up technique and jamming the guard very hard or lined up in a slight inside shake technique, the guard

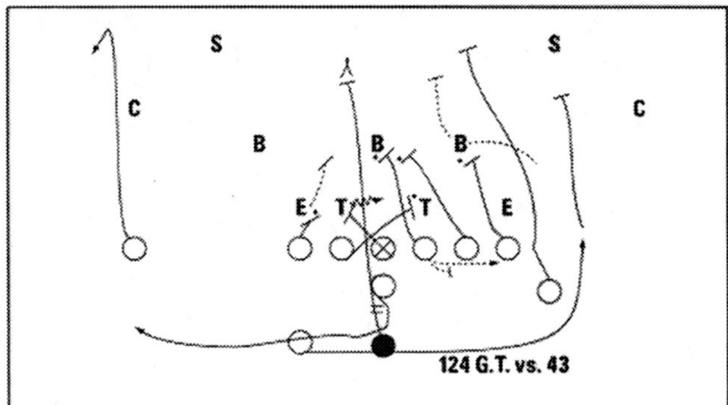

Diagram 2.5

would go to the influence part of the rule. The right guard can be influential in two different ways. You can pull him as done on the sweep play, or you can have him pass set to the outside and block the defensive end.

The center has to block back to the left for the pulling guard. The defensive linemen's technique will dictate whether he uses a gap technique on his assignment or uses a down technique. The left guard is going to pull and trap. Actually, on this play, you are going to trap the first man who shows outside the right guard's block. In the 4-3 defense, it would be the man head up on the guard. The left tackle is going to block the second man, so he will block the defensive end if he squeezes. If the end is an upfield player, he can release and try to look for the backside linebacker scraping to the play.

The right tackle's rule is to block first backer from five. He will go to the middle linebacker in the 4-3 defense. Versus the 4-3 defense, two people are assigned to the middle linebacker, which is great, because the guard may have to interpret his rule and use his influence assignment. You still have one lineman assigned to block the middle linebacker. The middle backer is the guy who can stop the trap faster than anyone.

The wingback will take a step as if to block on the sweep and then go to the cutoff. He must not get in a hurry. He must fake the sweep block and then go to cutoff. The spread end can either block at the cutoff or continue to work on his waggle-out technique.

The fullback has an even defense. His first step in an even defense is with his right foot for the left foot of the center. The quarterback will reverse pivot with two steps on the midline. He hands the fullback the ball, and the fullback stays tight to the block back by the center on the defensive tackle. The fullback could conceivably receive the handoff with the defensive tackle or nose fighting across the face of the center's block. The fullback can run right through the backside of the center's block in that case.

The left halfback fakes the 21 sweep, makes a 90-degree cut, and goes to be a cutoff blocker. The quarterback takes two steps on the midline, makes the sweep fake, and then attacks the flank, reading the free safety.

124-126 Guard Trap vs. 4-4 Defense

When blocking this play against the eight-man front or the 4-4 defense (Diagram 2.6), the rules still hold up just fine. If you look at the tight end, he still blocks backer to cutoff. If he can get inside the defensive end, then he will get inside and look to go block the backer. If he can't block the backer, then he's going to go to cutoff. Right tackle, again, is first backer from five and is going to block the frontside linebacker. He is going to try to block that man with his head to the inside (in Diagram 2.6, this block would be with the right shoulder).

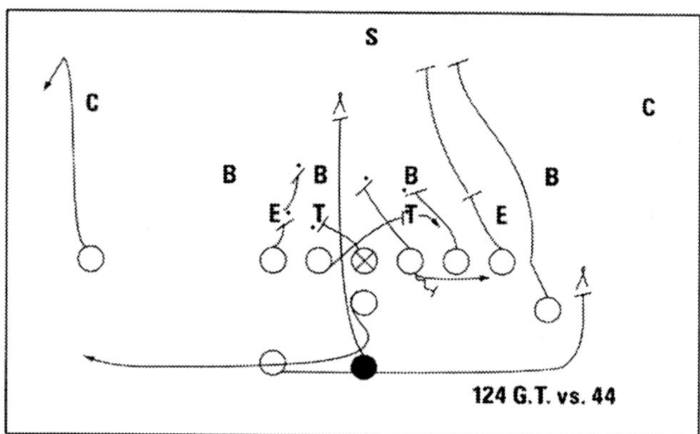

Diagram 2.6

The right guard has gap, lead, backer, or influence. In the 4-4 defense, no defender is in the inside gap, and no one is on the center for him to lead. He is going to have to try to get inside and block the backside linebacker, since the tackle has the frontside linebacker. Notice again, all the linebackers are accounted for. If the defensive tackle were a 2 technique or an inside shade and was not going to let anyone inside, then the right guard would use one of his two influence assignments. He will either influence by pass setting and kick out the defensive end or pull influence and make the play look just like 21 sweep. If that event happens, then the right tackle needs to go to that backside linebacker and the tight end needs to go to the frontside linebacker. Two people are always going to be assigned to block the inside backers.

The center has to block back on the defensive lineman to his left to secure him for the pulling guard. The left guard is going to pull and trap using his right shoulder inside out and finishing the block back toward the line of scrimmage. The left tackle blocks the second man. If the defensive end is squeezing, he'll block him. If not, he's going to be upfield to block the linebacker.

The wingback will fake his sweep block and then block at the cutoff. The fullback, versus an even defense, takes off with his right foot to the left foot of center. He stays tight to the center's block and makes the cut wherever he finds the seam. The left halfback fakes the 21 sweep. The quarterback takes his two steps on the midline, gives the ball between the first and second step to the fullback, fakes to the halfback on waggle, and then attacks the flank. Finally, the split end can block at the cutoff, or you can have him running an out route. The out route is preferred because it keeps one less body from the cutoff and also establishes how the defense is going to play the waggle pass.

Variations for 124-126

Some blocking scheme variations exist for 24. It's important that you run the base offense and not give up on it if a defensive scheme might stop one particular blocking scheme. You should always find a way to have the 24 play in your game plan, and it should be in there every week. You should figure out the best way to block it. One of the best ways to block this play against a 50 defense is to just block on. Basically, any seven-man front can be blocked with "on blocking." The tight end, playside tackle, frontside guard, center, backside guard, and backside tackle are all using "on" technique. When they use that technique, their head is going to go to the called point of attack. The center will use his left-shoulder block, and the left guard and left tackle will use left-shoulder blocks. Everybody on the right is using a right shoulder block. Each lineman is attempting to get his head inside and block the man on him. One of the things to tell your guards is to step down to the nose on both sides, giving him the feeling of someone coming down on him, and then climb vertically to the linebackers. That technique also gives you good inside-out position on each linebacker, which is what you want.

Everyone else runs the play exactly the same. That play can be used against any seven-man front, whether the seven-man front is odd or even (Diagram 2.7 and 2.8).

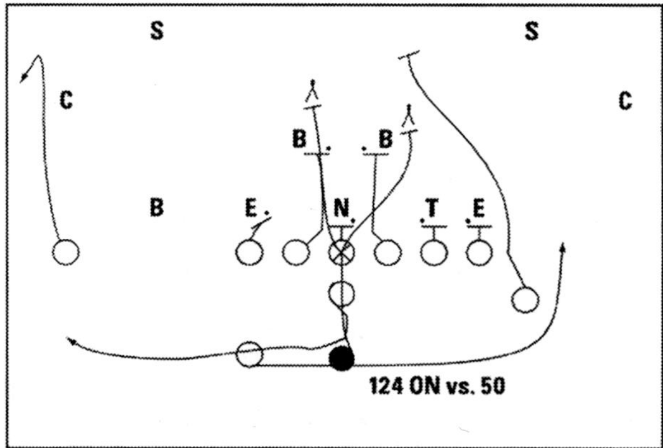

Diagram 2.7

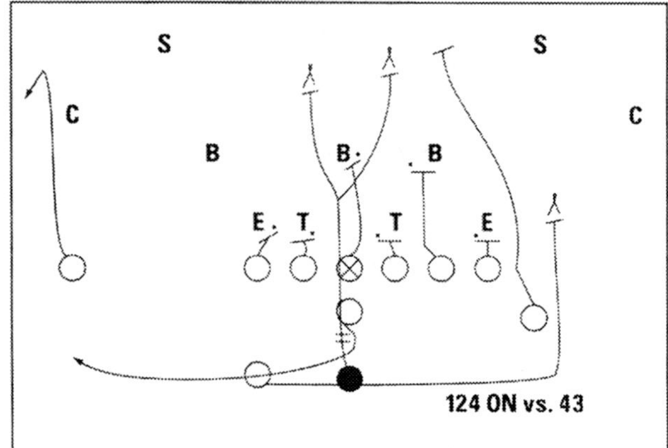

Diagram 2.8

Another thing you can do against even defenses is block 124 Gut with what is called gut blocking. You can run it against any defense, but especially against an even defense (Diagram 2.9). Anytime you add gut to a call, the word gut tells you that the man who was pulling to trap is now going to fold up around the center's block through the hole gut, and you are not going to trap. You can block on the linebacker. The right guard would use his influence assignment. If a defensive tackle, as soon as he sees the guard pull, reacts out to the offensive tackle, then he is susceptible to the influence blocking scheme. He's a great guy to run gut against. Also, if you see a linebacker scraping too fast to the sweep, then he's a great guy to run "gut" against. This play will look exactly like the sweep to the defense. Even the blocking scheme will look exactly the same. The right guard is going to pull, execute 21, and pull to block the fourth defender. If the outside linebacker or fourth defender comes hard on the sweep fake, and the guard's action, then you have a chance to draw one more person away from the play and get the other blockers up the field. It's important to have the backside defensive end blocked because he's too close to the mesh point with the quarterback and the fullback. You do not want anything disrupting that. You can use an on

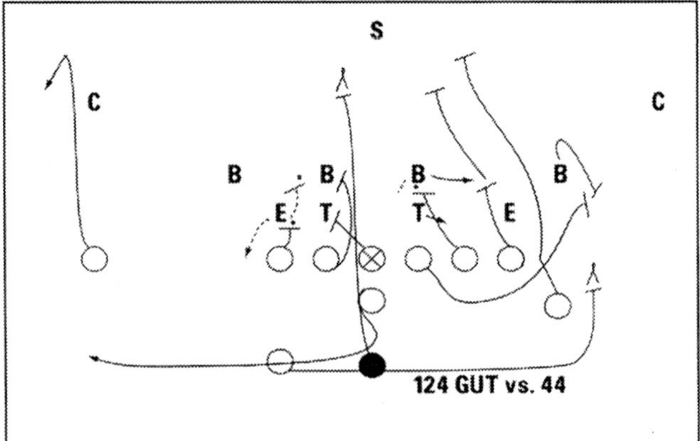

Diagram 2.9

technique, and, if the defensive end is an upfield player, then you can work upfield and cut off the backside linebacker. If the defense plays a 4-3 (Diagram 2.10), then the blocking scheme does not change. This play influences the frontside defensive tackle in even defensive schemes, especially when he is reading the sweep pull.

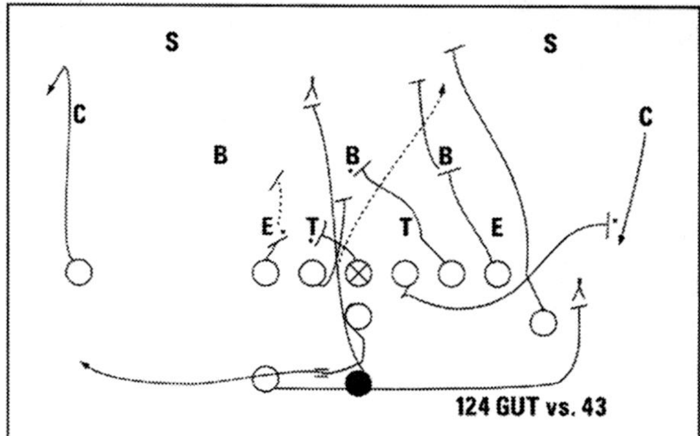

Diagram 2.10

You can run 124 gut against a 50 defense, as well as using the same rules (Diagram 2.11). Against an off defense, you want to use it as a key breaker for people who might be keying the guards. The right guard is going to pull, and he practices his sweep kick-out. Kicking out the corner should make the play look like the sweep and, hopefully, should divide the defense a little bit. The fullback's cuts on 124 gut should be north and south and more vertical.

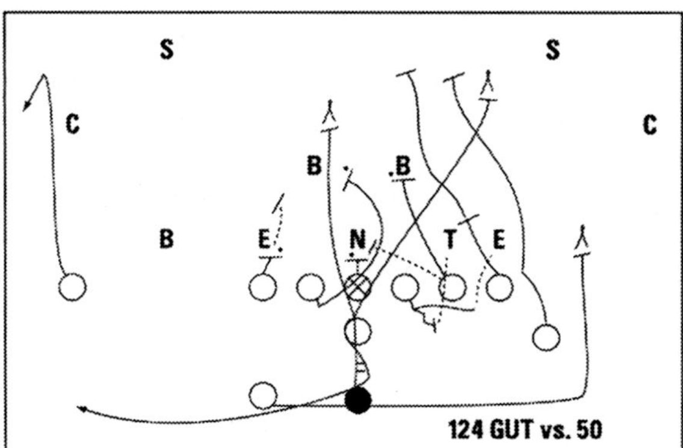

Diagram 2.11

These methods are probably the most popular to block the 24 gut play up the middle. Two different ways are normally used to block this play in every game plan. It's a basic staple of the wing-T offense, and you don't want one defensive reaction to stop the play, especially if that defensive reaction probably sets up another play.

121-129 Waggle Pass vs. 50 Defense

One of the classic plays in the 20 series is the waggle (Diagram 2.12). The 21 waggle means you are going to fake 21 sweep. The line knows the word waggle means you are faking the sweep to the right, but the quarterback is actually going to keep the ball after the fake and attack the opposite flank with a waggle pass. As explained earlier, the last number indicates the point of attack or the hole number where you are attacking. If you add the word waggle, the actual point of attack is exactly opposite the 1 hole – in this case, the 9 hole.

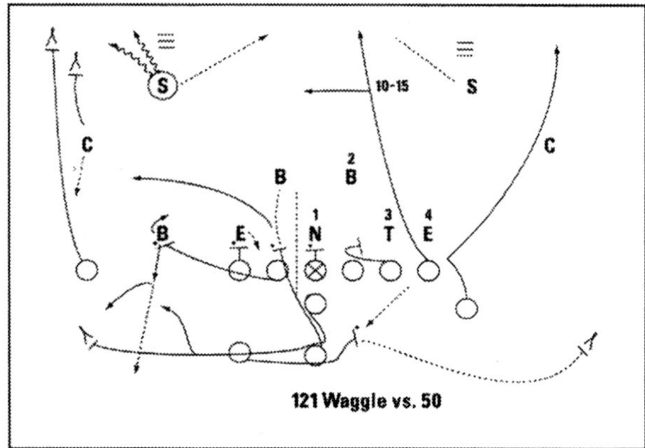

Diagram 2.12

The rules for the offensive linemen are very important. The rule for the left tackle, or the playside tackle, is gap down on. If a defender is in the inside gap, then the tackle will come down to block him. If a defender is down over the guard, then the tackle will come down and block on him. If not, then the playside left tackle will block on. One thing you want is the lineman's head to the outside. The first step is with the left foot, which facilitates blocking with the right shoulder and using on technique. If the defensive lineman (end or tackle) pinches inside, then the tackle must be able to swing his tail and finish the block inside, staying on the defensive end or tackle.

The left guard is going to pull and log. You want to come on an inside-out path similar to a kick-out. Rather than kick-out, you use a wrong-shoulder kick-out, which means you're going to log block the end man by putting your head to the outside. It is a right-shoulder block. The pulling guard also wants to swing his tail and finish the block back upfield, or to the inside, if he can.

The center's rule is to block one or cup to the right. As you know from the discussion on how to count defenders, on the backside of the play, the first defender from the attackside A gap would be #1. In this example, the 50 defense, a noseguard is #1, the right inside linebacker is #2, the backside defensive tackle is #3, and the backside defensive end or backer is #4. They are the defenders to the right, away from the point of attack. If a #1, a noseguard, is on the center, then the center will also use an aggressive technique, just as the left tackle did. He will use a right-shoulder right block, actually described in the individual technique as on right.

The backside right guard will pull, cross over for depth, and block at the flank. The right tackle is going to short pull and check #2, the second defender, off the backside of the play. He will pull all the way down to the center if he has to, checking the #2 defender. If #2 is not coming on any kind of a blitz, then the tackle will turn immediately back and block the #3 defender, thus preventing pursuit.

The fullback and the halfback who fakes the sweep are also important parts of the blocking protection. The fullback steps with his right foot to the left foot of center and, on his second step, widens his path slightly. As he comes through the hole, he is going to block the playside inside linebacker. If the linebacker happens to blitz in either the A gap or the B gap, then the fullback is assigned to block him. The fullback also uses a right-shoulder block, with his head to the outside. If the linebacker is not blitzing, then the fullback can now be a receiver in the left flat. The fullback is asked to climb to a depth of four to six yards as he goes out to the flat.

The left halfback is also a blocker. After the quarterback fakes the sweep to him, and after he passes the mesh, the halfback will gear down and get inside out. He has the first man who shows outside of the backside right tackle's block. If no one comes at all, the halfback becomes a fifth receiver, flaring out wide to the right. Depending on what happens with the coverage, the quarterback may have to actually throw back and hit the halfback on the backside. This action also helps set up the waggle screen play, where you screen back to the halfback. But most important, the halfback must be a blocker first. He must block any defender chasing off the backside of the quarterback, in case the quarterback has to pull up to throw.

As the quarterback attacks the flank, he is going to read the safety on the weakside. He is going to read him for his reaction. As he's doing that, a couple of things can happen at the flank. You could get penetration, if the outside linebacker comes upfield, which may force the quarterback to pull up. If the outside defender squeezes down to the sweep, he will get log blocked, and the quarterback can continue outside to the flank. The linebacker may also drop in coverage.

The fullback, as mentioned earlier, is in the flat. Whoever is the inside man on the backside will run a crossing route. Whoever is the outside man will go deep. You can switch those routes by adding a call. If you split the end out wide, and your halfback is still in his position in a slot or a spread formation, then the halfback becomes the inside receiver and will run the crossing route. When coaching the crossing route, you want the backside receiver to take the quickest release he can off the ball. You want him to push up the field between the hash marks. As he sprints down the field, he should attack the area between the hash marks. If he sees no safety between the hashes, since he is running right down the middle, he's going to stay on that course and gives the quarterback a home run threat. If either one of the two safeties rotates to the middle between the hash marks, then around 10 yards, you want that crossing receiver to break it off and stay in an open area. You do not want him to cross the far hash. He will be open most of the time on the backside of the quarterback. The outside receiver on the backside, if he is split wide, would run a post and stay outside the hash mark so the field is divided and good pattern distribution exists. If the outside receiver is a tight receiver, he runs a fly route. You coach him to step one step down inside, like he's going to fake the sweep block, and then get deep. If the backside corner over commits to the sweep fake, then the wingback will run right past him and be wide open.

As the quarterback attacks the flank, he's been reading the free safety. Every time he hands the ball off on sweep, ever time he hands the ball off on guard trap or gut, he has been reading the free safety. By the time you call the waggle play, he should have a pretty good feel for how that free safety is reacting to the sweep. Whoever in the press box is watching the secondary should also have a pretty good feel for the reaction of that free safety. Is he chasing? Is he staying weak? What is he doing?

As the quarterback attacks the flank, if the free safety goes to the middle, then you are going to stay on the playside with the reads by the quarterback. The quarterback's progression is to look deep, and if he has the touchdown, take it. If not, look short, which is the flat. If nothing short exists, then the quarterback can run the ball. The defense is in a real bind to cover these things. If the playside corner rotates forward while the safety stays in the middle and tries to come up to stop the fullback in the flat, then the quarterback has a potential touchdown with the wide receiver deep. The quarterback should take the touchdown and hit it. Even in college football, people make that mistake a lot. If the corner stays deep, which is what he will normally do, then he will cover the deep. Sometimes if your receiver outmatches their corner in speed, you can still run right past the corner and can take the ball deep. So the quarterback will always check it. With the corner deep, he has the option to throw the ball short to the fullback in the flat or run the ball. The decision is based on the outside linebacker on the defense. If he is a dropper, you should have a great flank run, because he will cover the fullback in the flat. The defense, then, has no one to pull up the quarterback, who should have a great run. If the outside linebacker is coming upfield and the corner is going to be in the deep third, then no one is covering the flat, which is the first part of your read. When the weak safety rotates to the middle, your progression is playside deep-short-run.

If the free safety stays on the frontside hash or rotates weak to the waggle action, you know that the throwback possibilities are outstanding. As the quarterback gets out to the flank, he now has three receivers he can throw back to. He can hit the tight end down the middle, he can throw to the deep route on the backside, or he can actually throw all the way back to the halfback. Normally, what should happen is that the tight end is open on the crossing route. What you tell the tight end to do is to split the middle if no one is between the hashes. If the free safety rotates to the middle, the tight end should break it off at about 10-15 yards, somewhere in that vicinity, and gear down so he does not cross the hash mark, but also find an open seam and sit in it. He is the receiver the quarterback is probably going to try to throw back to. Many touchdowns have been made with the throwback off the waggle.

121-129 Waggle vs. 4-3 Defense

The play does not change significantly against an even seven-man front, such as the 4-3 defense (Diagram 2.13). The patterns are the same. The blocking rules are the same. The playside left tackle blocks gap-down-on. At this time, he must come down and block the defensive tackle, using either gap technique or down technique, depending on the tackle's reaction. The left guard is going to pull and log the defensive end. The center is going to block one or cup right. Since no 1 is on him, he will cup right. The center will take a step to the left and help in case the defensive tackle is pinched to the inside. If no threat exists, the center can look for the backside tackle pinching, the linebacker on a run-through, or the backside defensive tackle scraping or pursuing. The center will help with anything he sees. He's going to reach-step with his left foot and, as that foot gets in place, drop his right foot back and block whatever comes to him. The fullback widens his path and can block either the middle linebacker or the outside linebacker if they stunt in A or B gap. If not, he can go on to the flat and be part of the route.

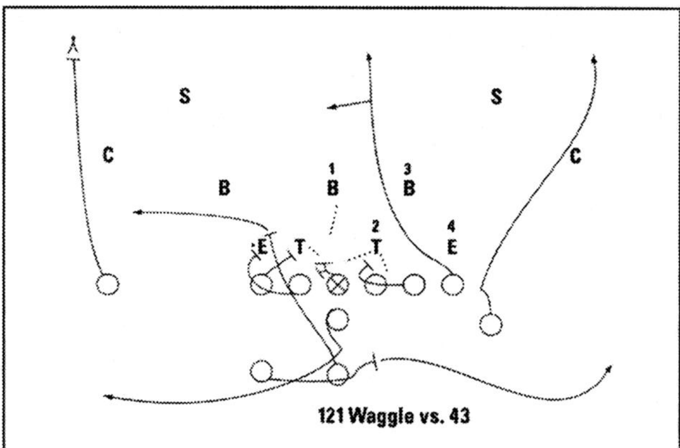

Diagram 2.13

The right guard is still going to pull, cross over, get depth, and lead the quarterback around the flank. The right tackle is pull-check, also. The right tackle's assignment is a little tougher. He must pull down all the way to the center if he has to and check the second man. The second man, the defensive tackle, can go vertically upfield, or he can go inside, depending on whether he is a reader, a pitcher, or a penetrator. If the defensive tackle goes inside, the center should pick him up. If he's straight up the field, the tackle should be able to get his head inside and cut it off. If that tackle becomes a real big problem, you can adjust the blocking scheme or run the play to the other side.

The left halfback is still faking the sweep. After the fake, he blocks the first guy who shows outside the right tackle's block. The routes are the same for all the receivers. The crossing route is still run by the tight end, the fly route by the halfback, and a possible flare route by the halfback, who fakes the sweep. The quarterback still makes the same read progression.

121-129 Waggle vs. 4-4 Defense

Thus far, all the 20 series plays have been blocked, with the action going to the tight end wing. But you can show action going to the split end diveback side, as well. These plays can be run to all flanks from all formations. No significant differences exist in blocking a 4-4 defense (Diagram 2.14). The left guard is going to pull and log the end man. When blocking an even defense, the log block is going to happen faster. The center is again going to step to his left and has responsibility for anyone working through the frontside A gap. The right tackle is pull and check two. Two players could be #2, depending on who aligns the widest. The backer could be wider and be #2, or the tackle could be wider and then would be #2. If the right tackle has an upfield reaction from the defensive tackle, then he'll block it. If not, the linebacker is expected to blitz, and, if none of those things occurs, then the tackle can turn back on the defensive end to his outside. The fullback again has the blocking assignment to block the inside linebacker, which is his first responsibility. If that man stunts in his A gap or B gap, he picks it up. If he blocks it, he blocks it with his head to the outside, and, in this case, it would be a right-shoulder block. As he goes through the hole, if no blocking

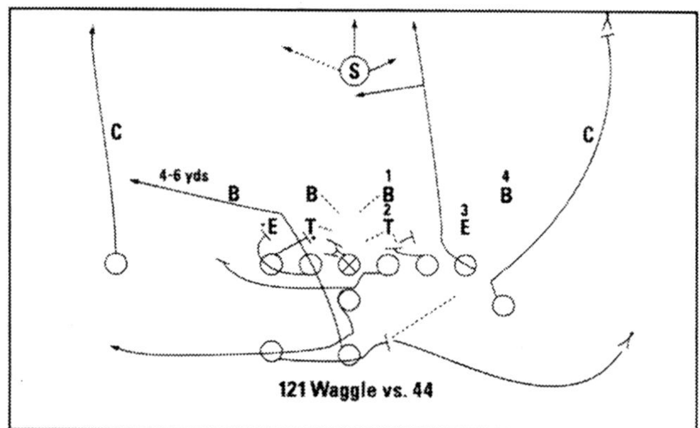

Diagram 2.14

assignment exists, he can work to the flat and climb to a depth of four to six yards. The quarterback makes the sweep fake, then sprints to the flank, and, again, makes the same reads. If the free safety rotates backside or stays in the middle, then the quarterback's reads are deep-short-run. If the free safety rotates to the weakside, you will have a throwback possibility.

Variations of Waggle Pass

Several variations exist to the waggle. You can do it a bunch of ways, but what will be illustrated are waggle out, waggle curl, and some different variations run with the waggle. The responsibilities of each position will not be detailed, since those details have already been explained. In this section, just the routes will be drawn up.

Diagram 2.15 illustrates a two-deep secondary and a seven-man front. This coverage can be halves, with the corners rotated up; can be three-deep rotation to either side; or can be what is called cover six, where both safeties are robbers and both corners play deep quarters of the field. In that case, each safety is either a robber or a deep one-quarter player, depending on the action. From a two-deep look, you can get a whole bunch of different coverages. You want to be able to run your waggle game, and you do not really care what the coverages are. You are going to try to execute the waggle plays anyway.

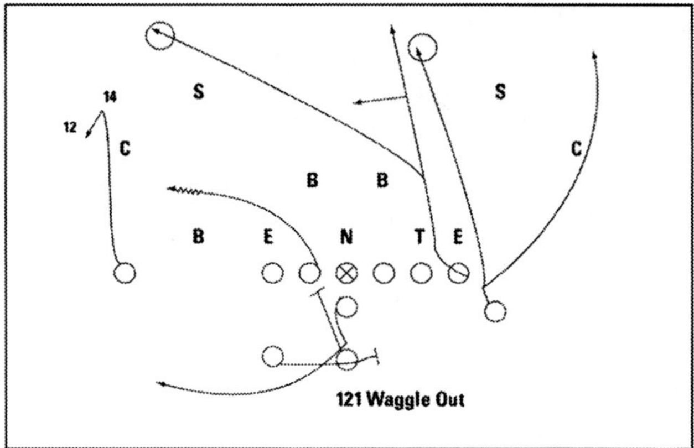

Diagram 2.15

121-129 Waggle Out

The waggle play can be run with an out call. You have the spit end running an out. When you do this, you simply call in the huddle, "121 waggle out" (Diagram 2.15). You take all of the split ends and have them run a fly in practice as fast as they can possibly run, and you film them. Stop the film when the quarterback is in a position to throw the ball after he's executed the proper footwork and technique. When the quarterback gets to the spot and plants his foot, freeze the film and measure how far down the field each spread end is. Some of the faster spread ends will be able to run this play at 16 yards back to 14. Some of the players will go 14 back to 12, and some of the slower ones will go 12 back to 10. Normally, 14 back to 12 is about where most of your players should be, and so you begin there when you first teach the play.

When you call waggle out, the split end has the out route. If the fullback doesn't have to block, he is going to go towards the flat, but he gears down so that he doesn't bring the coverage underneath the out. You want him to gear down, to choke his speed down just a little bit. Two things are done with the tight end. He runs his crossing route, where he splits the middle or crosses the field, which actually keeps everything exactly the same for him. You can also tell him if he reads three deep, he can break across the field, try to get into the area behind the playside deep third corner, and try to pull him off the out coverage by threatening behind him. If you are going to cross the tight end all the way to the weakside deep third, you will put the halfback down the seam in the middle. If you do not put the tight end in the weakside third and run the crossing route with the tight end, then the halfback can still split or run deep. The wing must run the fly outside the hash mark. If you want the tight end to go across the field and pull the corner off the out route, you also run the halfback through the middle at the same time. On waggle out, you have two different options for the backside tight end and the backside halfback.

121-129 Waggle Curl

Waggle curl is going to be just exactly like it sounds. You are going to run a waggle route, with the spread end running the curl (Diagram 2.16). You teach the curl route to get to a certain depth with a certain step and then come back down the stem until you see where the open alley is. You then try to slide in that direction. Lately, the curl has been coached with a slight inside stem burst, hard to 12 yards, plant the foot, come right back down the stem, and then start to slide wherever you see the open area. The split end takes a wider split. He comes off the ball with a slight inside angle for two or three steps and then bursts vertically up the field until he gets to a point where you want to break. The break point is 12 yards, depending on the speed of the receiver. Next, he is going to come right back down the stem and slide if he can find an open area.

On the waggle curl play, if the fullback does not have to block the linebacker as he goes through the hole, you want him to really stretch to the flat and pull coverage away from the curl. The left halfback and tight end will do exactly the same as they did on the regular waggle routes. One of the things you could do is just tell the tight end to go right down the middle every time and make sure the free safety is not going to be nosy on the curl route. The right halfback fakes his sweep and goes deep, just like the regular waggle. When you call these variations, you're looking to try to get the ball to the players who are called, because you know the defense is doing something in particular.

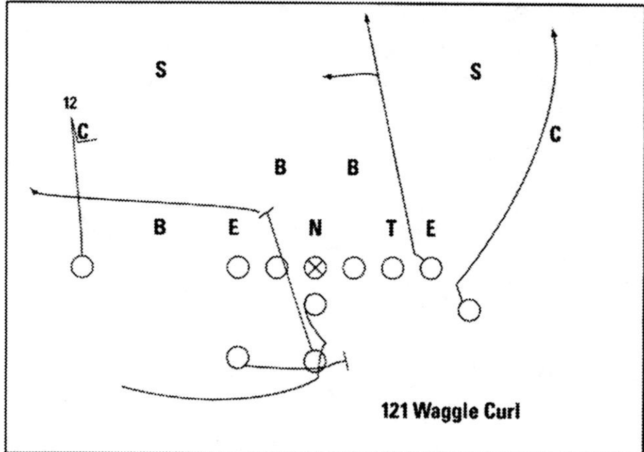

Diagram 2.16

121 Waggle Wing at Five

Two common way exist to break the wingback back over the center and switch the routes of the tight end and the wingback. This play is called 121 waggle, and then you're going to add wing at five (Diagram 2.17). The 121 waggle wing at five basically means the tight end and the halfback are going to switch assignments. When you run the 21 waggle, everyone is going to do the same thing he always does. The spread end will now run his out route or can run his fly. Having him on the fly is good, because the coverage tends to be cleaned out. The tight end takes his inside release and bursts

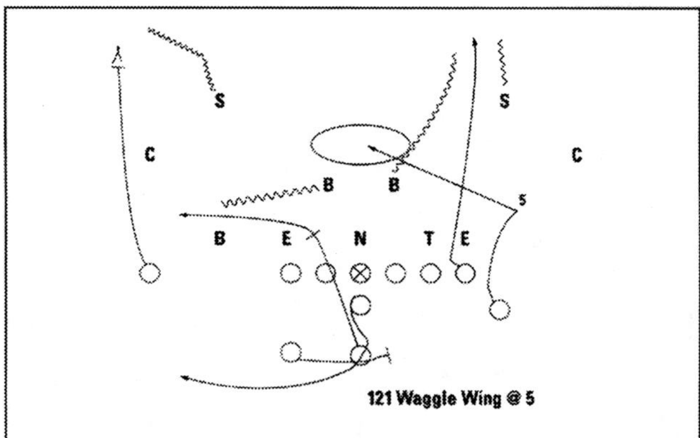

Diagram 2.17

right through the inside shoulder of the half safety. With the spread end running the fly and the tight end running up through the half safety, you are trying to divide the middle. You're trying to get a reaction in which one safety is going to have to cover the tight receiver and one safety is going to have to stretch to cover the spread end on the fly route. The wingback will fake his sweep block, climb to a point where he is about five yards deep, and then break across the middle. He is now going to run the crossing route. If the linebackers are taught that one of them walls off the tight end crossing and one of them plays the back in the flat, you can really split the middle for a nice play inside.

121 Waggle Screen Right

Another thing to do is show off of the motion series, by running the waggle screen. On waggle screen (Diagram 2.18), you are going to throw a screen back to the back who just faked the sweep. You want to make the play look like waggle. Everyone is going to do the same thing he does in the waggle. In this case, though, you want the tight end to take his down release, start through the middle, and definitely run that crossing route. You want full coverage away from where you are throwing. The wingback will fake his sweep block and go deep, but, again, you want to take the coverage deep and clear it out. The fullback does what he always does on waggle – he will either block or go to the flat. You want the spread end to run a fly, again, pulling coverage over the top. You want the halfback to fake the waggle and sit down, just as if he's going to block the first man off the backside of the tackle. The quarterback takes his two steps on the midline, comes on out, and sets up as if in the waggle. The halfback will block the first guy who shows outside off the tackle's block. He is then going to get four yards outside the wingback's original alignment and five yards deep. He is going to catch the ball here, and the quarterback will throw back to him on the waggle screen.

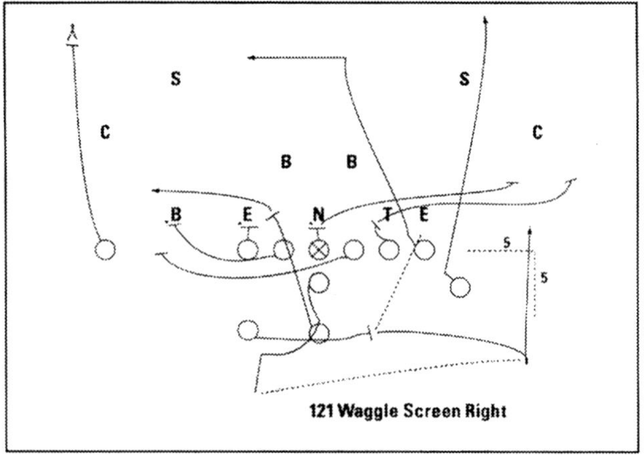

Diagram 2.18

The offensive linemen block exactly as they do in waggle. You have gut-down-on by the left tackle, pull and log by the left guard, block one and cup right by the center, pull and lead the quarterback to the flank by the right guard, and pull check by the right tackle – they all execute the same assignments. The center and the pull-check tackle, after they've blocked for two or three counts, will pull on out and lead the right halfback down the field after he catches the screen.

121 Waggle Switch

One more pattern variation is known as the 121 waggle switch (Diagram 2.19). The word switch tells the back who is running into the flat and the end who is on the side of the pattern to switch assignments. In the normal course of events, as you run 121 waggle, the fullback is normally the flat receiver and the spread end is normally the deep receiver. You can switch those routes by having the spread end run an out, while the fullback goes right down through the half safety. It is done against three deep if the playside corner is biting on the out route. The blocking and the rules are all the same. The tight end on the backside still runs his waggle route. He's going to split the safeties and break across. The halfback on the backside still has the fly. All you have done is switch the routes of the playside end and the fullback.

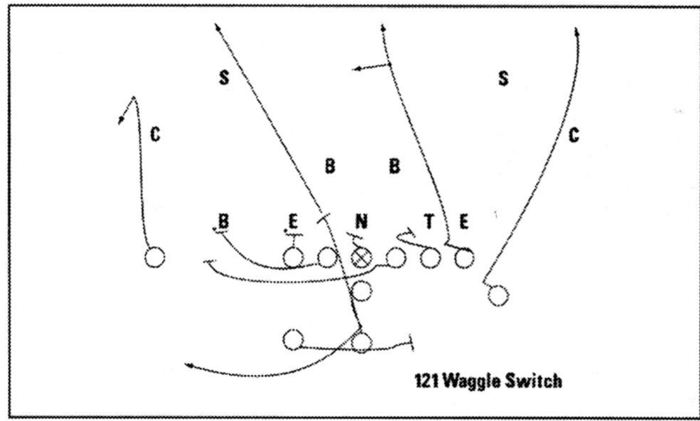

Diagram 2.19

Diagram 2.20 illustrates an eight-man front with three-deep coverage. If you run waggle switch versus three-deep coverage, the spread end breaks on the out, and the fullback (if he doesn't have to block) goes deep. The tight end goes down through the middle or breaks it off across, and the wingback goes deep. What can happen is that you can get a nice hole in behind the playside corner, because the safety covered the tight end and the corner jumped the out, because he did not see the fullback going deep.

The other time to use this play is when you can figure out that the defense is going to be a man-to-man. With the fake of the sweep and the fake of the trap, the linebacker tends to step up and get lost. As he gets lost, if he has the fullback in man-to-man coverage, the linebacker will have a hard time covering him. You can see that the fullback could be running right down through the seam untouched. This play is effective if you know that somebody will be in man-to-man coverage.

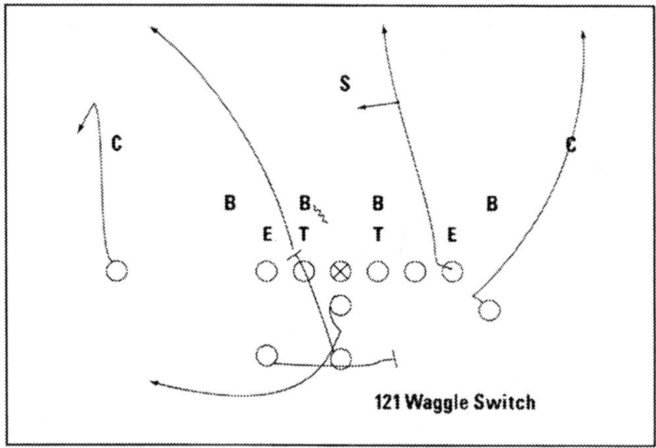

Diagram 2.20

Running to the Split Side

The next part of this entire package runs the wingback in motion and all the plays to the split end side. Basically, the blocking is the same as in the part of the package discussed previously, but with one exception – the lead back now is in the diveback position, rather than the wingback position. You can also run these plays from the double wing or can have the left half in the wing and the right half in the diveback spot and run these plays from slot.

If you put your offense in, out of two formations, you will have all the flanks that you need to run against. As shown in Diagram 2.21, you have three types of formations. Recall, if you put a spread end and a wingback on the same side, that formation is spread 100. What this change amounts to is the spread end is to the side of the wing. If you look at this formation and draw an imaginary line through the middle of the formation, to the right side of the formation, you can see that you have a split end and a wingback. This formation is called a split end-wingback flank. To the left side of the formation, you have a diveback and a tight end, which would be a tight end-diveback flank. Therefore, plays going left would go to the tight end-diveback flank. Compare this set up to the regular wing formation. To the right, you have a tight end and a wingback or a tight end-wingback flank. When you run to that side, you are running to the right end and wingback. On the left side of this formation, you have a diveback and a split end, known as a split end-diveback flank. In the wing-T offense, those flanks are all you will need to run the offense. When you first put the offense in, you do everything out of wing and slot formations only. You are attacking all four of the different flanks presented with only two formations. All of the other multiple formations will not create any different flank looks. You can have a split end and a diveback, a tight end and a wingback, a split end and a wingback, and, finally, a tight end and a diveback. You only have four different types of flanks, and as a coach, you can use the plays out of this offense that you choose to run. Most coaches are not going to want to run every single play shown in this book. But you are going to want to run your basic plays, along with their companion plays, and you do need to be able to run them out of all these flank looks, with or without motion, to strength or away from strength, whatever you have to do. This ability to vary is called formation integrity. It gives balance to your offense, and the defense can't say that you always run certain plays to the tight end wing and away from the tight end wing. You should be able to run all these plays to all these flanks.

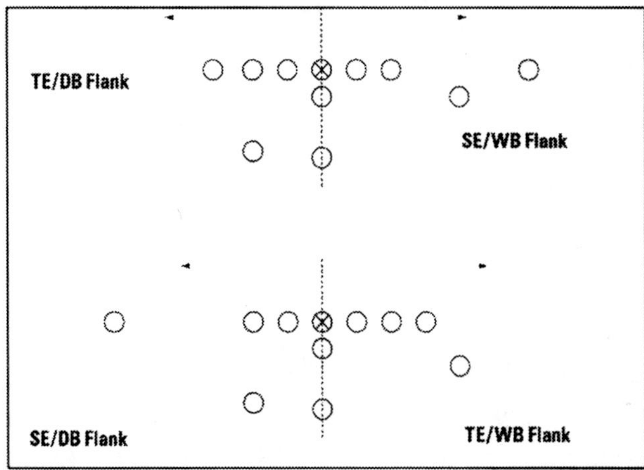

Diagram 2.21

129 Sweep to the Split End vs. 50 Defense

In keeping with that thought process, the next play is 29 sweep run to a split end and diveback (Diagram 2.22). You would say, "129," making the sweep call to the split end side. The left tackle is now the playside blocker. The left tackle's rule is gap-read-down. No one is in his inside gap, no one to block down on, so the first man to his inside is the defender he is going to block. You can interpret that assignment as either coming down to the nose or going to the inside linebacker. If the center can handle the nose alone and the tackle can rip through the defensive end and get a block at linebacker level, which would be optimal. When you do that, the left guard is going to pull and kick out the force.

The left halfback goes for a point one to 1.5 yards outside the tackle and blocks the first free man inside. He takes off for his landmark and then must read from there.

If the defensive end is working out, you will call guard trap. This block is tougher for the halfback, so, therefore, he has to adjust his path, work out, and be able to block the defensive end. If the end is staying on the line of scrimmage or going straight ahead, then the halfback will have to adjust his path in order to be able to block him. Obviously, if the end is squeezing the tackle, the left halfback will have to adjust even further. The defensive end should be the first free man inside. The diveback should use a rigt-shoulder block and keep his head to the outside.

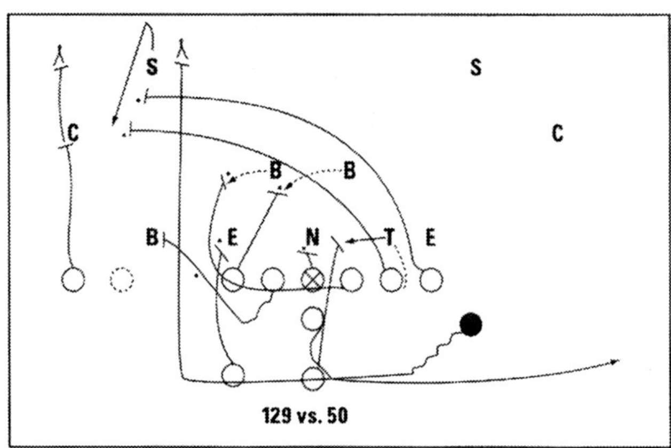

Diagram 2.22

The left guard is going to pull and take two steps of depth so that he does not run into the left halfback. He flattens out on the third step and can block the flank two different ways. You can bring the split end down to what is called a split alignment, and he can block down on the outside backer. The guard can then go and kick out the corner. You also can take the spread end and let him run the corner off or stalk block him, depending on what kind of reaction he gets. Then, the left guard can pull, trap the outside linebacker, and kick him out. It makes it a nice tight hole.

The center is reach-area-away, if he has a man on him. He uses an aggressive technique. You either reach him or cut him, depending on how far over he is shaded. The right guard is going to pull to the left guard's alignment and is looking at the playside inside linebacker. His assignment is to wall off nice and tight to the left halfback's block and to keep his eyes on that linebacker the whole time. If both backers scrape because they see the action and are both running with the action, then the tackle will not be able to get the first one, so he can turn back on the second one.

The right tackle must go across to the cutoff and is probably going to be blocking a safety, who is attempting to play support for the sweep. The tight end is a second cutoff blocker. He will go across the field and will also be blocking in that same manner. Both cutoff blocks are right-shoulder blocks, with the head across the front as the defender reacts forward.

The fullback will dive for the backside foot of the center. Against an odd defense, it will be his left foot for the right foot of the center. He is going to block the backside A gap. He is looking to pick up the defensive tackle, who may be chasing the ballcarrier down inside, or he is looking to pick up the linebacker, if the defensive tackle is penetrating instead.

The wingback must use three-step motion. His first step is back for depth, and his second and third steps indicate that he is going back to his diveback position. He should end up back in his diveback spot and then come across the backfield. The wingback is the ballcarrier, and he must make a sharp 90-degree cut and sweep-cut up into the alley formed by the guard's kick-out block. The quarterback takes two steps on the midline and, on his third step, gives the ball to the motioning wingback. The quarterback continues on to fake the waggle.

Each play in the wing-T offense can be mirrored and run to the split end and diveback side, to a tight end and diveback side, to a split end and wingback side, or to the wingback and tight end side. It makes no difference. All the plays can be run to each type of flank.

129 Sweep to the Split End vs. 4-3 Defense

The sweep to the split side against an even defense (Diagram 2.23) follows the same basic blocking rules. The left tackle has gap-read-down, therefore, he must come down to block the defensive tackle. The diveback dives for a point 1.5 yards outside the defensive end. He is going to block the first free man inside, which is the defensive end. The diveback will have to adjust his path on his second step, depending on the end's reaction. The center's rule is reach-area-away to secure the inside gaps. Both guards are going to pull. The first guard pulls and, in this case, will probably kick out the outside linebacker, who should be forcing. The right guard is going to pull to the left

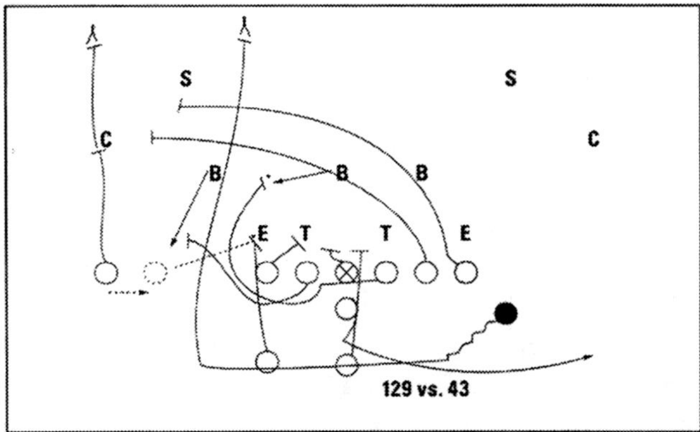

Diagram 2.23

guard's alignment and is going to wall off the inside linebacker as he scrapes. The right tackle and tight end are going to cross to the cutoff. The split end can either run the corner off or can stalk him, depending on the reaction he gets. The fullback is taking the fake and blocking the backside A gap. The right halfback is in three-step motion and then is going to come across the backfield and run the sweep.

129 Sweep to the Split End vs. 4-4 Defense

As mentioned earlier, one option is to tighten the split of the split end to four to six yards and let him come down on the end man on the line of scrimmage. This little change-up can be used with your back and split end. Occasionally, this variation is done against eight-man fronts. All you say is, "Split 100," for a formation.

Against a 4-4 (Diagram 2.24), the two ways to go exist. The left tackle's rule is still gap-read-down. He will use the gap or down technique. The left guard is going to pull and kick out. The center still has reach-area-away. He will reach, first securing the frontside A gap. The right guard pulls, eyes up the inside backer on the playside, and walls him off. The right tackle and tight end are going to cut off – you have two cutoff blockers.

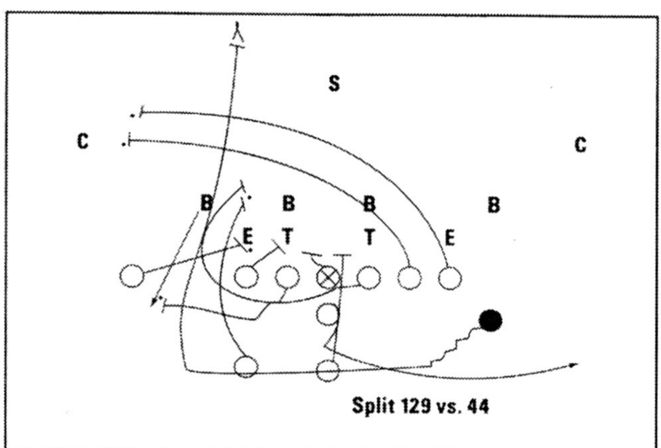

Diagram 2.24

The spread end and the halfback have to be able to communicate who is going to block the end man. You have two options. From the split alignment, you can come down on the defensive end. In that case, the diveback can come right off the split end's tail and can wall the first inside linebacker coming from inside out. The outside linebacker is going to be the force player and is the guy who is going to kick out with the offensive guard. The right guard is going to pull, get some depth, step around all the trash, and be an additional wall-off blocker. The right halfback is in three-step motion. The fullback is responsible for the backside A gap. The right halfback, who is the ballcarrier, makes a good north-south sweep cut. The quarterback fakes waggle.

The alternative to changing up the blocking is for the halfback and the split end to switch assignments (Diagram 2.25). In this case, the split end will come down and block the outside backer with his head across the backer's front and above his waist. As he comes to the point 1.5 yards outside the end man, the left halfback will block the first free man inside, which would be this defensive end. At this point, the guard can pull and kick out the corner. This blocking adjustment is different. The first one would be the split end down on the defensive end. The next one would be the split end cracking on the backer. Two different styles are used when running the sweep play to the split end side against the 4-4 defense.

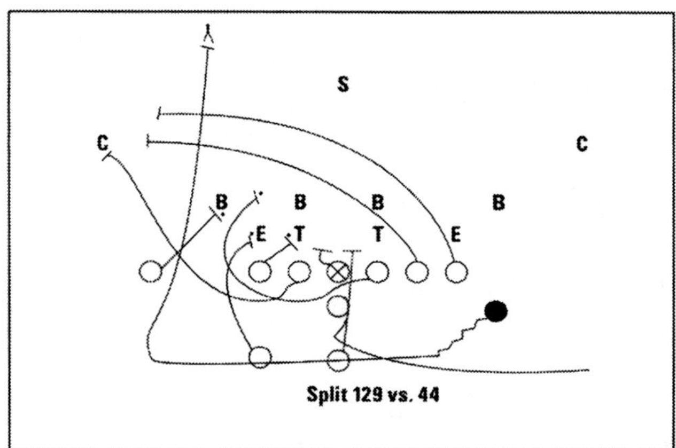

Diagram 2.25

126 Guard Trap vs. 50 Defense

Diagram 2.26 illustrates 126 guard trap back to the split end side of a 50 defense. You're not running back to the tight end side anymore; instead, you're running to the split end side. In this case, you have the post by the center and the lead by the left guard. The left tackle is blocking first backer from five, and the right guard is going to pull and trap. The guard trap to the split end side, with the action faking the sweep to the split end side, would be called 126 guard trap. The right halfback is going in three-step motion and faking the sweep to the left. The fullback is going to get the ball and run a 6-hole guard trap. The 6 man is the left guard, so a chance exists the fullback would have to veer to the left, hugging the double-team. Since it is an odd defense, the quarterback opens beyond the midline and gives the fullback the midline.

This play can be better more to a tight end side because, to a tight end side, you can send the playside tackle all the way to the backside linebacker and the tight end to the frontside backer. The guard and the center are going to post lead on the nose, creating the good double-team. The right guard pulls and traps inside out. He traps the first man from the nose of the offensive guard out. This maneuver actually amounts to trapping the first man beyond the offensive center, depending on what kind of defense you're going to see.

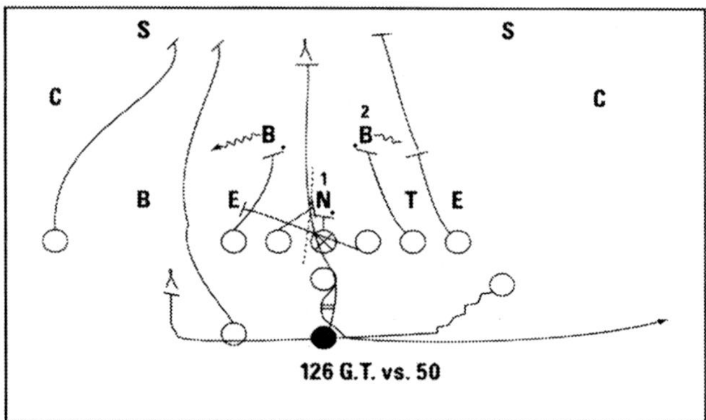

Diagram 2.26

The backside tackle's rule on guard trap is block the second man. If you count from the frontside A gap, the nose is one, and the linebacker is two, because those two are the backside of the defense. The tackle interprets his assignment and will go right to the backer trying to cut him off, and you will try to wash both backers outside. Hopefully, the quarterback's waggle fake will help to draw the backside backer with him, and the sweep fake by the right halfback will help to draw that backer with the sweep, thus splitting the defense. The fullback takes the ball and cuts tight to the center's block, right up the middle. The left halfback is going to fake his sweep block and then work from backer to cutoff down the field. The backside tight end will also work backer cutoff. You should have some good cutoff blockers down the field. Since the waggle fake is going away from him, the split end will go ahead and block at the cutoff.

126 Guard Trap to the Split End vs. 4-3 Defense

Against an even defense, 126 guard trap (Diagram 2.27) makes use of exactly the same rules. The center's rule is post right, so he is going to block to the right for the right guard, who will pull and trap the defensive tackle. The right tackle has first backer from five or the first backer from his side of the center. You are going to have three-step motion and be faking the sweep toward the split end, so you are figuring that the defense is going to react in that direction, which is what you're anticipating. The left tackle's rule, first backer from five, becomes the middle backer. You want him to try to get the middle linebacker and get his head across his front.

The left guard's rule is gap-lead-backer-or influence. A defender isn't in his gap. Nobody is on the center for him to double-team. The left guard must block the backside linebacker, or else he's got to influence. If he can get to the backside linebacker, that move is optimal, which is what you want. But, especially to a split end side, a lot of times you will see the defense line up in inside techniques. Those defensive players are now shaded to the inside. The left guard might not be able to get through to the backer, so now he is going to have to use his pass set influence or his pulling influence. On this play, you would like to pass set, then turn, and block out on the defensive end.

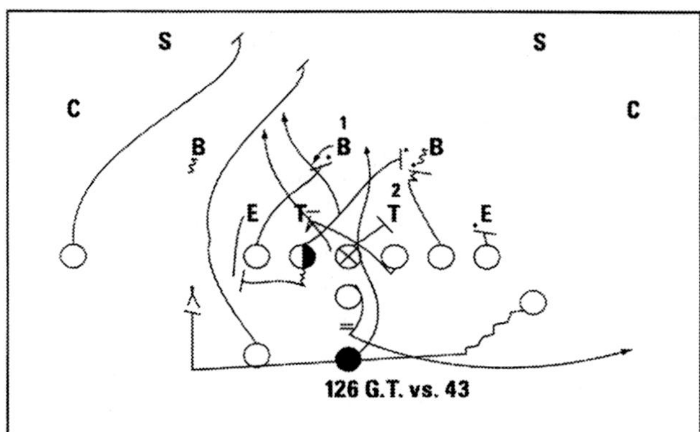

Diagram 2.27

The left halfback will dive for a point a 1.5 yards outside the end man, just as if he's going to run the sweep, and then he is going to go to the cutoff. Since the quarterback is faking waggle away from him, the split end will just go to the cutoff.

The right tackle normally blocks the second man, who is the defensive tackle on the backside, but he's already blocked by the center. Since he is freed up, the right tackle can be sent to cut off the strongside linebacker. The tight end on the backside can block on, because of the quarterback mesh. If you tell the tight end his rule is gap-on-backer-cutoff, then, in this case, nobody is in his gap. But a man is on him, so he will use his on assignment and block on.

The fullback is getting the ball. Versus an even defense, he can step with his right foot for the left foot of the center, receive the handoff from the quarterback, and stay tight to the center's block. He can cut off the block on the middle linebacker, or, if the defensive tackle fights all the way across the front of the center, he can also cut backside.

126 Guard Trap to the Split End vs. 4-4 Defense

Finally, Diagram 2.28 shows 126 guard trap against a 4-4 defense to the split end side. With the fullback getting the ball up the middle, you expect to get the defense to pursue to the left, because both halfbacks are faking sweep to the left. The quarterback is going to fake waggle away. The 6 hole requires the fullback to step with his right foot backside. He's going to step with his left foot for the right foot of the center. The quarterback has the midline, because it's an even defense. As the fullback receives the ball, he will break to the 6 hole, but he will stay tight to the center's block, which is his down block. He could even play off the backside of the center's block.

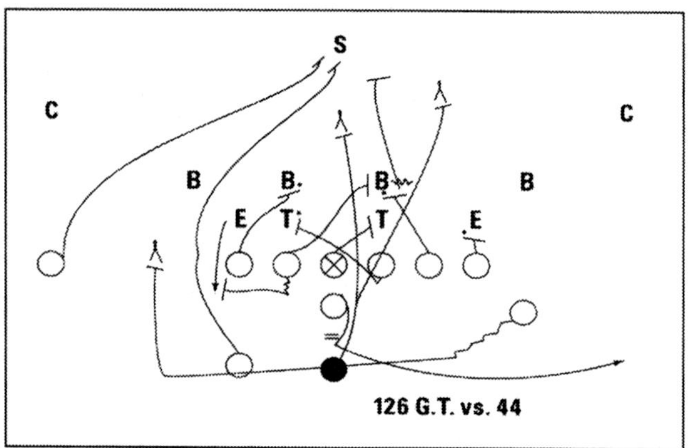

Diagram 2.28

The center is post to the right. The left guard has gap-lead-backer-or influence. In this case, no one is in the gap and no one exists to lead on, so he is going to go across to the linebacker, or he'll influence. If he influences, you have him pass set and kick out the defensive end on the left. The left tackle has the first backer from the center. You would like to get your head inside. The right guard is the trapper, so he is going to pull and adjust to the tail of the center, pulling tightly inside out on the trap.

The backside tackle blocks the second man. In this defense, you will try to get him to the inside linebacker, because if the left guard has to influence, no one will be there for that linebacker. Hopefully, the backside inside linebacker has some concern for the quarterback on the waggle fake, which allows the tackle to get inside of him. If the left guard has the linebacker blocked, then the tackle can go to cutoff.

The backside tight end has gap on backer cutoff. He has a man on him, so he will block on in this case and protect the quarterback-fullback mesh. The split end will block the safety. The left half is faking the sweep block and then going to the cutoff.

129 Waggle to the Tight End vs. 50 Defense

You can always run waggle back to the tight end side. This play is called 129 waggle and is illustrated in Diagram 2.29. The play is actually going back to the tight end side, even though you're faking action to the split end side. The word waggle tells the offensive linemen you are going opposite the number or opposite the called point of attack. Therefore, the fake of the sweep is going to the 9 hole, and you are then attacking to the right at the 1 hole.

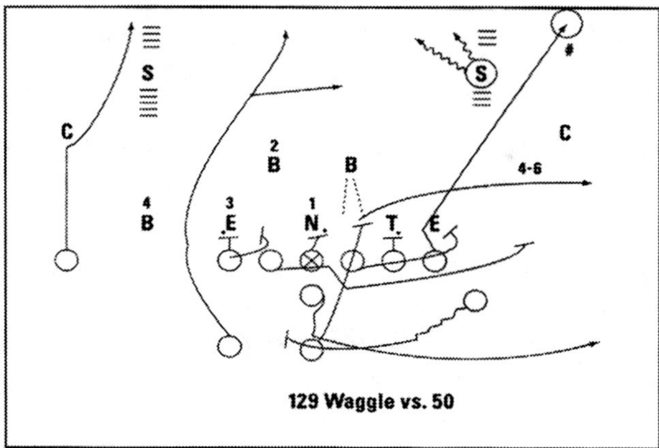

Diagram 2.29

The right tackle is gap-down-on and must block on since he is covered. The right guard pulls and logs the end man. The center blocks on because he is covered. The backside guard pulls, crosses over, and leads the quarterback around the flank. The backside tackle pulls and checks the second man. Those rules are exactly the same, as discussed earlier.

The right halfback is faking 29 sweep, so he will come across the backfield, gear down, and block inside out. The fullback is going to fake 29 sweep. His first step is his left foot for the right foot of the center. When you call waggle, you are attacking the other direction, so the fullback begins to widen his path a little bit and must block the frontside linebacker if he blitzes A or B gap. Even if the linebacker blitzes through C gap, the fullback can pick up the linebacker. He must be a blocker first. If the linebacker does not stunt, then the fullback is out in the flat and will climb to a depth of four to six yards.

You tell the tight end, "We dictate which release we want." He is going to use a down release, unless he has an inside shade from the defensive end playing on him. If he has an inside shade, then he uses what is called block release. Both releases will be explained in the receiver technique chapter (see Vol. 2). Normally, you use the down release. The tight end uses a fire step with his inside foot, rips through with his outside shoulder, and then gets deep on the numbers. The left halfback and the split end are the two backside receivers. Whichever one is aligned inside runs the crossing route, and the other one runs deep. The split end runs the deep route and is told to run a skinny post, yet stay outside the hash mark. The left halfback is releasing for a point one to 1.5 yards outside the end man. Instead of blocking the first free man inside, the halfback continues past them to get to the middle of the field. If he sees no safeties between the hashes, he stays deep in the middle for the touchdown. If he sees either safety, he should rotate to the middle of the hashes and then break off somewhere between 10 and 15 yards. You want to push the underneath coverage, break it across, and then sit down in an open area between the hash marks. The halfback should not come back running across the hash marks. He should stay in the middle.

The quarterback takes two steps on the midline, makes the sweep fake, and then gets on out to the waggle. If the safety happens to rotate away or stays deep in the middle, then you have a big play opportunity to the tight end deep on the numbers. The corner can cover the tight end, and the quarterback can drop it to the flat or else throw it deep over the corner coming up in the flat. If the defensive end drops off, you will have a great run possibility. The quarterback looks to the tight end side so he can anticipate a pretty good run flank. To the split end side, he could probably anticipate having to throw the ball. If the safety rotates to the waggle, then the quarterback works his backside reads, expecting to throw to the crossing halfback.

129 Waggle to the Tight End vs. 4-3 Defense

The next play is the same back to the tight end side against a different defense. You have already seen the base routes, so not a lot of time will be spent on them. You just need to see the blocking versus the 4-3 defense and how to block these plays coming back the other way (Diagram 2.30).

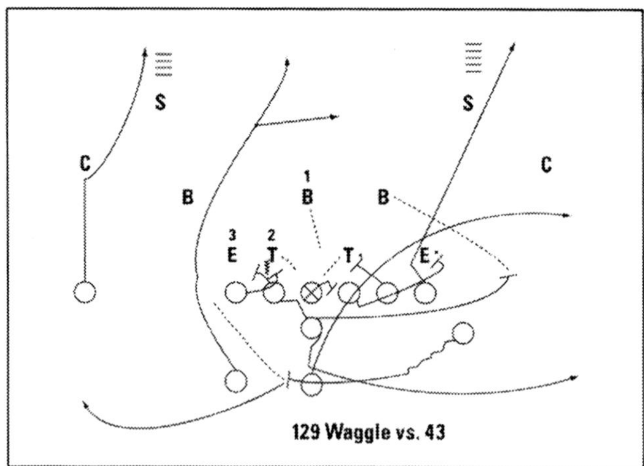

Diagram 2.30

The tight end again takes the down release and gets deep on the numbers. The right halfback is going in three-step motion and fake the sweep. The left halfback is going to fake the sweep block and then run the crossing route. On the backside, the split end is going to again run the skinny post and stay outside the hash marks. The fullback has a blocking assignment. He is going to block the linebacker in either A gap or B gap if he blitzes. If not, he is out in the flat.

The right tackle has no one in his gap, but a man is there to block down on. He will come down on the defensive tackle using down or gap technique. The center will block #1, which is the middle linebacker. The center is going to step with his right foot and check for 1; if he's not coming, the center drops his left foot back and holds right in the A gap area. He can help with either the tackle pinching inside or any linebacker on a run through, as he's looking for those.

The right guard will pull and log the end man. He uses an inside-out kick-out. The left guard pulls, crosses over, leads the quarterback to the flank, and reads the first guard's block. He must be ready to block any scraping backer who might come to the quarterback on a stunt, which is his biggest assignment. The left tackle will pull down to the center if he has to and check the second man, the defensive tackle over the guard. If that second man is giving a reaction vertically, he'll block him. If he's pinching inside, he can now turn back on the next defender, and the center will have to take him.

The right halfback fakes his sweep and blocks the first guy who shows outside that left tackle's block. If no one is there, then the right halfback can flare. You now have waggle to the split end and waggle to the tight end. It could be a whole passing offense all on its own.

129 Waggle to the Tight End vs. 4-4 Defense

Against the 4-4 defense (Diagram 2.31), you must teach a different release for the tight end. The action goes to the split end, the fake goes to the split end, and the waggle goes to the tight end. Most of the time, against eight-man fronts, the defensive end will be in an inside shade, or a 7 technique. You get a lot of guys lined up inside gap or inside shoulder. The difference on the release is you want the tight end to come off and do a block release, which is explained thoroughly in the receiver section (see Volume 2). Basically, the tight end is going to come off the ball and bang that 7 technique. He is not going to stand on the line of scrimmage and block him, but he will give him a good piece and then go on and get deep on the numbers.

The right tackle's rule is gap-down-on, and the right guard will pull and log. Just about the time the tight end releases off this block, the defender should get logged by the right guard. Everyone else is exactly the same.

The key is that the quarterback should be able to get to the flank, because the tight end has block released on the defensive end. The defensive end is slowed up enough so the guard can get on him before he has a real chance to get any penetration. What you do not want on this play is a lot of penetration.

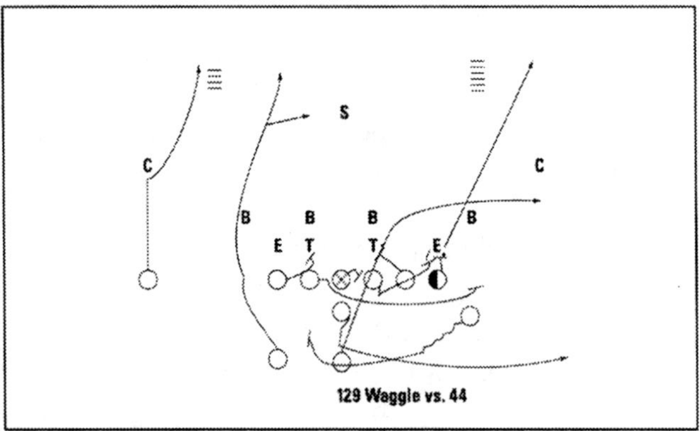

Diagram 2.31

129 Waggle Switch

Some variations are used when you have the waggle back to the tight end side. One of the first is called waggle switch (Diagram 2.32). If you recall, waggle switch means that you still fake the sweep, and the fullback, as he goes through the hole, will become the deep route, with the tight end now in the flat. To the tight end side, this play gives the defense a completely different look, especially when they are in man-to-man when you call switch. The fullback will run right through the line and be wide open, because the linebackers will get lost on all the action and misdirection. The 129 waggle switch is a good red zone change-up if people are blitzing you and also anytime you know that they will be in man-to-man coverage.

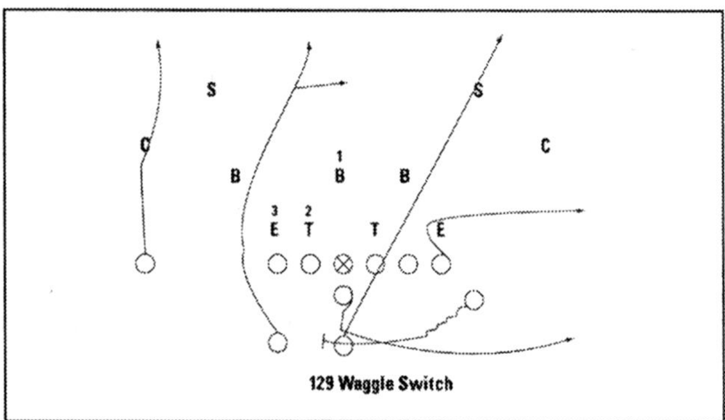

Diagram 2.32

129 Waggle Block

Waggle block (Diagram 2.33) can really help break some tendencies and get you to the flat. When you call waggle block, a lot of ways exist to run it, but you mainly use it without motion. You say, "No mo," in the huddle. The writing in the playbook is just NM, for no motion. This variation is a great key breaker for the defense, because on 29 waggle, the right half would normally go in motion, fake the sweep, and block the backside. When you say, "No mo waggle block," you are going to bring the wingback down and let him block the defensive end – the man you had been log blocking with the guard. The tight end and the split end still run the same routes. The fullback executes his blocking assignment and then goes to the flat. You can keep the backside guard in or can pull him and let him lead the quarterback around the flank.

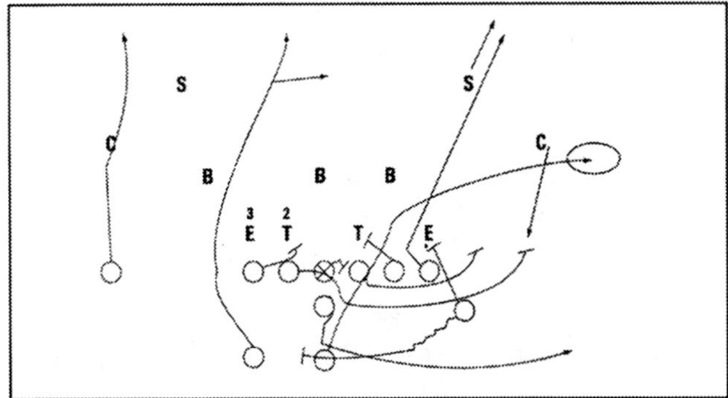

Diagram 2.33

This play does the following for you. The wingback blocks down. At this point, the key is broken. Is it sweep to the wing side? You hope the corner thinks it is sweep, because the wingback blocked down. You want him to fly up. The safety can try to cover the deep route, and the fullback is wide open. This play has gone for 80-yard touchdowns. This play breaks big sometimes, especially if the corner misreads it. A fast fullback can go right down the sideline. Sometimes you see a corner back up, and the safety take the deep route. Then the crossing route runs right down through the middle of the field for a touchdown. This play gives you a good little change-up. You can run this play to the spit end side as well, but you have to put your left halfback, or some running back, in the wingback spot and have him block down on the 5 technique defensive end.

129 Waggle Shovel

The last waggle variation is the waggle shovel pass (Diagram 2.34). Basically, you're going to run the waggle to the tight end side, but the offensive line is going to block

32 power, which will be discussed in another chapter. When the offensive line blocks 32 power, you can see you have post by the right tackle, lead by the tight end, area by the right guard, and fire on backer by the center. The backside guard is going to pull. He is going to wall off on the inside linebacker. The left tackle must pull-check two.

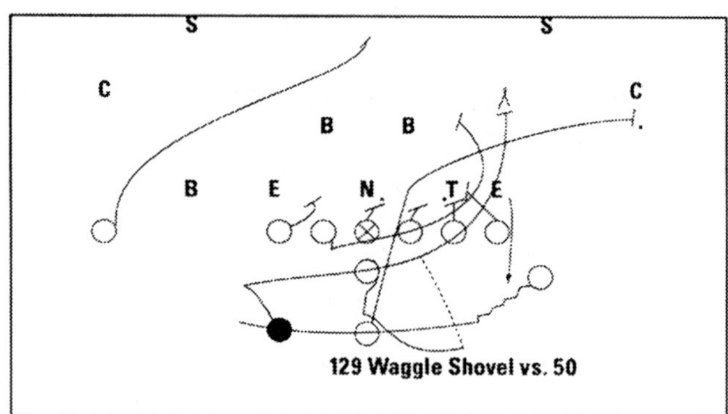

Diagram 2.34

When you call, "129 waggle shovel at two," you are going to run a little shovel pass at the 2 hole, using power blocking. Some defenses, when they see the wingback go in motion, know not much is coming back other than the waggle. They sometimes send the defensive end running straight up the field, looking for waggle by the quarterback when the wingback goes in motion away. They open up the off-tackle hole.

The quarterback is running 29 waggle and, as the fullback comes through, comes out to the flat to block the playside corner. The quarterback gets a little bit extra depth. The left halfback is the ballcarrier. He is going to cross over, plant, and then come running right for the off-tackle hole. The quarterback takes the ball and pitches it forward with his inside arm. In this case, it would be his left arm. The halfback catches the pitch and turns up in the off-tackle power hole. The split end goes to the cutoff. A waggle fake is not coming back to his side.

What you've done is to entice the off-tackle hole to open up by inviting the defensive end to come upfield. Some teams will do this naturally, as they try to stop the wing-T. As soon as they see a wingback go in motion away from them, they penetrate the defensive end, thinking the number one play coming back to them is waggle. They're right; it usually is. But with this play, you break all those keys. Then your sweep game, passing game, and everything else will start working even better.

129 Waggle Shovel vs. 4-3 Defense

Against the 4-3 (Diagram 2.35), everybody blocks using 32 rules, power off-tackle blocking. The post lead against an even defense is closer. The offensive line blocks power at two. The tight end is going to release inside, try to get his linebacker, or go to the middle linebacker. The center can block back, and the backside guard pulls through the hole and walls off on the first linebacker he sees. The left tackle is pull-check two. When the left guard is pulling, if the defensive end reacts up the field or outside, he's not going to stop the play so the left tackle can climb to the next backer.

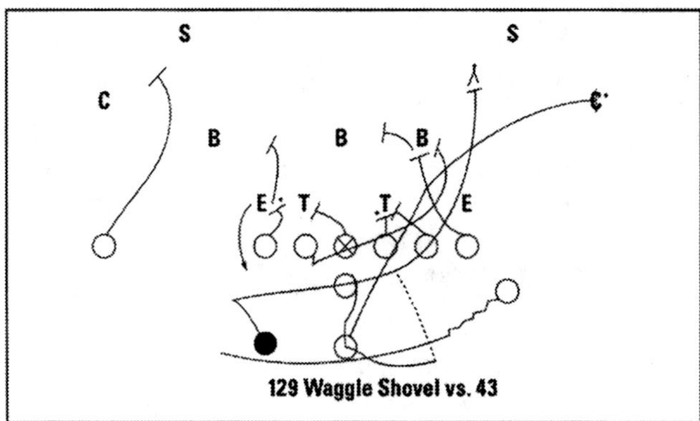

Diagram 2.35

The backfield action is unchanged. Again, you want to talk to the referees about this play before the game. Let them know that you have it so if the quarterback pitches it forward and the ball gets fumbled on the ground, the referee has waved it off as an incomplete pass. Even though the ball is pitched with an underhand motion, it still definitely constitutes a forward pass; so, if it is dropped on the ground, the risk of a fumble does not exist.

129 Waggle Shovel vs. 4-4 Defense

Finally, Diagram 2.36 shows you the 129 waggle shovel against the 4-4 defense. Against the 4-4 defense, when you have inside shade defensive ends, or 7 techniques, the tight end steps right to the defensive end and sets him up for the kick-out block. He then turns out and blocks the next man outside. The tight end influences and blocks the fourth defender. The right tackle's rule is gap-post-lead. Since, in this case, he has neither a man on nor inside gap, he becomes the lead blocker. The right guard in this case is going to post, and the right tackle is going to lead. The center is going to block on-area-left, so he blocks back to the left. The post blocker will look for the run-through by the backside linebacker. If that linebacker tries to run through the A gap, the post blocker comes off and blocks him. All the gaps are protected. The left guard pulls and wraps around for the linebacker. The left tackle's rule is pull and check the second man. Probably, in this case, he will have a chance to turn back. The only thing he's really looking for is stunts where the tackle might go inside into A gap and the backer to B gap or vice versa. The backfield action is the same as that versus the odd and even defenses.

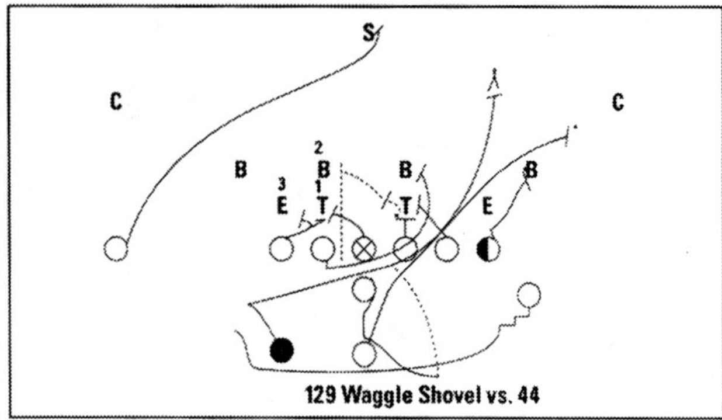

129 Waggle Shovel vs. 44

Diagram 2.36

122 Gut vs. 50 Defense

To finish off this package, three plays are left in the 20 series. The first one is a complement to the sweep. When you get the sweep going, you read the third defender. If he is a seal-conscious player, you can block him down and get outside of him. A lot of places I go, people ask me, "What do you do when that defensive end is really penetrating upfield?" The answer is, "We don't run the sweep," because you are putting your wingback in a tough position to block the defensive end. You have coaches assigned to watch the people on the defense, which is explained in the chapter on game planning (see Volume 2). Each coach is assigned to watch a player on the defense, and, as he observes him, the coach has got to know if the man that he's responsible for watching is penetrating, sealing, or whatever. As long as the tight end goes down inside and the defensive end seals, you can stay to the outside with your attack. You can run the flank attack, 21 sweep, 29 waggle, 82 down option, whatever you need to do in order to run outside. As soon as the #3 man becomes a penetrator into the backfield, you are better served if you run inside of him. The answer is 22 (Diagram 2.37).

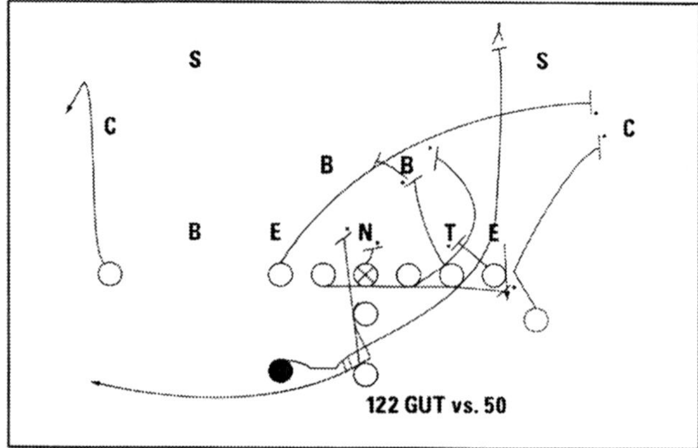

122 GUT vs. 50

Diagram 2.37

Although two primary methods are used blocking it, you can call, "122 gut," which tells you that you are going to do everything just as with the sweep, but with a very small exception. The right halfback, who is in the wing position, steps hard right at the # 3 defender to influence him and get him coming up the field. Next, the right halfback turns out on the player who's in the fourth position. The tight end is gap-read-down, as on the sweep. He is going to come down and block the defensive tackle. The right tackle is also gap-read-down, so he is also coming down and either going to block the nose (if you interpret his rule that way) or rip through and go from frontside backer to backside backer.

The right guard, who normally on the sweep would pull and kick out, changes when you say, "22 gut," and is going to pull and wall off. He is going to gut through the hole and wall off on the frontside backer. You can see in Diagram 2.37 that you have a very good chance to get both backers blocked. The center is reach-area away, just as he is on the sweep. He has a noseguard on him, so he will go ahead and either use reach or fire technique, depending on the width of the shade. The backside guard, who normally pulls and walls, also changes and is going to pull and kick out the penetrating defensive end.

The fullback will fake, just as he does on the sweep, and block the backside A gap. The left tackle still goes to cutoff. The spread end will run his out route and set up waggle with the quarterback.

The quarterback and the left halfback are the only two people, other than the guards, who vary their moves at all. Since you are going to run off-tackle, you do not want to ask the quarterback to give the ball to the halfback over the top, as in sweep, because that move would force a severe cut by the halfback. The halfback will still cross over on his first step and then take one more step. Next, he will run right for the off-tackle hole. He is the ballcarrier. The quarterback comes back two steps on the midline, just like a sweep. Then, as he crosses over on his third step, he hands the ball off inside of him and fakes waggle at the flank. As a result, you have an effective complement to the sweep, which looks just like the sweep. Between 121 sweep, 122 gut, and 124 gut, you have plays that look like the sweep that all hit at different points of attack, which is a good combination.

122 Gut vs. 4-3 Defense

Not much changes on 122 gut versus the even 4-3 defense (Diagram 2.38). Again, the wingback steps hard at the defensive lineman, as if he is going to come down on the sweep block. He influences him and then turns out on the player in the force position. The tight end is coming down inside and works from frontside backer to middle backer against the 4-3 defense. The right tackle is also coming down and will block the man over the guard, using gap technique, unless the man is not a penetrator. The right guard will pull and gut. Between the guard on the gut and the tight end, two blockers will be on the two linebackers as quickly as possible. The center reaches to the frontside A gap. The backside guard pulls if the defensive end is the penetrator and is the man you are going to kick out.

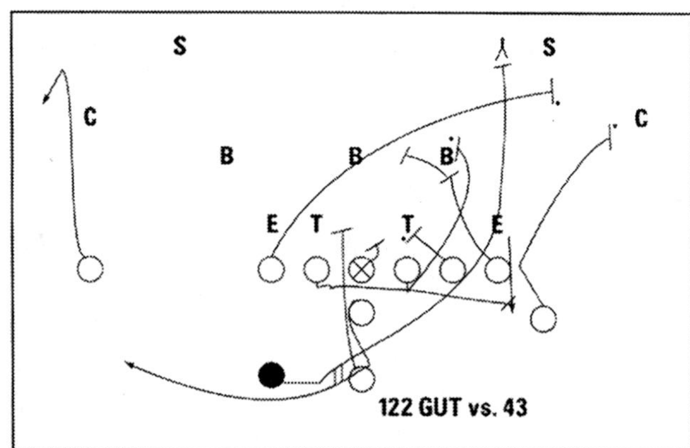

Diagram 2.38

Nothing changes for the fullback and backside tackle. The quarterback and split end set up the waggle. You should constantly set up the waggle. You should always try to make all these plays look alike, yet hit different points of attack.

122 Gut vs. 4-4 Defense

The only change on 122 gut versus the 4-4 defense (Diagram 2.39) is the tight end, if he has a 7 technique or an inside shade on the backer, will also influence. He is going to influence, as well as the wing. In a 4-4, two guys are outside who have to be blocked anyway. The tight end will step, influence, and turn out to the outside backer. The

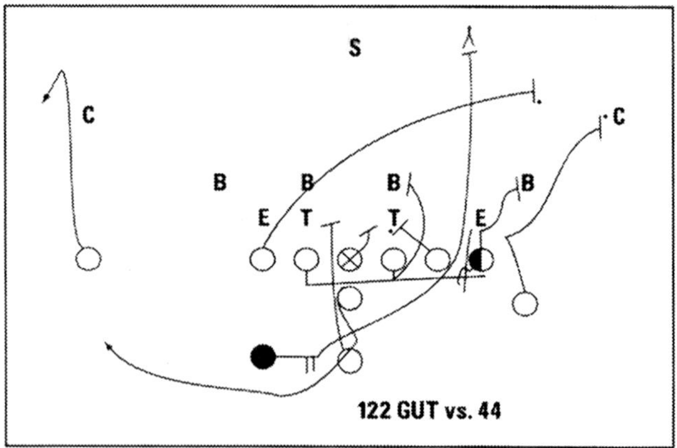

Diagram 2.39

wingback will step into influence and can turn out to the corner. Those two can switch blocks around if they want. If it's easier for the halfback to block the backer and the tight end to block the corner, that change is fine.

As explained earlier, everyone else blocks the same. Remember you are running this play because you know the third defender is penetrating. If he is not penetrating and is sealing down inside instead, then you should be running the sweep. This play is not usually run to the split end side. You could find a blocking scheme to do it, but some coaches don't like to hand the ball to a wingback. Also, the gut play is not usually run to the split end side because the tight end is needed to block gap-read-down.

122 Tag vs. 50 Defense

One more blocking scheme is used with the 22 play. You are going to add tag, which means the backside tackle and guard are going to pull instead of both guards. You can block tag a couple of different ways against the odd defense. If you just say, "122 tag," then it's a 2 hole play in which you have the true counter-gap blocking. You also block the play to actually hit one hole tighter. You will double-team the noseguard with the right guard and the center. The left tackle will influence, and the tight end will block the inside linebacker. Remember, this play was called because you knew that the #3 defender is penetrating. The right tackle will pass influence and turn out on the defensive end, who is penetrating up the field. The guard pulls and traps the 5 technique or the defensive tackle, who will also be influenced up the field by the pass set of the tackle. When you run the play this way, you will call in the huddle, "122 tag at 3" (Diagram 2.40). The wingback will step at the defensive end to influence him and then will go block above the hole. The backside tackle is going to pull and wall off on the first backer he can find. The fullback is going to block the backside A gap area. The halfback crosses over, takes a second step, and then runs for the off-tackle hole. Which is a slightly tighter hole when you say, "Tag at 3." The quarterback takes two steps

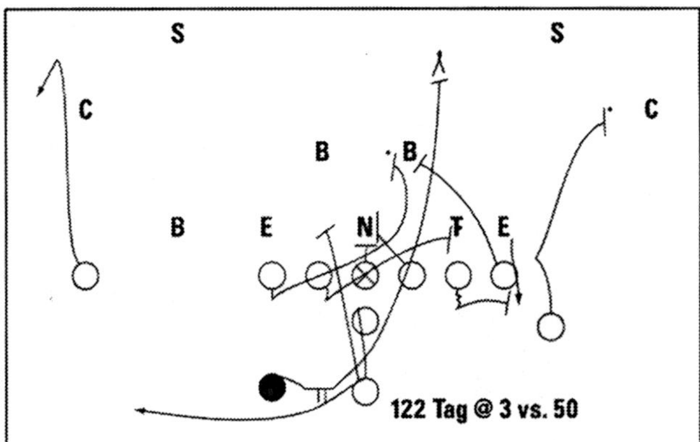

Diagram 2.40

on the midline, fakes waggle, and hands off inside to the left half. The spread end will go ahead and fake waggle with the quarterback. You only run 122 tag at 3 against an odd defense.

The other way to run counter gap, or tag, against the odd defense is to go ahead and block the play all the way out to the 2 hole (Diagram 2.41). At this point, you want to attack and kick out the defensive end, who is penetrating up the field. The wing will still influence and block out. You use regular counter-gap blocking, or tag blocking, where the center will post with his right shoulder. His eyes are on the backside defensive end, and he turns back on the defensive end once he feels the lead from the offensive guard. The guard comes down on the nose. The same thing happens with the tight end and right tackle. The right tackle will post. He will come down and go block the backside linebacker when he feels the lead from the tight end. You get two double-teams, and then the post blockers from both the double-teams will come off on backside players. You are calling this play, again, because you know that #3 is penetrating. The backside guard pulls and kicks out #3, who is penetrating.

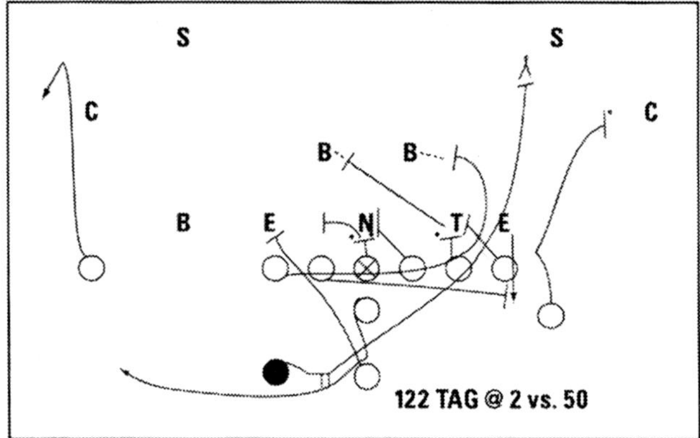

Diagram 2.41

The fullback, when you call tag, is going to run to seal the A gap. The defender he has to watch is the tackle. When the tackle pulls to wall off on the linebacker, the fullback may have to adjust just a little bit in order to come right off the tackle's tail. The tackle pulls, comes around the double-team, and walls off of the frontside linebacker.

Therefore, you can block the 50 with one of two different schemes: one, where you trap the man who is over the tackle, and, two, where you trap the man who is over the end. Both schemes are effective. It's simply a matter of whether you want to hit the tighter hole or the wider hole.

122 Tag vs. 4-3 Defense

122 tag against the 4-3 defense is illustrated in Diagram 2.42. All the even defenses are pretty much blocked the same way. The tight end's role is that of lead-backer-influence, and, since no one is there to lead on, he's going to go to the backer. His head should be across the front when he makes his blocks. The right tackle and the right guard are going to post-lead, so they are going to double-team the defender over the guard. You want the post blocker to be able to come off all the way to the backside linebacker. He does not, however, have to come off really quickly, because he has time. The center is going to post left. The left guard is going to pull and trap the penetrator, which is why you're running the play. The wingback will influence and block out. The left tackle will pull the hole and wall off the backer. The fullback is going to block the backside A gap area. He should not alter his path very much at all. If the fullback has to adjust as the tackle pulls, you want him to come tight off the tackle's tail and be ready to block whoever shows in that area. If the defensive end penetrates way up the field, you do not have to worry about him. If he seals down inside, then the fullback is going to have to block him, keeping his head inside and using a left-shoulder block. The ballcarrier crosses over, plants, and then runs straight for the off-tackle hole. The quarterback and the spread end fake the waggle.

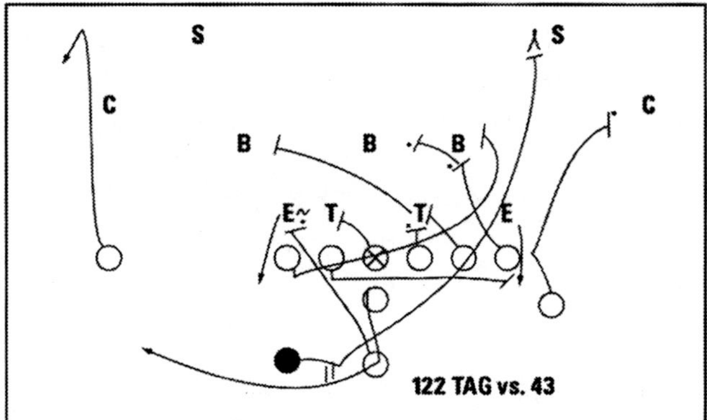

Diagram 2.42

122 Tag vs. 4-4 Defense

Finally, 122 tag against a 4-4 defense is really no different (Diagram 2.43). As noted earlier, the tight end's rule against a 7-technique defensive end requires him to influence. He will step at the technique and then block out. The wingback influences and also blocks out, which gives you two players for defensive players #4 and #5 in the defensive count system. The right guard and the right tackle are going to post lead, with the right guard, after his post, coming off on the weakside linebacker. The center blocks left. The left guard pulls and traps, and the left tackle pulls and walls off the frontside backer. The rest of the play is exactly as discussed earlier.

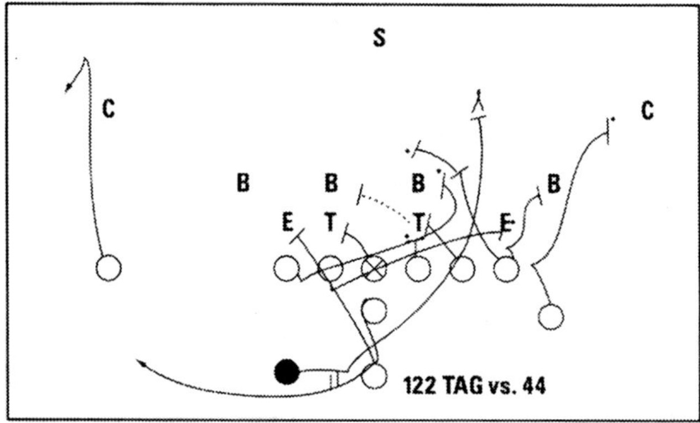

Diagram 2.43

127 Guard Trap vs. 4-3 Defense

The last play in the 20 series is 23 and 27 guard trap. This play can be run either to the split end side or to the tight end side. It can be run against any defense. Against even defenses, you get a slightly wider trap play, but against an odd defense, the play looks just like 26 guard trap. The play can be incorporated into the 20 series, and your quarterback can fake waggle off the sweep fake. You can use the play in the 60 series as part of the trap option series in order to set up your trap option. The quarterback, in that case, would fake trap option instead of the waggle. The 23 and 27 guard trap can also be used as part of the split end side package when you're attacking the split end side with the sweep fake and running the waggle back to the tight end.

When you run 127 guard trap (Diagram 2.44), you are going to trap a little wider at the 7 hole, which is over the left tackle. Therefore, you are going to show three-step motion by the wingback and are going to use the sweep fake to the wingback around the left end. Calling 27 guard trap means you are going to trap the first man beyond the guard. You're going to trap one hole wider. Against the 4-3 defense, if the play were 26 guard trap, you would trap the first man past the center — 27 means you will trap the first man past the guard.

You know the center is going to block back. The left guard is going to post, if he has a 2 technique man on him, and then is going to execute a wheel technique, where he takes the defender by himself with his left shoulder, swings his tail, and takes him down the line. The left guard will have the help of a bump lead by the left tackle. The left tackle's rule is bump-lead-or-backer. He will come down, block the defensive tackle, then come off him, and go to the backer. If the defensive tackle is in an inside shade or a 1 technique, then that tackle is responsible for the A gap. At that point, the guard can come down and block that tackle by himself. But what you need here is some help from the left tackle. He comes down, bangs the defensive tackle, then goes to the linebacker. The left guard turns the block into a wheel block. The center is post right, so he is going back immediately. The right guard is still going to trap, except now he is going to trap all the way out on the 5 technique. It is a longer trap.

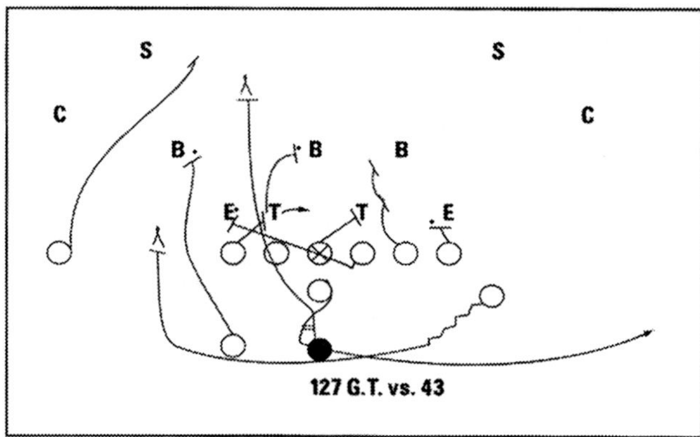

Diagram 2.44

The backside tackle can pull-check the second man. If no pressure exists, he can either turn back or climb to the backside linebacker. You would prefer for the tackle to climb to cut off the linebacker against the 4-3 defense. The tight end can either go to cutoff or block the man on him. Facing 4-3 penetrating defenses, the on technique can be used to protect the quarterback and fullback mesh point. If the defensive end is pinching down inside fast and you do not cut him off, then he can stop this play before it ever really gets started.

The left halfback fakes his sweep blocking assignment because you are showing the picture of split-side sweep. The first guy at the cutoff is going to be the outside backer. Against these even defenses, the diveback is coached to block the outside linebacker, and the spread end will take care of any problems at the cutoff. The fullback is going to get the ball. Normally, on a 6 hole guard trap, the fullback takes his left foot and steps for the right foot of the center, and then he bends it back. In this case, he has to bend wider because his aiming point is wider, so you coach him to step with his left foot for the left foot of the center. Consequently, the quarterback must come beyond the midline a little bit. The quarterback reverse pivots beyond the midline, and the exchange is made on the second step. After the exchange is made, the fullback will veer tightly to the left tackle's down block and the left guard's wheel block and stay away from the trapper's feet. The quarterback is going to fake waggle, which is the difference between the 20 series and the 60 series. If the play were 67 guard trap, the quarterback would turn downhill and fake the trap option.

127 Guard Trap vs. 4-4 Defense

Against the 4-4 defense, this play really should look exactly the same as it does against the 4-3 (Diagram 2.45). The blocking rules are the same. The playside is blocked exactly the same, with the only slight difference being that the backside tackle, who checks two and climbs for the backside backer, has a tighter inside linebacker to climb to.

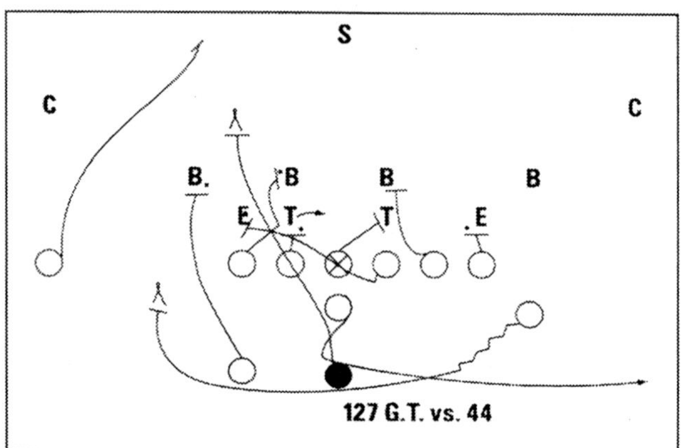

Diagram 2.45

The left halfback blocks at the cutoff, which, in this defense, has to be the outside linebacker. The split end is at the cutoff. The fullback uses the same footwork and veers to the left, staying tight to the down block by the left tackle. The quarterback must reverse pivot a little bit beyond the midline in order to give the fullback, who's the ballcarrier, the opportunity to make his cut. The right half uses three-step motion, makes a good sweep fake, and the quarterback fakes waggle. The play really does look the same against the 4-4 as it does against the 4-3. It works better against the 4-3 and not quite as well against the 4-4. It all depends on what you are going to do with the trap option and what kind of defensive techniques you are facing.

127 Guard Trap vs. 50 Defense

Against the 50 defense, 127 guard trap ends up looking exactly like 126 guard trap (Diagram 2.46). The blocking rules keep the schemes consistent. The center has post or right, and, since he is now covered with a noseguard, he is going to post. He will step with his right foot and block with his left shoulder. He is going to elevate to the numbers on the noseguard. The left guard's rule is gap-post-lead. Therefore, since he is not covered, he will double-team. You will try to take the noseguard flat down the line. The tackle's rule is bump-lead or backer. Since in the 50 defense no one aligns over the guard, he goes to backer. The right guard is going to pull and trap. The right tackle is pull-check two; therefore, he ends up trying to block the linebacker. With the quarterback faking waggle, and the right half faking sweep, you hope to get the linebackers to take a step with each fake and divide the middle.

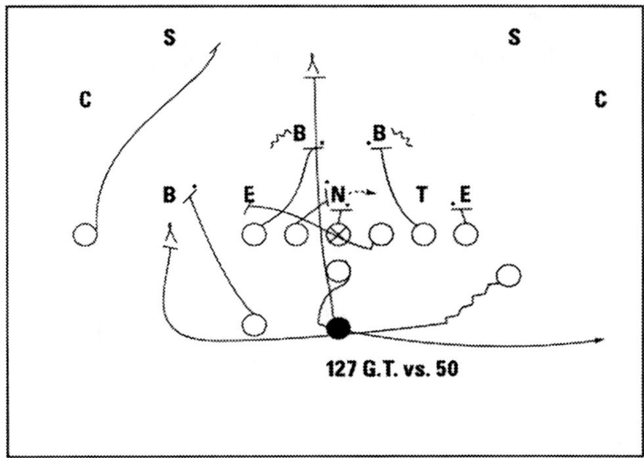

Diagram 2.46

As you look at Diagram 2.46, something should become clear. Against a 50 defense, no difference exists in 126 or 127 guard trap. You want the play to actually be the same because you want to trap the first defender outside the guard. Against the 50 defense, the defensive end is the same player. The way the rules are constructed, the plan and rules are good for the 4-3, 4-4, or any even defense. The rules also incorporate the basic trap rules, so that, if the defense is a 50, you can go right back and trap the 50 defense.

123 Guard Trap vs. 50 Defense

The wider trap play is also effective when you attack the tight end side. On 123 guard trap, you are going to show action with the sweep fake going to the tight end wing side (Diagram 2.47). The play ends up using the same blocking scheme as 24 guard trap against the 50 defense. In this case, the quarterback is going to fake waggle to his left with the split end. The tight end, when the play comes to his side, is to block the backer. The same rules are in effect. The playside right tackle will bump-lead-backer. No one is there for him to bump-lead on, so he will go to the backside backer, giving you two blockers for the two linebackers.

The playside guard has no one in his gap. A man is on the center in the 50 defense, so he leads. You have a double-team with the center and the guard. The center is post or left, so he will post. You attempt to drive the noseguard flat down the line. The right guard pulls and traps. The left tackle has to pull and check the second man, who is inside the linebacker. If the linebacker happens to blitz, the tackle takes care of him. The nose is the first man. The backer is the second man. As the tackle pulls, if that backer blitzes, he has to block him. If no blitz happens, the tackle can either continue on to the backer or can turn back on the defensive end. You would like him to block the defensive end in this case. The wingback is going to fake his sweep and go to cutoff. The playside defensive end should not be able to stop the play, regardless of what he does – he is too far away from the inside trap. If he becomes a serious factor, you then have to block him.

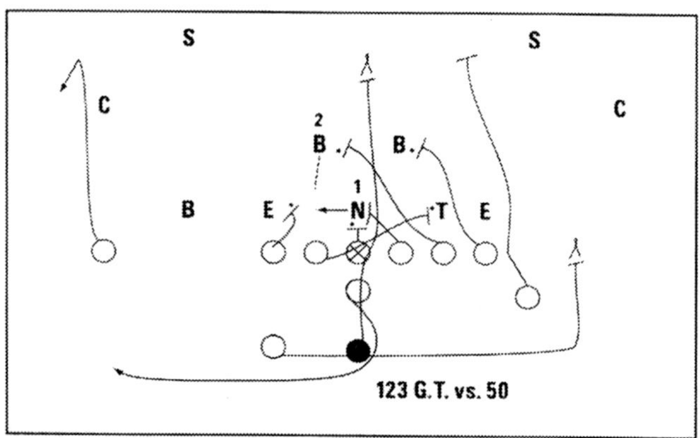

Diagram 2.47

The fullback normally steps with his right foot for the left foot of center on 24 guard trap. On 23 guard trap, he will step right for right foot, with the quarterback reverse pivoting beyond the midline. The fullback stays tight and hugs the post-lead block by the right guard and the center. The left halfback fakes the sweep and makes a good sweep cut. The quarterback fakes waggle, and the fullback has the ball. If a 50 defense shows itself, 24 guard trap will give you the same blocking scheme as 23 guard trap. This way is how the rules are constructed and why they are meant to be that way.

123 Guard Trap vs. 4-3 Defense

Against the 4-3 scheme, 23 guard trap to a tight end and wing side is actually a pretty good play (Diagram 2.48). It is a good complement to the sweep. Again, you're going to trap the first man past the guard. The tight end's rule is to block the backer. You're going to release him inside, and he is going to go to the playside backer and try to block him with his head inside. If the linebacker scrapes really fast, then the tight end will block the middle backer. The right tackle's rule is bump-lead-backer. If a man is on the guard, he is going to come down on him and bump him as if he is a double-team blocker. What bump-lead means is to come down like a double-team blocker, but to bump and come off the block and go to the backer. Bump-lead-blocker is interpreted this way. The right guard's rule is gap-post-lead-backer. He has no one in his gap, so his next priority is to post. When he feels the bump – and it should be a good hard bump by the right tackle – he should then take the defensive tackle and execute a wheel block down the line. The center is going to block back on the defensive tackle, and the left guard is going to pull and trap the defensive end. This strategy creates a nice little conflict for the sweep, especially if the playside linebacker scrapes too fast for the sweep.

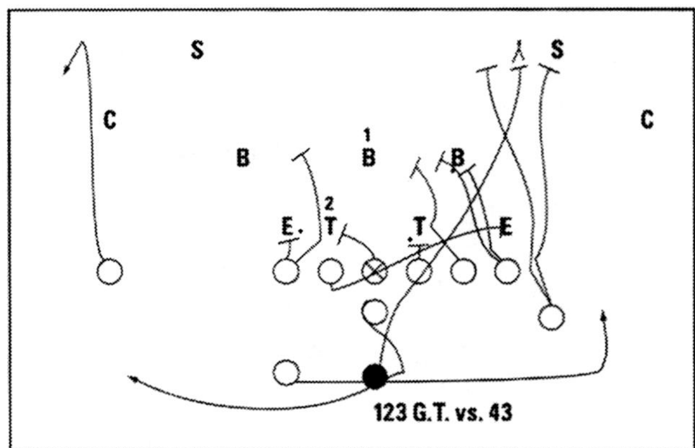

Diagram 2.48

The fullback uses right-foot-for-right-foot footwork, and the quarterback reverse pivots beyond the midline. The left half fakes the sweep. The fullback, with that footwork, can veer tightly off of the bump-lead block, providing a good trap hole under the defensive end. Remember, you are running the play because the defensive end is penetrating upfield and stopping the sweep. He should be set up for the trap underneath him. If he were squeezing down, you would simply run sweep and get outside. The important thing is to get the backers blocked.

The left tackle will pull-check the second defender backside. As he pull-checks, you should already have blocked the defensive tackle with the center, so he should climb to the backside linebacker or can turn back on the defensive end. The right half fakes his sweep block and goes to cutoff. The quarterback, after he hands the ball to the fullback, is going to fake the waggle with the spread end.

123 Guard Trap vs. 4-4 Defense

123 guard trap versus the 4-4 defense should be pretty much the same as against the 4-3 (Diagram 2.49). The only difference is you tell the tight end that, if a 7 technique won't allow him to release inside, he'll have to release outside to block his backer. He is not going to block the man on or inside him, because he is the man you're going to trap, since he is penetrating upfield and hurting the sweep.

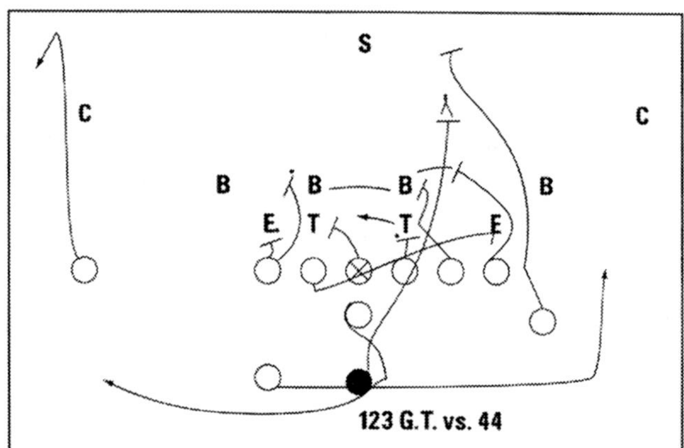

Diagram 2.49

The right tackle will come down with the good hard lead and go to backer. If he can't get the first one, then he will let the tight end take care of him and will block the backside backer. The right guard has a man on him and nobody in his gap. He will post and, when he feels the lead, will turn back into a wheel block. The center blocks back on the man covering the left guard. The left guard pulls and traps the end, who is penetrating upfield. The left tackle has pull-check. You can either get him up to the backer to cut off pursuit or block him on, depending on whether the defensive end is a factor in the play.

The right halfback in the wingback position fakes the sweep and goes to block at the cutoff. The fullback is the ballcarrier. When you make the exchange, the fullback is going to veer and stay tight to his down blocks. The left halfback will fake the sweep. The quarterback, after he hands the ball off to the fullback, will fake the waggle with the split end.

These plays are the 20 package. It is a complete package, utilizing sweep action in the backfield. The package contains a complementary play to attack each defender, depending on his reaction to the sweep. This package is the heart and soul of the wing-T concept of offensive football.

3

60 Series

This chapter will discuss the 60 series – the trap-option series – and all the plays associated with this series. Many people continue to call these plays 20s, but some call them 60s because you can call plays at the line of scrimmage and attack the weakest part of the defense or the best place to run these trap-option plays. You would like to be able to check on the line. What number do you use for 21 trap option, 21 wide-roll, 21 sweep, 21 trap-option pass when they are all different plays? Using the same number for all of these plays could be a bit confusing to the players. Therefore, instead of 21 trap option, you call 61 trap option, to clarify it for your players. A new series number also alerts the quarterback that he has different footwork. It helps the quarterback know that his footwork is for trap option, rather than for buck sweep. The plays are interrelated with the 20 series. The 60 series uses the same buck action in the backfield, with a different footwork for the quarterback. You can use these plays to complement each other and will cross the series boundaries all the time. 21 wide roll helps to set up 61 trap-option pass, and vice versa. These plays, even though they are numbered differently, are very closely related to each other.

169 Trap Option vs. 4-4 Defense

Starting with 169 trap option, this play calls for several different blocking schemes at the flank. If you say, "Option," and nothing else, then you are going to option the third defender and are also going to block #4 and #5 with the men closest to them. If you add option crack, you are going to change the blocking. You are still going to option the third defender and block #4 and #5, but, at this time, you will crack #4 with the widest receiver, or the widest back, provided he is in a crackable position. If you say, "Option load," you are going to block #3 and bring the ball out one man farther to option the fourth defender. Other calls can be used use: option gap changes the inside blocking, but you still option #3; option pitch, you will option #3 and change the blocking a little bit.

To start, the eight-man front is illustrated in Diagram 3.1. You can run this play to the split end side from 100 formation or can put the right halfback, who is normally in the wing, back in the diveback position. That formation is 900 for the backs, but the split end is on the same side as the wing, so the formation is called spread 900. You can run the trap option out of spread 900, as well. You can run the trap option as a weakside play out of either the wing formation or a slot formation, which gives you a chance to run the play on sound, without motioning. In this offense, you have many formation variables that you can use to attack the defense.

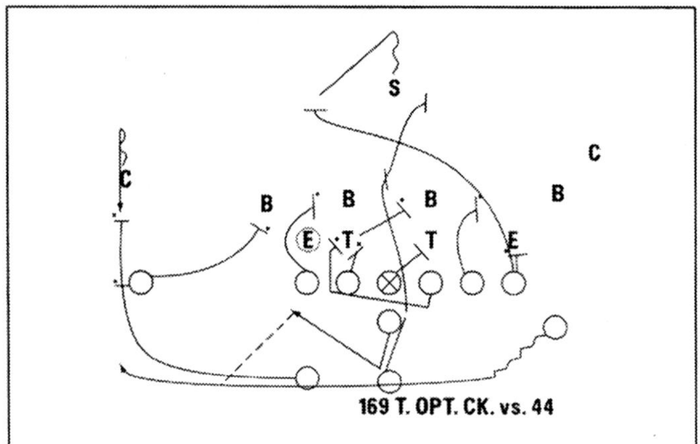

Diagram 3.1

If you count the defense, you know to option the third defender. A favorite way to run trap option is 169 trap-option crack, setting up the trap-option pass, where a slant route is run, looking like the crack. On this play, the fourth defender gets put into a conflict. He must decide if he wants to come flying across the line of scrimmage to defeat the crack by beating the crack before the crack can get there. If he does that, as he flies across the line of scrimmage, he knows the slant route behind him should be exceptional. If the fourth defender decides to play soft because he is worrying about the trap-option pass, then it is much easier to crack him. The fourth defender is in a real conflict, and you have already decided that, whatever way he reacts, you will call the opposite play.

At the University of South Dakota, we gave our whole offensive line an alternative way to block this kind of defense. The left guard and the left tackle were told if the defense had three people on our two, then they were going to make a call and block the trap option with what we called shadow blocking. In that case, we would post with the left guard and shadow with the left tackle. In the playbook, the rule for the tackle said, "Bump-lead backer," and then, in parentheses, we put an asterisk next to his rule. In the parentheses, we told him that he could shadow versus 3-on-2.

The frontside guard's rule is gap-post-lead-backer. Nothing has really changed for him. He doesn't have anyone in his gap, but he does have a man on him and, therefore, will post. As he comes off the line, he steps with his right foot. He will post with his left shoulder. The center's rule is post-or-right. He is going to block back to the right, and the right guard is going to pull and log. You tell the pulling guard that he is going to pull and log the first man outside the center, who usually is the defensive tackle. In this case, the pulling guard will pull and log the first man outside of the guard, because of the 3-on-2 problem. As the right guard pulls, he has the 3-on-2 problem, so he logs the first man on or outside the offensive guard. The left guard is going to post long enough for the pulling guard to get over and wheel block it. Then, he comes off the post and blocks the backside linebacker. The backside tackle's rule is second man. You tell him to look for the second man. If no problems exist with him and he is blocked, then the tackle can climb or turn back. The backside tight end leaves inside and goes to cutoff. If you feel the defensive end is going to be a problem on the backside of trap option, then you will get him blocked with either the right tackle or the tight end. If you feel the end is a real problem, you will go ahead and block him with the tight end. Normally, the tight end on the cutoff block is looking for the safety as he drives to the play.

On this play, you are going to call trap option crack. You don't have to add the word crack. You can have the halfback and the split end block #4 and #5, whomever they are closer to. Crack is good because it sets up the pass. The split end is going to post up on his first step so he can see what the reaction is from the fourth defender. The receivers are taught that they need to run flat down the line first and then adjust to the backer after that. When you crack the backer, you want the receiver to get his head across the front and want him above the waist, so he is legal. Those points are stressed from the first day you do anything – punt returns, any kind of crack blocks, or whatever blocks you're working on. The split end's rule is crack #4, and the halfback's rule is flare and block #5. The diveback is told to get as wide as the outside leg of the spread end's initial alignment before he turns up on the corner. In Diagram 3.1, the back appears to go up the field and run after the corner, but in reality, the corner is going to be coming toward the line of scrimmage. That movement is fine, as long as you have the proper width. You need to get as wide as possible with the halfback. You want the block to occur as wide as possible. The back is taught to make sure he gets the width first, before he chases people up the field.

The fullback is going to dive for the backside foot of the center, using his 20 series footwork. He takes his left foot and dives for the right foot of the center. The quarterback will have the midline. He will take two steps on the midline, just as he does when you fake or hand the ball off on the sweep. On his third step, he starts to pivot his toes and snaps his chin to his right shoulder. He comes downhill and then options the playside defensive end. When you have a 3-on-2 situation, the defensive end or third defender is pretty close to the quarterback. The quarterback needs to get his head snapped quickly, because if that third defender squeezes down quickly, the quarterback must turn and pitch the ball immediately. The halfback has to get going. He has to generate momentum, and you want a five-by-three pitch relationship.

169 Trap-Option Crack vs. 4-3 Defense

The 169 trap-option crack against the 4-3 defense is different than it is against the 4-4 (Diagram 3.2). Normally, in the 4-3 defense, the defensive tackle to the split end side is going to align in either an inside shade or a gap technique. That defensive tackle is #1. The defensive end is #2. The outside linebacker is #3 and is also the pitch key. You are going to block #4 and #5. The spread end knows that he is going to crack #4 if he is in a crackable position. Against a two-deep coverage, #4 is the corner and #5 is the safety. The split end is told to push off the ball and go block the safety. It is not necessarily a crack anymore, but the safety is the man the split end would normally crack if he were up. The halfback will go ahead and arc to the corner. Those two blockers have not really changed much in their blocking scheme. You could tell the spread end that the corner is #4, so he can block him; and you could tell the halfback that the safety is #5, so he can block him. You may not want to do that, however, because you may still want to try to keep the crack look so that the slant pass is set up.

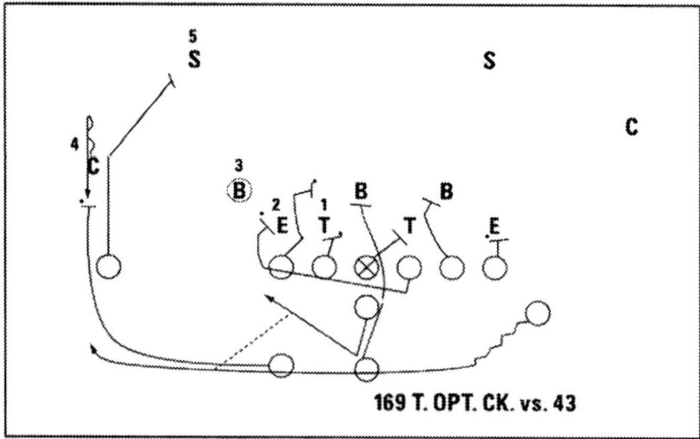

Diagram 3.2

You will be positioning #3, so you will block #1 and #2. You must figure out how you are going to get that blocking done. If you go by the rules, the offensive tackle's rule is gap-bump-lead-backer. No one is in his gap, so he would come down and bump-lead. In other words, he is going to get a good piece of the defensive tackle. Lead means he is a double-team blocker, and, if you say, "Bump-lead," he comes down, strikes the man inside, and then goes to the backer.

The left guard's rule is gap-post-lead-backer. No one is in his gap. If the defensive tackle were in his gap, obviously, he would block him. If not, then he needs to execute what is called a wheel technique. He executes a post block. When he feels the bump leave the left tackle, he will turn and take the tackle by himself with his left shoulder. But that maneuver is difficult to do unless the defensive tackle is pinching or you get a good bump lead from the tackle as he comes down.

The center's rule is post-right, and the right guard's rule is to pull and log the first man on or outside the left tackle. The backside tackle's rule is to block the second man, and the tight end is either going to go to the cutoff or block the defensive end, if he is a problem.

The fullback is going to look to block the first backer as he comes through the hole that he finds. The right halfback is the pitch back. The quarterback takes two steps on the midline, comes downhill, and will be stretched a little farther as he options the third defender. He can keep the ball or pitch it. What he is told is to get in the third defender's face and pitch the ball. That outcome is how you would like to have this unfold. Obviously, if the third defender sprints straight across to the pitch, then you want the quarterback to take it up into the option alley.

The first question that coaches ask about this kind of blocking scheme is, "How do we get the defensive end logged when he is that far outside?" The key is to put this man in a conflict. You are going to bring the offensive tackle down inside. If the defensive end is a penetrator, you won't run trap option; instead, you'll kick him out and run the trap underneath him. You have already seen 23 and 27 guard trap. Next is 63 and 67 guard trap, which is part of this series. The two are interrelated. You can use either trap play to set up the trap option and vice versa.

169 Trap-Option Crack vs. 50 Defense

Finally, against the 50 defense, 169 trap-option crack (Diagram 3.3) can be run using the same blocking rules. The spread end cracks #4, if he's in a crackable position. In this diagram, #4 is not in a crackable position because of the two-deep secondary look. The split end is going to the safety and is going to block him. He will push that corner first and then will block the safety. He will block with his head to the inside. The left halfback will flare and block the corner.

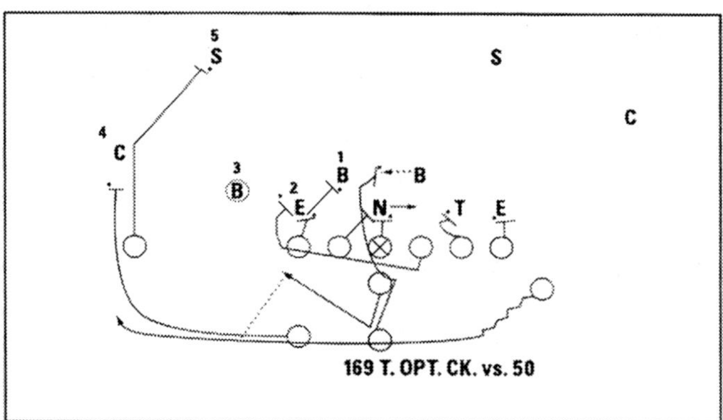

Diagram 3.3

The left tackle has no one in his gap and no one on the guard to bump-lead, so the tackle will now go to block the inside linebacker. Against the 50 defense, you want him to go to this linebacker. If the defense is a reading type of defense and the defensive end is going to squeeze really hard, one of the things you can do is give the end a little post technique before the tackle goes to the linebacker. That technique makes the defensive end squeeze hard and also sets up the log block by the right guard. You can use 24 and 26 on, which gives the ball to the fullback straight up the middle with on blocking to help set up this technique. This defensive end will start to squeeze, because he wants to get to where the fullback is going to run. As he squeezes the 26, the on block is setting up this log block in 169 trap option. This little post move before you go to the backer really causes the defensive end to squeeze. Even if he were a penetrator, it would slow down his penetration and allow the guard a better chance to log block him. If you do not like that technique and don't want to use it because you want to get the tackle up inside on the backer right away, that choice is fine, too.

The left guard has no one in his gap and no one on him to post. The next part of his rule is lead, which means double-team, so he would come down and double-team the noseguard. The center's rule is post-right. The center uses right foot, left shoulder, while the left guard uses left foot, right shoulder. You coach them to swing their tails and take the noseguard down the line of scrimmage. The right guard is going to pull and log the defensive end. Just about the time he gets off the post by the tackle, the guard should be there to log him. The right tackle blocks the second man. He will pull inside, look for the second man, and turn and block the defensive tackle. He has to pull and fill space for the pulling guard. The tight end would go to cutoff, and, again, if that defensive end is a real problem in the play, you can block him on.

Against an odd defense, the fullback uses left foot forward for the center footwork and, as he comes through, blocks the backside linebacker. One of the things he can do is bend just like the guard trap to give the impression of a guard trap and then get an angle on the backside linebacker as he scrapes. At this point, the backer should be somewhat hesitant, because you are using buck action coming across the backfield, and the quarterback is on the midline for two steps. Is that trap, is it sweep, or is it trap option? What is it? All those plays look identical. The right halfback comes across and gets in pitch relationship as the quarterback comes downhill and options the third defender.

167 Guard Trap vs. 50 Defense

The play setting up option is either 23 or 27 guard trap or 63 or 67 guard trap. Play 23 was discussed in Chapter 2, with the 20 series package. Of course, 63 and 67 are basically the same. The next play is 167 guard trap (Diagram 3.4). This play sets up the trap option. You can run this one first. You can run trap-option first. By film analysis, you would watch the reactions of the defenders. You would then know which play probably would be the best one to begin with. As the game goes on, you need to watch the defenders you are putting in assignment conflicts. You constantly want to find out: Are these defenders penetrating, or they trying to seal? Which way should the attack go? Coaches should be assigned to watch all that. This method will be explained in depth in the game-planning chapter, where you will see how to set up game plans and how to determine who is responsible for watching what.

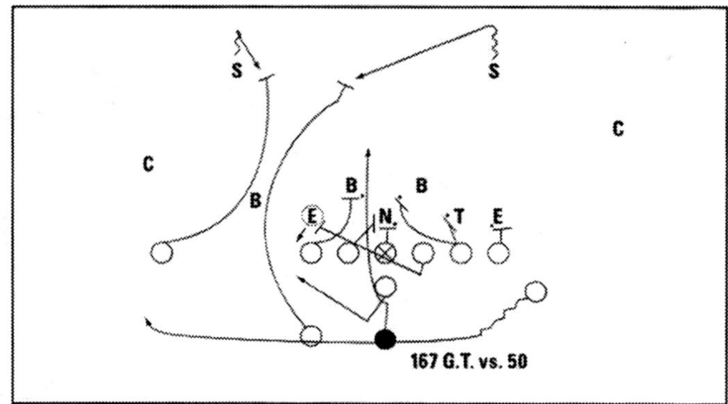

Diagram 3.4

The blocking rules for 167 guard trap are similar to 26 in the 20 series. The center has post-area-right. With the nose on him, he will go ahead and post. The guard's rule is gap-post-lead-backer. Since no one is in his gap and no one is on him to post, he will block down and lead. A double-team is created to run behind for the trap. You're going to take the noseguard down the line when you swing your tail. The right guard is going to pull and trap the defensive end. The left tackle's assignment is bump-lead-backer. If a man was over the guard, he would bump-lead him. Since no one is over the guard, the tackle goes straight through to the backer immediately.

The decision-making process determining which play to run is very clear. It is determined by the defensive end's reactions. If you try to run trap option and the defensive end is penetrating through the line of scrimmage, he will make trap option a very tough assignment. What will happen is that the log blocker will see that he can't log the end penetrating upfield, so he will kick him out, and the quarterback will keep the ball up through the middle. The trap option really turns into a quarterback trap. You do not want your quarterback running quarterback trap all day long. He is going to take a lot of hits. If the defensive end is going to be a penetrator, then the heck with him. You will just run 67 guard trap and will trap him. You let him go ahead and penetrate and then run right up inside of him with the trap. As he penetrates, he allows the tackle to have a free release to the linebacker.

The backside tackle is going to pull-check and block the second man. If no problem exists with the second man on the backside, then he will climb for the backside backer and try to get to him. The tight end goes to cutoff, and, if you are having problems with the defensive end, you might have to block both the tackle and end on. The quarterback-fullback mesh is going to be exposed to any penetration off the backside. The quarterback-fullback mesh should work itself out. Because it's 67 guard and the hole is one man wider, the fullback takes his right foot and steps for the left foot of the center. The quarterback has to reverse pivot beyond the midline slightly. As the quarterback hands him the ball, the fullback can veer to where the trap is going to be. Against the odd defense, the quarterback has to get beyond the midline. The spread end, when the play comes to his side, has to go to cutoff and is probably going to get the near safety. The right halfback is going to go in three-step motion and fake trap option with the quarterback. You are going to come downhill and try to pull defenders with you by faking the option. The left halfback fakes his sweep block. He goes to a point a yard to a yard and a half outside the end and then runs to the cutoff. You have a blocker for both of the safeties. If both safeties want to collapse, you have somebody who can get a hat on each of them. With two cutoff blockers, you have a chance to get a big play, if you break the line of scrimmage.

As you saw with the guard trap rules in the 20 package, they can handle every defensive front. The rules are written for the trap play to be useable versus any defense and to be the same whether 26 or 67 is called. Other than the trap-option action by the quarterback, the blocking schemes are the same. Therefore, 67 guard trap really looks just like a 26 guard trap, except for the quarterback. Initially, the point of attack was going to be one man wider, but against the 50 defense, everything reverts back to a normal guard trap.

167 Guard Trap vs. 4-3 Defense

In the 4-3 defense, you still have a seven-man front, but you also have a man covering the guards, so the trap hole on 167 guard trap will be wider (Diagram 3.5). The defensive tackle on the split end side is normally an inside shade or a gap player. The left tackle, the onside tackle, has bump-lead-backer. As he comes down, he's going to get a good piece of the tackle over the guard and go to the backer. If that defensive tackle is way down inside in the gap, then the guard can take him by himself, and the tackle can go right through to the linebacker.

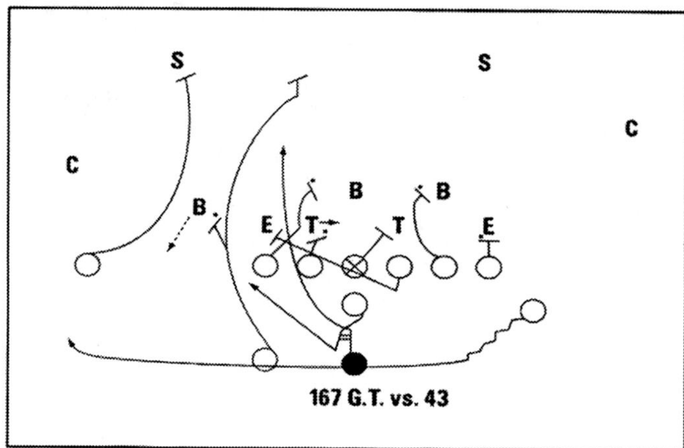

Diagram 3.5

The left guard has a man in his gap. If that defensive tackle is lined in or near the A gap, then the tackle is the gap assignment for him, and he blocks that defender. You still want the tackle to come down and act like he's going to bump-lead, because even though a guy might be lined up inside, he might loop to the outside, and you still want that bump-lead. If the tackle is head up, then the guard will execute his post assignment. The tackle will bump him hard, and the guard will use his wheel block technique and take that man down the line. The center will block back on the defensive tackle so that the guard can pull inside out and trap the defensive end. The right tackle has to block the second man, who is the inside linebacker. The tight end can go to cutoff or he can block his defensive end if the end is going to be a real problem.

The fullback is going to step with his left foot for the frontside leg of the center. The quarterback will come off the midline and allow the fullback to run for the left foot of the center and then veer tightly to the double-team. You do not want him too wide as he runs, because you don't want him running into his trapper.

The split end is at the cutoff. The left half fakes 29 sweep and then is at the cutoff. The right halfback is in three-step motion, and he and the quarterback are going to come downhill and fake trap option. This instance is where you want to take the outside linebacker and draw him on the trap-option fake. If the outside linebacker is filling to the trap, then the halfback needs to change the man he's going to block and go to the outside linebacker. You are going to have the outside linebacker taken care of, one way or the other. If he won't honor the trap-option fake with the quarterback or is not particularly fast running toward the line of scrimmage, then you'll go ahead and block him with the left halfback. This play is great looking, especially considering the recent popularity of the 4-3 defense.

167 Guard Trap vs. 4-4 Defense

The 167 trap option is run a lot against the eight-man front (Diagram 3.6). You should be confident that the guard trap can work. It does have some problems, but it depends on how the defense reacts as to whether or not you can solve those problems. The left guard and the left tackle can execute their post and bump lead assignments, with the left guard taking over by himself if his defensive tackle is lined up in the gap. Most defensive tackles in the 4-4 to the split end side are either an inside shade or down in the gap.

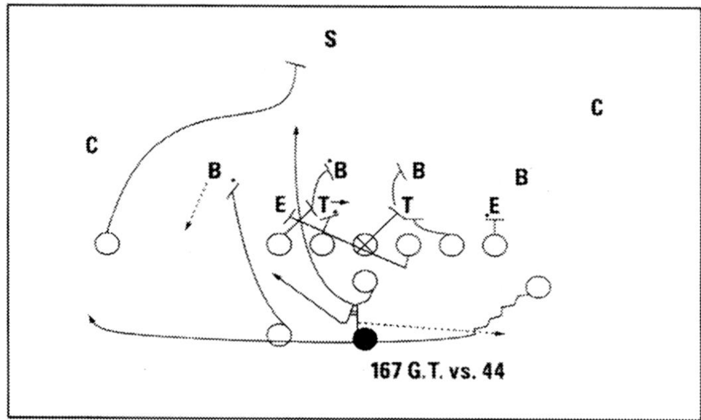

Diagram 3.6

As you pull to trap, you have a problem on the backside. You can block the center back to the tackle and have the right tackle come off and try to block the linebacker, who is the second man. If the linebacker is frozen by the action, then you've got a chance to get that blocking done. The tight end can then block on. The other problem you can have is when the linebacker flows quickly and you can't get to him with the right tackle. You should interpret the center's rule as area. The right tackle can interpret his rule, as the second man is the defensive tackle because of the linebacker's flow. He can pull down to the inside and help seal on the tackle. At that point, you have eliminated the chance of a run-through by the backside linebacker. One way or the other, you must have the center and the backside tackle take care of the backside tackle-linebacker stack – whatever is the easiest way for you to get it done. If the tackle is in loose 3 technique, then you should block him with a tackle and have the center execute an area technique. You never want the linebacker running through and stopping the play.

The split end is going to go to cutoff, and you want him to look for the middle safety. The left halfback is going to block the outside linebacker. If the outside linebacker is really aggressive into the backfield, then you can run to the cutoff with the left half and will not have to block the outside linebacker at all. The right halfback is in three-step motion and comes downhill and fakes trap option with the quarterback.

In Chapter 2, you saw this play out of the 20 series. It can be run to both the tight end side and the split end side with either quarterback action. If you want the quarterback faking trap option, then that play is the guard trap out of the 60 series package. It is the wider guard trap and is a great play to set up or complement the trap option.

169 Trap Option Pass vs. 4-4 Defense

Another play complements the trap option, which is the trap-option pass. This play is called 169 trap-option pass. You've seen how the #3 defender can be put in conflict because he can stop trap, or he can stop trap option. You call the play on the basis of how #3 reacts. Another player you also need to put in assignment conflict is the fourth defender. If you are running trap-option pass against the eight-man front (Diagram 3.7) and you count defenders, the outside linebacker is #4, and you need to put him in conflict. If he is going to run straight across the line of scrimmage and stop trap option all the time, he is vulnerable and leaves the defense vulnerable to the slant route by the split end. Putting that fourth defender into conflict is what trap-option pass is all about. You first look at the #3 defender you put into conflict. If he is going to play trap, you will run trap option. If he's going to play trap option, then you will trap him. Once you have a pretty feel for what #3 is going to do, then you have to put #4 in conflict. If he is aggressive against the run and has been a factor in stopping both the trap option and the trap, then, obviously, the trap-option pass should open up.

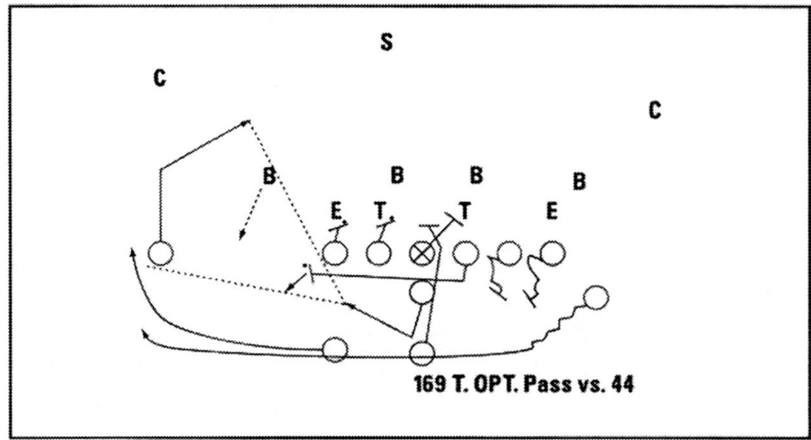

Diagram 3.7

On the front side of the play, both the guard's rules and tackle's rules are gap-on-area, and they are going to block the man on them. Even though it is called 169 trap-option pass, with nine for the point of attack, you are going to have these linemen put their heads inside in order to protect the quarterback. If they put their heads outside and their man beats them inside, the quarterback gets hit in the backfield. If they make him release around outside, at least the quarterback has time to take his footwork.

The center is going to be on or right. In this case, he blocks to the right. The right guard is going to pull and is going to trap the first man who shows outside the left tackle. While like a trap, it has a slightly different technique. You teach the guard to just come down the line and run right through the top of the defender's numbers. You want to run right through his numbers and want to have him concerned with defeating the block so he is not sticking his hands up in the air and knocking down the pass.

The right tackle, or the backside tackle, and the tight end on the backside are both going to step and cut. They take a good reach step inside and then hinge back to protect the back side of the quarterback. Notice you're building a nice wall of protection here on the backside of the quarterback. The fullback is also a part of that. He will fake 236 guard trap and then block the backside A-gap area. Specifically, he will look for any kind of linebacker run-throughs. Basically, he is going to block the right guard's area. Since the center is blocking back on the man covering the right guard, you let the fullback bend into the front side of the center. If the center were blocking on, you'd let the fullback block the area off his back side. The playbook indicates, "Block 4's area," which means to block the right guard's area.

The split end is going to burst off the ball with a little bit of an outside technique. You're going to try to capture his outside shoulder. When the split end gets to about five or six yards, he is going to plant and drive inside. You do not want a 45-degree angle, nor do you want a 90-degree angle. You want an angle somewhere in between – not quite straight across and not quite on a 45, but somewhere in the middle of those two angles. You're running this play because you know the fourth defender is coming hard to stop option, and you can easily see the void area left if that fourth defender does come hard like that.

The left halfback is going to flare to the outside foot of the split end so that he becomes a pass receiver. He's going to come downhill, and, if the #4 defender is aggressive and the corner is chasing the slant, then the quarterback will pop the ball to the left halfback running the flare. At the University of South Dakota, we have actually thrown that ball more times than we have the slant route. Normally, if the corner stays deep and a #4 is aggressive when catching the slant, you are going to get at least a 20-yard play. We've had some go 80 yards, because the free safety missed the tackle.

The right half is in three-step motion, is going to come across the backfield, and still be the pitch back. If #4 is really soft and the corner stays back, then you have nobody to throw to. You can pitch the ball to the halfback and do the best you can on the option.

The quarterback takes his two steps on the midline. He comes downhill – not quite as downhill as he is on the trap option, but still downhill enough so the right guard, as he pulls, can block his defender with his head inside and his left shoulder. The trap-option pass is basically a two-man route, and you can also pitch the ball to the halfback if nowhere exists to throw the ball.

169 Trap-Option Pass vs. 50 Defense

The trap-option pass creates the same conflicts against the 50 defense as it does against the 4-4 (Diagram 3.8). In this case, the blocking rules for the linemen are all the same, except for the center. Since he is covered, the center must block on, and the fullback must bend back to the backside A-gap to protect the quarterback. The left guard cannot chase the linebacker downfield, so he simply checks for the run-through and helps the center. Everyone else runs the play exactly the same. The quarterback has the same choices: slant, flare, or pitch. You now put the #3 defender, the outside linebacker, in an assignment conflict, thus complementing the trap option.

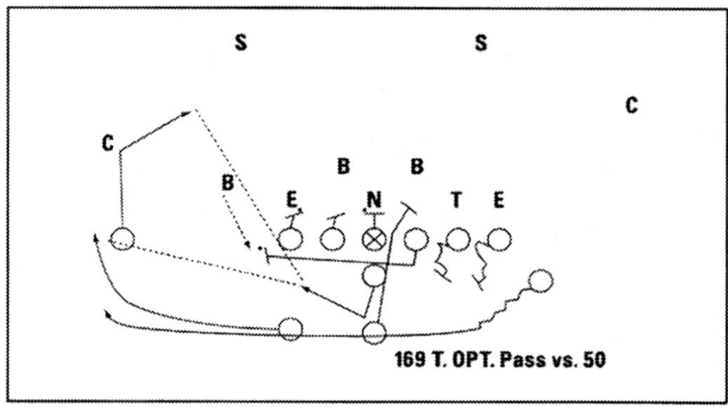

Diagram 3.8

169 Trap-Option Pass vs. 4-3 Defense

Once again, against the 4-3 defense, you can follow the blocking rules with no exceptions (Diagram 3.9). Nothing changes except that the center is not covered, so he will block back, and the fullback will block to the front side of the center. The slant should be good, because you are still putting the #3 defender in conflict. If the corner chases the slant, then the left halfback is the choice, and he flares as wide as the spread end's outside foot of his alignment.

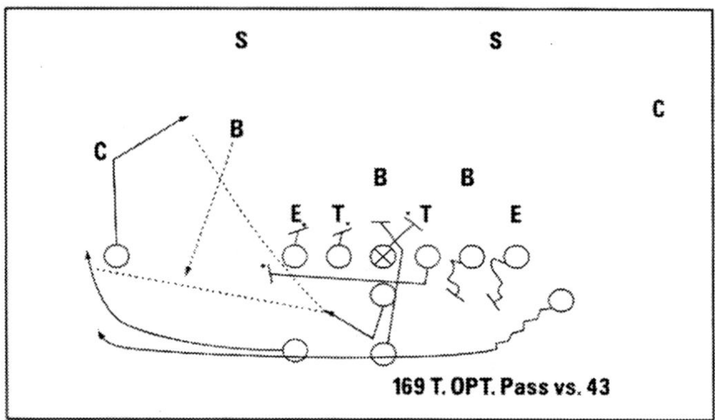

Diagram 3.9

You can run this package out of several different formations. You can put the onside halfback in a wing or the backside halfback in a diveback spot. You can leave them both as wings, because it doesn't matter. You should try to run this to a split end, although you could run it to a tight end. You may not like the blocking angles to that side as well, but you can do it. Your pass play would be trap-option release, as opposed to trap-option slant. The tight end and the wing would release upfield rather than run slants. You can run this out of loose formations with both ends out wide. You have multiple formations and multiple ways to run this same play. It is one of the basic staples in this offense and should be considered during every game plan.

161 Trap Option vs. 50 Defense

Diagram 3.10 illustrates how to run the trap option back to the wingback side. The play is called 161 trap option. The two blockers at the point of attack are not called to crack, because you do not have a flanking angle where you can crack from outside in. The tight end and wing are now reassigned to simply release and block the 4th and 5th defenders. The tackle will post and go to the inside linebacker. You can use the post technique first to help set up the defender for the log block. The center and the guard will post-lead on the nose. The left guard will pull and log the defensive tackle. You will pitch off the third defender, who is the defensive end. The backside tackle is going to block the second man or block on, depending on what your problems are.

The fullback is going to be a blocker and wrap around the double-team so it looks like trap. He can help on the backside linebacker. The split end goes to cutoff. The quarterback and the left halfback are coming downhill and optioning #3. Notice that all the assignments carry over to running the play to the tight end and wing. Very few adjustments are needed, other than the blocks on #4 and #5. Although you may not be crazy about the blocking angles, this play does set up a nice little pass.

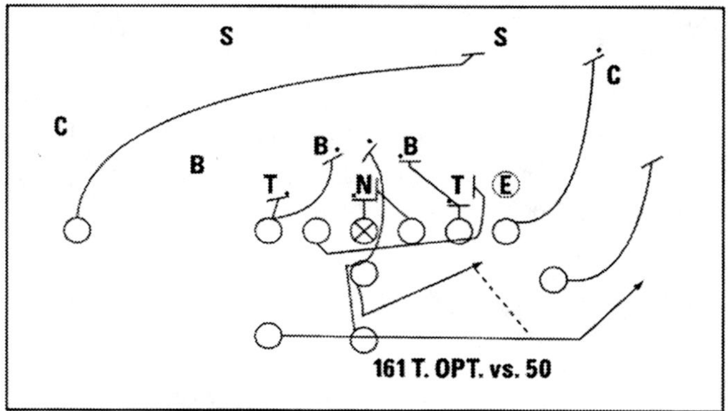

Diagram 3.10

161 Trap-Option Pass Release

Diagram 3.11 illustrates 161 trap-option pass release, which is like a pop pass out of the old veer. You just add the word release, which tells the halfback and the tight end that they are going to release exactly as they do on the trap-option action. Those releases become their pass routes. They are basically running vertically. Remember that you call the trap-option pass because the fourth defender is too aggressive trying to stop the trap option. His aggressiveness creates a void area behind him.

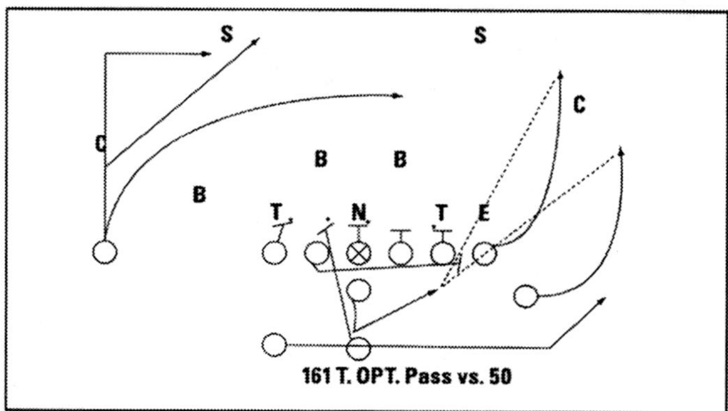

Diagram 3.11

The line blocking is all the same as on the trap-option pass to the split side, except you do not have the tight end on the backside. You have one less step and cup blocker. The fullback has the left guard's area, and the left half is going to be a pitch back and get in pitch relationship with the quarterback.

The quarterback takes two steps on the midline, comes downhill, and then can pop the ball in the seam to either of the receivers releasing vertically. It depends on how the safety reacts. The corner is coming to the trap-option fake, so whichever receiver the safety covers, the other receiver should be open. The quarterback should look to get rid of the ball quickly because no step and cup exists on the backside.

You can do virtually anything you want with your spread end. He can run a post, a slant, a dig route, or a crossing pattern – whatever you like. Or you can just have him run off and clear out the back side of the coverage.

169 Trap-Option Reverse vs. 50 Defense

The trap option sets up a real cute, favorite, little play. We've been running this play and scoring touchdowns with it since 1979. It is not a play that you use very often, but one that you save for just the right moment. It can be a momentum changer for you, or it's a great play to call after you have created a turnover on your opponent's end of the field and want to take advantage of the opposing players' emotional letdown.

The play is called 169 trap-option reverse at 1 (Diagram 3.12). If you are going to run it from the wing formation, you set up the play by faking the trap option to the split end side. Therefore, you call this 169 trap option and then simply add the words, "Reverse at 1," which tell you the spread end will run the reverse to the 1 hole.

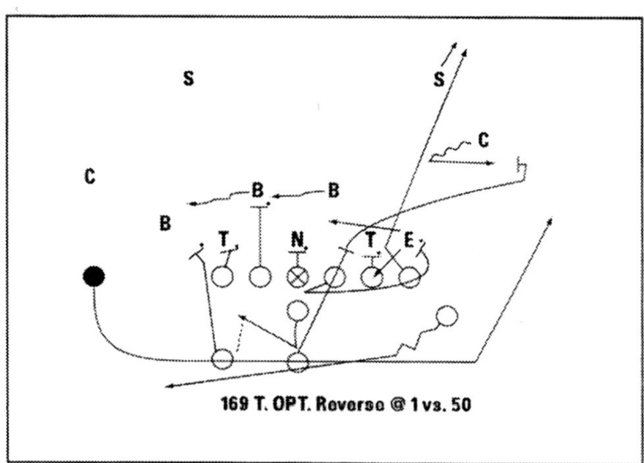

Diagram 3.12

On trap-option reverse, the tight end is going to run a waggle route. He is going to use a down release against the 50 defense and then will burst deep on the numbers, as if he's running waggle. Waggle is definitely a play intermingled with the 60s, because both 20s and 60s use buck actions. If the safety will run deep with him and go all the way to the goal line with him, then you tell the tight end to run him all the way to the goal line, because he isn't going to help the play. If the safety eventually recognizes the play and starts to react, back up, then the tight end becomes a stalk blocker and blocks the safety.

The right tackle is actually the onside tackle on this play. His rule is gap-down-on, just as it is for waggle pass. He has no one in the gap, or down on the guard; therefore, he blocks on. The tackle keeps his head to the outside because the play is going there.

The playside right guard is going to pull and log the end man, just like waggle. You give him a guard key breaker to set up the trap option or make this play look like trap option. You coach him to pull to the left with two flat steps, then reverse his field, and execute the log block. If the defensive end is a chase player, or what is called a cutback player, where he is folding back behind the defensive line, then he has really set himself up for this block. If he is trying to jam the tight end as he releases, he is set up for the log block. If he penetrates and runs flat down the line, he is still set up for the log block. Any of those reactions is beneficial. A bad reaction is if he penetrates straight back into the backfield, making it hard to log him. You try to call this play only after you know what the end's reaction to the trap option will be.

The center's rule is follow-on-backer. He has a man directly on him. He will block on. The left tackle and the left guard will block gap-on-backer. The left guard has no one in his gap and no one on him, so he's going to come off and block the linebacker. The left tackle comes off and blocks his man on. They all have their heads to the inside.

The left halfback has to block the first man who shows outside the left tackle. He is going to a point right off the tackle's tail and will block the first thing showing, with his head to the inside. In Diagram 3.12, it is a left-shoulder block. The right halfback has to be a great actor. He must win an Oscar. He's going to come in three-step motion, come across in pitch relationship, get depth, and make a great fake. When the quarterback pitches the ball, he's going to put his hands up in the air and act like he is catching the pitch.

The fullback's assignment is just like waggle. He's going to dive left foot for the right foot of center, take his second step wide into the guard's area, and then come through the hole. If the inside linebacker blitzes, the fullback has to pick him up. If the blitz doesn't happen, he's going to run out to the flat on his waggle route. Once he gets outside all the defenders, he gets himself set up to block the corner, who will probably start to react and then come back up.

You actually have a hat for everyone on the defense. What you're looking for is for the two inside linebackers to run fast and run themselves out of the play. The left guard can actually block the backside inside backer, while the frontside backer runs himself out of the play and is no help.

The split end takes a pull step and is going to run as fast as he can right through the left halfback's alignment. He intercepts the pitch and runs around the end to the one hole. The quarterback will take two steps on the midline and come downhill. If he were pitching the ball to the right halfback, he would pitch the ball five yards out in front of him and three yards deep. But when he pitches the ball to the spread end, that spread end's momentum is going in the other direction, so now he needs to pitch the ball straight back. This coaching point on the reverse is important.

Contrary to some reverses, where you hope that the trail player runs himself out of the play, on this play, you have a blocker for everyone. That fact is why this play is liked the most. It is not risky to pitch the ball backward. After just a few reps, they will get the feel for it. Once the quarterback understands not to pitch the ball out in front, but rather pitch the ball straight back, the pitch part of it is really pretty easy to execute. You want a nice, soft pitch without a lot of spin. The split end, as he comes through the backfield, will almost intercept the pitch.

169 Trap-Option Reverse at 1 vs. 4-3 Defense

The 4-3 defense is still a seven-man front, so the rules are the same (Diagram 3.13). No one needs to change a thing. The right tackle now has a man to block down on, so he's going to come down using gap or down technique, depending on what his man's reaction is going to be. In this case, the center is going to follow the outside backer as he scrapes with the trap-option fake. The guard and the tackle are both going to come off and block the men on them. The left halfback has to block the first man who shows outside the left tackle's block, probably a scraping or filling linebacker. The rest of the action stays the same. Nothing really changes. The defense has a different spacing, but all the rules hold up.

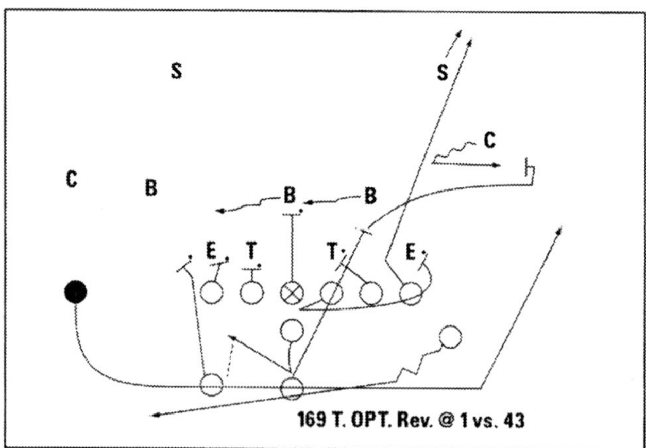

Diagram 3.13

169 Trap-Option Reverse at 1 vs. 4-4 Defense

Diagram 3.14 shows 169 trap option reverse against the eight-man front. Again, the rules hold up, but with some minor adjustments. The tight end now uses a block release because of the inside shade of the defensive end. He comes off and gets a piece of that man with his left shoulder. His head wants to remain outside, and, from there, he runs his waggle route. You should prefer to run the waggle route against a 7 technique more often than any other technique that you see. The block release by the tight end really slows the end down and allows him to be logged.

As the center follows and goes to backer level, the backer he's going to block is probably going to the backside inside linebacker, because the backers should be reacting to the flow of the trap option. The fullback, as he gets in the flat, must be ready to block the outside linebacker, because he will be the one who will react to the play. The corner should be the defender covering the tight end.

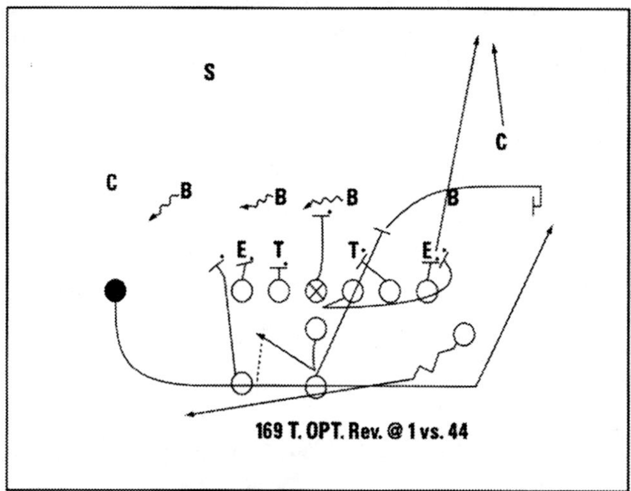

Diagram 3.14

The trap-option reverse is a great football play. It is not a play you're going to run a lot of times, but a play that you can really change momentum with. It is good in plus yardage and has scored a bunch of touchdowns over the years.

Trap-Option Series from the Spread Formation

This series is the trap option the way most people traditionally know. A couple of other things can go with it pretty well. Adapted from other series, they complement those series, if you can run the trap option out of spread 100 formation (Diagram 3.15).

This series is good out of spread 100 formation. You'll run spread 161 trap option to the split end side. You can crack block it or employ whatever blocking you want to use. You want to run spread 163 guard trap to set up the trap option. Then, you will run spread 161 trap-option pass, and put the fourth defender in a conflict. You said you would run spread 161 trap-option reverse. Those plays are the first four in this series.

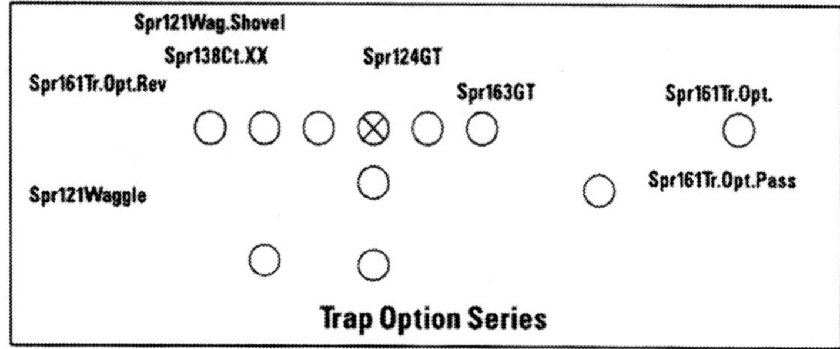

Diagram 3.15

Now, if you'd like to, you can intermingle plays from other series. You can put the fullback up the middle and run spread 124 guard trap. You can fake any kind of option or any kind of footwork you want with the quarterback, but those plays are intermingled, too. You could run 24 and use any blocking scheme you want. Then, you could run back to the tight end with spread 121 waggle, which is part of the package. You've seen spread 121 waggle shovel. That play could be part of this package. Then another play is called spread 138 counter-crisscross, which will be explained in the 30s chapter (Chapter 4). With the trap-option package, you now have a whole series of offense. You have flank-to-flank offense, with everything looking exactly the same for the first two steps. The beauty of the wing-T offense is you can create many formation packages, just as illustrated here.

167 Counter vs. 50 Defense

The next couple of plays can mix with the trap-option series really well and have been in the playbook for a long time. These plays are being recycled and looked at again. The first one is called 167 counter (Diagram 3.16).

The offensive line uses counter-crisscross blocking. That blocking is covered extensively in the 30s chapter and with 87 counter. You can use this counter blocking with any series you want. Depending on the kinds of defenses that you're seeing, you can run the counters and choose to pull the guard and tackle, pull the guard and tight end, or pull the tight end and the tackle. You can pull two backside people and take care of any defensive problem you have. You can do that depending on what the frontside problems are. Against the 4-3 teams, a lot of times, if your center's going to block back on the backside 3 technique, sometimes he has trouble getting there. You can keep him and the guard in, let the center do something else, and pull the tight end and the tackle. Or you can use the tag scheme that you saw in the 20s chapter. Finally, you can use the normal, counter-crisscross blocking. In the wing-T, you have many choices of blocking schemes to be used with a play.

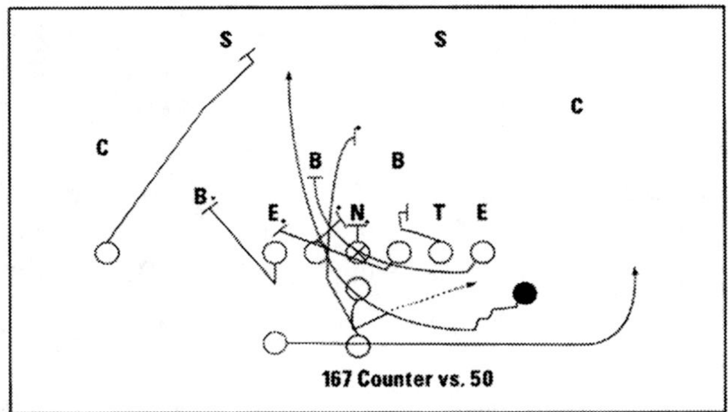

Diagram 3.16

This play is shown here with the normal counter-crisscross blocking. The call 167 counter means the right halfback is going to get the ball and the rest of the backs are going to fake 61 trap option. Counter-crisscross has a specific set of rules, and those rules can be used for any type of 7-hole counter. The 7 man, or left tackle, is going to be the playside, or onside, blocker. He has gap-lead-influence. No one is in his gap, and no one is on the guard for him to double-team, so he will influence and block outside. He can fake fire on the defensive end and try to get him to widen, or he can pass the defensive end and try to get him to come upfield. In either case, he turns and kicks out the next man, the outside linebacker.

The left guard's rule is gap-post-lead. He has no one in his gap and no one on him to post, so he will go to double-team the nose. The center's rule is post-area right. He has a noseguard on him, so he will post. You want the guard and center to swing their tails and take the nose down the line. The right guard's rule is pull and trap. He's going to trap inside out and trap the end who has been influenced. The right tackle's rule is pull-check 2. He will step down inside. If the linebacker is on any kind of blitz, the tackle can take care of him; if not, he'll turn back.

On 37 counter, 87 counter, 67 counter, 37 counter-crisscross, or any 7-hole counter, the tight end is assigned to pull through the hole and wall off. Obviously, in Diagram 3.16, which shows the play versus a 50 defense, if the tight end pulls through the hole and walls off, nobody is there to block the backside defensive end. This play shouldn't be run if the defensive end is going to cause a disruption in your backfield. If he's not that kind of player, or if he's a slow play player, you can run this play, and you'll be okay.

The fullback is going to run 61 trap option. He will step with his right foot for the left foot of the center. As the quarterback reverse pivots for two steps on the midline and starts downhill, the fullback will wrap around and block the backside linebacker. You have a hat for both linebackers and have a pretty good-looking football play.

The left half is going to fake trap option, and the right half is going to be the ballcarrier. The right halfback's technique is to retrace, to leave on the snap, not go in motion, but run like he is going in three-step motion. You tell him that you want him to come back as if he were going in three-step motion, but not to leave until the ball is snapped. When he plants his left foot on his third step, he is going to turn for the 7 man, staying tight to his lead-post double-team. He'll receive an inside handoff from the quarterback, who then will continue faking trap option. The spread end goes to the cutoff and blocks the safety down the field.

The right half gets the ball on 67 counter, which is another complementary part of the trap option package. If the backside defensive end is giving you problems, you have ways to handle it. You can pull the guard and the tackle and let the tight end stay back home with the center turning back on the defensive tackle, which is one possible solution.

167 Counter vs. 4-3 Defense

Diagram 3.17 shows 167 counter against the 4-3 defense. The rules are the same counter-crisscross blocking for the offensive line. The left tackle now has a defender to lead on, so he will come down and double-team with the left guard. The center has to block right. You'd like him to be able to block right, as long as no run-through exists for the linebacker. The post blocker's assignment is to take care of any run-through. If the middle backer tries to run through, the post blocker, the guard, must come off the post, turn, and gap block the blitzing linebacker.

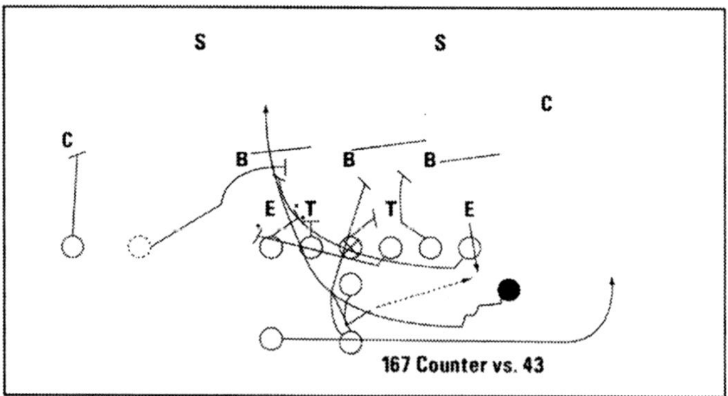

Diagram 3.17

The right guard is going to pull and trap end. The right tackle is to block the second man, or pull-check, whichever way you want to say it. He's going to pull for the tackle; if the tackle is not a problem, then he can climb for the backside linebacker. If the center has the defensive tackle handled, then you can climb for the linebacker. The tight end is going to pull through the hole and wall off. If the linebacker is really scraping, you should be able to block the outside linebacker with the tight end pulling through the hole. You should be able to block the backside linebacker with the right tackle. One other alternative you can use is to run 67 counter from split formation. You can put the split end in a four-to-six-yard split, at this point, bring him down inside, and give yourself another hat for the linebackers.

The backfield action is all the same. The 7-man, or the left tackle, is the man who establishes the point of attack with his down block. That action should give you plenty of hats for the linebackers, and you should have a pretty good football play. You should not run this play if the backside defensive end is especially penetration conscious. Instead, you should use a different blocking scheme. What you do in that case is use tag blocking and pull the guard and the tackle or the tackle and the guard. Tag stands for this and lets the tight end stay home and block on the defensive end.

167 Counter Tag vs. 4-4 Defense

Finally, Diagram 3.18 illustrates how to block the 67 counter play against the eight-man front. In the diagram, tag blocking is used with this, so you can get a feel for exactly how you can change the blocking. The addition of the word tag to the call tells you that the tackle and the guard are going to pull. You can change up the blocking schemes and take care of the defensive end problems.

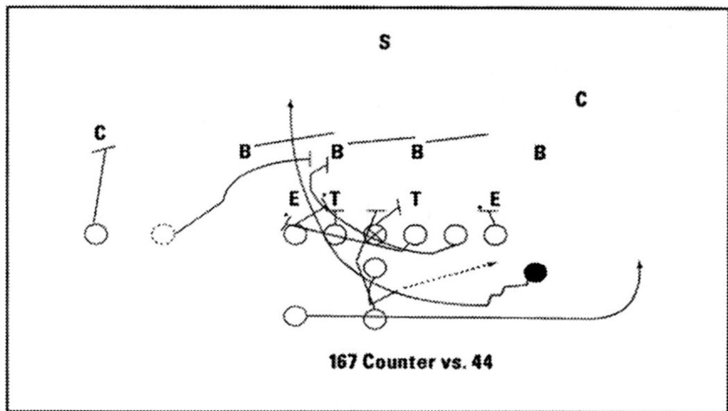

Diagram 3.18

Nothing changes for the left tackle and the left guard on the double-team. The center is gong to block to the right, and the post blocker, the left guard, has the responsibility for any run-through by either inside. He has to come off the post if any backer runs through inside. The right guard can pull and trap the defensive end. Remember that you are calling this play because the end is a penetrator and is giving you problems. You trap the end and pull the tackle through the hole, and he can wall off on the linebacker. You also have the fullback, who winds through the hole, for blocking the linebackers. You should get a hat on the linebackers. If you get what you want, you will get each of the linebackers to flow with the play. If you get that kind of action, the tackle pulling through the hole can block the outside linebacker. The tackle will get position on the inside linebacker, who flows, and wall him off. The fullback then has the backside inside linebacker as he overflows. By using this approach, you can force the linebackers to essentially run themselves out of the play.

You have the tight end to block the defensive end and take care of those problems. This block is the answer if the end is causing you problems in other blocking schemes. If you need more hats for the linebackers, then you can bring the split end down, put him in what is called split 100 formation – which gives him a four-to-six-yard alignment – and bring him down. Now you'll have hats for all the backers. The backfield action does not change, and all the checking problems are taken care of. You have hats for all the linebackers. These changes are why you should not give up on football plays. Just try to help your players with a better blocking scheme.

169 Counter Sweep

The next two variations are good little change-ups to the 67 counter play, the counter sweep and the counter bootleg off the 60 action. 67 counter, 169 counter sweep, and 167 counter bootleg are good against the 4-3 defense. All of these plays have been good against 4-3 defenses, since the 4-3 has become so popular these days.

The first play, 169 counter sweep, looks just like 67 counter, except that you are going to run a sweep around to the left end to the 9 hole (Diagram 3.19). In order to block this play, what you want to do is to have the offensive tackle on the left side execute his bump-lead-backer assignment. The offensive guard usually gets a defender in some kind of an inside shade, or gap, in the 4-3 defense. He and the tackle are going to post and bump-lead this defender, while the tackle is going to go to the backer. Remember, you are starting trap-option action away, so you are hoping for good flow out of the linebackers. The backs are faking 61 trap option.

The center is going to block to his right, and the right guard, when he pulls instead of trapping the backside defensive end, will pull and log him. You have created the same kind of conflicts for the end that you have with 61 trap option and 67 guard trap. If the end squeezes on the counter, he opens himself up to the log block on the sweep. If he widens for the sweep, he is more easily kicked out on the counter.

The right tackle will step to ensure the B gap is protected and then go back on the defensive end. You now have an answer for that defensive end. The tight end is going to pull, but instead of pulling up through the hole to wall off, he is going to pull all the way around the right guard's block and wall off on the outside linebacker.

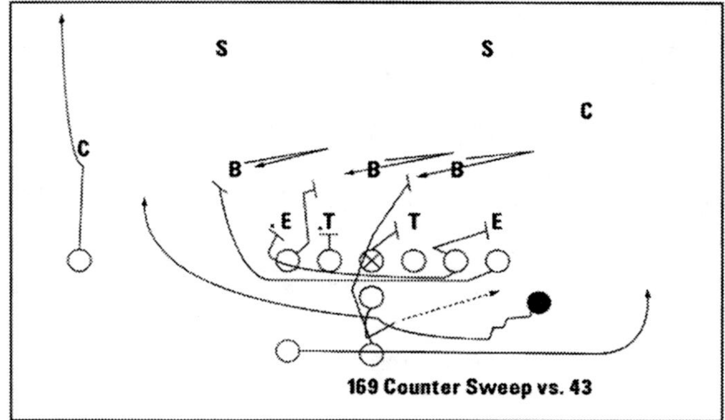

Diagram 3.19

The fullback is still going to fake 61 trap option, so you have another blocker for the linebackers. If you get any kind of flow, you have all three linebackers accounted for. The split end takes his corner through the end zone and runs him off.

Again, the right halfback will take the same footwork that he would take if going in three-step motion, but instead of leaving early, he goes on the snap. He turns and receives the inside handoff from the quarterback, who starts downhill. As soon as the handoff exchange is made, you want the halfback to get depth and run his sweep around the end. This play is similar to any counter sweep play that people run out of the I formation, except that you're just handing the ball off to the wingback.

The quarterback continues to fake his trap option. If you have run trap option release once to the wingback, it will help to set all this up. This play is just a special thing that we're in the process of looking at right now. It's an old play, but we are refreshing it, dusting it off, and trying to go with it against some of the defenses that we're seeing now.

167 Counter Bootleg

The last play is the bootleg, which looks just like this whole package (Diagram 3.20). The play is called 167 counter bootleg. When you say bootleg, you mean that the offensive line blocks the run and the quarterback keeps the ball on a run-pass action. You use this to attack the defensive end, who has been a problem chasing or penetrating and stopping the 60 counter game. You let him chase the counter fake and let the quarterback keep the ball. When you do that, the halfback, who fakes trap option as he comes across the backfield and passes the quarterback mesh, will have to turn up and become a log blocker at the flank. You should have the end pinned down pretty well, if you even have to block him at all. If he chases himself out of the play and the linebacker is flowing, then the left halfback can block the linebacker. The halfback is going to block the first free man at the flank from outside in.

You want to show the picture of 67 counter, but the only difference is that you cannot send the linemen down to the linebackers, because the play is a pass. The guard will block his defensive tackle, the tackle will block his defensive end, and both of them will put their heads to the inside. If the guard's man is in the gap, you will just come down on him. The center is going to block back. The right guard, as he pulls, can block anything showing off the backside of the play. If the defense is going to run the outside linebacker to counter sweep, you have a blocker to take care of the back side of the quarterback on any kind of blitz.

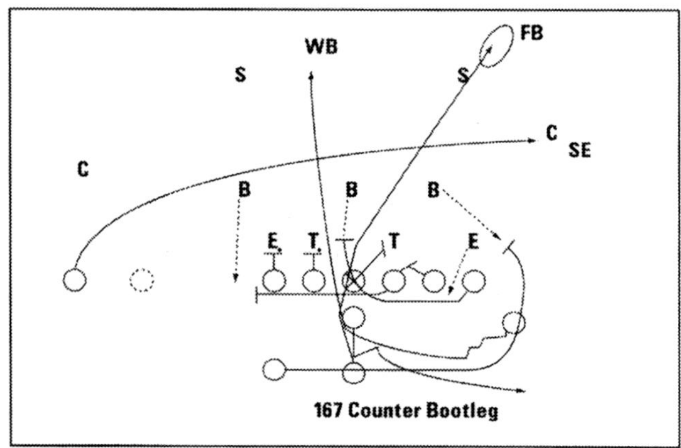

Diagram 3.20

The fullback is going to go up through the line, just as he always does when he's going to go block backers. Next, you are going to have him go to the deep outside one-third in the pass pattern. Depending on how the defense reacts, the fullback is going to be wide open or the safety is going to run back there with him. In either case, you have cleared the coverage out with the fullback. But what tends to happen is the fullback will get lost, and, if you get a reaction by the secondary to the run play, he will run right past the secondary the way he does on a waggle switch.

The spread end on the backside can come down to a split alignment, which helps this play, and run a crossing route. You want him to get all the way across the field as fast as he can.

The right tackle is going to step down inside and help on the second man. The tight end is going to pull, just as he did on the 67 counter, and is going to come up through the hole, because he's basically assigned to block the backside backer.

As the halfback fakes the counter, you want him to sprint right through the hole and go right down through the middle. The quarterback will come two steps on the midline, start downhill, and get depth after the fake as he attacks the flank. This action gives you three receivers out on the route. It is something we are experimenting with right now, and something that we're going to probably evolve into, depending on how the 4-3 defense evolves, and whether or not coaches continue to use that defense. We feel that this play provides the opportunity for several people to get lost in the action and come open deep.

Summary

The 60 package contains trap option, trap-option pass, the wider guard trap (either 63 or 23), the 27 or 67 guard trap, and the reverse. Those four plays complete the package. The 21 waggle or 29 waggle out of the same formation you run the tap option from is a big part of this. If teams line up in two deep and rotate, or if they just line in three deep, the middle safety will not be able to play both trap-option pass to one side and waggle back to the other side. He cannot play both. If he is stopping the trap-option pass, the waggle route back to the other side will hurt him. If he's staying in the middle and stopping waggle, then trap-option pass should work successfully. Those plays must be run. You have the package, and you have to execute those plays. To be executed correctly, they all need to look like they are the same play for the first two steps.

4

30 Series

This next chapter features the 30 series package, which is basically power sweep and power off tackle. The package consists of direct shots and is full flow. The 30 package also has some nice counters. But, basically, this package is direct flow. You are going to use this package of plays just as you would use the 20 series. You have a sweep, off-tackle plays, a counter, and play-action passing. You have all those things in this package. Some might wonder why not just stay with the 20 series. Many defenses will do a lot of blitzing on wing-T teams – especially in eight-man fronts, where they are going to send backers through A gaps and B gaps and be blitzing you all over the place. What you want to be able to do with this package is to pick up all those blitzes with what is called solid, or fire on backer, blocking. When you do that, you don't have to worry about keys. The defense is not keying the full flow; they're not keying the guards. They are just blitzing and trying to run through the gaps and stop plays. When keys are no longer important and direct power blocking becomes important, you go to the 30 series. Many times in goal line situations, you use the 30 sweep, as opposed to the 20 sweep, because you can fire block everything and solid block everything and pick up all the stunts. First, you should look at the power sweep, and then go on from there and evolve through the whole package.

131 Power Sweep vs. 50 Defense

The power sweep is called 31 and 39. In a wing formation, the call would be 131 (Diagram 4.1). You are going to run power sweep to the right, and, instead of the right guard pulling and kicking out the force, as in the 20 package, the fullback will kick out the force, and the line will block fire on backer. The line will be very solid in terms of their blocking. For those running the zone play, this blocking would be the same, where all the inside stunts are pretty well picked up. You also get a good lead at the point of attack. The defense can blitz all they want, because you can pick up all the blitzes and still get outside them.

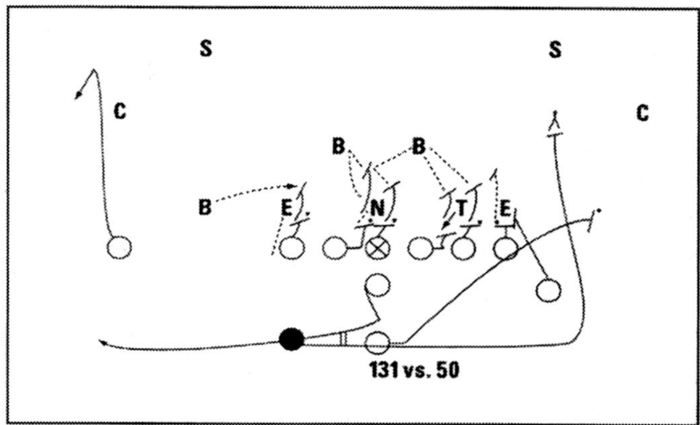

Diagram 4.1

The rules are pretty easy for the five linemen. The frontside three are all in fire on backer blocking. All they have to remember is fire on backer. If the defensive tackle is inside, in the gap, and even though the rule is fire on backer, you could tell the tackle to block down on it. He would make a 4 call, which tells the right guard, the 4 man, to pull through the hole and block the linebacker by folding around the tackle's block. That adjustment is just one which could be made to the blocking. Another call to make is for the center to make a 6 call. The center has no possible threat to the frontside A gap, so he can allow the left guard to pull around and provide another wall off blocker. The left tackle would then pull-check. Remember, you're not running this play for this reason. You are running this play to have fire on backer blocking, because you know the defense is trying to stunt and run through.

When you have fire on backer blocking with no calls, you will not get scoop blocks. The offensive tackle will take a fire step and use fire technique. He is the covered man, so he will use fire technique. The guard is uncovered, so he uses reach technique. The guard's first step is a reach step. From there, one of those two blockers is going to come off on the linebacker. Normally, the guard will take a reach step first and then climb on a 45-degree angle to try to cut the linebacker off by running right through the inside hip of the defensive lineman. He needs to get on an angle to cut the linebacker off at the flank. Remember, you are calling this play because they are blitzing and running through on you, so you do not really anticipate much flowing action. You do, however, anticipate some kind of blitzing action. As the guard takes his reach step, if the defensive tackle slants inside, the guard blocks the tackle. The offensive tackle then comes off on the linebacker. He takes his inside arm and punches the nearest shoulder of the defensive tackle on the way to the linebacker. Now, you have any stunt picked. If for some reason the tackle was coming to the outside and the linebacker was blitzing B gap, then the tackle stays with this man, and the guard comes off and blocks the linebacker on the B gap stunt. One of those two will block the defensive tackle. The other one will block the linebacker, and then all the stunts are picked up.

The center also blocks fire on backer against the noseguard. He comes off with a fire step because he is a covered man. If you are getting a lot of blitzing, the center should never use the 6 call. The center shouldn't make the 6 call because he knows you take a chance of getting the nose going one way and the linebacker going the other way. If you are getting a lot of different stunts, then you've got to be able to pick up those stunts with fire on backer blocking, rather than making calls. If the nose slants left to the backside, the center can now let that man go, can climb to linebacker level, and cut the backside linebacker off. Since the left guard's rule is also fire on backer and is uncovered, he will take a reach step. The guard reads the noseguard. If the noseguard comes toward his side, the guard blocks him. If the noseguard stays frontside, then the guard comes off and picks up the linebacker.

The backside tackle is fire on backer and takes a fire step. If the defensive end is working outside and up the field, then the tackle would keep climbing and look for the backside linebacker, who would be the cutback player. If the defensive end locks on to him, then the tackle will lock on the end and just block him.

All five linemen are basically using the fire on backer blocking scheme, which is your version of zone blocking. You have some exceptions. You can pull or fold guard around at times, if no threats exist to your gaps. But for the most part, you are running this play because you know the defense is going to be stunting on you, and you need to be able to pick up all those stunts.

The tight end's rule is gap-post-read-down. If a man was in his gap, he would block him. If a man was on him, he would post him. In the 50 defense, a man is on him; therefore, he will post.

The right halfback's rule is a lot like it is on 21 sweep. He's going to block the first free man to his inside. In this case, he is going to come down and block the defensive end. If that tight end will post the end and raise his center of gravity up, elevate his numbers, and expose his hip, then the right halfback can come down and get a lethal shot on him. The other thing to tell the tight end is, as you knock the end off the ball, he must keep his eyes up and be ready for any run-through in the C gap. He also has to be ready to come off on the linebacker. You should be able to take care of the defensive end. If the defense is blitzing and running linebackers through inside, then you can keep the tight end on the post block and get great movement on the defensive end.

The fullback takes one lead step and comes downhill. He stays tight, off the right halfback's lead block, and blocks whichever defensive back is coming to force the sweep. If it's a linebacker who has overrun, the fullback is going to turn and kick him out. In this example, it would be a right-shoulder block when you run 131 sweep to the right.

The left halfback is going to run the sweep. He is going to come across the backfield, cross over, and run through the heels of the tailback, exactly as he would on 21 sweep. The quarterback comes back two steps on the midline, again, as in 21, hands the ball off, comes out, and fakes waggle. The left half is going to get outside the down block and then is going to burst north and south under the kick-out block. In this case, he has to make the safety miss. The safety should be in some kind of man coverage if the defense is blitzing, and you're going to have to make him miss.

The spread end can run his waggle out route. He and the quarterback are going to fake the waggle. The waggle out, waggle curl, waggle fly, whatever route is being run for that game.

Another thing that you can do is run this play from unbalanced and bring the spread end over to the playside. Now, you have one less defensive back to worry about because the corner will have to move out. Then your fullback can concentrate on kicking out the safety, and you still have a good play. In this play, the halfback has to make the safety miss, because if you keep all the linemen in, someone is probably going to get to the halfback, or the safety will make the play. Once in a while, your back is going to have to be asked to make a second-level guy miss. As long as you can take care of the front, at least, you will not have a minus-yardage play. Once you get back to the line of scrimmage, you can go from there and let the halfbacks use their ability.

131 Sweep vs. 4-3 Defense

Diagram 4.2 illustrates 131 against the 4-3 defense. A lot of time was spent explaining fire on backer blocking, which is your form of zone blocking. When the defensive front changes, the blocking scheme accounts for the front. In essence, what happens is a change in who is covered and who is uncovered; as such, a change will also happen in who is taking the fire step and who is taking the reach step. Everybody is still fire on backer. Remember, you are running this play because the defense is stunting on. You probably will not be using the calls; instead, the line will be firing off and reading those stunts to pick them up.

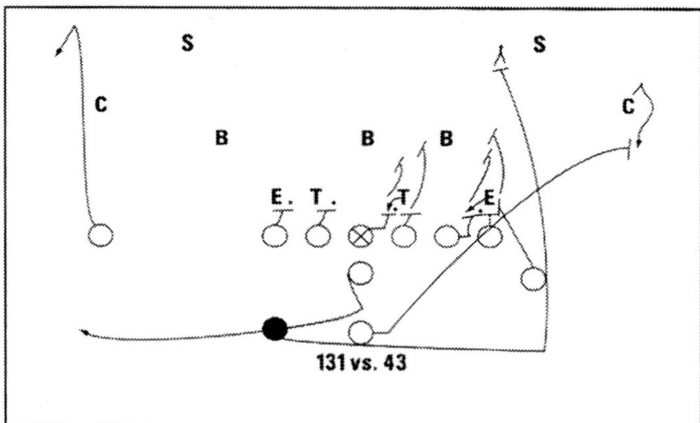

Diagram 4.2

The tight end has a man to post, and the right halfback is going to block the first free man to his inside, so you have a nice double-team right at the point of attack. Since fire on backer is the rule for all the linemen, a case exists where your right tackle could make a 4 call, block down on the defensive tackle, and have the guard pull around. If the defense is doing a lot of blitzing, you should prefer to fire on backer and keep it that way. In this case, the right tackle is uncovered and takes a reach step. If the defensive end is slanting down inside, the lead blocker (wing) should go to the linebacker, and you should have both the right tackle and the tight end staying on the defensive end, slanting down inside. If the defensive end does not slant down inside, the right tackle will climb on a cutoff angle on the linebacker.

The right guard and center will work together and execute fire on backer blocking on the defensive tackle and middle linebacker, reading the tackle's charge to determine who will come off on the linebacker. The left guard and the left tackle use fire on backer technique, and both take a step and block the defenders aligned on them.

The backfield action and assignments are identical. You may have a chance to get a blocker down the field. If one of the linebackers blitzes away, then one of the offensive linemen can get down the field and maybe block the safety. Otherwise, except for using unbalanced formations, the ballcarrier is going to have to make the safety miss.

131 Sweep vs. 4-4 Defense

Diagram 4.3 shows 131 against the 4-4 defense, or the eight-man front. The rules are fine. Every lineman is a fire on backer blocker. Each is going to execute scoop technique, so if he's uncovered, he should reach; if he is covered, he should fire. Everyone takes that first step and then reads what happens from there. The only slight difference is for the tight end, who has the defensive end in an inside shade or maybe even down in the gap. The tight end will come down and block with his head across the front, and the further inside the defensive end goes, the flatter the tight end will have to step. If it is a gap situation, the tight end and right tackle should take care of the end, and the wingback should be able to come off and look for the linebacker scraping.

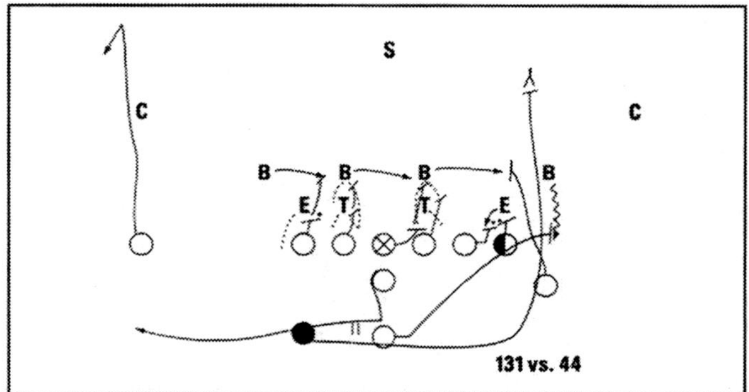

Diagram 4.3

The right guard and center work together on the tackle and inside linebacker, reading the tackle for whoever comes off to the linebacker. If for some reason the linebacker did flow fast and the wingback picked him up, then the right guard and center would be looking for the backside linebacker. The left guard and tackle are both covered. Each executes fire technique, and, if the defender pinches inside, you block him. If the defender loops away, they climb for the backer. Sometimes, that man will be the backside backer all the way from the outside.

The fullback takes his lead step and blocks tight to the wingback's down block. Against the 4-4 defense, you're probably going to have a tighter force angle because the outside linebacker is closer to the play. The ballcarrier needs to know that and also needs to make a sharp sweep cut.

132 vs. 50 Defense

Oftentimes, the defensive end is a real penetrator, and you cannot get him blocked. In that case, you want to use the 32 play and run off-tackle. Again, as in the other packages, you want to put the #3 defender in an assignment conflict. In this series, you do that with 31 sweep outside and 32 inside the defender, if he begins to penetrate upfield to stop the sweep. Just as the sweep action out of the 20 series has a 21 and a 22, the 30 series also has a 31 and a 32. Both put the defensive end in an assignment conflict. The only difference is how the offensive linemen block the front. In the 20 series, you pull linemen; in the 30 series, you use more direct blocking to account for defensive blitzes and stunts.

Diagram 4.4 shows how to block 132 against the 50 defense. Basically, it is a power off-tackle play. You want to double-team down, kick out, and run the ball off-tackle. You can do this from the I, from split backs, and from the wing-T. You can do it from virtually any backfield set you want. It is a universal play, and you should have it in your offense as well. It is not a big staple plan. But it definitely answers a problem when you need it, and it gives you another way to handle the penetrating defensive end that is stopping the sweep.

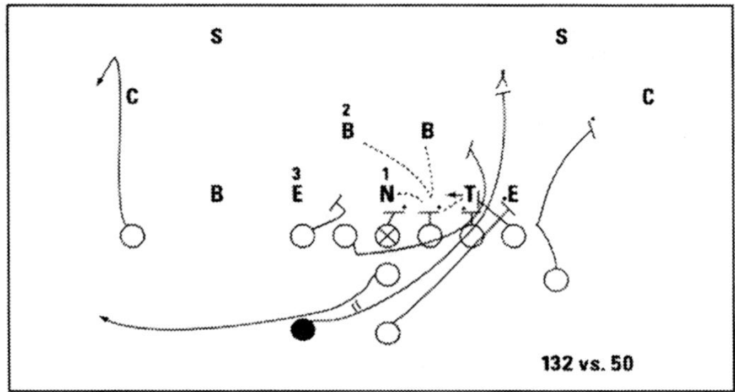

Diagram 4.4

The tight end's rule is lead-backer-or influence. Since a defender is over the tackle, he is going to double-team him. The right tackle has gap-post-lead. Since nobody is in his gap and a man is on him, he will post. You would like that double-team to take the defensive tackle down the line. You want to create lateral openings in the line.

The right guard's rule is gap-area-post. Since he has no one in his gap, he will step up and block the area by stepping with his right foot up, bringing the left foot up even, and holding in the area. He is looking for the defensive tackle to slant in, the nose to slant out, or any linebacker to run through his area. He will just protect the area and make sure that no one runs through that area.

The center's rule is on-area-left. He has the nose on him, so he is going to block on, using his left shoulder and putting his head to the side of the hole. The left guard's rule is to pull and wall off tight to the double-team. The fullback is going to be the kick-out blocker from the inside out, and so those two will form the hole. The left tackle has to block the second man. He should pull and check #2, who is the inside linebacker. If the linebacker is not posing a problem, then he will turn back and block the defensive end.

The right halfback is going to influence the defensive end. You want the wing to step right at the end as if it's the sweep block. Then he turns outside and blocks above the hole in the cutoff area. The fullback gets to the quickest path he can in order to get inside out on the defensive end, and you tell him to dive for the outside foot of the tackle. He can cross over, so he gets there the fastest way possible His aiming point is the outside foot of the tackle, and he kicks out from there.

The halfback is going to carry the ball. You do not want him to go all the way around and try to vertically cut into the off-tackle hole. You tell him to go and cross over as he would on a sweep and run right to the off-tackle hole. He also will run right to the outside leg of the tackle. When he takes his second step, the handoff will be made. His hips will be open to the quarterback, and then he will run right through the off-tackle area.

The quarterback takes the ball and steps right to the halfback. The handoff should occur on the second step, and then the quarterback will fake waggle. It looks a little bit different, but the purpose is to gain the yardage off-tackle, not necessarily to fool the defense. The spread end can either fake the waggle or go to the cutoff if you think you need the extra blockers down the field.

If everyone on the defensive front is blitzing all the time, the answer is fire on backer for all assignments. Give all five linemen fire on backer, except the right tackle, who will post because of the tight end lead. That method is how you handle the continuous blitzing. But this blocking scheme isn't bad either, because it will pick up a lot of the blitzes. So you shouldn't mind just staying with the main blocking scheme. In goal line situations, a lot of times, you will call 32 gap and change the assignments a little bit. You will be a little bit more gap oriented on the frontside.

132 vs. 4-3 Defense

Against the 4-3, the rules hole up on 132 (Diagram 4.5). The tight end's rule is lead-blocker-or influence. If the tackle is not covered, he doesn't have anybody to lead on, so you want him to go for the playside linebacker. The frontside tackle's rule is gap-post-lead. No one is in his gap, and no one is there for him to post, so he's going to come down and double-team with the right guard. The right guard will post block. He steps with his left foot, posts with his right shoulder, and makes contact in the numbers, elevating the defender's hip so the right tackle can lead on him at the hip. You want good movement down the line.

The center's rule is on-area-left. You can tell him to block left if you have no problems with run-through. You will also tell the post blocker, the right guard, that if you get a run-through by the middle backer or the backside backer in the A gap, then the guard must come off the post and take care of it. The lead blocker will handle the defensive tackle by himself. Sometimes, you'll even tell the post blocker to come off the post and go get those backers; it depends on how fast they flow.

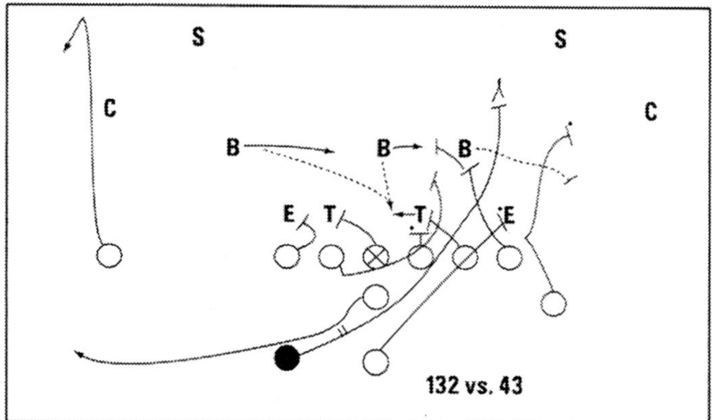

Diagram 4.5

The left guard is still going to pull and wall tight to the double-team. The left tackle is going to pull and check 2, which should be pretty well taken care of because the center is blocking back on him. This maneuver will enable the left tackle to turn back on the defensive end very quickly. If you're worried about that and think you are going to open up a gate on the backside, tell the left tackle to block on. If the center has to use his area assignment, then you definitely have to pull check the left tackle. But, if the center is using his left assignment, then the tackle can go ahead and block on.

The wingback will step right at the defensive end, making him think it's a sweep, and then he can block out or above the hole, which is the influence technique. The fullback crosses over for the outside leg of the tackle and goes to kick out the defensive end. The halfback is going to run the ball. This time, he can bend his path a little bit tighter because the post lead is a one-man move inside. He takes a tight aiming point after he receives the handoff. The quarterback will make the exchange on the second step, and he and the spread end will go ahead and fake waggle.

A couple things can happen on this play. The outside linebacker to the playside can flow quickly and run himself out of the play. If he does that, you tell the tight end not to chase him. He simply goes on inside and blocks the middle backer. You can also tell the tight end to just go block the middle backer and then tell the offensive guard pulling through the hole to get the outside backer. That change-up is another you can use. If the outside linebacker is running himself completely out of the play and the tight end blocks the middle backer scraping, you can tell the pulling guard to go ahead and block the backside backer who is scraping. You have ways to get hats for each of the linebackers. You should be able to get those people blocked.

The tight end, anytime you plan an even front, can take a five- or six-foot split for internal and off-tackle plays. That widens the defensive technique playing on him. Now, you have even more room off-tackle. The game-planning section (see Volume 2) shows exactly how to take these splits, exactly how to get lined up, and what you are trying to do in all these game plans. The game plan for the 50, the 4-4, the 4-3, and the overshift is also illustrated.

132 vs. 4-4 Defense

132 versus the 4-4 defense, or eight-men front, is shown in Diagram 4.6. As you can see, at this time, the major difference is the fact that you have two influence blockers to deal with the defense's outside support players. The tight end has no one on the tackle to double-team. If he has a 7 technique on a gap defensive end, someone who won't let him inside, it makes it very difficult to block the inside backer. Now, he uses his influence rule. A lot of times against eight-man fronts, he will use his influence rule. He steps hard at the defensive end and then turns out. The wingback also influences and blocks out. You have two blockers for the two people who could make the tackle outside the kick-out block. Each will block whoever is easiest to get it blocked. If the wing is closer to the outside linebacker and feels he can block the linebacker better, then he can block him, and the tight end releases for the corner. Otherwise, they can call out the guy they are going to block and block the defender closest to them.

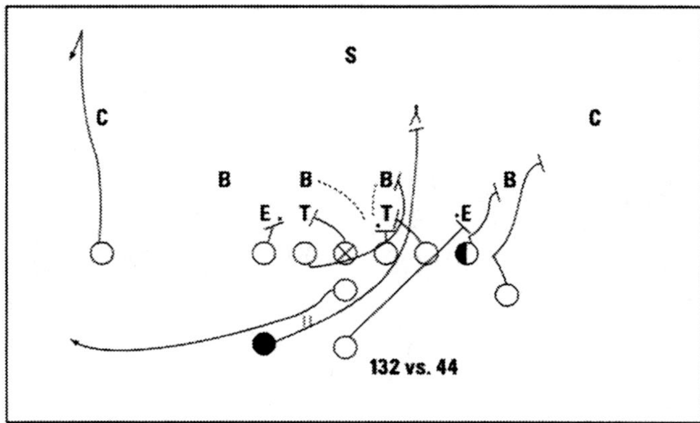

Diagram 4.6

The right tackle and guard form the double-team. The right guard, as he post blocks, needs to have his eyes up, looking for run-throughs by the linebackers. If a run-through does occur, the post blocker comes off and blocks it. The center can block left, or, if you have real problems with checking, you can use him to block area, and you can pull check the tackle. As long as the center is blocking left, the tackle can block on. The left guard is going to pull and wall off. The fullback crosses over for the outside leg of the tackle and is going to stay on a kick-out course and kick out the defensive end.

You can run 32 to the split end side, absolutely. But, you should never do it against the 50 defense. Only do it against even fronts. A 32 to the off-tackle hole on the tight end side is a good short-yardage play. It also is not a bad play against the even fronts, especially if the third defender is penetrating.

134 Blast vs. 50 Defense

The next play in this package is 34 blast, which continues with the power aspect of the package (Diagram 4.7). A blast play is where you are going to double-team the nose, pull the backside guard around for the backside backer, and lead the fullback straight up through on the frontside linebacker. It's like any I formation isolation play that you've seen. The other linemen block on assignment. The offensive line has one set of rules for blast, and you can run the play with any kind of backfield action you want. It works well with 80 footwork and also to the halfback with 30 action.

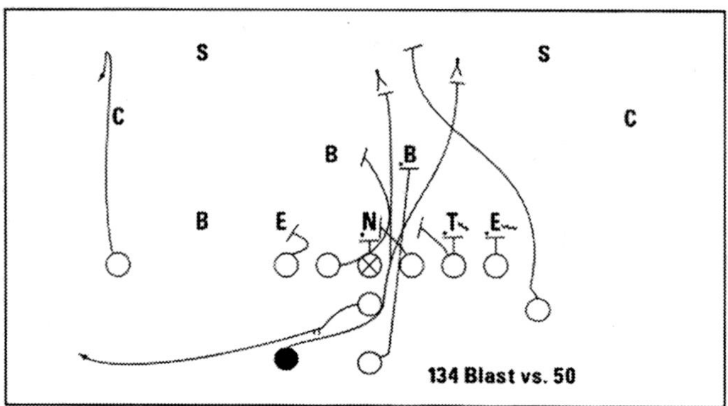

Diagram 4.7

The tight end's rule is going to be on-outside-backer. In this case, he has a man on him, so he blocks on. The 4 hole is the point of attack, so his head is to the inside. The tackle's rule is on-outside gap-backer. He will also block the man on him and use on technique, which puts his head to the inside. The playside guard's rule is gap-on-lead. That rule means block your gap; if no one is there, you block the man on you; and, if no one is there, you double-team down with the center. The guard will execute his lead assignment with the center. The center's rule is post-left. Against the 50 defense, with a nose, he will post. The left guard's rule is to pull and wall around the tail of the lead blocker, looking for the backside linebacker. If you think that blocking puts too many bodies in the hole or you can get the backside linebacker without walling off and pulling, then just take a good angle and cut him off. If you feel your guards could do that, you should not pull around. You do not want to have too many bodies in the hole. The backside tackle's rule is pull and check. He's going to quickly check the second man, the linebacker, and then turn back on the defensive end. If you are worried about the defensive end being in the backfield all the time, then have the left tackle block him on.

The fullback is going to take a quick lead step and dive right for the inside foot of the guard. He is gong to block the playside linebacker with his head inside. It is just a good, old-fashioned fullback isolation block. The left halfback is going to receive the ball. He wants to show 32 action. With the 32 action and the quarterback bringing him the ball initially, the defense sees the play more outside. The halfback, as he clears the mesh, starts to turn and stays tight to the double-team. He can bounce outside from there or stay between the left guard and the fullback's block. He has to run where he finds daylight. If the defensive people are thinking outside the end, or even sweep, working that way, the blockers just turn them outside. You use an on technique, which means you finish to the right, anyway. The fullback has some very good run lanes, especially if you get a good post-lead by the center and right guard. The quarterback continues on and fakes the waggle with the split end. The wingback will fake the sweep block and is assigned to be a cutoff blocker.

134 Blast vs. 4-3 Defense

Now, 134 blast against the even defense is illustrated in Diagram 4.8. The rules hold up quite nicely. The tight end has a man on him; therefore, he will block on. The tackle has no one on him or to his outside gap, so he can go block the linebacker. He takes an inside-out course because the 4 hole is the point of attack. You want to get your hat on the inside of the linebacker. The linebacker, if he sees 31-32 sweep action and reacts to 31-32 with a little outside flow, can be blocked by the guard, who can take a straight path to him. If the linebacker reads blast and comes down inside, the guard must use the inside-out path on him. You are thus putting your head to the inside and taking the path to get you there the fastest.

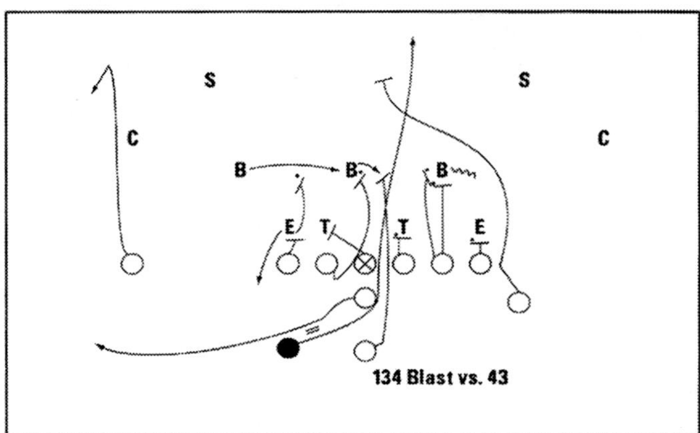

Diagram 4.8

The right guard does have a defender on him, so he uses on technique to block the defensive tackle. The right guard is the 4 man, and, since this play is 34 blast, he is the point of attack. His head goes to the inside. The center is going to block back to the left, and the left guard is going to pull around and wall off on the middle backer. The guard will take the first opening he can find to the middle linebacker. The left tackle can block on, since the center is going to use his left assignment. If the defensive end is an upfield player and running up into the backfield, the tackle can start with on technique and then work to the outside linebacker, who will be flowing to the play.

The wingback will fake the sweep block and then go to cutoff. The fullback is going to isolate on the middle backer. He takes his lead step, dives for the inside foot of the guard, and is going to the middle backer. Who will actually block the middle linebacker depends on whether he steps up or flows. You would like to have the fullback be able to take care of him, so the pulling guard can block the backside linebacker as he gets through the hole. In any case, at least three hats exist for the three linebackers, and maybe a fourth, depending on whether or not the left tackle will shift or block on.

The left halfback is the ballcarrier. He starts right, as if he is going to go for the off-tackle hole. The quarterback brings the ball straight to him and makes the exchange. As the quarterback fakes waggle, the ballcarrier will turn up inside, find the opening, and go. The spread end fakes the waggle play, along with the quarterback.

The 34 blast is a good-looking play, especially if the defense sees 32 or 31 and starts to react outside too much. You are going to turn right up inside of them and make some big things happen.

134 Blast vs. 4-4 Defense

The rules still hold up well against a 4-4 defense (Diagram 4.9). The tight end's rule is on-outside-or backer. Against the 4-4 defense, he has a defensive end inside him, whether he's in a 7 technique or an inside shade. The defender could be down in the gap. Regardless, the defender is inside him, so he blocks outside on the outside linebacker. If the end were a head-up 6 technique, you should go ahead and interpret the rule as on. Most of the time, you find that the defensive end is inside shade or gap conscious. If he is, the tight end blocks his outside rule. Because that defender is an inside shade, the offensive tackle, who doesn't have a man on him, will turn out on him.

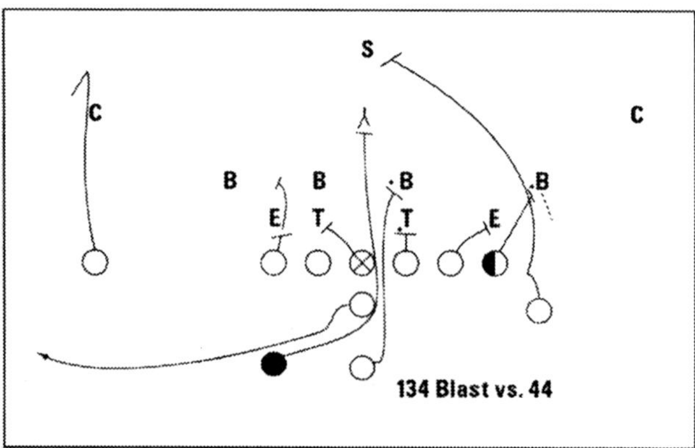

Diagram 4.9

The right guard has no one in his gap, but he does have a defender on him, so he will block on, with his head to the inside again. The center has no one on him to post, so he is going to block left. Since he is doing that, the left tackle can block on, or else he can shift to the backside backer. The left guard is going to be pulling to wall off. He pulls right off the center's tail and has the backside inside linebacker. The fullback takes a quick lead step, isolates through, and takes the frontside middle linebacker.

You will find that this play and blocking scheme is pretty good against the eight-man fronts. You see people attack them this way all the time. The backfield action is all the same. The wingback is the cutoff blocker, or you can have him influence and block out on the corner. Since 34 blast is an internal play, you coach the wing to go to the safety on the cutoff.

This play completes the power package. You have a power sweep (31), where you double-team the defensive end, kick out the corner, and run out wide. You have a power off-tackle play (32), where you double-team the defensive tackle, kick out the defensive end, and run off-tackle. And, you have a blast play (34), where you double-team the noseguard, lead through on the inside backer, and run right up over the center. This combination gives you an inside, an off tackle, and an outside play, all in that series, with the same backfield action for the first two steps.

131 Keep Pass (Flood) vs. 50 Defense

Along with the 31 sweep, 32 off tackle, and 34 blast, you have a pass play in which the quarterback keeps the ball in the same direction and throws a flood route. That play is called 131 keep pass flood (Diagram 4.10). You use this play to take advantage of a defense in which the corners are overreacting to the sweep. Oftentimes, when they see sweep fake, they are going to come flying, so, at this time, you are going to run keep pass flood on them.

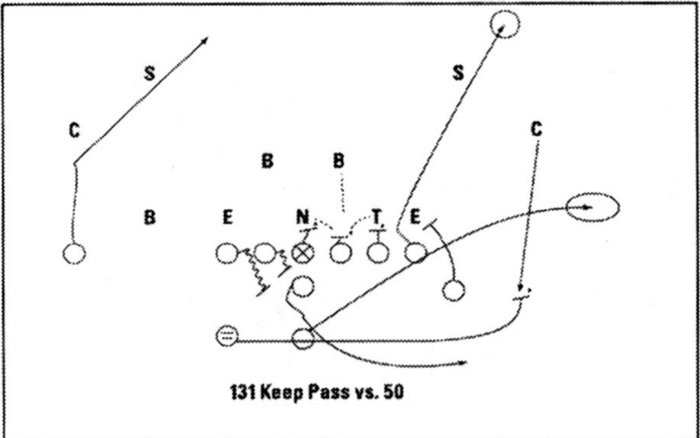

Diagram 4.10

The right tackle and right guard's rules are gap-on-area. You do not want to say linebacker, because they cannot go downfield on a pass. If a man is in their gap, they will block him; if not and a man is on them, they will block that. Therefore, the right tackle is going to block the man on him. The right guard has no gap and has no one on him, so he blocks area. He steps with the right foot, brings the left foot up even, and holds in his area. He is looking for pinches by the tackle, slants by the nose, or run-throughs by the linebackers. Any of those things are his responsibility. The rest of the offensive line is step and cup. The one thing you do is tell the center that if he has an odd defense, where a noseguard is on him, even though the rule is step and cup, you want him to block aggressively. You tell the center to block aggressively with a left-shoulder block. Next, the left guard and the tackle will step and cup back, as you protect the backside of the quarterback by building a solid wall of protection.

You can run this as keep pass or keep pass flood. If it is keep pass flood, then the wingback shows block and releases out, too. You can run all sorts of routes. If you go to the playbook, it will say for the wingback to run a fly, the tight end to run a clearing pattern, and the fullback to go out into the flat. The wingback fakes his sweep block and runs a fly (flood), or he can actually make the block (keep pass). When you run this play, what you want to accomplish is to break the key. So, you want the wingback to come down and actually block the end a little bit, to make contact on him before you actually run the route. If you need to block the defensive end with the wingback, then you will just come down and stay on that block. You tell the tight end to run the deep route.

The fullback, who would normally be kicking out when the corner reacts to the sweep, goes out to the flat. He releases tightly off the wingback's tail and then right into the flat, behind the corner, who is forcing the sweep. The corner has now been put into an assignment conflict. If he comes to support the sweep too aggressively, you throw the pass. If he is soft, playing for the pass, he cannot support the sweep effectively.

The left halfback is faking the 31 sweep. Then, he becomes the blocker at the flank and protects the quarterback. The spread end on the backside runs a post. You'd like him to run a post through the middle and get in the quarterback's vision.

The quarterback takes two steps on the midline, but instead of faking waggle, he is just going to roll behind the left halfback's block. He will have either the flat or the tight end wide open. Remember that you call this play because the corner is forcing the sweep. You look deep to short. If one of them is not there, you'll go ahead and run. If for some reason the corner stays off and covers, rather than forcing the sweep, the quarterback has the option to run the ball.

131 Keep Pass (Flood) vs. 4-3 Defense

If you look at 131 keep pass or keep pass flood versus the 4-3 defense, the play is unchanged (Diagram 4.11). The wingback is going to come down and block the defensive end. If you call, "Flood," he will come down, show the block, and then run his route. The tight end is going to burst and run the deep clearing route. All the linemen on the frontside block gap-on-area. The only difference is that, at this point, the right tackle blocks area and the right guard blocks on. Their heads are to the outside since the 1 hole is the point of attack. The rest of the offensive line will step and cup. Again, you build a wall of protection behind the backside of the keep pass. The rest of the assignments are identical. The only difference in the routes is whether the wingback is releasing or blocking, depending on the call.

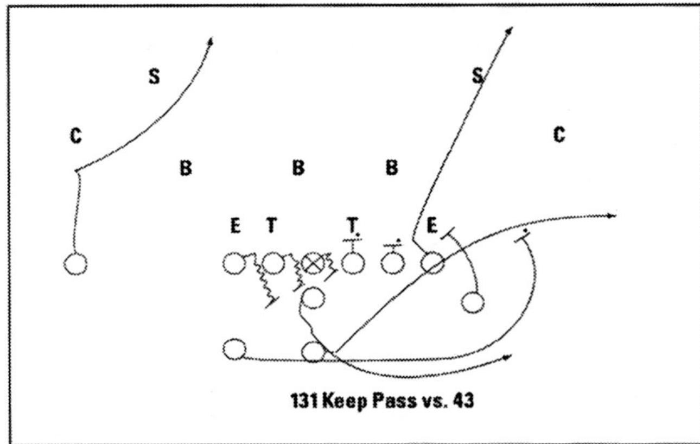

Diagram 4.11

Keep Pass (Flood) vs. 4-4 Defense

131 keep pass or keep pass flood versus a 4-4 defense does not call for any significant changes (Diagram 4.12). The tight end is going to run the clearing route. You want him to use a block release, just as he would on waggle. The wingback is going to come down and will block the defensive end, who should be pretty well set up for him by the tight end. The offensive line blocks with the same rules as before. The routes stay the same. The only slight difference has to do with the halfback. He is going to be faking the sweep and be the blocker at the flank. He'll block the first free man from the outside in. Against the 4-4 defense, you can see you have the wingback to block the defensive end and the halfback coming across the backfield to block the outside linebacker. The corner should be playing the deep one-third, which should help open up a passing opportunity to the fullback out in the flat. If the corner comes up short, the tight end will be open deep. You still have deep, short, run the ball for the quarterback.

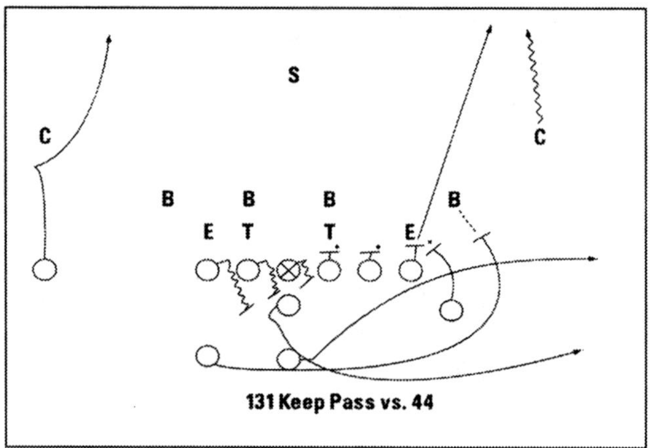

Diagram 4.12

131 Option (Wall) vs. 50 Defense

One final thing in the 30 package in terms of the sweep action is 31 option (Diagram 4.13). The 31 option play is similar to trap option. You can run this play if you do not want to run trap option. If you are getting a lot of internal blitzing and crossfire stunts and want to use a fire on backer blocking scheme to pick all that stuff up, you can do that and run 31 option. When you add the word wall, it means that one of your normal option blockers will wall off inside, as opposed to blocking at the flank.

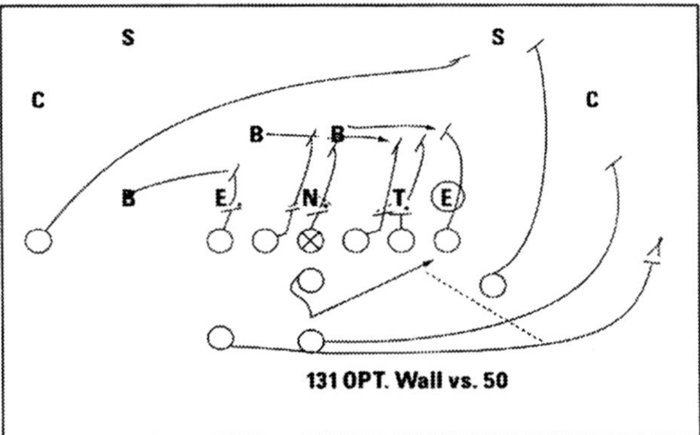

Diagram 4.13

What happens for the linemen are fire on backer rules, which make up the form of zone blocking to pick up all stunts. Thus, each one of the linemen will fire if he is covered, or else he will reach on his first step if he is uncovered. The first steps look like that all the way across the line. If your rule is fire on backer and you are one of the five offensive linemen, then a good chance exists that you will be using scoop technique.

The right guard and right tackle work together on the defensive tackle and inside linebacker. If the defensive tackle comes upfield or outside, then the tackle blocks him and the offensive guard stays on the angle to cut off the linebacker. If the defensive tackle is pinching inside, the offensive guard takes him over and the tackle climbs for the linebacker.

The same thing is true backside for the center and left guard working against the nose and inside linebacker. The center will fire on the nose, and the backside guard will take a reach step. If the nose locks on to the center, then the backside guard keeps going off the hip of the nose and tries to cut the linebacker off on the angle. If the nose is going to slant to the weakside, the guard picks him up. The center bench-presses the nose into the guard and then climbs for the linebacker. The left tackle will fire step and block the defensive end if he works to the tackle. If he loops away, the tackle will get to the next level and look for the cutback player.

At the flank, what happens is the fullback will flare and block #4. One of the two remaining option blocks can wall off inside, and the other one will go ahead and block #5. Whichever of the two is the inside man will go ahead and wall off inside, and the other player will release and stalk #5. In this diagram, the halfback will release and stalk #5, and the tight end will take the fastest release he can and wall off on the linebackers. Now, look at all the hats you have for the linebackers. If the playside linebacker beats both the guard and the tackle, he still has the tight end to wall him off. If the center and left guard don't pick up the backside backer, the right guard and right tackle will. The left tackle may still come upfield and block the cutback player.

The split end is going to cutoff. You're going to try to get him across to the cutoff on the opposite side. No waggle fake is to his side, so he needs to go to cutoff. The quarterback and left halfback will run trap option technique. The halfback will cross over, run through the fullback's heels, and become the pitchback. The quarterback takes two steps on the midline, then works downhill, and options the third defender. The defensive end is the pitch key. This play is the same as trap option, and it gives you basically the same things, except now you can take care of all the stunting problems.

131 Option (Wall) vs. 4-3 Defense

Diagram 4.14 gives you a look at 131 option wall against the 4-3 defense. The fullback is a flank blocker. The inside man between the tight end and wingback will wall off, and the outside man will be involved in the option blocking. You then have two flank blockers. All the linemen are using fire on backer rules to create a good zone blocking front. If they're uncovered, they reach. If they're covered, they fire. The only small difference is on the backside, where both the guard and tackle will fire and work upfield if their defenders slant backside. The tight end takes his fastest release and walls off on the first backer from the center. The defensive end is unblocked and is the pitch key.

The backfield action does not change. The fullback blocks #4, and the wing blocks #5. The quarterback options #3, and the left halfback gets in pitch phase to receive the pitch.

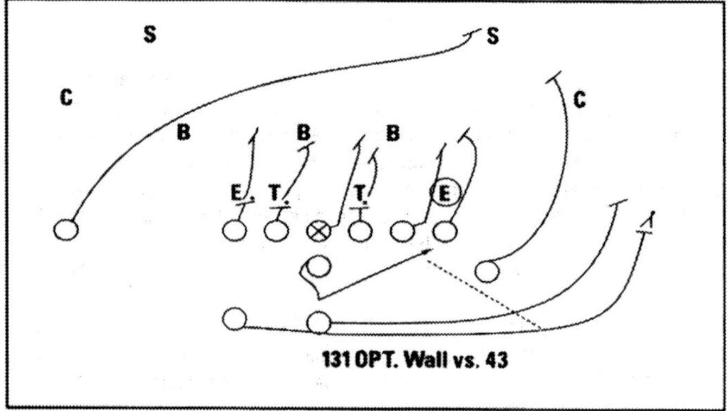

Diagram 4.14

131 Option (Wall) vs. 4-4 Defense

Against the eight-man front, 131 option wall has to account for the different alignment of the outside linebacker (Diagram 4.15). The wing is the widest aligned, so he takes care of #5, and the fullback blocks #4, the outside linebacker. You're going to option #3. Usually, the defensive end will be an inside shade in the eight-man front, and the tight end is taught to take the quickest release to block the nearest backer from the center. He uses an outside release and should be looking to cut off the playside inside

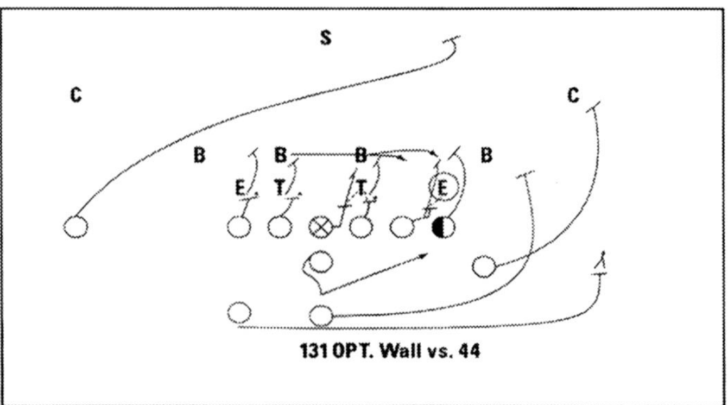

Diagram 4.15

linebacker. The wall tells him, instead of option blocking, he is going to wall off. If this formation was spread 100, with the spread end playside, or loose 100, or any formation where the end is out wide, it would be the wingback who executes the wall-off assignment.

If the defensive end comes pinching down inside, you will actually block him with the tackle and really not have a defender to pitch off of. If he does not, then the tackle climbs upfield looking for the first linebacker, which might be the backside backer scraping, because this play is full flow. Nothing slows down the reads by the linebackers. Recall that the only reason you're calling this play, or any of the 30 series, is that you're getting a lot of blitzing and stunting inside, and they're not reading anybody. You're not really worried about the keys, because you run this play for a definite reason. The rest of the line uses fire on backer technique and could go to linebackers, depending on the reaction of the defensive linemen. So it is pure zone blocking. The backfield assignments are no different. You can do this from a lot of different formations. The illustration is out of the tight end and wing, but it's the same rules versus any other formation. If you use a spread 100 formation or a loose formation, it's all the same. You can run this strong; you can run it weak. You can run it with motion; you can run it without motion. It is simply an alternative to trap option if you need it.

137 Counter-Crisscross vs. 50 Defense

Next, the counter game is discussed. The 30 series counters are an integral part of the offense. The first play is 37 counter-crisscross (Diagram 4.16). This play can be handed off halfback to halfback, or you can have the quarterback hand it off, just as he did on the 67 counter. If you call 137 counter-crisscross, you use "XX" to abbreviate crisscross. If you want to change the blocking, you'll add a suffix to the play. You can say, "Counter-

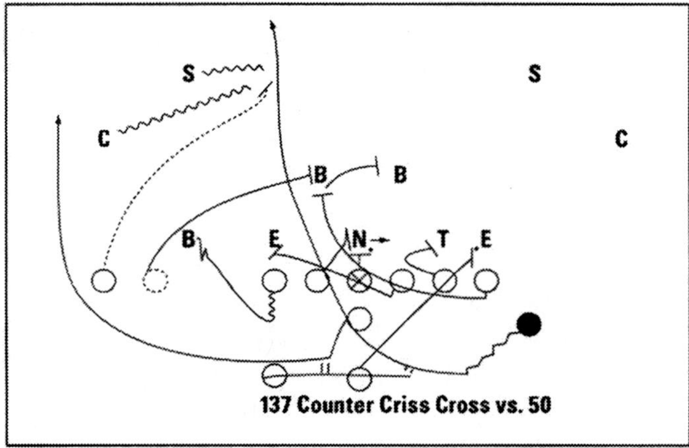

Diagram 4.16

crisscross-tag," and that suffix will pull the guard and tackle instead of the guard and tight end. Or, you can use whatever code words you choose and can pull any two out of three offensive linemen who are actually backside, since the 7-hole, or left tackle, is where the counter is going to attack.

The rules for the counter-crisscross begin by looking at the 7 man, or the left tackle. He is the point of attack. His rule is gap-lead-or influence and block out. In the 50 defense, no one is in his gap for him to block. No one is on the guard for him to double-team. Therefore, he will influence and block out. He can use two kinds of influences before he releases and blocks out. He can fake fire, where he takes a fire step to the outside of the defensive end and tries to widen him if the end is fighting the fire block. Or he can pass set, invite an upfield rush, and then kick out.

The left guard's rule is gap-post-lead. No defender is in his gap, and no one is on him for him to post. He is going to lead as the double-team blocker with the center. The center's rule is post-area-right. Against the nose in a 50 defense, he is going to post. The center and the left guard will be the post-lead block; they're the double-team block, and they want to take the noseguard parallel to the line of scrimmage.

The right guard is going to pull and trap the end. The right tackle is going to pull inside, check the backer, and then turn back on his defensive tackle, if no threat exists from the inside linebacker. The tight end will pull through the hole and wall off. This scheme is the exact same blocking as in 67 counter.

The wingback will be the ballcarrier. He does not go in three-step motion; he leaves on the snap. But, he will run a course similar to what he would run if he were in three-step motion. The fullback, unlike 67 counter, where he fakes the 20 series up the middle, now fakes the kick-out block in the 30 series – the power off-tackle play. This change gives you a blocker for the defensive end, and you don't have to worry about his chasing the play or penetrating the backfield and doing disruptive things. So the fullback will just cross over, run for the outside leg of the tackle, and block the first thing showing off the tight end's tail as he pulls. His head will be inside, so this block would be with a right shoulder, in this case. The spread end can block at the cutoff, or, again, you can put him down in what is called a split alignment. Then he will come across on the first inside backer, allowing the wall-off blocker to look for the other linebacker.

The quarterback executes a technique similar to 32, but the halfback is using his 31 footwork. The halfback is going to cross over and receive the handoff from the quarterback, and the quarterback will get the ball to him as quickly as possible. The defense will react to the sweep fake. You want the defense to react to the tight end wing side. As the left halfback comes across the backfield, he hands the wingback the ball. The quarterback will fake waggle and run down the sideline. He will be an option for the ballcarrier as he breaks through the hole. The running back receives the handoff from the left half. The left halfback has his inside hand down, inside thumb down, receives the handoff, and pushes the ball straight to the right halfback without having to turn it over. So, the right halfback gets the ball and runs tight through his double-team, and he's going to get north and south. As he gets down the field, the quarterback trails him in a pitch relationship. What you could do if you wanted to let your players do it, is, if all the defensive backs collapse on the ballcarrier, he could option pitch the ball to the quarterback. We let our guys do it in practice, so they can have a little fun and joke about it. We really won't let them do it in the game unless we're up by quite a bit. I have seen the back pitch the ball right to the defensive corner and watched the corner ramble 60 yards for a touchdown. I don't want that to happen to us. On one occasion, one of our backs at the University of South Dakota did pitch it, and he pitched it as he was getting tackled. He wound up pitching the ball to the dirt. We ended up recovering our own fumble, but it was scary enough that we don't want to be doing that very often. We just try to take the play as it exists. Hopefully, as the quarterback comes out on the waggle fake, he will draw some people with him, which will create some help for the wingback as he breaks through the hole on the counter-crisscross play.

137 Counter-Crisscross vs. 4-3 Defense

Against the 4-3 defense, 137 counter-crisscross will look a little different because of the spacing problems of this front, but the rules will stay the same (Diagram 4.17). The 7 man, the left tackle, has a defender covering the guard, so he will come down and lead. The left guard posts. You should get a good double-team between the left tackle and the left guard. The center will block to his right. The post blocker will take care of any linebacker run-throughs. If you get the middle backer running through, then the left guard needs to be able to come off and make that block. He is responsible for any linebacker run-throughs.

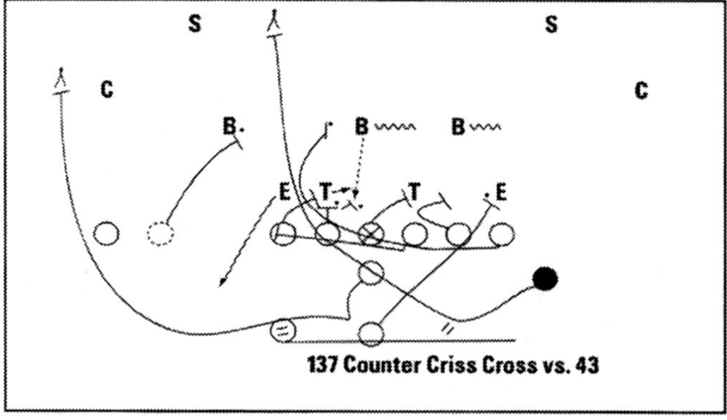

Diagram 4.17

The right guard pulls and traps the end. Remember that the quarterback is going to come on out and fake waggle in an effort to draw the defensive end with him. If that defensive end sees the near halfback go away and figures no run plays are coming back except waggle, then he starts running to the quarterback. This play can kick his tail. The right tackle is going to check the second man, turn back, and help backside. The fullback blocks the first thing showing off the pulling tight end's tail. The tight end is going to pull and wall off through the hole. As he walls off, he's looking for the linebacker, who should be flowing with the sweep fake.

Again, you can run this with the split end four to six yards from the tackle and bring him down on the linebacker. Then, you have an extra hat for the linebackers, since they're the toughest guys to get blocked. The backs' assignments are not changed versus the 4-3 defense.

Counter-Crisscross vs. 4-4 Defense

137 counter-crisscross against the 4-4 defense is illustrated in Diagram 4.18. The same rules as usual apply for the offensive linemen. The left tackle has a defender for him to lead on, so he will come down. The left guard will post and, again, is responsible for any linebacker run-throughs. The center is going to block to the right. He can use gap technique and put his head across the front or use down technique and put his head behind. It just depends on what kind of player he is blocking. The right guard pulls and traps the defensive end, who should be somewhat influenced by the quarterback's fake on the waggle. You have the right tackle blocking the second man. You have the tight end pulling through the hole and walling off.

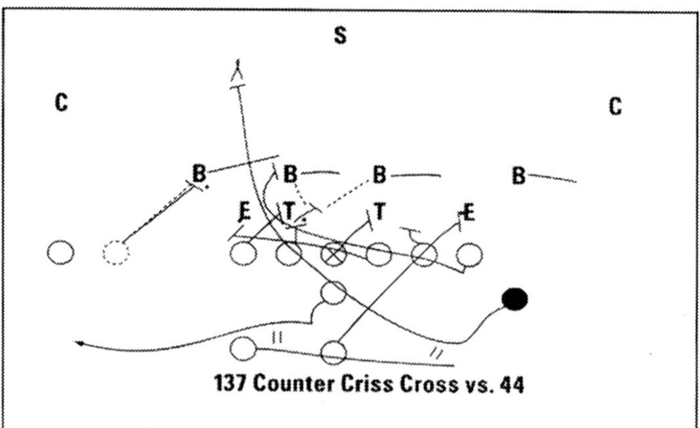

Diagram 4.18

You have the fullback going through the tight end's tail and blocking the first thing showing outside, with his right shoulder. The left half gets the handoff from the quarterback and hands the ball to the right halfback. If the linebackers are really fast and are really flowing hard, the outside backer might be the guy the tight end blocks. The inside linebacker might run himself right out of the play. If that instance does not happen and you're having problems, bring the split end down to a split position. Change the call to split 137 counter-crisscross and let that split end take care of one of those blocks on a linebacker. He can now come down and block the outside backer; the tight end, who is walling off through the hole, can wall off on the inside backer. You get hats for everybody and have a sound football play.

137 Counter-Crisscross Tat

This play is for the 4-3 defense, because many times you know that the defensive tackle is a 3 technique, and the center can't always get back to him. To counter the defense, you change who is pulling on the counter-crisscross. The linemen playside block the same, but the right guard will stay and block the defensive tackle. Now the tackle and the tight end are pulling (Diagram 4.19). You can call it tat, or give it any name you want. The center can now climb to the linebacker level. If the linebackers are influenced by the flow, which they should be, then the middle linebacker, as he starts back, should be the backer whom the center can block. The right tackle, meanwhile, pulls and traps the end, and the tight end pulls through the hole and walls off on the first backer who shows. Everything else remains the same. You simply change who pulls to get a better seal at the line of scrimmage on the 3 technique defensive tackle. This adjustment is good when you face 4-3 defenses.

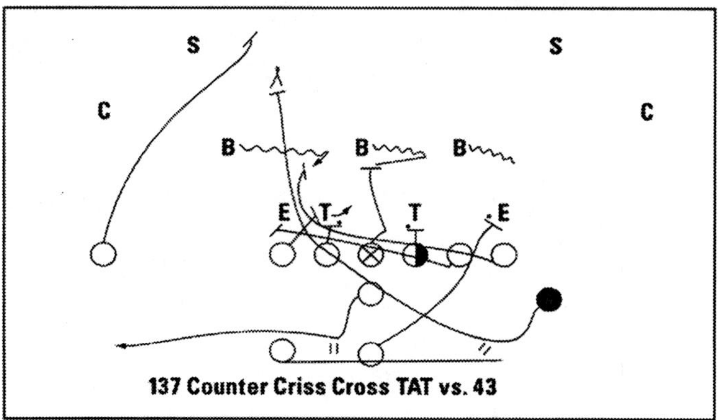

Diagram 4.19

137 Counter-Crisscross Tag

The other change-up you can make is to let the guard and tackle pull by adding the word tag (Diagram 4.20). Again, you use this against the 4-3 defenses you face. With this adjustment, you have the guard and tackle pulling and the tight end staying home. The tight end can block on, which helps when the fullback is mismatched against an aggressive, penetrating defensive end. The center blocks to his right for the pulling guard. The right guard pulls and traps. The right tackle pulls through the hole and walls off.

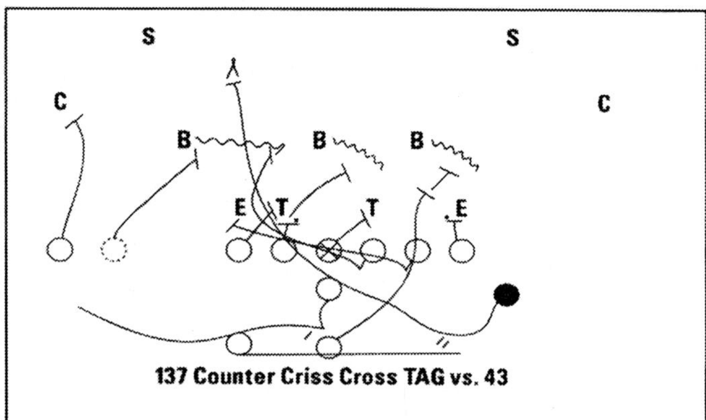

Diagram 4.20

The fullback can actually go through the hole and help with some of the linebackers. As the linebackers start to run and come back, the fullback can block one of them and the post blocker can come off on one. The wall-off blocker, as he comes through the hole, can get the other one. If you need the split end, in a split alignment, you can get one more hat for the linebackers. These variations give you a bunch of different ways to run counter-crisscross.

137 Counter

Sometimes a back handing off to another back is a little dangerous. Some coaches are uncomfortable with that. If you feel that way, you would just call 137 counter, with no crisscross action added to it. If you say, "137 counter," the counter blocking is still intact (Diagram 4.21). Counter blocking is good for a lot of these plays. Everybody does exactly the same thing, except the quarterback. The quarterback comes back two steps on the midline, as in the 30 series, except now, instead of handing the ball to the left halfback on sweep, the quarterback can come downhill like trap option, and the left halfback can continue across like trap option. The quarterback can hand the ball off using 67 counter, including the fullback. You must call this 37 counter, because you want your fullback to block as if it is the 30 series. That blocking is another way to run the same play, and, again, you can use tag blocking, use tat blocking, use whatever you need to get the front blocked. Do whatever you have to do in the backfield, and you're guaranteed, if you really get the defense running, these counters work and work well.

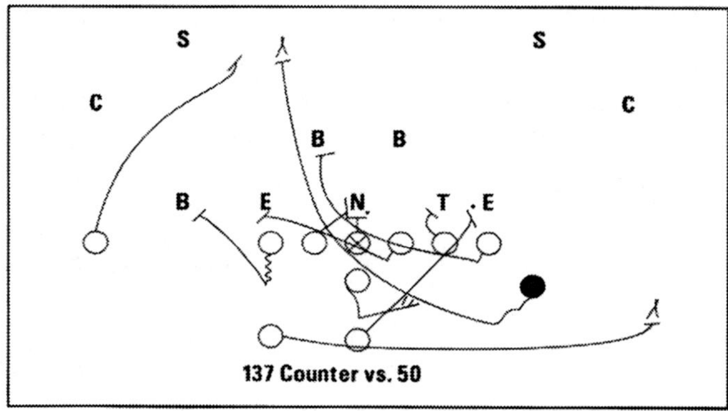

Diagram 4.21

138 Counter-Crisscross

Counter-crisscross can be run to the backside of a spread formation. Note that, earlier, it was mentioned this play could be used as part of the 60 trap-option series (Diagram 4.22). Using a spread 100 formation and a 50 defense, you can see what would be called spread 138 counter-crisscross, or counter, if the quarterback were to hand the ball off. This play is a good mix with the trap-option series. Since it's an 8-hole play, you just use the power off-tackle blocking rules. You will double-team outside with the tight end and tackle. You have the guard and center block on. The right tackle will pull check. The fullback blocks the first guy who shows outside the right tackle. The right guard will pull and trap the defensive end or will off, depending on what the defensive reaction is. The quarterback brings the ball back, hands it to the left half, and then fakes the waggle. You should get some kind of a pulling effect on the defensive end, who is checking for waggle. Now he gets trapped outside. The left half hands the ball to the right half, who bends it just a little bit wider and stays tight to his double-team. You send the spread end to the cutoff. Now, you have 38 counter-crisscross, with the right halfback carrying the football. It's just a little bit wider, but it's also a little bit of a

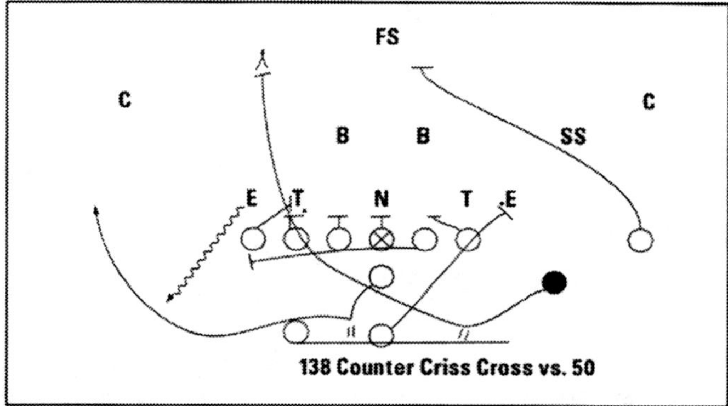

Diagram 4.22

different blocking scheme. This adjustment gives you a chance to run the play back to a tight end. You can run this play to the split end side or to the tight end side. If you look at the diagram again, for the first few steps, the defense could be thinking trap option. You can use this change-up as part of your trap-option package or as a conflict for any type of waggle back to the tight end side.

134 Counter vs. 50 Defense

Two plays are left in the 30 series package: the tackle trap counter and the tackle trap counter bootleg. Starting with 134 counter (Diagram 4.23), this play is a tackle trap counter. The word counter tells all of the backs, except the ballcarrier, to go away from the point of attack.

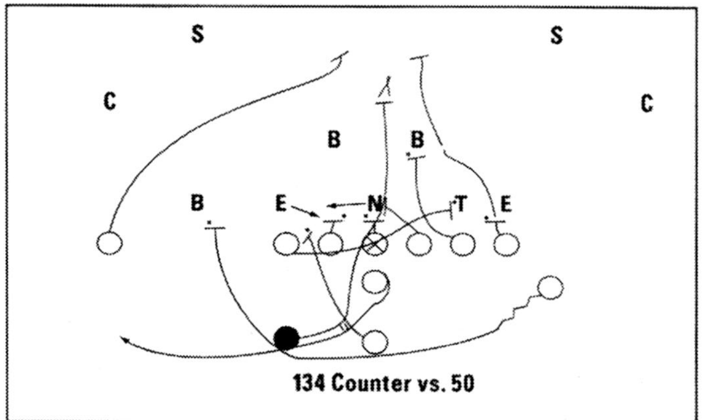

Diagram 4.23

You want to start out the play with three-step motion by the wing so you can start some kind of flowing action. Initially, you are going to make this play look a little bit like belly. The fullback is going to fake over an imaginary ball. The quarterback is going to reverse pivot, almost as he would on belly. The halfback is going to rock his weight to the outside to give the impression that he is taking the jab step on cross buck.

The right tackle is the playside tackle. He is going to use evasive technique and go block the first backer from five. He has the first linebacker on his side of the center. The tackle will post up down inside, dip his outside shoulder, and rip through with his outside arm. If he has to pull all the way to the center to get away from the defensive tackle, then he will pull to the center. He must not go straight up the field and let the defender jam him and close off the counter hole.

The right guard's rule is lead-backer. If he gets a man in his gap who prevents him from getting to the backer, then he will influence. In this defense, because the center is covered, the right guard leads. A double-team exists, too, and the center is post-lead-backer. So, if he has a nose on him, he's going to post him. You want the nose driven down the line of scrimmage to create the lateral opening.

The left guard's rule is area-post. If he has a man on him, he posts him. If he does not have a man on him, he blocks area. Against the 50 defense, he will just block his area. The reason is that, many times, the backside 5 technique defensive tackle will chase as the tackle pulls to execute his trap block. When he does, if the guard stays home and is blocking his area, he can help pick that up. If, on the other hand, you allow the guard to go straight out to the linebacker, the man chasing the tackle pulling is going to come right off his tail and stop the play.

The fullback is going to run right for the outside leg of the guard and block the first thing showing when the tackle pulls. He will come right off the tail of the tackle and block the first thing that he shows, head inside, with a left-shoulder block. As he goes through the hole, the fullback crosses over on his first step and fakes over an imaginary ball on his second step. The left halfback is the ballcarrier. You tell him to rock his weight so that he shows cross buck, simulating taking the short jab step out and up with his left foot. So, as he rocks that weight, his first step is actually with his inside foot. He leads, which means he is going to have his inside foot gain about six inches of ground, keeping his toes and shoulders pointing north and south. Next, he squares up as he receives the handoff. The quarterback is going to reverse pivot, bring the ball to him, and then fake counter bootleg.

If it's an odd defense, you want the halfback to bend his path for the near foot of the center. You're expecting the noseguard will be double-teamed by the center and right guard and will be moved down the line, which means the running back can stay tight to the lead-post block as he bursts up the middle. If it is an even defense, it's a shorter hole. The quarterback knows, if it is an odd defense, the halfback is going to bend his path for the near foot of the center. Therefore, the quarterback's first step can be right on the midline. His second step is going to wrap tight around the tail of the fullback. And on the third step, the exchange is made, and now he will fake counter bootleg at the flank.

The spread end will run to the cutoff. He'll set the counter bootleg play up by doing this. The right halfback is in three-step motion. He's going as fast as he can, and when he passes the quarterback-halfback mesh, he starts downhill and is going to block the first free man on the flank from outside in. He's going to set up counter bootleg. Now, the tight end can block backer-cutoff or can block on.

The left tackle is going to pull and trap. He's going to tackle trap that first guy past the center. If the defensive end is penetrating and coming down inside and disrupting the play – or if he's coming back over the top and disrupting the play – you will use the tight end to block him on assignment. You have to ask yourself what problems the defenses that you play present to you and then solve them whichever way you think is necessary. A lot of defensive ends can stop this football play, so you should not be hesitant to use the on assignment for the tight end.

134 Counter vs. 4-3 Defense

Diagram 4.24 shows 134 counter against the 4-3 defense. Counter tells you that you're going to tackle trap. If you want a different blocking scheme, you could just suffix the call. You could say, "Counter at 8," or, "Counter short." Again, the play goes to the left halfback at the 4 hole, so all other backfield people are going to run away from the play.

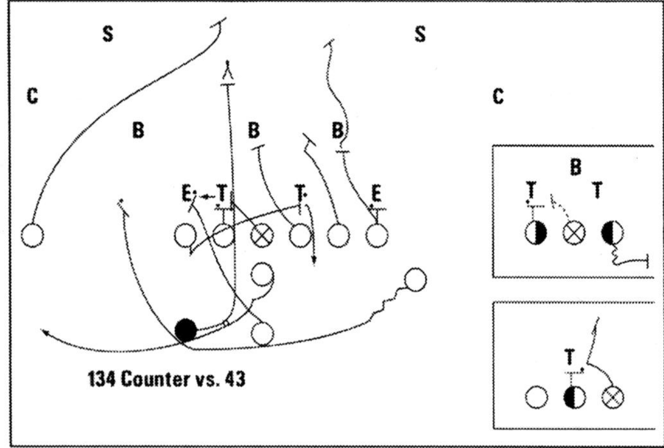

Diagram 4.24

The tight end will go backer to cutoff unless the defensive end is a real problem. The right tackle blocks the first backer from 5, who happens to be the middle backer. The right guard, as long as he can get inside the defensive tackle, leads inside and goes to the middle linebacker. The center will come backside and block the defensive tackle. The left guard will post with his right shoulder. The center blocks with his left shoulder, and the two of them work the defensive tackle down the line of scrimmage.

The fullback blocks the first thing showing off the tail of the tackle who pulls. He blocks with his head to the inside and with a left-shoulder block. The left tackle pulls and traps the defensive tackle. You can see you are set up for the linebackers. You have the tight end, the right tackle, and the center.

One more coaching point exists. If the defensive tackle you are going to double-team is all the way out on a 3 technique outside the left guard, the left guard will take him by himself and use on technique with his head inside. The center will then climb right upfield and block the linebacker (side diagram).

The spread end goes to cutoff. The left half is the ballcarrier. As he hits the hole, his aiming point is the inside foot of the nearest guard. Because the double-team has moved over a man, you use a shorter hole. At this point, the quarterback reverse pivots beyond the midline, because it's going to be a shorter hole. His second step again wraps tight around the fullback, and he hands the ball off on the third step. The right half should be out in front of the quarterback, because he's coming in three-step motion, and, as he passes the quarterback-halfback mesh, he'll attack downhill and set up the counter bootleg by blocking at the flank.

One other thing can happen (side diagram). If you have a 2 technique on the tight end side, or an inside shade over the guard so that he cannot get inside to block the backer, then he uses the influence part of his rule. He can pull to the right, as if on a sweep, or can pass set and influence his tackle and then turn out on somebody else. If the backside guard has a 3 technique he can handle by himself, then the center knows he must go right to the linebacker. You want to keep as many blockers available for the linebackers as you can. But you have little problems to worry about sometimes, so it depends on how you want to solve those problems.

134 Counter vs. 4-4 Defense

The next play is the counter versus the 4-4 defense (Diagram 4.25). This play is the tackle trap counter. The rules should hold up well for this defense. The guards and center have some interpreting to do, depending on the exact spacing of the two defensive tackles on the inside. If the defensive tackle away from the play is inside gap conscious, then you'll have to double-team him with the center and the guard. If the tackle is a 3 technique, the guard should handle him by himself and the center can go to the linebacker. The right guard knows if he can get inside to the linebacker, he's going to do that. If he can't get inside, then he's got to influence. And, you should have

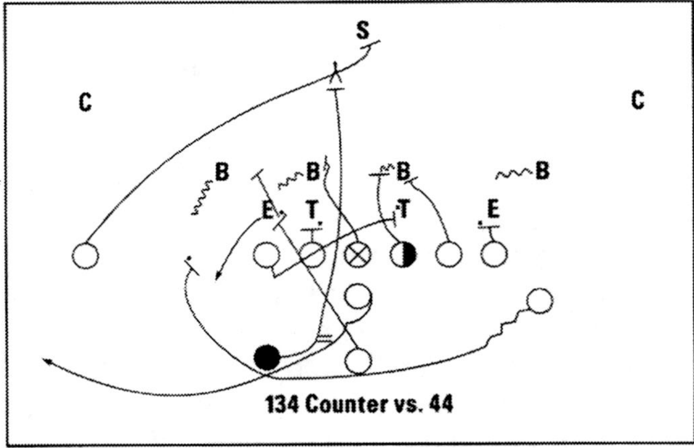

Diagram 4.25

a lot of blockers for those linebackers. The backfield action is the same. Nothing changes except possibly keeping the tight end to block on so you do not get penetration from the defensive end.

136 Counter vs. 50 Defense

The next play has been really successful – running the counter to the motion halfback, as opposed to running the counter to the stationary halfback. This change ends up being the opposite play. It would be 136 counter, but, at this point, instead of handing the ball to the left halfback on 34 counter from wing right formation, you are going to use wing right formation and hand the ball to the wingback going in motion (Diagram 4.26). You could tie this play into your trap option series because it looks very similar to others.

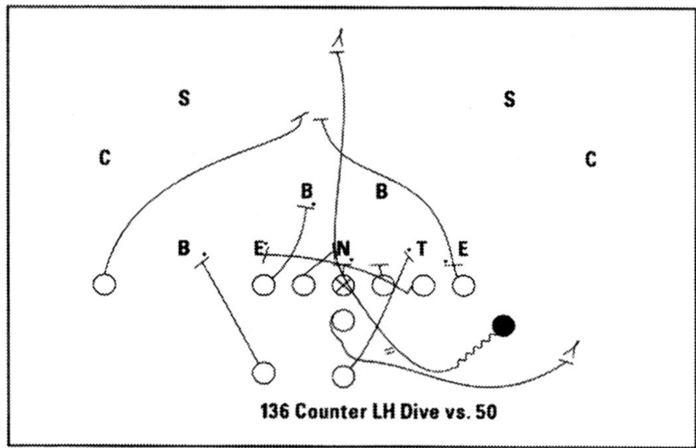

Diagram 4.26

What you will do when running this play is normally tell the left halfback to dive and block the outside linebacker to the call. If you didn't say left half dive, he would come across the backfield, be a log blocker, and set up counter bootleg with the quarterback. You call, "Counter left half dive," most of the time when running this.

The playside tackle blocks the first backer from the center. The playside guard has lead-backer-or influence. In this case, he's going to lead. The center has post-lead-backer. He will post and, thus, help the double-team create movement. The right guard, or backside guard in this case, would be area. The right tackle is going to pull and trap.

The fullback is going to dive for the outside leg of the guard and block the first free man who shows inside. The rule for the tight end when he is on the backside is to go to cutoff. But again, don't hesitate to use on technique if you feel that the defensive end is going to be a really disruptive force.

The quarterback's footwork is exactly the same. He'll reverse pivot and wrap his second step tight around the tail of the fullback. As the halfback goes in three-step motion, he'll turn and come underneath the quarterback. The wing is the ballcarrier. The quarterback will come on out and fake counter bootleg after the handoff. The wing uses the near foot of the center for his aiming point and breaks vertically up the field.

It's the same blocking as before for all the linemen, except, at this point, you're going to give the ball to the right halfback going in three-step motion. You coach the halfback to go in three-step motion and simply work out the details of the mesh with the quarterback. You tell him to use the same motion technique he always does. The only little addendum you give the halfback is to aim for a spot a little deeper than his diveback spot. He should go in three-step motion, go a little deeper, square his shoulders to the hole, adjust to the quarterback, and find the play. You don't want to be telling him, "Left foot, right foot," all that kind of stuff. Basically, you let him and the quarterback adjust it and work it out, and you won't have too many problems with it.

One thing you have to guard against is the halfback coming back too slowly when he comes in motion. As he comes in motion, he still needs to come fast, just as he does on all the other three-step motion plays, so he does not rip this play off to the defense. Those guys come fast. They're cooking as they come up through there.

136 Counter Short

These schemes are a couple of blocking variations. Counter short is a fine variation. When you run 136 counter short against the 50 defense, you are actually going to trap the noseguard (Diagram 4.27). As the tackle pulls, he's going to trap the noseguard, as opposed to coming all the way across and trapping the backside tackle. When you trap the noseguard, the tight end is going to go to cutoff. You can go to cutoff with him, or else you can block on with him. It just depends on what you need. The right tackle

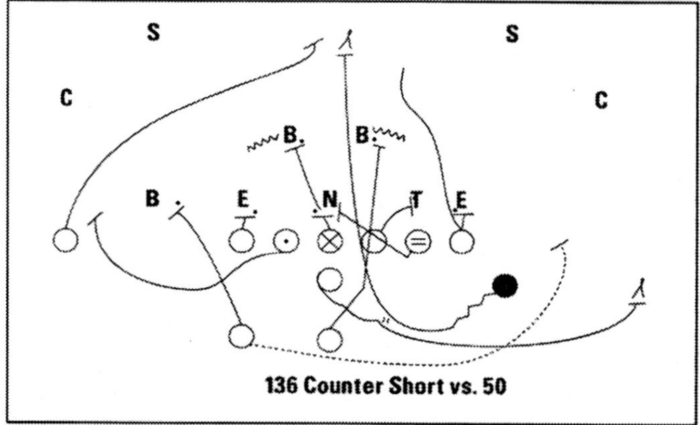

Diagram 4.27

is the trapper, because it's a 36 counter. The right guard is going to block outside. If he has a man on him, he'll post and not block outside. Against the 50 defense, the guard is going to come out on the tackle. That change, in itself, gives you a little misdirection. The center's rule is fire-release to backer-or lead. Lead is for the even defenses, so he is going to fire block that nose as if the play were going to the left and then go to the linebacker. The left guard pulls away just as he does on 29 sweep. So, at this point, you have both guards moving in opposite directions. If any chance the backers are keying guards, they're going to get pulled in opposite directions, and the middle should get split. You should get a kind of split-flow reaction in the middle.

The left tackle's rule is on-backer. He is going to come off and block the man on him, head to the inside. The 6 hole is normally over the left guard, but the counter short tells the ballcarrier – who is the right halfback – that he's going to get the ball and use his short-hole technique, even though against an odd defense. The word short tells him that, plus it also tells him you are trapping the nose. The fullback's normal assignment is to dive for the outside foot of the guard, which he begins to do initially. He fakes over the imaginary ball, but, as the tackle pulls to trap the nose, the fullback fills right off his tail and will, at this point, be the blocker for the linebacker.

The quarterback steps across the midline, because you say short-hole footwork. The halfback and quarterback are going to adjust their footwork to a shorter hole. The second step for the quarterback wraps tight around the fullback's tail. He hands the ball off on the third step, then comes on out, and fakes the counter bootleg. The ballcarrier runs right up over the inside leg of the guard and busts right up through the middle. The spread end is going to cutoff. The left halfback can do anything you want him to do. You like to dive for the outside backer when you run the counter to the motion halfback. He doesn't have to do that. He can be in his diveback position and can come across to set up counter bootleg. He can be a log blocker and block the first free man at the backside flank. It's up to you as a coach to give your play a better chance to work. If you're trying to set things up, you probably want to set the counter bootleg up and then bring him across.

134 Counter Short

You can also run 134 counter short and hand the ball to the left halfback. On this play, you trap in the other direction and the left tackle traps the nose. The rules remain the same, as you use short-hole techniques.

Oftentimes, you anticipate seeing a 50 defense, but all of a sudden, the defense jumps into a 4-3 look (Diagram 4.28). You build in answers to that problem on this play. Remember that 34 counter is handed off to the left halfback. The right half is coming in three-step motion. The fullback is crossing over and running through, as if it is belly. He fakes over an imaginary ball. All is still the same. The rules you build into

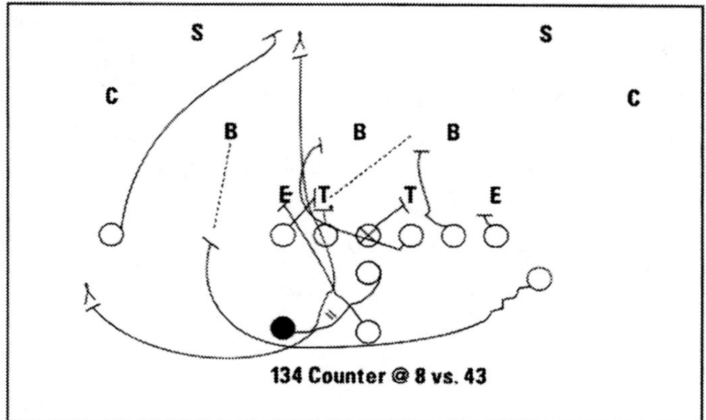

Diagram 4.28

this are meant to account for the even defense. The playside guard's rule is going to be block outside on the counter short-or post with his head inside, if he's covered. If the tackle is covered, his rule is on or backer. But, at this point, because of the even defense, you're going to have this play changed to counter at 8. What happens is you now get the post and the lead from the left guard and the left tackle. The fullback now comes right off the guard's tail and kicks the defender over the tackle out. What you're going to see is the play reverts to power blocking. When the ballcarrier, the left halfback, takes his footwork, he's aiming for that short hole, but he's going to bend it off-tackle. The play, 34 counter short, is changed to 34 counter at 8 versus an even defense. Really, it's nothing more than 38 power blocking.

The spread end is at the cutoff. The center can block to the right. The right guard pulls through the hole and walls off. The right tackle blocks the second man. The tight end can block on. If the right tackle has no problems, he can go to backer.

The quarterback reverse pivots to his short-hole footwork beyond the midline, gives the ball, and then fakes counter bootleg with the wing in motion. The post blocker has responsibility for the backside backer, so you have at least three hats for the backers. The right halfback, coming around in motion, has the responsibility for his linebacker.

134 Counter at 8

Counter at 8 does not have to be an adjustment to counter short. You can call this play anytime you want. You will call this play and not hesitate if you're going to run counter at 8 to the split end side. You can call it to the split end side as long as the defense is even. You can run the play to the tight end side against any defense you want.

Diagram 4.29 shows 134 counter at 8 versus the 4-4 defense. You can see in the diagram that you have a post-lead, a double-team, which is 38 power blocking, by the left tackle and the left guard. The backs are running 34 counter action into this 38 power blocking scheme by the line at the 8 hole. The backfield technique is 34 counter. The line technique is 38 power blocking. The left guard will come off and block any run-throughs from the backers. The center blocks back to the right. The right guard pulls and walls off through the hole. At this point, the fullback is going to dive for the outside leg of the guard and be the kick-out blocker. The right tackle pulls and checks, and the tight end can either block on or go to cutoff. This scheme is simply power blocking.

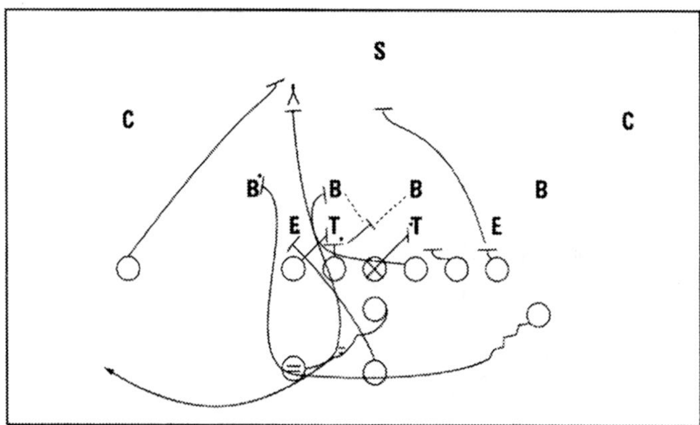

Diagram 4.29

The right halfback and the fullback are showing the picture of belly. The fullback is faking over an imaginary ball as he makes his kick-out block. The quarterback is going to use the short-hole technique and reverse pivot beyond the midline. The left halfback is going to rock his weight, lead, cross over, square up, and run short-hole footwork. He is the ballcarrier. As he receives the handoff, he just bends his path outside for the off-tackle play. So, at this time, you're running an off-tackle power play, but with misdirection. It is important for the wing to know this. Normally, on counter plays, he just log blocks at the flank and sets up counter bootleg. But, on the counter at 8, he has to really take off, really get going in motion, get upfield, and block the #4 defender inside out. He cannot let #4 fall in and make the play. His is a key block. The spread end goes to the cutoff. The quarterback will go ahead and fake counter bootleg by himself.

136 Counter at 2 vs. 50 Defense

The next play is used against a 50 defense, which is an odd defense. You can run this play right back to the tight end side. What you do is try to run this to a diveback. It's a better play if the ballcarrier is in a diveback position than if he's in a wingback position. You simply have to run it from a different formation. But, nothing says you cannot do both. First, look at this play using the wingback as the ballcarrier, which would be 136 counter at 2 (Diagram 4.30).

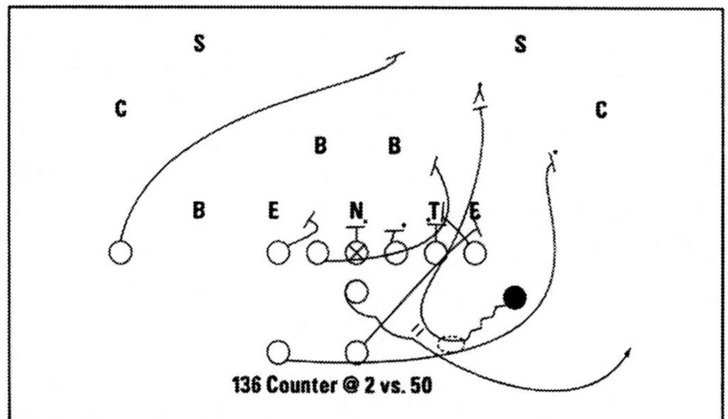

Diagram 4.30

Remember, it is really easy for the line, because they're running 32 power off-tackle blocking. They are simply creating a double-team at the point of attack, which is the 2 hole. The blocking rules for the line are all the 32 rules. You have a post-lead at the 2 hole with the tight end and right tackle. You have an area assignment by the right guard. The center has an on assignment. The left guard pulling is through the hole to wall off, and the left tackle is going to pull-check 2.

The fullback is going to cross over for the outside foot of the tackle. He's going to be the kick-out blocker on the end. If the left halfback is in a wingback position, he should be coming in three-step motion, coming around, and blocking the #4 defender. If he's in a diveback motion, he does the same thing. He can cheat his alignment a little bit inside and come around on the snap block inside out on the #4 defender, who is the corner. The spread end is at the cutoff. The quarterback is using short-hole technique, because you're going to bend this play off-tackle to the 2 hole. He reverse pivots beyond the midline. If the ballcarrier is in a diveback position, he rocks his weight, leads, crosses over, and squares up for the inside foot of the guard, a maneuver using short-hole footwork. As he takes the football, he bends it right off-tackle. The diagram illustrates how you can run this to the wingback coming in three-step motion and hand the ball off back underneath. The wingback just bends his path back for the off-tackle hole. The quarterback continues on out and fakes counter bootleg. The right halfback is the ballcarrier, regardless of whether he is in a diveback position or a wingback position. You can run counter at 8 to the tight end side, against the even front, and use the same power rules.

136 Counter at 2 vs. 4-4 Defense

Play 136 counter at 2 versus the 4-4 defense or eight-man is shown in Diagram 4.31. Again, it is just power off-tackle blocking in which the tight end influences whenever he gets a 7 technique. You have the post and lead, with the right tackle and guard creating the double-team. The center blocks left, and the left guard pulls and walls off. The fullback is the kick-out blocker. The left tackle can block on because the center blocked #2. The wingback is the ballcarrier. He can be aligned as either a diveback or a wingback. The quarterback will reverse pivot beyond the midline and use short-hole technique, as will the ballcarrier. Upon receiving the handoff, the wing breaks outside the double-team and stays tight to the double-team. The spread end works to the cutoff. The left half can dive or come across the backfield and block the #4 defender. Whether it is the outside backer or the corner, you need that extra blocker at the flank. The quarterback fakes the counter bootleg.

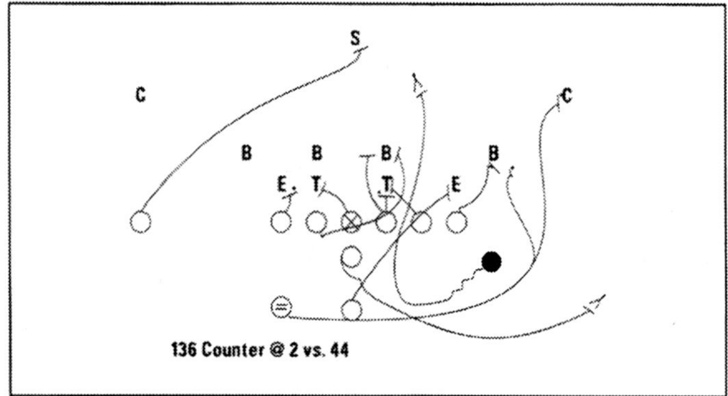

Diagram 4.31

134 Counter Special vs. 50 Defense

Several blocking adjustments can be made with the counter play. One change is called counter special, which is used against 50 defenses. The play call is, "134 counter special" (Diagram 4.32). The blocking on this play is the same for everyone, except you are going to kick out with the pulling tackle rather than wall off. You still have the post-lead on the nose by the right guard and center. You still have the area assignment by the offensive guard. The tackle will still pull, but he traps the defensive tackle. The only other difference is the right tackle and the tight end are going to basically switch assignments. The right tackle is going to cup back and show pass, and the tight end is going inside to the linebacker. Next, the right tackle will kick out the defensive end as he comes upfield. You have the pass set influence on the defensive tackle to trap him. You must be able to get the tight end to the linebacker, and he must be able to block the linebacker with his head across the front in order to really make this play go.

Again, you're going to come in three-step motion. The fullback is going to dive for the outside leg of the guard, taking over an imaginary ball. The fullback blocks the first thing showing, and the right halfback log blocks the first free man at the flank to set up counter bootleg. The spread end goes to cutoff. The halfback on the left is the ballcarrier. He does the same thing he does on all counters — rocks his weight, leads, crosses over, squares up, and, in an odd defense, uses the near foot of the center as an aiming point. Then, he has to make a nice cut tight to the double-team. The quarterback reverse pivots to the midline, hands the ball off, and fakes counter bootleg. This counter special uses a pass-set influence and is an especially effective play against the 50 defense.

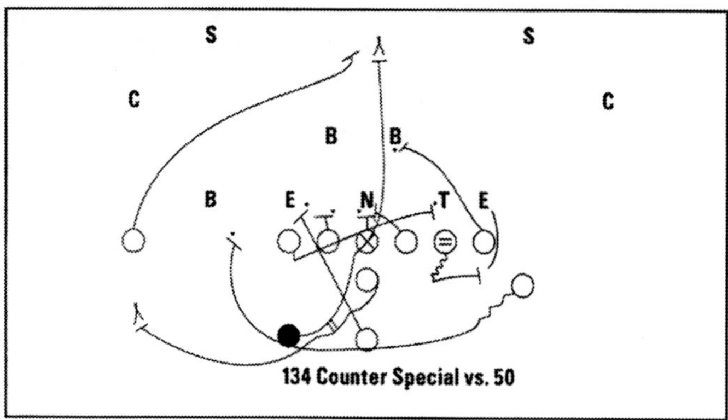

Diagram 4.32

134 Counter Gut

Another blocking adjustment you can make to counter plays is counter gut. As explained in other sections, the word gut tells the trapper to pull through the hole. This play is called 134 counter gut, with the trapping tackle pulling up through the 4 hole (Diagram 4.33). This whole play is exactly the same as 34 counter, with the exception of the two tackles, who are going to switch assignments. You still have the post-lead double-team with the guard and center. The left guard still blocks the area assignment. The left tackle pulls to trap and blocks through the hole on the linebacker. The right tackle normally goes for first backer from 5, but, at this point, blocks on. He blocks the man you would normally trap in 34 counter. The tight end also blocks on. The fullback runs for the outside leg of the backside guard, blocking the first thing showing. You

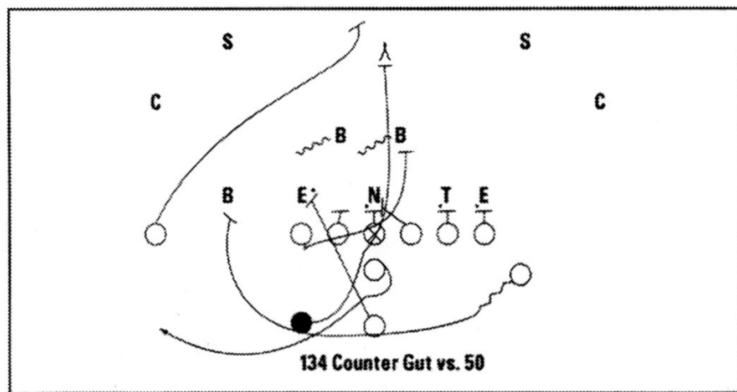

Diagram 4.33

have the motion, and the action of the play encourages the linebackers to flow. The left half is the ballcarrier. He rocks his weight, takes his footwork, and uses the near foot of the center as his aiming point. The spread end is going to go to the cutoff.

134 counter gut simply entails a small blocking adjustment to 134 counter by just exchanging assignments between the left tackle and the right tackle. If the defensive tackle is squeezing the heck out of the offensive tackle when he tries to go inside to block the linebacker, counter gut is a great little adjustment that you can use to still make yards. You should get some good flow by the linebackers. If you're doing a good job running the belly play, then this play looks like the belly. It starts like the belly play. The footwork starts like the belly play, and the backers should be really flowing. If they're not, you run the belly play forever.

Counter Draw

The last blocking adjustment to counter is considered one of the best. It is 34 counter draw (Diagram 4.34). If you are playing against great pass rushers and can't get a pass off because they are coming up the field so hard on you, counter draw might help you. It is just like all the other counters.

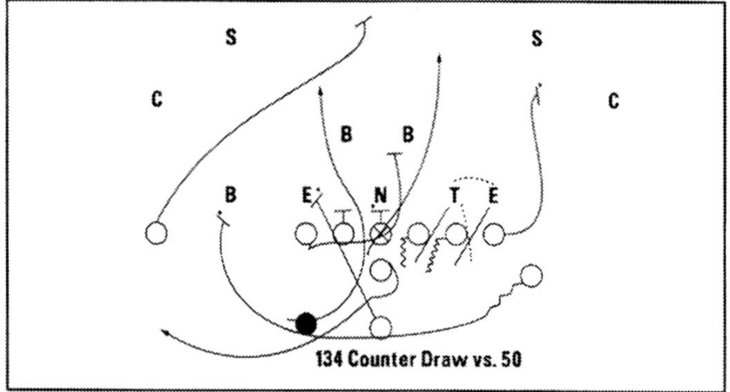

Diagram 4.34

The backfield technique is 34 counter. The fullback again dives for the outside leg of the guard, faking over the imaginary ball. The ballcarrier rocks his weight, takes his lead step-crossover-square-up footwork, and then bends his path for his aiming point. The right halfback is in three-step motion and is still logging the first free man at the flank. The quarterback reverse pivots to the midline on an odd defense, makes the handoff, and fakes counter bootleg.

In the 80 series chapter, you will see the scissors blocking. It is similar to Sally blocking, for those who run Sally. What you're going to do is show pass on the frontside of the play, so the right guard and the right tackle will cup back and show pass. The tight end is going to outside release and cut off the corner, which helps the pass illusion. The left tackle is going to pull and gut, just as he did on 34 counter gut. But, at this time, what is different is the left guard is on-area-or delay to the backer. The center is left-gap-on-right, so he has an on assignment on the nose. This block is one of the few times in the offense where you put the head of the center away from the point of attack. You do that in this case and block the nose with the right shoulder, only to protect the mesh of the quarterback and halfback.

The fullback blocks the first thing showing behind the pulling tackle. The left tackle pulls up over the tail of the center. The tackle and the ballcarrier will option run the center's block on this play. If the center takes the nose to the left, the tackle comes behind the block. If he takes the nose to the right, the tackle pulls up through the inside of the block. You just tell the tackle and the ballcarrier to run right up over the tail of the center, and the hole will show itself to them. As the tackle pulls through the hole, he has the first backer who shows in the hole. The ballcarrier uses the near foot of the center as his aiming point and breaks wherever he can find the opening. He's basically option running the noseguard.

On the frontside, when you show pass, what happens is the right guard is going to block the B gap rusher, and the right tackle is going to block the C gap rusher. So, if both defenders pinch, they will come right to them. If, for some reason, the tackle comes flying upfield and the end goes to cutback, again, they sort it out as the rush comes to them. The spread end goes to cutoff.

The counter series is a basic staple of the offense. You're going to have it in every game plan. You simply find the blocking scheme to use against that particular defense and then run it. These things go in cycles. Your power draw may be good one year; your tackle trap counter may be better the next. You may prefer counter gut at the beginning of one year and counter short as the season draws to a close. It's just that whatever the problems you're seeing are based on the defenses you're seeing. You should look at the play, but not eliminate the play if your tackle trap is not working. Just find a way to adjust blocking to handle the problems you are seeing. One other thing you can do is run 34 counter and just use guard trap blocking. All kinds of ways exist to make a play work. You're going to try to find a blocking scheme to use for that particular defense in order to run that counter play, because it is really a great complement to the belly series.

134 Counter Bootleg vs. 50 Defense

The last thing to discuss in the 30 series is 134 counter bootleg (Diagram 4.35). You abbreviate counter bootleg with "CT" for counter and "B/L" for bootleg. This play is where you fake the tackle trap to the right and run the bootleg back to the left.

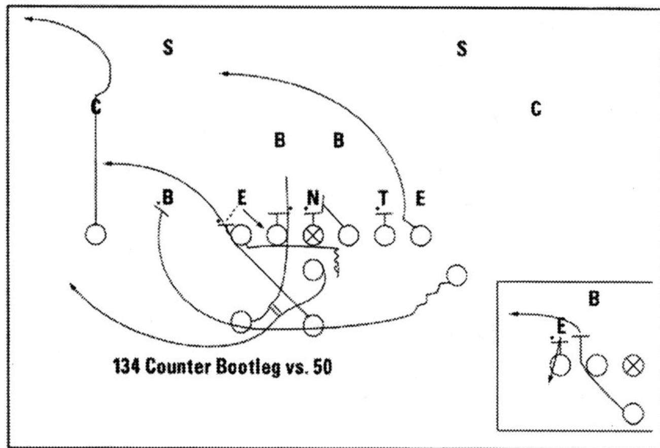

Diagram 4.35

A couple of different things need to be considered when you decide how you're going to block this play. First of all, the rules are pretty simple. You're not going to change the rules for the linemen at all. The only lineman who might change is the left tackle. Since you are going to fake 34 counter, you are faking a tackle trap to the right. The left tackle is going to pull and block chase. He pulls exactly the way he does on the tackle trap. He's going to fly down the line full speed. When he gets to the far offensive guard, he can break down and block any chase showing off the backside of the quarterback. It is very important that he does not break down until he passes the center. The reason is that, if he starts gearing down, the halfback faking the counter is going to run right into him, and you don't want that to happen.

The left guard is blocking area-post, so he's going to do just as he did on the counter play. Against the odd defense, he'll just be area blocking. The center has post-lead, so he's going to post on the noseguard. The guard on the side you're faking the play to – the right guard for 34 – has gap-on-lead. Against a 50 defense, he will lead. The quarterback is going to keep the ball to the left flank, so you don't want to be too strong on the double-team and kick the defender way down, where he can make the play on the quarterback. Actually, in fact, all you want to do is give him the feeling of post lead and control him right at the line of scrimmage. The right tackle's rule is gap-on-area-outside, since he can't go to backers because it's a pass play. In this 50 defense, he is blocking on.

The tight end is going to inside release and run the crossing route. He is the crossing receiver. The split end is going to run some kind of flag or corner route. We have been through this a number of different ways. When we initially coached the angle flag, we used to coach the split end to come down on an angle and then break deep on the numbers to the flag. We teach a different route lately, where our split end will bust upfield, then, at about 14 yards, give a little inside head fake and a little inside stick step, and then try to bend himself out to a 22-yard area. We call that a Q route, and it has been a pretty good route for us.

The fullback has a slightly different technique when it's counter bootleg than when it's counter. If you say, "Counter bootleg," he's going to cross over and run for the outside leg of the tackle. If any 5 technique penetration exists whatsoever, he must block it. You are running this play because the defensive end is running way down inside hard, trying to stop the 34 counter play. If he's going to chase down inside like that, when the tackle pulls on counter, then you want to be able to just pull the tackle, let him chase, and then have the quarterback keep the ball to the outside.

The wing is in three-step motion. When he passes the quarterback-halfback mesh, he's going to start downhill and block the first free man from outside in. He uses a right-shoulder block, head outside, and tries to turn and take the defender inside. Remember, you're running this play because the defensive end is chasing inside on tackle trap. So, as the fullback comes to the 5 technique area, he should be free from having to block anyone, can slip out into the flat, and become the second receiver to the flat. If, for some reason, the defensive end did not chase and, instead, went upfield, the fullback should recognize it and pick it up. He should block with his right shoulder and his head outside. The left halfback is going to fake being the ballcarrier. He will take his footwork and run for a short hole. He must always run for a short hole on counter bootleg for two reasons: one, you don't want him running into the pulling tackle, and, two, you want the quarterback to use short-hole footwork, where he reverse pivots beyond the midline, which gets him to the flank faster. As the quarterback makes the fake, he attacks the flank with the ball, and you have the deep-short-run the ball progression for the quarterback.

If you're playing a team that you know will not chase the pulling tackle because the defensive end is going to work hard up the field, then what you call is counter bootleg solid. You add the word solid to let the players know that this play can also be blocked with a solid call. This call simply allows the left tackle to block on with his head to the outside. The fullback now knows that he can go back to his original aiming point, which is the outside leg of the guard. He's responsible for the inside backer if he comes, just as in waggle. If he doesn't come, the fullback will then be out in the flat and running his pass route (side diagram).

One other thing to do is run the counter bootleg and fake the counter to the wingback coming in motion, as opposed to the diveback. This play really has the defense sitting there. The other thing this play will do is give you basically the same kind of play that you have on waggle, but without the guard keys. If a defense is trying to key guards on you and they are stopping your waggle because the linebackers are flowing with your guards, then you should run the counter bootleg. No guard keys exist. Especially if you go counter bootleg, no keys of any sort exist. At that point, the backfield becomes the only real key, and you know how tough it is as a linebacker to try to key the ball in a wing-T backfield.

134 Counter Bootleg vs. 4-3

Look at 134 counter bootleg versus the 4-3 (Diagram 4.36). You are going to show the picture of 87 cross block, so you're going to have the wing coming in three-step motion. The quarterback is going to reverse pivot across the midline because it's an even offense. On this counter bootleg play, the left tackle pulls to the right guard. The left guard is area-post, so he's going to post with his head to the outside, using his right shoulder. The center is going to lead. Those two blockers will just control the defensive tackle and not drive him. The right guard has gap-on-lead and will block on. The right tackle blocks an area assignment. The tight end is in the pattern. So, at this point, it looks like the backside defensive end is free, but you have the tackle pulling to block chase to take care of him. If you have to interpret the right tackle's rule as outside to get the end blocked, you can do that, too.

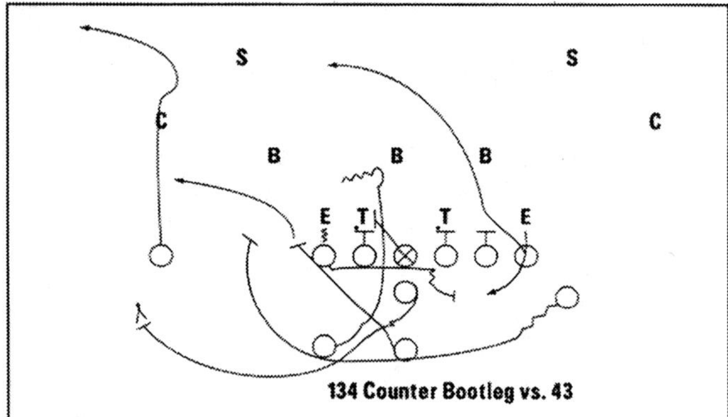

Diagram 4.36

The fullback is diving for the outside leg of the tackle. He will take care of any 5 technique penetration or be out in the flat. If you have to, you call, "Solid," and the left tackle stays in. The fullback then has linebacker responsibility, and you just go with everyone else doing the same thing. You want the left halfback to get tackled. If he does not get tackled, he will hook up over the middle. The spread end will run the Q route. The tight end has the crossing route. The right half is going to log the first free man at the flank. And the quarterback's coming out on the bootleg play.

136 Counter Bootleg vs. 4-4 Defense

Against the 4-4, the assignments are the same. The counter bootleg play is where you fake the counter to the motion halfback. That way you will get to see both variations. The call here is, "136 counter bootleg," with the bootleg coming to the tight end side (Diagram 4.37).

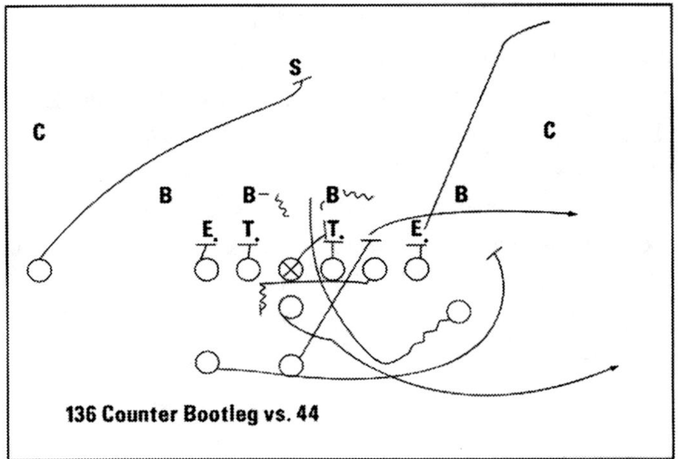

Diagram 4.37

The tight end now runs essentially the same route as the waggle route. He's going to block release, go deep to the numbers, and then can bend, depending on what the reaction of the corner is, to stay away from the safety. You tell him, "Don't run to get covered." The same holds true if the corner overlaps in the deep third. He can bend it a little bit, as opposed to running right into the corner, where he would run to get covered.

The right tackle will still pull and block the chase. The right guard will post, head to the outside, and the center will lead. When the center leads, those two blockers are going to control the defender, but not drive him back into the quarterback's bootleg course. The left guard and tackle block on.

The right halfback is going to come in three-step motion and is going to fake 36 counter. You want the linebackers to hold on him. The fullback will dive for the outside leg of the guard and block any linebacker who comes. If not, he is in the flat. The spread end runs the crossing route. The diveback needs to get around in front of the quarterback and be able to block any penetration coming off the edge. If he has to cheat his alignment over a little bit, then he cheats his assignment, but he still is responsible for being the log blocker at the flank. The quarterback's technique is the same, and, as you can see, this play gives you basically the same thing that waggle gives you. The key difference is no guard keys exist. No one is there for the linebackers to key. If they are looking in the backfield, they will not be able to read the play. They can run to the pass, and the counter will kill them. They can step up on the counter, and counter bootleg will kill them. Whatever those inside backers react to, simply run the other play. Our guys are told to do it that way, and it has worked quite well for us.

Summary

As you have seen, the 30 series offers the offense multiple adjustments to the counter game with power off-tackle blocking. You can attack with power or deception. The package has an answer for each of the problems you encounter. Defenders are put into assignment conflicts, which is the heart and soul of wing-T philosophy. Finally, this series offers you the ability to pick up stunts with zone blocking concepts and run several types of plays with a backfield action appearing the same for the first two steps. Each of these advantages helps to strengthen the idea that the wing-T is one of the most difficult defenses to defend. You will enjoy running it a great deal.

5

80 Series

The next package of plays is the 80 series, which basically centers on the fullback belly game. Most wing-T teams use at least two different types of belly actions. Throughout the history with the wing-T, a third one has even been used.

The first play in this package is the fullback belly play, which is possibly the best play in the series. If not the best, the fullback belly is certainly one of the top three plays in this offense. Year in and year out, you should find a way to make this fullback belly play work. Your fullback is going to be near or over 1,000 yards every single season, and, of course, this play is one of the big reasons why.

187 Cross-Block vs. 50 Defense

Looking at the fullback belly play, you have many of ways to block. A favorite way is called cross-block. When you run this play to the weakside, or the split end side, this play is called 187 cross-block (Diagram 5.1). You can abbreviate cross-block by just saying, "XB." The playside tackle's assignment is gap-down-on. If he has a man in his gap or a man on the guard, he blocks him. Since neither of those exists against the 50, he blocks on. The left tackle is the 7 man, and the play is 87, so he is the point of attack. As he blocks on, his head goes to the inside. The left guard's rule is to pull and trap, which creates the cross-block. He will pull and kick from the inside out and block the next man outside the left tackle's block. The only time he will not do that block is if he has a guy in his gap. You really could say his rule is gap-or pull and kick out, but you don't do that. Your rule on cross block is to pull and kick out. If a defender is in the gap, you will know that by the line calls, and then you change the play to 87 on and just block with on blocking.

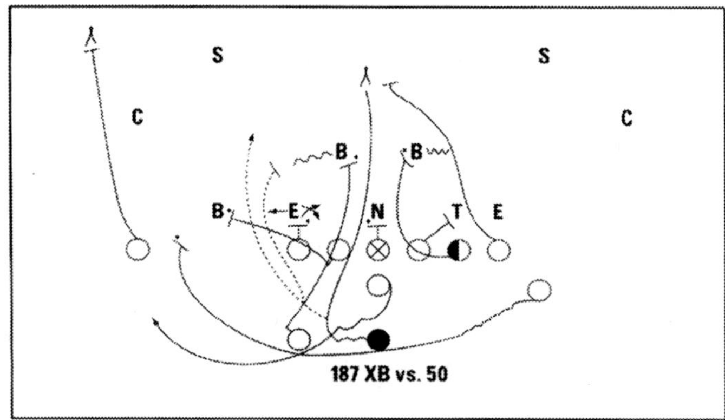

Diagram 5.1

The offensive center's rule is to block on-or right. Against the 50 defense, he has the noseguard on him, so he must block on. He puts his head to the side of the hole, so he will put his head to the left and block with the right shoulder. You give the rest of the linemen the blocking rule fire on backer, which is a form of zone blocking. The linemen have calls that they use to gain leverage for blocks and fold around for linebackers, but they make those at the line of scrimmage according to their needs. The backside guard can pull and wall off or fire on backer. It depends on how you're blocking the frontside and how the center is going to block. If the center blocks using his on rule, then the guard is going to block fire on backer. If the center is going to use his right rule, then the guard will pull and gut. His rule in the playbook is fire on backer, but he has a parenthesis saying he can also pull and gut. He can also odd block. What happens on an odd block is, if the defensive tackle on the backside tackle (right tackle) is an inside shade player, then you can block back to the inside shade technique with the guard. The tackle will pull, gut through the hole, and take care of the backside backer. One way or the other, between the backside tackle and guard, somebody's going to be responsible for the linebacker and somebody will be responsible for the defensive tackle. If it's fire on backer by the guard and block on with the tackle, those rules are fine, too.

You can do many things with the tight end. You can show step and cup, which is the same look as the keep pass, and make the defensive end rush, running up the field. You can block the tight end on or send the tight end to the cutoff. For this illustration, he is being sent to the cutoff.

A couple things can be done with the split end. He can go block at the cutoff or can fake keep pass. The routes on keep pass are either out or fly, so you can take the corner and try to run him to the goal line to eliminate a defender.

It's important that the backfield executes this play with correct technique. As long as the front is executing cross-block, the left halfback needs to allow for the lineman to execute the cross-block. Therefore, they need just a little bit more time than if they were all firing straight ahead. In this case, the left halfback will take a short jab-step up and out with his left foot. From there, he's going to run right for the outside leg of the guard as his initial takeoff point. He reads the first man from head up on the guard out, the first defensive lineman from on the guard to the outside. The fullback does the same thing. He is the ballcarrier. He's going to take his footwork and also going to make the read on that first down lineman from the guard out. In this case, in the 50 defense, it's the defensive end coming over the playside tackle. If the tackle gets his head inside and uses his on technique to turn the end to the outside, then both backs are going to pull up inside of that block. If the defensive end lines up in a wide 5 technique, you can go ahead and count on the tackle turning him out so the backs can actually read the noseguard. That reason is why you odd block the backside with an inside shade, because you might wind up all the way back behind the center's block. Basically, this play is your pro I formation sprint draw in the wing-T. This play is going to be given to your best back, deep in the backfield, to allow him to find the hole, wherever it might be. If the defensive end pinches and runs inside, the playside offensive tackle just swings his tail and finishes the block down inside. Both backs will read that and break to the outside. Both backs, with the halfback leading through the ballcarrier, are reading the first down lineman, the defensive end, for their route. This coaching point is very important. The other important point is, when the halfback starts off, he runs for the outside leg of the guard. It is also very important for the fullback to be patient with his footwork. He shouldn't abbreviate the footwork. He is going to take a lead step, a crossover step, and a square up step. As he bends his path for the inside foot of the tackle, which is his aiming point, he will have a nice relationship with the lead back. You want him a good yard behind the lead back going through the hole. If everything is normal and the left halfback blocks the linebacker, then the fullback can follow him through the hole, cut, and make yardage.

The right halfback is going to come in three-step motion and is going to log block the first free man at the flank to set up the keep pass. The quarterback is going to come out and set up the keep pass, as well. The quarterback's technique on this play is to reverse pivot behind the midline, mesh up with the fullback on the second step, then come behind the fullback, and fake the keep pass after the ball has been handed off.

If you get a team keying guards, then you've got one guard going to the outside, which should widen a backer, and the other guard is going to the outside, which should widen the other backer. Now you're splitting the middle. This play is a great guard key breaker as well, and you can run it regardless of whether they key guards.

187 Cross-Block vs. 4-3 Defense

Most of the time, the 4-3 defenses have the weakside tackle inside, in the gap, or down over the center, even in a 1 shade (Diagram 5.2). If you block down and pull the guard, a lot of times the weakside A gap on the frontside of the play is exposed. You won't want to pull the guard if the defensive tackle is down inside in the gap or down on the center, since you are not sure you can get all the way down to him with the offensive tackle. Two things can be done.

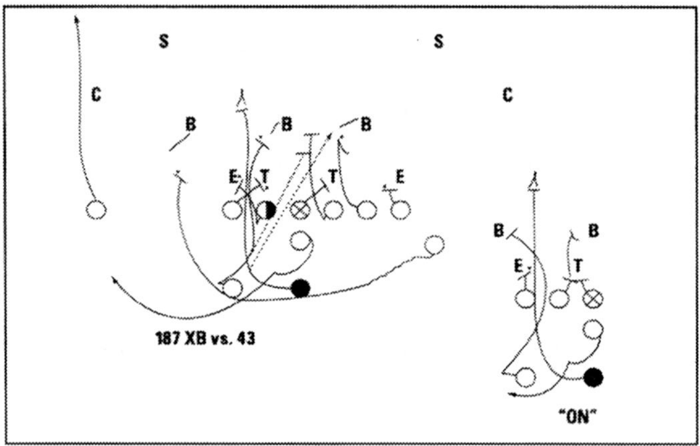

Diagram 5.2

First of all, if the defensive tackle is still a 2 technique and you can execute the cross-block, you'll go ahead and do that. After you execute the cross-block, you're going to block down on the defensive tackle and pull and trap the defensive end. As the backs go through the hole, the halfback starts to the outside foot of the guard, and the fullback starts to the inside foot of the tackle. As they go through the hole, wherever it shows, the halfback will block the linebacker and the fullback will make the read and run through the hole. They're going to read the defensive tackle, who is the first man from head up on the guard to the outside, the first down man. They're going to read him and, if he fights outside against the down block, can wind this play back over center. The blocker can go back inside, and the ballcarrier can break back inside. You can do many things with the center. His rule on this play is on-right. In this case, he'd block back to the right. The right guard is going to pull and wall off on the middle linebacker. The right tackle is fire on backer, so he's going to come up and block the strongside backer. The tight end will again step and cup drag, go to the cutoff, or block on, whatever you think your problems are. You interpret the rule for him, whichever way you need to solve whatever problems you encounter.

The right half is in three-step motion. He's going to attack the first free man at the flank. Hopefully, with this action and with the quarterback faking keep pass, you'll get some flow out of the linebackers. The split end and the quarterback will then go ahead and set up the keep pass play.

If the frontside tackle cannot block down on the defensive tackle because he's too far inside, you will adjust the blocking (side diagram). When the defensive tackle is either a gap player or a 1 shade on the center, then the line checks the play to on technique. The center and the left guard double-team the defensive tackle and keep their eyes on the linebacker. Depending on the reactions of the defensive tackle and the linebackers, one of them will take over the defensive tackle as the other one comes off on the linebacker. What you would like to have happen is for the center to take over the defensive tackle and the offensive guard to come off on the middle linebacker. The tackle then would block on outside to the defensive end. The fullback can go ahead and read the first down lineman, the halfback can go through the hole on the backer, and you have a hat for everybody.

If you have an inside technique defender to the split end side, checking into on blocking is how you would handle the problem. You would rather do that than try to cross-block and have the center reach and end up with the noseguard in the backfield making the play. That adjustment is quite a bit against the 4-3 defenses. Lately, some coaches have gone to just calling 87 on and not even worrying about the cross-block. But, if the defense is mixing it up on you at all, then just call 87 cross-block in the huddle and let the players adjust on the line of scrimmage.

187 Cross-Block vs. 4-4 Defense

Diagram 5.3 illustrates 187 cross-block versus the 4-4 defense. Again, if the defensive tackle on the split end side is too far inside to cross-block him, then you'll check the play to on assignments again. If you check to on assignments, the halfback will take care of the outside linebacker, the center and left guard will take care of the defensive tackle and the inside backer, and the tackle will block on.

If you can cross-block, you should. You'll come down with the tackle. You'll pull and trap with the guard. The center's rule takes him right, and the right guard will pull and gut through the hole. The backside tackle is reach-on-backer-away. If he has someone inside him, he'll reach; if someone is on him, he'll block on; and, if he's got a backer, he'll go to the backer. Against the 4-4, he could block away. He could block to the right and let the tight end go to cutoff. If he's uncovered, you would rather he go to the backer. He should be looking for the backside linebacker in any kind of chase situation, because it is a full-flow play.

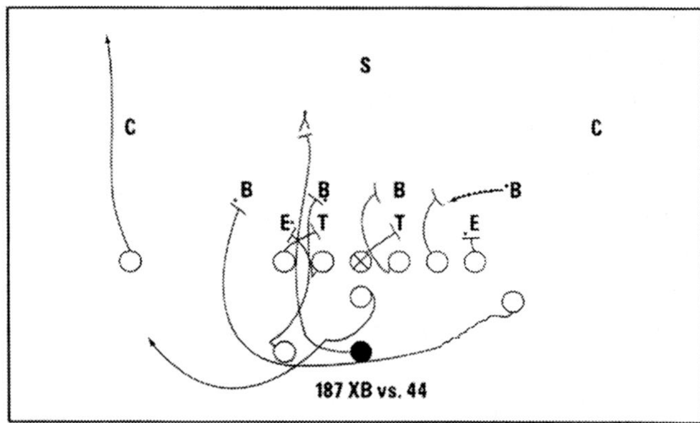

Diagram 5.3

The wing, coming in three-step motion, will come around and fake keep pass with the quarterback. He has got the first free man at the flank. Hopefully, with the quarterback's fake, you get the outside backer concerned about the keep pass. The backs do not change. They read the left tackle's block. If he's blocking the guy inside, they go to the outside. If the defender is fighting outside, they go inside. In the diagram, you've got hats for all four linebackers and still have the tight end able to block on the defensive end.

Again, if the defensive tackle is too far inside to cross-block, you'll check the play to on. At this point, this play can be run to a diveback side on the tight end side. If you run it to a tight end side, the tight end's rule will be to go inside and block the backer. You could call cross-block release and release the tight end outside, having him go for the corner. That move would influence the man you're going to trap with the cross-block. This play can be run to either side: tight end side or split end side. It is best as part of the split end side attack. You don't want to overload the tight end side because you'd be stuck with running only to the tight end. You want to be able to have balance and formation integrity with all formations.

187 Blast vs. 50 Defense

Now, the blast scheme will be illustrated, which was shown when discussing 34 blast. If you run 87 blast, you use the same rules for the linemen (Diagram 5.4). You are going to run this play weak against odd defenses. You are going to double-team the nose and lead the halfback through on the linebacker. It's just one of those good, old-fashioned, double-team, lead-through, power-type plays. But, now, it's not only run out of the 30 series, it's also run out of the 80 series.

The playside tackle, or 7 man, has on-outside-gap-or-blocker. In this case, he blocks on, with his head inside. He is the point of attack. The onside guard has gap-on-lead,

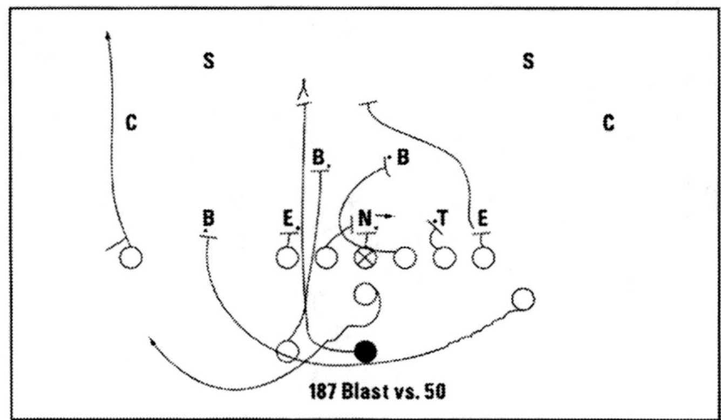

Diagram 5.4

so he's double-teaming. The center is post or right. He is going to post and create the double-team. You want to move the nose on down the line of scrimmage. The left halfback continues to go for the outside leg of the guard as an aiming point. He's going to block on the inside linebacker.

The right halfback, in three-step motion, is going to block the first free man at the flank and set up the keep pass. He is responsible for the outside backer in the 50 defense. The backside right guard will pull and wall off. He can block the inside backer by pulling around the double-team and walling off. If you know the guard can get him by going straight ahead, you'll allow him to do that. But, if you're getting a good push by the center and the left guard, that nose is going to be moved and the right guard shouldn't be able to go straight upfield because he's going to get knocked off by the movement. This reason is why he should pull around the nose. The playside tackle is pull-check and, if no threat exists out of the linebacker, is going to block back. Finally, the tight end will go to cutoff or can block on. You can do either of those things, depending on what your biggest problem is.

The fullback is the ballcarrier. His footwork is lead, crossover, and square up. The quarterback reverse pivots beyond the midline, hands him the ball, comes on out, and fakes keep pass along with the split end. The fullback reads the first down man from the guard out. This play is an isolation, or blast, just like an I-formation blast.

Spread 187 Blast vs. 4-4 Defense

Against even defenses, this play is good to run to the tight end side because it creates an extra blocker at the point of attack, meaning the tight end. This same play will be illustrated from a different formation, using a spread end to the side of the wing, instead of the tight end to the side of the wing. So, this play would be spread 187 blast. Showing this play against the 4-4 defense will prove the point that, even in eight-man fronts, you have hats for everybody (Diagram 5.5).

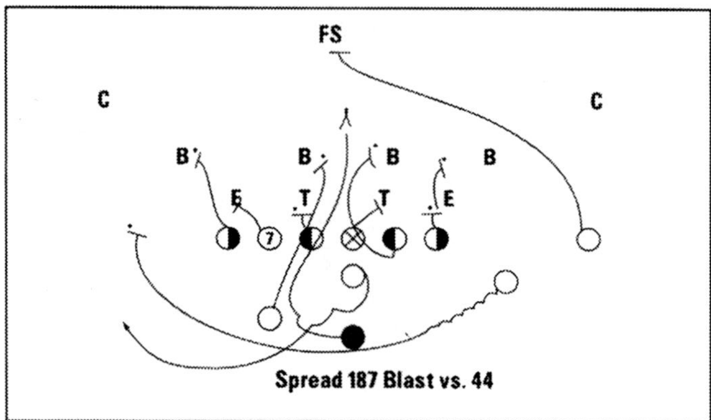

Diagram 5.5

The tight end, if the blast play is coming to him, is on-outside-or backer. So, if he has a man on him, he'll block him. If the defender is on an inside shade or is gap conscious, you will not block him. Instead, you will go to the outside part of the rule and turn out on the outside linebacker. The playside tackle's rule is on-outside-gap-backer. Now, in this diagram, you can see the defensive end has the outside gap – he's the C gap player, so the tackle must block him. The left guard is gap-on-lead. He will block on with his head to the side of the point of attack, which means he will block with his right shoulder. The center is post or right. The right guard is pull and wall off. The right tackle is pull-check. With the center's block right, he doesn't need to, so he can just block on the 5-technique defensive end.

The fullback is going to be the ballcarrier. His initial aiming point is for the inside leg of the tackle. The left halfback's initial point of aim is the outside leg of the guard. Both of those guys are going to read the left guard's block. If he takes the man outside, they'll cut inside. If he takes the man inside, they'll cut outside.

The quarterback is going to reverse pivot, hand the ball off, and fake the keep pass. The right half, if you don't call anything else, will log block the first free man at the flank. If you say, "No mo," he will go to cutoff with no motion. The spread end now needs to go to cutoff, because he's away from the keep pass fake. That setup is another way to run the same play against the eight-man front and have a hat for every single player. If you are worried about the backside linebacker, then your right tackle can shift to him. One of those defenders has to be a trail player; they can't both go to cut back. If they do, you can run some kind of reverse on them.

187 Blast vs. 4-3 Defense

Diagram 5.6 shows 187 blast to the split end side versus the 4-3 defense, which is a seven-man front. The playside tackle has a man on him, so he's going to come off and block with his left shoulder, head inside. The left guard is going to block the defensive tackle. If the defensive tackle is down in a shade or on the center, the guard has a good angle on him. If not, he still blocks on, his head goes to the outside, and he's going to use his right shoulder. The center is going to block to the right. The right guard is going to pull and wall off. The right tackle's rule is pull and check, and, in this situation, if you block the tight end on, you can try and get the right tackle up to the linebacker.

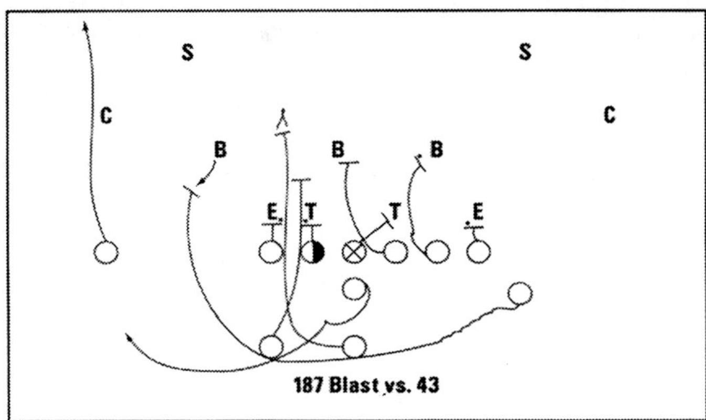

Diagram 5.6

The halfback makes the read on the left guard's block and, as he goes through, blocks the first backer who shows in the hole. The fullback also makes the guard's block his read. The wing is in three-step motion and fakes keep pass at the flank. You want him to get over and make the outside linebacker have some concern for him, so you have enough hats to block all the backers. The quarterback will reverse pivot beyond the midline, mesh up with the fullback, and then attack the flank. He and the spread end will go ahead and fake the keep pass.

You can run 87 blast, 87 on, or 87 cross block. Same thing can be run to the right: 83 cross block, 83 blast, or 83 on. Those plays are mirrored, and you will feel the belly play is a great football play. You're going to find a blocking scheme. You are going to find a way to make that play work. If they're shutting it down, something else is probably going to be open – either keep pass, counter, or counter bootleg. Regardless, something in the package will be open.

189 Keep Pass vs. 50 Defense

The next play in the package is the keep pass, which is used to put the secondary support defenders into an assignment conflict, making them come up aggressively versus playing soft for the pass. This particular play is 189 keep pass to the split side (Diagram 5.7). A couple of different alternatives for blocking the 50 defense will be shown. If you play against a reading defense and they really seal with you, then this method is how you block the keep pass. The frontside tackle's rule is gap-down. He's going to come down as if he's going to block the nose. The guard is going to pull and log the end man. As you can see, no blocker exists for the defensive end. Well, if he's reading, squeezing and sealing, then he is a line of scrimmage player, and the fullback will take care of that as he fakes the belly. So, this method is the first way you would block the keep pass. The fullback, instead of aiming for the inside foot of the tackle, widens just a little bit to the outside foot of the tackle and blocks the 5 technique area, or the offensive tackle's area. The guard is blocking the 9 technique or the ghost tight end area.

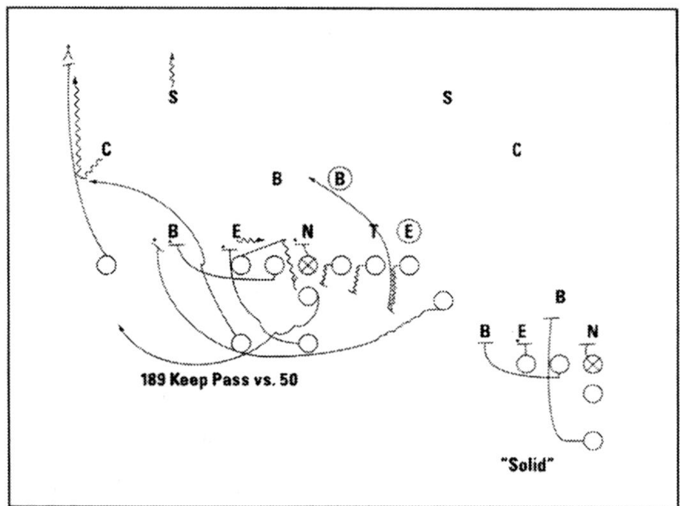

Diagram 5.7

The center, right guard, right tackle, and tight end are all step and cup on this play. The center has a noseguard on him, so he will use aggressive technique, instead of step and cup. He is going to come off and block the nose with his right shoulder. The left tackle, as he steps down, will either finish that block for the center or, if the center has him handled, can drop behind the line of scrimmage and take care of anybody chasing the quarterback behind the line. The step and cup by the right guard, right tackle, and tight end should build a solid wall off the backside of the quarterback. The tight end's assignment on this play is step and cup-drag. That rule means, as he cups, the only time he actually has to block is when both the inside linebacker and the outside backer are both rushing. If either one of those people drops, only two people are left, so the guard and tackle can handle them. But if they both rush, you need the third blocker. As he cups, all the tight end does is simply check inside backer to outside backer. If he sees either player drop, he's going to run a delayed drag route over the football.

The wingback is going to come in three-step motion and is going to set up the keep pass by log blocking at the flank. He starts turning upfield as soon as he passes the quarterback-fullback mesh. The quarterback reverse pivots beyond the midline, makes a quick arms-length ride to the fullback, and then is going to get on out and attack the flank with the keep pass. The left halfback and the split end are the two primary receivers. You can do a lot of things with the spread end. If you are getting hard corners squatting on you, you'd like to have the spread end outside release and run a fly. You tell the quarterback to pop him a ball as quickly as he can in the hole, as long as the corner rotates up and the safety's a hash player. If you see that kind of rotation, as the quarterback comes off the mesh, you'd like him to quickly pop the ball in the hole. The left halfback is going for a point one to 1.5 yards outside the end man. He's going to work to about four to six yards of depth out in the flat, and he's the flat receiver. The wing is a log blocker. He's going to protect the quarterback. The quarterback's progression is deep, flat, or run the ball.

You can also suffix the pass pattern and say, "Keep pass curl," "Keep pass out," "Keep pass post," or anything you want to do. Against two-deep teams, you should hit the pass in the hole, if you can get it. If the corner is sinking in the hole and taking that pass away, you instantly know the halfback in the flat is going to be huge. If the defense wants to give five or six yards and tackle all the time, you'll take the five or six yards. If you have really good halfbacks and they break that tackle, you've got a big play. You won't mind taking that five-yard play anytime. This play is good on first and second down. It is also good on third-and-medium. If you get five yards, then you're going to have the first down or are going to have an efficient play enabling you to stay on schedule. You also have the quarterback ready to throw quickly to the flat all the time. On his third step, the ball is up in the passing position. And, within a few steps after that, the ball can be gone, and you can really get rid of it fast. If you do succeed in getting rid of the ball quickly, you give the halfback the ball sooner, giving him a chance to run the ball, break tackles, and make a big play.

One last problem with this keep pass play needs to be talked about: what if the defensive end is not sealing, is penetrating, and is just knocking the dog out of your fullback? Or, what if the fullback cannot handle him and is overmatched in size and strength, and it's just not going to happen for you (side diagram)? Tell the linemen to block with keep pass solid rules. Solid means, in this case, instead of the tackle coming down, he will block on. He blocks with his head outside, since it's a 9 hole play. At this point, the fullback will go back to his normal aiming point and will take care of the linebacker, if the linebacker comes. If not, he can get into a route or help on someone else. The guard will still pull and log the 9 technique area. The center can still block the noseguard, and everybody else can still be step and cup. It really only changes the fullback and the left tackle if you use a solid call.

189 Keep Pass vs. 4-3 Defense

Very little changes on 189 keep pass versus a 4-3 defense (Diagram 5.8). The backside of the protection is identical, but you do modify the frontside slightly. The left tackle's rule is gap-down, so he's coming down on the first defender inside him, unless you call solid. You can have the left guard pull and log the end man on the line or can continue to have the left guard pull and log the 9 technique area. The fullback will then have to take care of the 5 technique area. You don't mind letting the fullback be the 5 technique blocker, as long as the end is squeezing and is trying to jam the offensive tackle, and is not overly concerned with getting upfield. That match is even. If he is a penetrator and is coming upfield into the backfield, even the guard log blocking him is a tough block to execute. So, again, you have the possibility of a solid call. Or, you can use a fire call, which means the tackle fire blocks on him, the guard stays home, and nobody pulls. So, if you have a head-up technique, that adjustment isn't bad either (side diagram). The fullback will take care of the linebacker in the B gap.

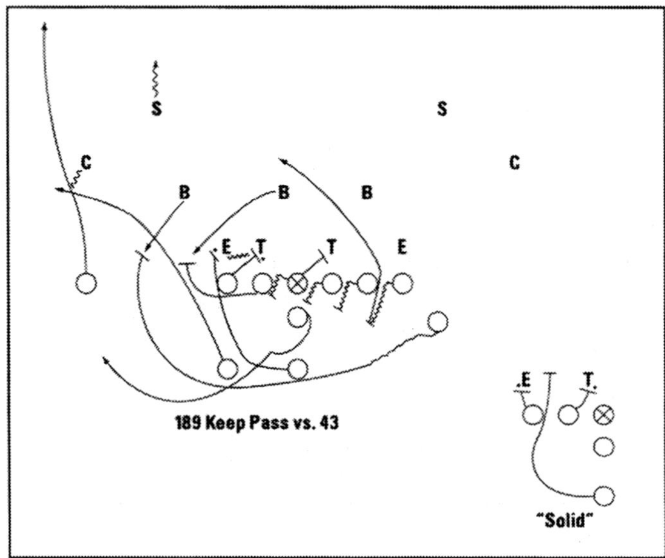

Diagram 5.8

The backfield action and the routes remain the same. The only adjustment against the 4-3 defense is on the frontside blocking adjustments. Even if you've called keep pass out, where the spread end should run an out route, if the corner squats, the out turns into a fly as well.

For the backside linemen who are in step and cup, one more quick point is, if they are uncovered as they step and cup, they can hold their ground a little bit. Whereas, if they're covered, they should step, cup, and give a lot of ground, in case the defense is running some kind of inside-outside stunt. The man inside, the uncovered man, holds his ground. Now he can pick up the inside rush and, as the covered man gives a little ground, also pick up the outside rush, and the moment will play itself out for you fairly quickly. If uncovered, hold your ground; if covered, give ground. This technique is how you coach the technique for the backside linemen.

189 Keep Pass vs. 4-4 Defense

Diagram 5.9 illustrates 189 keep pass versus a 4-4. As you can easily see, no rule changes are needed to protect against the 4-4. The frontside can log or block solid. The backside, including the center, are all step and cup. The fullback's aiming point is a little bit wider. He is going to aim for the outside leg of the tackle, instead of the inside leg, and block the 5 technique area. If the end skates out and the backer plugs, you can see how the blockers will pick up those guys wherever they show. The wingback is going in three-step motion and blocking the first free man at the flank. In this defense, the wing is responsible for the fourth defender. He must get that block made. The rest of the backfield action is identical.

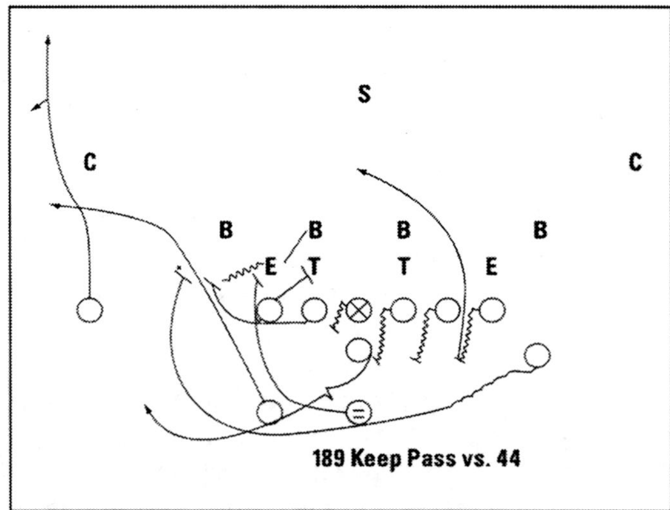

Diagram 5.9

The spread end can run the fly, or, against three-deep coverage, keep pass out is good to call, or some kind of individual cut to him, where he can take advantage of the deep third corner. That multiplicity has been a real staple of the offense. It's one of the base plays. It's one of the core plays. You are going to find ways to run this play each game.

181 Keep Pass vs. 50 Defense

Keep pass has only been shown to the split end side. It is also a very effective play to the tight end side. Diagram 5.10 gives an example of 181 keep pass to the tight end side. On any 80 series play, if you're going to run to the tight end side and the left halfback is the diveback, then he'll use his one-step motion. He will leave about a count to a count and a half early and will be into his second step when the ball gets snapped.

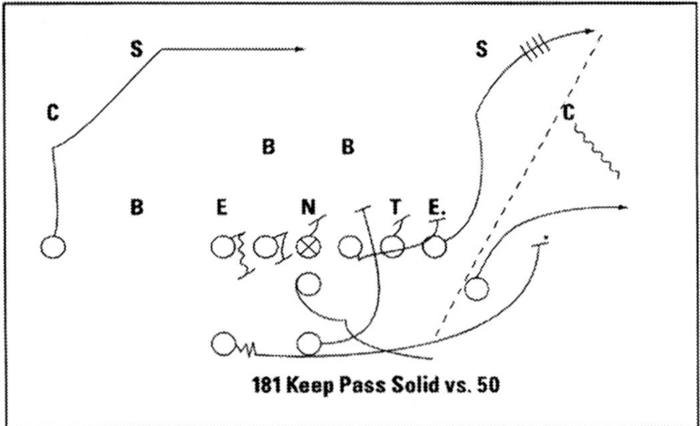

Diagram 5.10

When you run the keep pass to the tight end side, you want the tight end to release outside and run a seam route. As he releases outside, he's going to a point about three yards outside of his alignment and about seven yards deep, then look over his outside shoulder, and try to bend in the hole between the safety and the corner. The wing is going quick to the flat. The spread end is going to run a dig route. You are going to bring him across the middle and, hopefully, get him in the quarterback's vision, in case the quarterback has to come off to an outlet receiver. The blocking and backfield action is exactly the same.

What you want to do is out-leverage the corner with the halfback in the flat. If he's open quick, get him the ball quick and let him run. A lot of times, quarterbacks will be hesitant to pull the trigger, but they can't be. This play has to be like a long handoff. It has to be part of your running game. You have to be confident that you can complete this every single time. This play is a big catalyst for the wing-T offense. At South Dakota, we made this play go so many different ways, it was unbelievable, but it's always best when you hit the halfback in the flat quickly. Then you'll start getting corners to jump up on you. Those flat players will start really trying to get to that halfback in a hurry. If they do, then the seam route right should be a heck of a throw – especially if he bends away from the safety and the corner reacts up tight. That throw should be outstanding. You can almost read this backwards. You can almost look for the flat first, then throw the deeper ball, and then run.

181 Keep Pass vs. 4-3 Defense

Diagram 5.11 shows 181 keep pass versus the 4-3 defense. As you can see, absolutely nothing has changed. The tackle is going to block down, and the guard is going to pull and log. The rest of the linemen are still step and cup. The routes are all still the same. The quarterback has the same action, and all the backs have the same assignments.

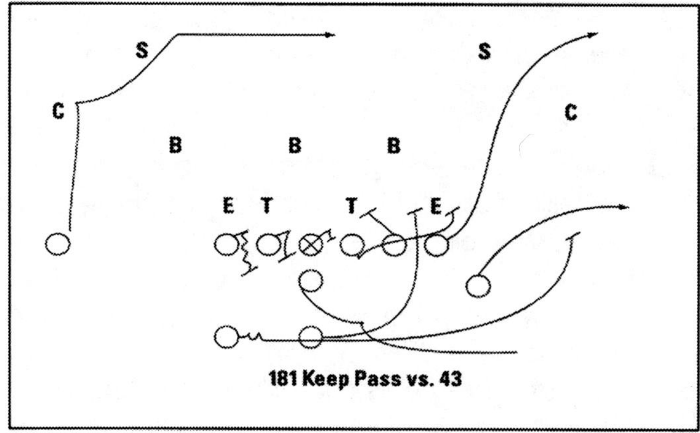

Diagram 5.11

181 Keep Pass vs. 4-4 Defense

You need to see the 181 keep pass against the 4-4 defense because the fourth defender should be the player in conflict (Diagram 5.12). He is either going to have to cover the flat or take the quarterback on the run, but he can't do both effectively. As long as the defensive backs are one-third conscious, then the fourth defender, the outside linebacker, has a real conflict on the keep pass. Once the defense starts rotating their coverages, if they rotate the corner up, the safety over, and the backside corner back, then you have exactly what you want, but, at this time, to the split end side rather than the tight end side. If they're going to do that kind of stuff, how will they ever stop keep pass out? They can't.

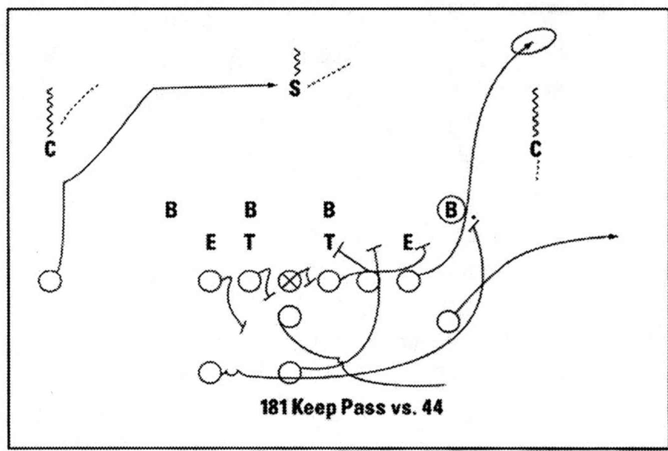

Diagram 5.12

The offensive line blocking is the same. Also, the backfield action and the routes have not changed. The quarterback has the ball ready to throw quickly. He's going to look in the flat and get that ball to the halfback in the flat very quickly, if the outside linebacker is out-leveraged. If the linebacker has any concern for your belly game whatsoever, he might step up or inside, and you'll have beaten him to the flat. If the corner rotates up, you should still be able to hit the tight end, even with the safety rotating over. He should not be able to cover. He's going to have to cover it from behind, if at all, and it's still a pass the quarterback can complete. Even though the tight end might get tackled, you're going to get 15 yards out of it.

As mentioned earlier, you can run several pattern variations with the keep pass. Everyone is really doing the same thing, but the pattern variations tell the spread end to run some different routes. Keep pass out is liked a lot. Keep pass curl is not a bad thought. You can run keep pass with some kind of individual deep route, whether it is post, corner, or the Q route. All those plans are good for keep pass, depending on what coverage you get.

Basically, it's effective when the corner and the spread end are going to be locked in a 1-on-1 battle. Then, the spread end should be allowed to work that defender a little bit. Work him to the outside, cut inside. Work him to the inside, cut outside. Work him outside, cut outside. Do all those things to him. And everybody else stays the same. Your halfback can adjust his route according to what individual route you call to the split end. Change up the routes as much as you want and be as multiple with that play as you need to be.

183 Pass Y Drag

The next play is another pass just like 81 keep pass. Instead of the quarterback attacking the flank, though, the quarterback is going to drop, because, at this point, he'll drop back on the outside leg of the guard or the inside leg of the tackle. The pass protection now becomes the same pass protection that every I formation team in the country uses on sprint draw pass. They use what is called backside gap protection, or turnback protection. This 83 pass package still creates a little bit of flow. Diagram 5.13 gives an example of the way to use 183 pass with a tag added of Y drag. The tight end is Y, and, obviously, you are telling him to run a drag route across the field.

The pass protection rules are very simple and extremely versatile in blocking the defensive fronts. The right tackle's rule is gap-on-area-outside. Against the 50 defense, he's going to pass block on. But, what you tell him is, in order to sell the run, he must be in control and be ready to pass set. You do that by coming off like a high drive block. You come off a little higher than normal, up in the numbers. But, initially, you're going to come off hard on the run. The right guard's rule is gap-on-lead. So, he's coming down to the nose against a 50 defense, and you're going to show run action. The center's rule is post-left. Again, you're going to show run action. Now, both the right guard and the center, as they post and lead on the nose, are eyeing up the backside linebacker. If anything happens where the nose and the backside linebacker stunt, then those two blockers pick up those two players wherever they show. The right guard is responsible for the inside A gap – the A gap right inside of him – and the center is responsible for the A gap to the backside.

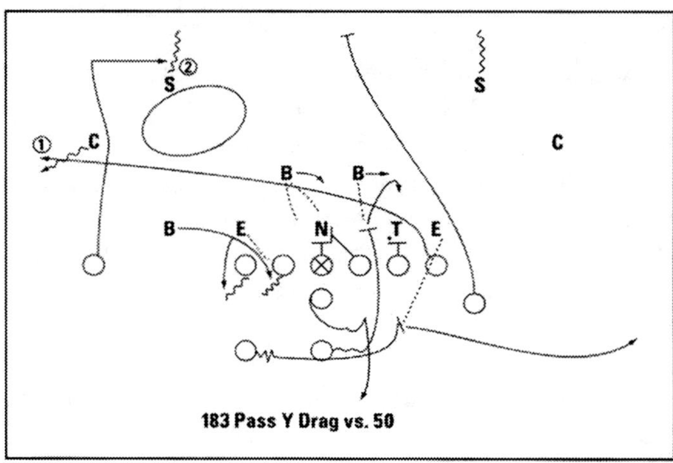

Diagram 5.13

The rule for the backside left guard and left tackle is going to be step and fan. They are basically going to block the gap to their outside. You have them kick-step and block the B and C gaps. If you have some kind of a stunt where the defensive end goes upfield and the outside linebacker loops behind him, those players block those defenders the way they show. The guard has the B gap rusher; the tackle has the C gap rusher. If they pinch, you can see the guard now has the end and the tackle has the outside backer. So, they basically block the defenders where they find them – in the B and C gaps.

Y drag tells the tight end to run a crossing route and intersect the far sideline at about six yards up the field. It's a shallow drag. You're going to have the spread end work to at least 16 yards, break in, find an open seam, and sit down in it. The wingback is going to run right down through the middle of the defense. He's going to run right through the middle and take out the safeties. Hopefully, both safeties will be backing up in halves, thus, allowing the drag route to occur.

You should get some action with the linebackers because of the action of the backs. If you've been running 81 keep pass or any kind of 80 action, then you're going to get some flow out of the linebackers, and, hopefully, the tight end running the drag route should be wide open. The fullback takes that same footwork – lead, crossover, square up – and, at this point, attacks through the hole. He's going to block the frontside linebacker if he should happen to blitz. His man is in B gap or C gap. He must adjust his footwork and get his man. If the linebacker doesn't come, you turn the fullback out, and he sits down in the underneath hook zone to hold the backers. The left halfback is going to show 181 keep pass, so he's in one-step motion, comes across the backfield, and, when he passes the fullback, gears down and gets an inside-out block on the defensive end. If, for some reason, the defensive end drops and doesn't come, the halfback can flare. The halfback flaring becomes the fifth eligible receiver on the play.

The quarterback reverse pivots, meshes with the fullback on the second step, and rides the fullback on the third step. Then he sits down, pushes off his left foot, and drops back. The difference between 83 pass and 81 keep pass is you are no longer attacking the flank with the quarterback. He is now pass setting behind the offensive guard and inside the offensive tackle, and everyone is using backside gap protection, so you should be able to pick up any blitzes. It doesn't matter what pattern you run; the linemen have the same blocking rules all the time.

As the quarterback drops, he'll look to hit the drag route first, if he can. He has to look out in front of the drag route and make sure an outside linebacker isn't dropping under it, or a corner squatting on it, before he throws the ball. If he doesn't see any defenders there, he should hit the drag route quickly. If not, he can throw to the dig. The dig route should be open because, if someone covers the drag, whether it's a corner or an outside backer and the two inside linebackers react at all to the flow, a big seam is inside for the split end to sit down in. You can run variations of this same pass pattern, but the quarterback reads it the same way every time.

The pass protection rules do not change against a 4-3 defense (Diagram 5.14). The right tackle will block area with a pass set technique. He will end up blocking the defensive end. The tackle can take care of the backer, and the halfback can come around in motion and take care of the end. Or you can switch, letting the tackle take

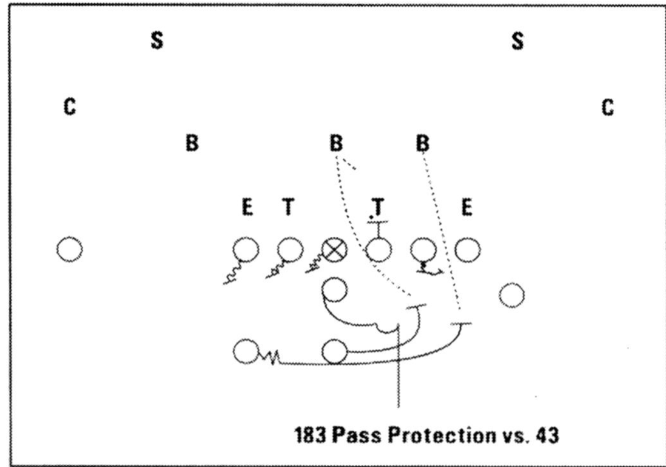

Diagram 5.14

care of the end and the halfback, as he comes around, take care of the backer. The right guard must block on, head inside, and sell the run, but it's a high drive block, and, when the defender reacts, then he turns into a pass block. The center is going to block to his left and just kick-steps to his left. He's got the A gap on the left. The left guard kick-steps to his left and has the B gap on the left. The left tackle kick-steps to the left and has the C gap. No matter what kind of a blitz the defense tries to run with the backside three defenders, you're going to pick it up, because the center, the left guard, and the left tackle are basically going to block their gaps.

The fullback will lead, cross over, square up, and take the middle backer. The halfback is in one-step motion, gears down, and has the outside backer. Everyone is handled in that defense.

Taking a look at the pass-protection blocking versus the 4-4 (Diagram 5.15), basically, it's the same as the 4-3. In this pass protection, it's almost exactly the same. The right tackle will kick-step right to the defensive end, who will probably be a 7 technique. The right guard is going to block on. The center left guard and left tackle are blocking the backside three gaps. They are stepping and fanning to the backside gaps. The fullback takes his footwork and is responsible for the inside linebacker. The left half goes in one-step motion and, when he passes the quarterback-fullback mesh, has the outside linebacker.

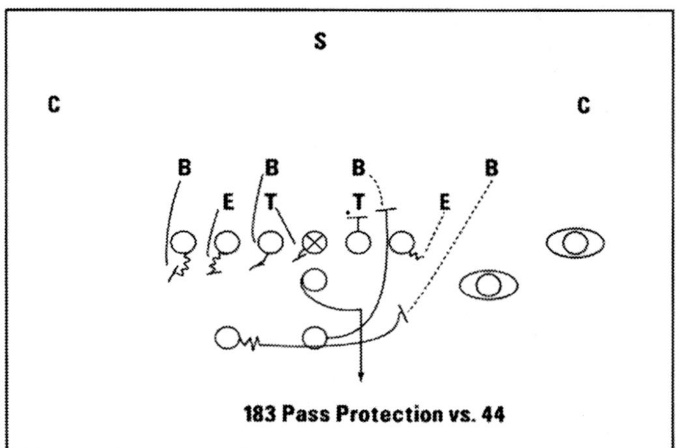

Diagram 5.15

If the defense brings four rushers off the weakside, the center can pick up the A gap, the guard picks up the B gap, the tackle picks up the C gap, and nobody is there for D gap. In this situation, if you are playing an eight-man front, you will change the formation. You will bring the split end from a split position to a tight position. If they have a tendency to blitz four off a side, you just keep the tight end in and make sure the backside of the quarterback is protected. That change means you would align with the spread end to the playside and the tight end to the backside. It would be a two-man route, and you would have eight pass protectors to block eight defenders. If they don't blitze four rushers off a side, you do not necessarily have to worry about this. Even if they like to blitz, it's usually just one of the two linebackers coming; therefore, you don't need to worry about this. You can go ahead and run the pass with the backside end split. But when in doubt, be safe. If they are an eight-man front and show any four man side blitzes, then go ahead and keep the tight end in on the backside.

On 183 pass Y drag, the tight end is going to run the drag, someone is going to go through the middle, and someone is going to dig in the open area. One thing you can do is just switch the routes of the spread end and the wingback. At this point, you'll let the split end go through the middle on the post and let the wing dig across and find a way to sit down in the middle. This read is the same for the quarterback. He looks for the cross, the dig, and then the post, in that order. It looks like something different to the defense. You would simply call 183 pass X post (Diagram 5.16). Use your imagination on the routes and come up with whatever you like.

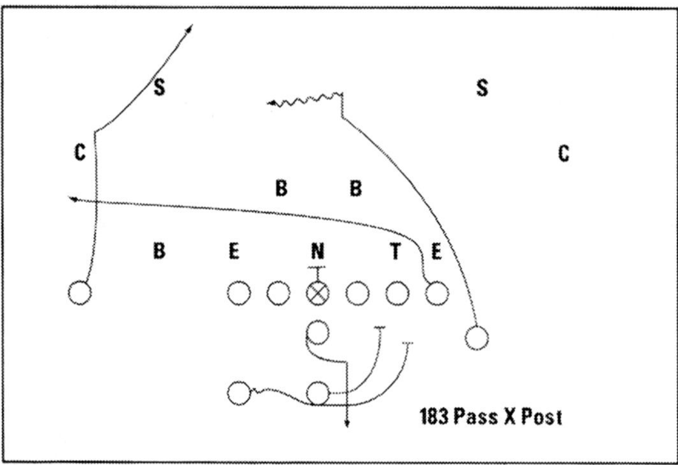

Diagram 5.16

A couple of routes are good to the split end side. If you were going to run this play to the split end side and were going to keep the tight end in on the backside, then you would run this out of a spread 100 formation. You simply call spread 183 pass and attach the routes (Diagram 5.17). At this point, you have a different look and can keep the tight end in on the backside for the eight-man front protection. You just run two-man routes. You will like a bunch of these. One route is where the spread end goes deep and the halfback runs a banana type of a route, where he just bends over the outside shoulder and goes in the seams when the corner covers the spread end deep. With the play-action, it should hold the strong safety. If it doesn't, you have other routes. You can call the same play and switch the routes, drive the split end to the flat, and drive the wing to the corner in the deep outside one-third. You also can run the right half to the banana route and the spread end to the post route, if you see free safeties who are overactive against the run. You can run those three-man and two-man routes.

This past year, we started to work with post and wheel and curl and wheel, as opposed to three basic routes. But our first three choices are the fly and the banana, the out and the corner, and the banana and the post.

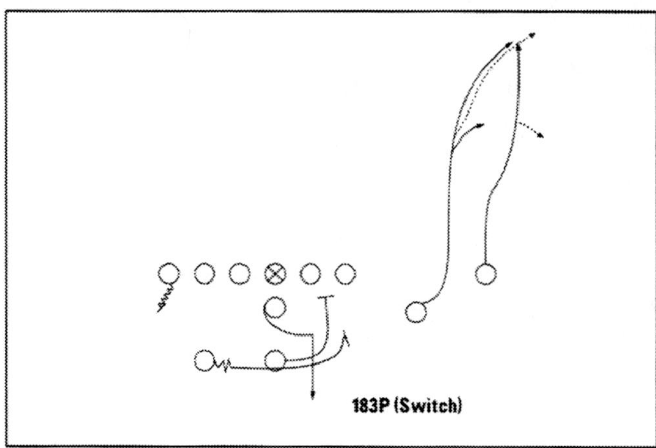

Diagram 5.17

187 Counter vs. 50 Defense

The final part of this belly package, with the fullback taking the lead, crossover, square-up footwork, is the 87 counter play. All the blocking schemes to the 7 hole are the same. You have seen different actions by the backs in the 60 package, the 30 package, and now the 80 package. But, the blocking for the line has been the same. Again, as depicted in Diagram 5.18, on the 7 hole counter lay, you could pull the guard and the tackle – which is called tag. You could pull tackle and tight end – which is tat. Or, you could use out counter-crisscross blocking rules, where you pull the guard and the tight end. In any of those blocking schemes, you need to answer the questions the defense presents you with your preferred backfield action. Just continue to run the play and make it work.

The 87 counter has been a great play. It is a favorite counter. Using it a bunch, it can be blocked a lot of different ways. The illustration (Diagram 5.18) features counter-crisscross blocking. The play call is 187-counter-crisscross. Again, you've seen the counter blocking in other series, which are basically all the same. The key is to determine what kind of backfield action you want to use to set up your counter play. It is also a question of which blocking scheme you select to solve the problems caused by the defense.

In Diagram 5.18, the line is blocking counter-crisscross rules against the 50 front. Nothing has changed from any other time you apply counter-crisscross blocking to a particular backfield action, so the focus will be on the differences in the backfield, which is 187 counter. The word counter tells all the backs who are not getting the ball to go

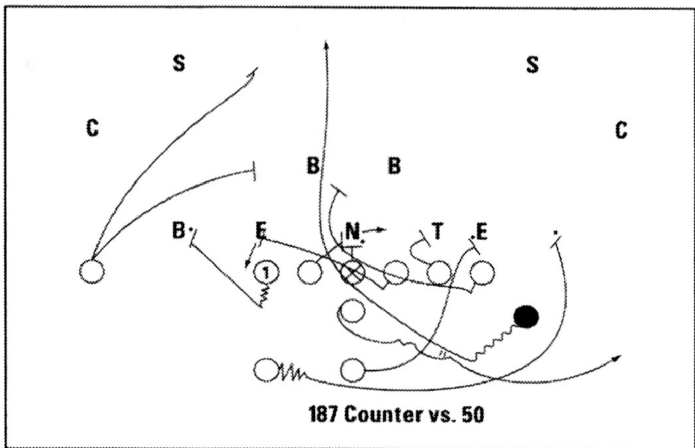

Diagram 5.18

away from the play. The 7 man is the left tackle, so the fullback is going to fake 83 away from the play. He will use his 80 steps, belly action and lead, cross over, and square up. To the fullback, the play is 83 away. The fullback is going to come off the 83 fake and block the first defender who shows off the tight end's tail because of crisscross blocking. He blocks with the right shoulder, his head inside. The left half is in one-step motion, is coming around the quarterback-fullback mesh, and blocking just as he would on 181 keep pass. He's going to block the first free man at the flank. The quarterback reverse pivots, meshes with the fullback, steps back, and hands the ball to the wingback on the counter. The wingback is the ballcarrier. He does not go in motion. He leaves on the snap, but comes back three steps, as if he is going in three-step motion, and then breaks for the 7 hole and accepts the handoff inside the quarterback. The quarterback will then go and fake keep pass. The ballcarrier is going to stay tight to his double-team and burst up through the field.

187 Counter vs. 4-3 Defense

Diagram 5.19 illustrates what the play looks like against the 4-3 defense with counter-crisscross blocking. The rules are the same. The linemen use their blocking rules for counter-crisscross, which have been detailed. The backfield action is now 87 action. Notice, you should get pretty good flow out of this. The linebackers should be committing to 81 keep pass, 83 pass, or 82 down option, whatever it is that you're running to the flank to set this up. Again, the split end comes down and cracks one of the linebackers, if you need an extra blocker.

The fullback is going to take his 83 footwork, come right off the tight end's tail, and block the first defender who shows with his head inside. The left half is in one-step motion. He comes on around and the blocks the flank. The action of the quarterback and the wingback is identical to the action discussed earlier. The action will not change just because the defense is, at this point, in a 4-3.

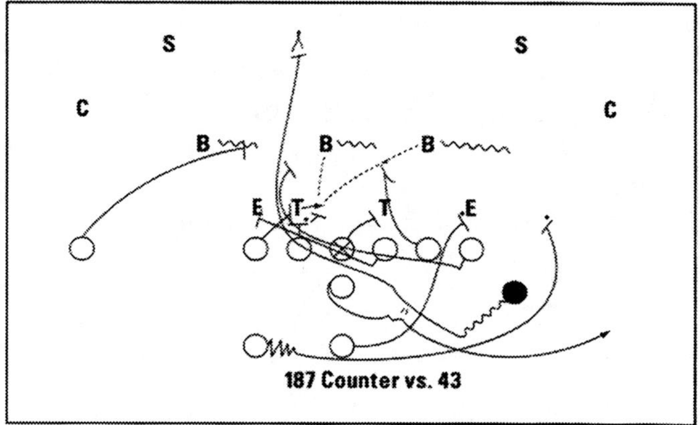

Diagram 5.19

187 Counter vs. 4-4 Defense

You will probably need the split end to come down and help against the 4-4. He gives you four hats for the linebackers. You can pretty much guarantee that you're going to call split 187 counter (Diagram 5.20). For the linemen, nothing is different. They simply apply counter-crisscross rules to the 4-4 front, just as they have many times before in other series. At this time, the spread end can come down and block the outside backer as he reacts to the play. The backfield action remains the same. The left half must make his block on the fourth linebacker, especially if you get some flow.

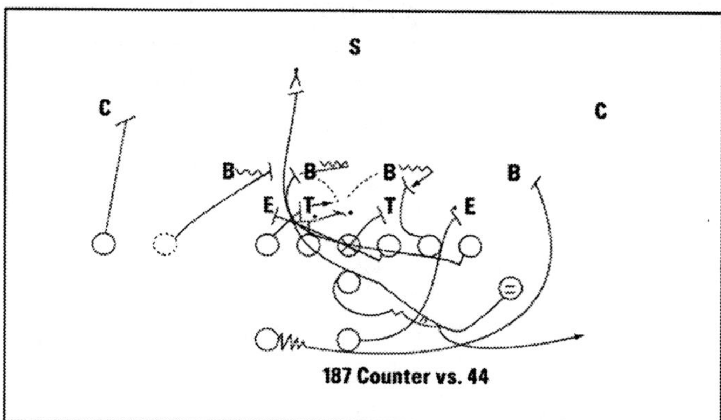

Diagram 5.20

The counters are all good — it just depends on what play you are running to set up the counter. You should use 87 counter and 37 counter, as they are favorites. The

67 counter really needs to be blocked, with tag blocking the most effective, because you have the problem of the defensive end, if he penetrates. You can also help keep the end honest with the 67 counter bootleg play, so, if the defensive end flies down inside, you have the bootleg to go back to.

182 Down Option vs. 50 Defense

The next part of the 80 package employs different footwork and a different aiming point for the fullback. It also uses different footwork for the quarterback. The package is the 82 down option package. This package has only two plays. It mixes well with keep pass and some other things, but it is definitely different for the fullback and the quarterback.

As you look at 82 down (Diagram 5.21), examine what the rules are and how you are going to block all the defenses. The tight end rule is down-backer. You do not include a gap assignment in his rule. You do not want him blocking anybody who is on his inside shoulder or in the gap. If a man is covering the offensive tackle, he will come down. Against a 50 defense, the tight end has to come down. He will put his head across the front and use gap technique, if the defensive tackle is a penetrator, if any threat exists that he might penetrate, or if you are unsure. If you know, for sure, he is a reader, the tight end will put the head behind. The rule for the right tackle, the playside tackle, is gap-down. He's going to block any defender to his inside, if in his gap. If not, he is blocking down. Just like the sweep, you can interpret gap-down to mean block the backer or come all the way down to the nose and finish off the block with the center. It's up to you, whatever you want to do. If you know the center can handle the noseguard, then you'll let the center, whose rule is fire on backer, take the noseguard by himself. You will try to get the tackle through to the backer and, if he can't get the frontside backer, have him go to the backside linebacker.

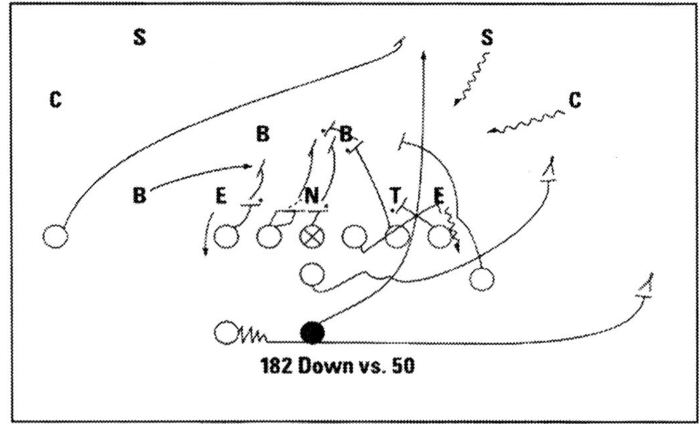

Diagram 5.21

The right guard is going to pull and trap the defensive end, with his head inside and a right-shoulder block. The left guard and the left tackle all fire on backer. If they are covered, they use a fire step; if uncovered, they use a reach step. If the nose loops or angles to the weakside, then the guard blocks him and the center bench presses him into the guard, and the guard climbs for the backside backer. If the nose and the center stay locked up, then the backside guard will climb for the backside linebacker. One of those two will climb for the backside linebacker. The tackle is going to fire on the defensive end, and, if he rushes upfield, he will never stop the down play. The tackle can go to the next level and look for the cutback player, probably from the outside linebacker position.

You are going to call 82 down whenever you know the third defender is either working out into the wingback's block or penetrating the line of scrimmage. If the #3 defender is going to seal and jam the defensive tackle, the companion play is 82 down option, which hits outside. If he is upfield, you're going to trap him out. Trying to help the trap, the wingback will step right out to the end and then can either turn out on the corner or can have him go across to the inside backer. This play is good from an unbalanced formation in order to remove the corner. Unbalanced formation allows you to send the wingback inside to the inside linebacker. The reason for sending the wingback in there is because the linebacker will stop the play faster than anyone. If the corner makes the play, you usually don't have lost yardage. The split end is going to cutoff.

The backfield is where the action becomes a little bit different. In 80 series, the backside left halfback is going in one-step motion, if he's in a diveback position. He will do the same on 82 down, but, as he comes across the backfield, he is no longer a log blocker at the flank. He is going to fake 82 down option and show the picture of being the pitch back on the option play. The fullback is going to run for the inside foot of the tight end as fast as he can. On an even defense, he will run for the inside foot of the tackle because the double-team or the down block is going to be a man closer. As he goes to that aiming point, the quarterback will reverse pivot flat down the line of scrimmage. When the fullback and the quarterback mesh up, you want the quarterback to ride the fullback and shuffle with him. You want the fullback to turn his shoulders north and south and stay away from the defensive backs, who want to come running in and make the tackle. The quarterback will continue on out and fake option with the left halfback. The 82 down is a fast, quick-hitting play. It's an off-tackle play. It's a good play in games where you feel that you can get the down blocks or when the third defenders are reacting upfield to stop other parts of the offense.

One other thing that you can do is call Z down (Diagram 5.22). On Z down, you are going to run 182 down, but, if you put the prefix Z in front of the play, the backs who are not ballcarriers are going in motion or running away from the ballcarrier. You trap the defensive end. You hand the ball off to the fullback. The fullback and the quarterback do the exact same thing, but, at this time, the backs go away. The left halfback dives and blocks the backside backer, and the wingback is in three-step motion and comes around as a log blocker. What you get is a full-flow play with misdirection. This play ends up being a nice little complement to some of the other plays, especially if the defensive end, when he sees the wingback motion away from him, runs upfield to stop waggle. Then, Z down is a great play under the end, who is being trapped. Keep this play in mind as a complement to the down play.

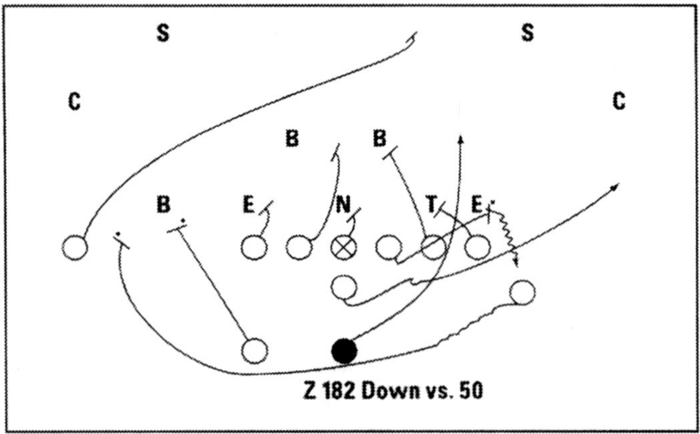

Diagram 5.22

182 Down vs. 4-3 Defense

Diagram 5.23 illustrates 182 down versus the 4-3 defense. The tight end winds up going to the linebacker. The right tackle, or the playside tackle, will block down. The right guard is going to pull and trap. The rest of the line is fire on backer. The center takes a reach step and, if the defensive tackle happens to be coming down inside hard, picks him up. As the tackle comes down, the center can climb to the backer. If the tackle blocks the defensive tackle, then the center can climb to the backer.

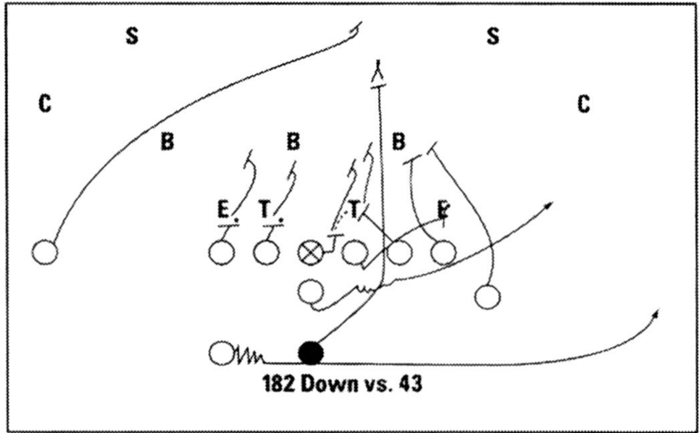

Diagram 5.23

The wingback will block the first backer inside of him. The fullback, because it's a shorter hole, runs a tighter course to the tackle's leg. When the quarterback meshes with him, he can square up and find the hole. If the tackle is going to fight outside the down block, you use a cross-block. But, if you feel good about blocking down on him and can get him walled off, you should feel better about down, because it is faster.

182 Down vs. 4-4 Defense

A fact worth mentioning is, against any even, the tight end knows if the tackle is uncovered, he is going to stretch his split to five feet. A few small exceptions exist to that rule. When he does this, he also widens the off-tackle hole. That change makes the down play hit that much quicker and also makes it much harder to defend, because the defensive end has to close so far to get to it. This fact clearly helps when you run 182 down against the 4-4 defense (Diagram 5.24). Here, the tight end goes to the linebacker. The right tackle will block down. The right guard will pull, trap the defensive end, who has been widened by the tight end's split, and release to the backer. Again, the center will pick up the defensive tackle, if he loops inside, and the tackle will go to backer. If the tackle does not loop inside, then the center goes to the linebacker.

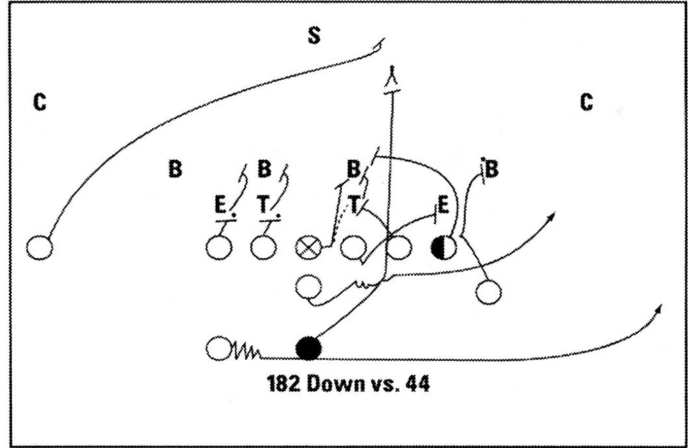

Diagram 5.24

The wingback is going to step down, influence the defensive end, and then turn out on the outside backer, so you have hats for everybody. The spread end goes to the cutoff. The fullback is the ballcarrier, is going to run for the inside foot of the tackle, and squares his shoulders on the mesh when he gets the ball from the quarterback. And, the quarterback and the left half, the latter of whom is going in one-step motion, are going to fake the option play. Anytime you can cave the tackle down, then down is one of the best plays. If you are having trouble with the tackle blocking down, then you run cross block so the backs can read him and cut off his reaction.

182 Down Option vs. 50 Defense

182 down option is a play to attack the #4 defender, if the #3 defender is going to seal all the time (Diagram 5.25). If you block the tight end down inside and the defensive end is going to squeeze or jam the tight end, then down option is a good play to run. You are going to log the defensive end instead of kicking him out and go outside and option the fourth defender. You are going to block #3 and option #4. He's the guy who you pitch or keep the ball off of. That blocking is a little different from normal.

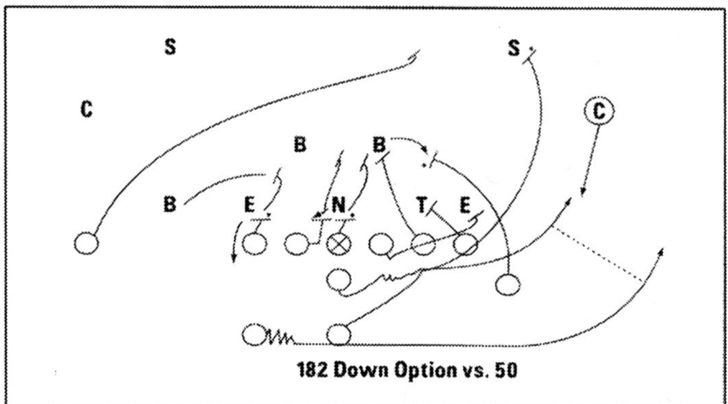

Diagram 5.25

On the down option play, the rules for the linemen are similar to down, but you will tell the tight end he does have a gap assignment. His rule is gap-down-backer. A man is on the tackle, so he's going to come down on him. It's going to look a lot like the down play. The right tackle's rule is gap-down-backer, also. He has no one in his gap and no one to block down on, so he will go to the linebacker. Again, the center, the left guard, and the left tackle are all fire on backer. The center will come off on the nose, while the left guard will read the nose and go to the linebacker, if the center blocks him. The left tackle blocks on. If the nose comes weakside, the guard ends up blocking him and the center comes off to the backer. If the defensive end runs up into the backfield, he's not going to stop this play. The backside tackle can now look for the cutback player. That technique is called sift by the left tackle, and you should practice that all the time. The spread end is going to cutoff.

Next, you're going to option the #4 defender. In this diagram, he is the corner. What you would like to do is have a way to block the #5 defender, who is the safety. You would also like to have the frontside linebacker blocked. When you call down option, the guard knows the defensive end is sealing, so he's coming down to log the defensive end, instead of kicking the defensive end out. You can send the wing inside and make sure the inside linebacker definitely gets blocked, or you can send him down the field and block the free safety or the #5 run defender. The corner is the option key, since he's #4. He's the guy you will keep or pitch the ball off of. You'd like to outside release on him and get the wingback up to the safety. But, a more immediate threat is the linebacker, because, if the tackle squeezes your offensive tackle and the backer scrapes over the top, then you're not able to block him with your right tackle. The wingback can take care of that. So, you don't get the safety blocked, but you don't have a minus-yardage play either.

The fullback is going to run for the inside leg of the tight end, just as he did on 82 down. As he meshes with the quarterback, he's going to bounce and become another blocker in the option alley. If the defensive end is squeezing like you think he will and you call this play and get him logged, then the fullback can bounce, become an extra blocker, and get the safety, and you still have exactly what you need on down option. You have everybody blocked and one guy to pitch off of.

If you like the unbalanced formation, you put the split end over on the tight end-wing side. At this time, you have an extra blocker. Sometimes, a defender doesn't exist to pitch off of.

182 Down Option vs. 4-3 Defense

182 down option versus the 4-3 is illustrated in Diagram 5.26. No difference exists in the play against this defense. In fact, when the tight end blocks on the outside linebacker, he knows, if he cannot get the backer, he can continue on for the middle linebacker because the wing is blocking the outside linebacker, also. The rest of the offensive line is blocking the same rules as 82 down. You are getting a good zone blocking scheme, which accounts for all the stunts. The backfield action remains unchanged. The fullback will again try to be the blocker on the #5 run defender. Again, you keep the ball or pitch the ball off the #4 defender.

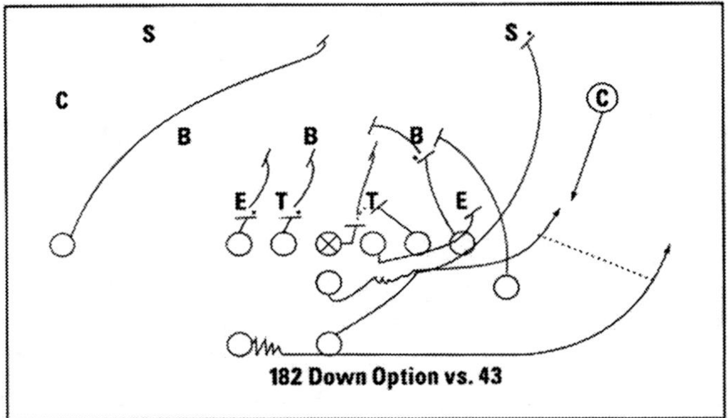

Diagram 5.26

182 Down Option vs. 4-4 Defense

A couple more things need to be discussed about against the 4-4 (Diagram 5.27). The tight end will probably have a gap assignment, since the defensive end is usually an inside shade. He has to make some sort of a call to let his guard know. If the tight end blocks him and the tackle comes down on his assignment, then the guard, as he pulls, doesn't have to log the defensive end; he can wall off inside, at this point. The wing is also an inside blocker, so you have two hats for the first two linebackers who show. The outside linebacker is #4, so he's the defender you're going to keep the ball or pitch the ball off of. The fullback, again, will run his course, and, when he meshes with the quarterback as the quarterback shuffles him up into the line, he's going to block the #5 defender. That assignment is fairly tough and is exactly why you play a lot of unbalanced in order to get an extra blocker to the playside.

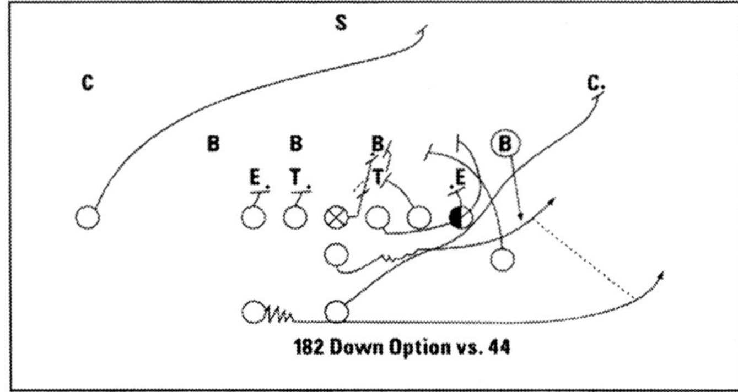

Diagram 5.27

182 down option completes the down option plays. They are a great complement to the offense. They also mix well with 181 keep, when you run keep pass to the tight end and wing. They mix well with 83 pass and 87 counter. You should use them as an integral part of the whole 80 series package.

186 Quick Belly vs. 50 Defense

The last series to discuss in the 80s is called the quick belly. Not a lot of teams, especially a lot of wing-T teams, run this package. But, it is a good package and is the best way to run the belly option.

The 186, the quick belly, is a good play to run to the split end side (Diagram 5.28). You're going to set up the 81 and 89 option plays with this quick belly footwork. The left guard and left tackle are the frontside of the play and have gap-on-backer. The left tackle does have a man on. The left guard is going to come off and block the inside linebacker. Everyone else is fire on backer. So, you zone block the backside of the play. The tight end will have to release outside and cut off the corner.

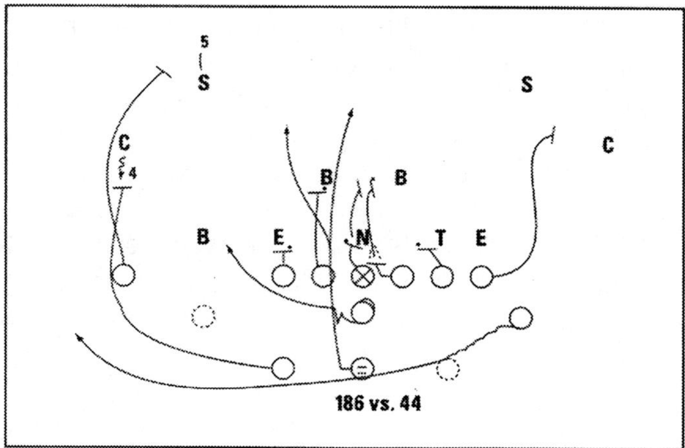

Diagram 5.28

You're going to fake 89 option with the backs, but the fullback and the quarterback have slightly different footwork. The fullback is going to take his lead step, just as he does on 87, but, from then on, he's just going to burst right up over the tail of the guard and option run the linebacker. He is the ballcarrier. This move is the quick belly. The quarterback will jab step with his left foot, reverse pivot, reach the ball back to the fullback, ride him up into the line, then come down, and fake option. The backs and the ends on the side of the play are option blockers. The widest player is to release and stalk #5. The inside player is to flare and block #4. In this diagram, if the corner is going to rotate up, he is the #4 defender, and, when the safety is covering deep, he becomes the #5 defender. The halfback flares and blocks the #4 defender.

The backs are going to do the same thing when you hand the ball off on 86. They are going to show the picture of the option. The only thing you might do differently is put the head to the inside so you can cut off the support angles. Other than that, the backs are going to block the same defenders they block on option, because you want all these plays to look identical. The wing is in three-step motion and is the pitch back.

You could also run 86 from spread 900 formation. You could run it from double-wing formation. It doesn't make any difference what the formation is. You can run all these plays the same way.

186 Quick Belly vs. 4-3 Defense

Diagram 5.29 shows 186, the quick belly versus the 4-3 defense. The line and backfield assignments are all the same. One area of note is the playside guard and center working against the tackle and middle linebacker. The left guard is going to block on, with his head inside, and, most of the time, the defensive tackle is an inside shade. The center can help with the left guard's gap block, if he has to execute this. If not, the center can climb for the middle backer. The fullback has the opportunity to option run the left guard's block and run inside of it or outside of it, depending on where he needs to be. The outside linebacker can step right back inside and make the play. That fact is true. But, it also means he is not going to be aggressive against the option or honor the option fake by the quarterback and wing. If you have to, if you're having a lot of trouble getting that outside backer, you can have the left tackle fake fire, go to the backer, and just let the left defensive end run. If he will run outside with the fake option, you'll do that and just hand the ball right off inside of him. Do not spend a lot of reps on this play. But, if you're going to run the belly option, it's a viable alternative for the quick belly package.

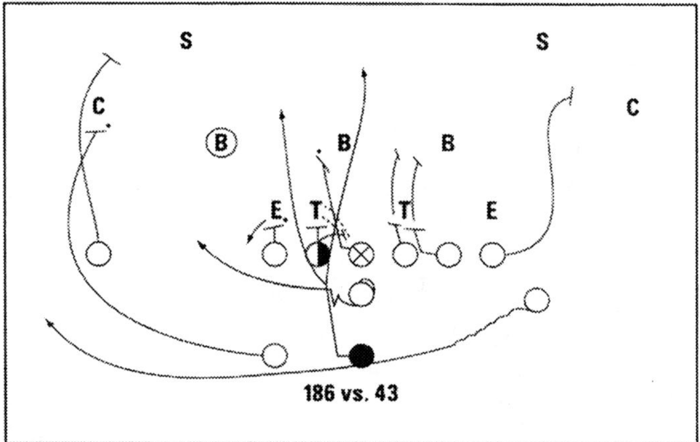

Diagram 5.29

186 Quick Belly vs. 4-4 Defense

When you run 186 against a 4-4 defense, the key is dealing with the playside stack of the tackle and inside linebacker (Diagram 5.30). If you follow the rules, both frontside linemen are gap-on-blocker. They are blocking on, head inside. The center takes his

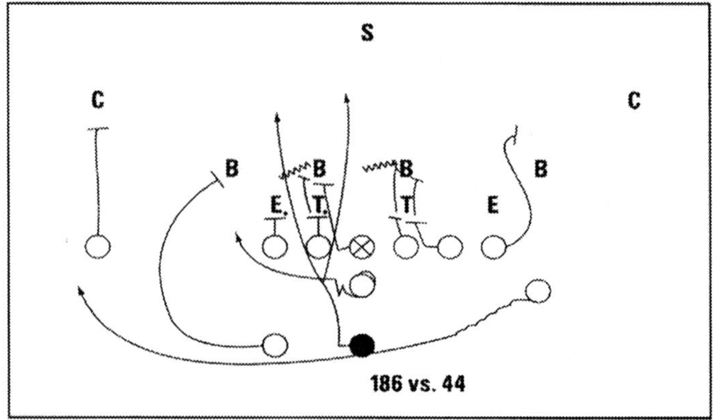

Diagram 5.30

reach step and either climbs to the backer or takes over the defensive tackle, if he slants inside. If he does slant inside, the center will take him while the guard comes off on the linebacker. One of those two has to come off on the inside linebacker.

The spread end releases and stalks #5. The left half flares and blocks #4, who is the outside linebacker in this defense. The rest of the line and backfield action is identical.

189 Option vs. 50 Defense

81 and 89 option, the belly option play (Diagram 5.31), come off of the quick belly and are really the only reason the quick belly is in the playbook. That play is a big part of the offense. You're going to need some kind of fast-flow option to the field, or to the boundary, every year. Sometimes, you can use the belly option; sometimes, you won't. But, the belly option is a great football play, and the quick belly is a little supplement to it, just to let the defense know you will run the quick belly to keep them honest.

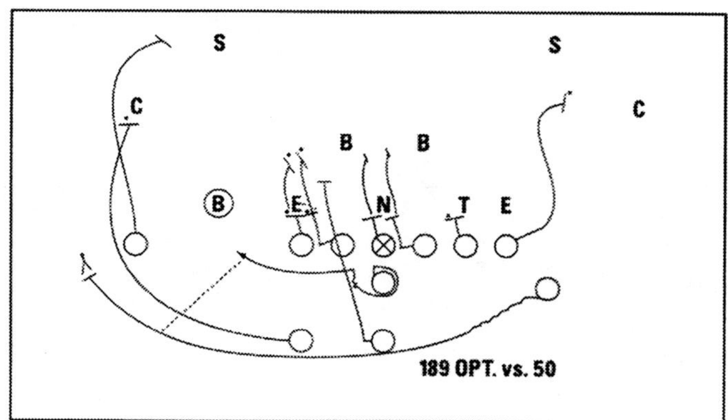

Diagram 5.31

The rules for the offensive linemen are very simple. Again, this play is one where everyone is just fire-on-backer across the entire line. The playside guard and tackle have a little bit of a rule change. If you have 3-on-2, with tackle and guard, then the tackle can shadow to the linebacker. Otherwise, everything you see is fire-on-backer blocking. So, if the defense is a 50 defense, the playside tackle and guard will work to and read the defensive end to the inside linebacker. If the end pinches, the guard takes him and the tackle is on up on the backer. If the end presses outside, the guard goes on up on the backer and the tackle locks on the end. You can pick up the stunts teams use very easily with this scheme. The center and backside guard team together on the backer and nose, and the backside tackle blocks on. The tight end will outside release and cut off the corner.

The fullback uses his quick belly steps, dives hard right for the butt of the guard, and should get tackled. You should make a good fake, but the fullback is another back who can slide through the hole and block linebackers. But, you want the great fake first. You want the quarterback to jab-step forward, reverse pivot, reach the ball back to that fullback, really ride him up into the hole, make people collapse inside, then come on down, and option the third defender. The outside linebacker is #3. He is the defender you're going to keep or pitch off of. The split end is to release and block #5. In this diagram, the corner will probably be #4, so the split end will release outside of him and block the safety. The halfback is assigned to flare and block #4. The outside man has #5, the inside man has #4, and you option #3. If you call option load, then the inside man will load #3, the outside man will block #5, and you still option #4. If you call option crack, which you could do, the outside guy cracks #4, the inside guy flares on #5, and you still option #3. A lot of different option blocking schemes can be used. The right half is in three-step motion, comes across the backfield, and gets in pitch relationship with the quarterback. The quarterback will come on down the line and option the third defender.

189 Option vs. 4-3 Defense

Against the 4-3 defense (Diagram 5.32), 189 option options the #3 player, the outside linebacker. Still a seven-man front and a four-deep secondary, it uses all the same blocking rules. You don't have a 3-on-2 frontside, so you don't have anything to worry about in terms of a shadow technique by the tackle. The tackle is on the defensive end, the center and left guard work their fire on backer rules together, and the guard and backside tackle team together to read the backside tackle and linebacker. The tight end will outside release and cut off corner support. The backfield assignments and action remain the same.

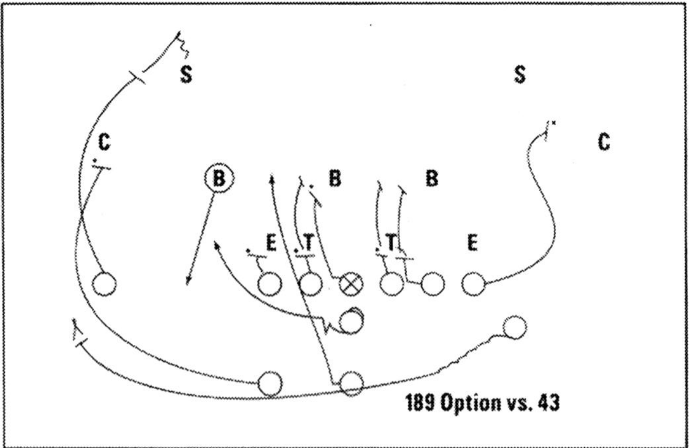

Diagram 5.32

These plays can all be run from spread 900. You can run them to a spread end and a wingback. You can put both halfbacks in the wing. You can put either halfback in the wing and the other one in a diveback position – it doesn't really make much difference. The rules take care of it, and you block it the same way every time.

189 Option vs. 4-4 Defense

Against a 4-4 in this example, 189 option encounters a 3-over-2 situation to the playside when running to the split end side (Diagram 5.33). The left tackle has three on two with him and the left guard. At this point, you would allow the tackle to shadow. He will go ahead, shadow, and block the inside linebacker using shadow technique, meaning he will pull outside the defensive end and cut off the inside linebacker as he scrapes. If the defensive end is wide, then the tackle takes one step, goes inside, and blocks the linebacker. He shouldn't try to go around an end. The end isn't going to let the tackle around him. But, you are going to be three on two. The third defender is the one you're going to option, so you don't need to block the third defender, anyway. You want to block #1 and #2 with the tackle and the guard, option the third defender, and block #4 and #5 with the halfback and the end. Everybody else is fire-on-backer. The tight end is going to release outside and cut off the backside support.

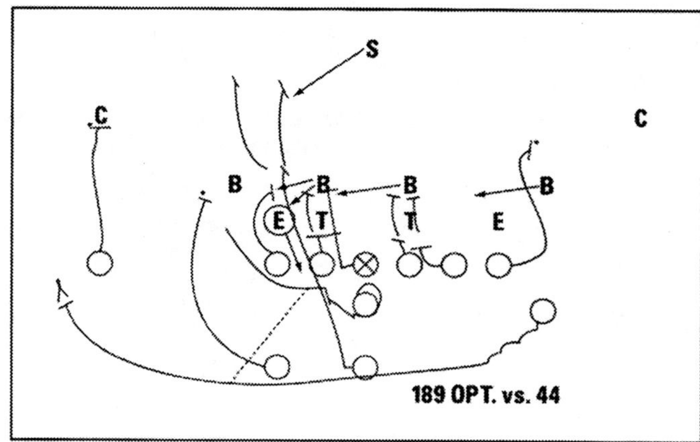

Diagram 5.33

The line and the backs execute the play using all the same rules. The halfback flares and blocks #4. The outside linebacker is #4 and is potentially much closer in this defense. After taking the fake, the fullback can almost come through and block the safety. The tackle, as he shadows (if the inside linebacker steps up and plays the fullback), can then go to the safety. If you can get one of those two players to be an alley blocker for you, then you can take care of any active safety trying to run through the alley on the option. So, you've got answers for most everything that they'll do to you. In this case, against the 4-4, #3 is closer to the quarterback. The quarterback must get his eyes snapped around and look at him quickly. You might have to make a quick pitch. You might have to even abort the fake to the fullback and pitch the ball early. If that defensive end who's getting shadowed crashes down inside quickly, you forget the ride to the fullback, just snap your hands back and get the ball pitched to the halfback quickly.

189 Option Gut

A couple of adjustments can be made with option blocking, and a few exist for inside problems. For outside problems, you can use load or crack. For inside problems, using either gut or pitch is recommended. Following are examples of 189 option with gut and pitch. If you call 189 option gut (Diagram 5.34), what you're doing is taking advantage of a defender playing on the offensive tackle, who's really reading and riding releases hard and not going to let the tackle down inside. In this case, you're going to have the tackle come down inside and try to get the frontside linebacker. Between those two, you're going to make sure you get two linebackers blocked. You're doing this because the defensive 5 technique is squeezing your tackle hard. The fullback takes that lead step, dives hard for the outside leg of the guard, then adjusts his path, and blocks the defensive end. In college, you can cut him; in high school, you can only block him at the hip. If he's squeezing really hard and won't let your tackle off on the linebackers, then this little adjustment is nice for him. If they're squeezing, where the ends squeeze and the backer scrapes really fast on that natural X principle, this adjustment pretty well handles natural X teams. Everybody else in the option blocking scheme is blocking the same. The only difference here is the left guard and the left tackle, or the playside guard and tackle, are going to execute a gut scheme. As that tackle comes down inside, you want him to try to get the first backer. If he can't, then go ahead and get the backside backer, and even possibly a safety, if necessary. This alteration is an option gut change-up in the blocking scheme.

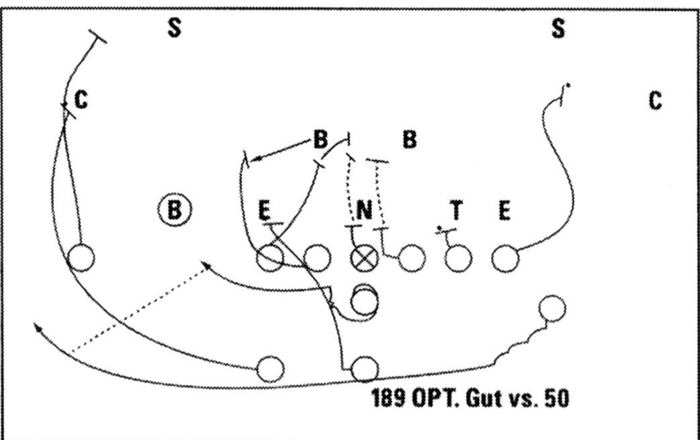

Diagram 5.34

189 Option Pitch

The last change is 189 option pitch (Diagram 5.35). On this play, the halfback and the guard are going to switch assignments. The halfback, instead of being a flank blocker and blocking the fourth man in the option, will now block inside on the linebacker. The guard will now block the fourth guy. If you have a halfback who is having a whole lot of trouble blocking the fourth defender, you can call 189 option pitch. The word pitch alerts the quarterback you'll probably get the ball pitched because you're not going to flare across the face of the option key. Rather, you're going to actually go down inside of him and probably make him squeeze. So, the ball will probably get pitched. Pitch alerts the quarterback a little bit and also adjusts the blocking. Normally, the left halfback is coming out to block the corner. In pitch, he is going to come inside and block the linebacker. You know the guard is going to pull and then block #4. He's going to kick out #4, or he can try to log him, depending on how wide he is. You are probably going to pitch the ball. If you kick the corner out, the halfback can take the cutback alley.

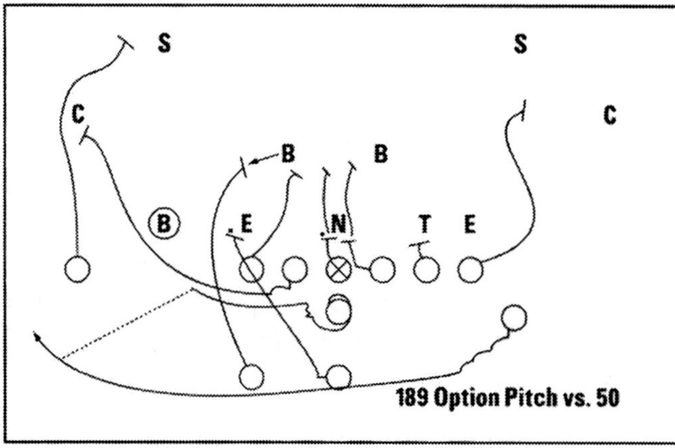

Diagram 5.35

The left tackle has two alternatives on option pitch. You can have him block on and have the fullback go through, like he always does. Or, if you know the tackle is a seal player, you can have him release inside and let the fullback take care of the defensive end again. You are still going to option off the third defender, who is the outside linebacker. With this block by the left halfback, you're pretty sure the ball will be pitched, or at least think it will. If the defensive end, that third defensive player, runs to the pitch right, you've got the inside pretty well sealed, and you're going to be off to the races with the quarterback running down through the option alley.

Those change-ups are what you can do to block the option game. You've seen crack blocking on trap option crack. Load blocking occurs when you load #3 and pitch off of #4. These changes give you a good handle on the different ways to run the option and make sure, no matter what the defensive problems are, you've got a way to run the option successfully.

186 Scissors at 4 vs. 50 Defense

The scissors play is a great little play off of this action. Some people call this play Sally. You block it just a little bit differently from Sally and call it scissors to designate the difference. On this play, you start the 89 option, or the 868 quick belly action, and then hand the ball on a counter coming back inside. You've already learned the blocking scheme with counter draw, and scissors is blocked with the same scheme and called 186 scissors at 4 (Diagram 5.36).

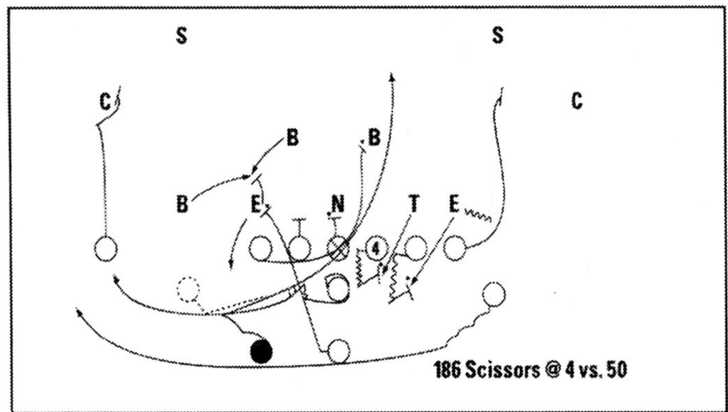

Diagram 5.36

The right guard and right tackle are to the playside, and the rule is outside, so they are going to step inside, show pass, and invite the two defensive linemen to sprint up the field. They basically block the defender where they show, meaning the guard is going to block the defender rushing in the B gap and the tackle is going to block the defender who goes to the C gap. They will show pass and will stay in their pass protection until they see the defenders flying upfield. As soon as they see that, it turns into a run block. In that case, it would be right shoulder, right direction. You want to invite those people up the field – get them to create a cavity in the defense.

The center's rule is left-gap-on-right. He does have a man on him, but he will move his head away from the called point of attack. He does put his head to the left on this play and on counter draw, only to protect the quarterback mesh. The backside guard, who would be the left guard in this case, has on-area-or delayed to the backer. So, he steps up, blocks the area, and goes delayed to the backer. The fullback takes his quick-belly footwork, dives for the outside leg of the guard, and blocks the first defender who shows in the B gap area. If the defensive linemen run up the field, then the fullback is not going to be a factor in the play. However, he can keep going and look for a defender coming at the next level, possibly a cutback linebacker or a fast-flow linebacker. The fullback can help block those people. The left tackle's rule is to pull and gut. He's the backside tackle, so you tell him to turn right up over the center. If the center blocks the nose to the left, he is going to come all the way around them. If he blocks the nose to the right, the tackle is going to pull up short of him. His job is to come up through the hole and block the backside linebacker. The spread end is going to release down the field like he's going to stalk the corner and slide to inside-out position on him. Remember, you have the tight end release outside on this whole package of plays and want him to release outside on this play, especially because you want to loosen the technique of the backside end. If he's a reader or trying to jam the tight end, he's going to be way outside jamming before he tries to come back upfield, and the hole will be wider. This extra width in the hole slows his pursuit down tremendously.

The right half will come in three-step motion and fake the option, with the quarterback. The quarterback takes that good footwork – jab step, reverse pivot, ride that fullback in – but, at this point, instead of coming downhill or coming out and attacking the flank on the option, he's going to step back and hand the ball off to the left halfback. If the left halfback is in a wing position, he takes one step of gut and then runs right for the tail of the center. If he is in the diveback position, you tell him to take his right foot, cross over one step, take his left foot, continue on that same angle, then plant, and break back over the center. The quarterback then hands the ball off to the halfback coming right inside of him. As the quarterback reverse pivots and rides the fullback, all he has to do is step back, hand the ball off inside, then continue out, and fake option.

186 Scissors at 4 vs. 4-3 Defense

You can run this football play against any defense and from any formation. It makes no difference if the halfbacks are in the diveback spot or the wingback spot, because you can still run the play. Looking at 186 scissors at 4 versus a 4-3 defense (Diagram 5.37), the backfield action is exactly the same.

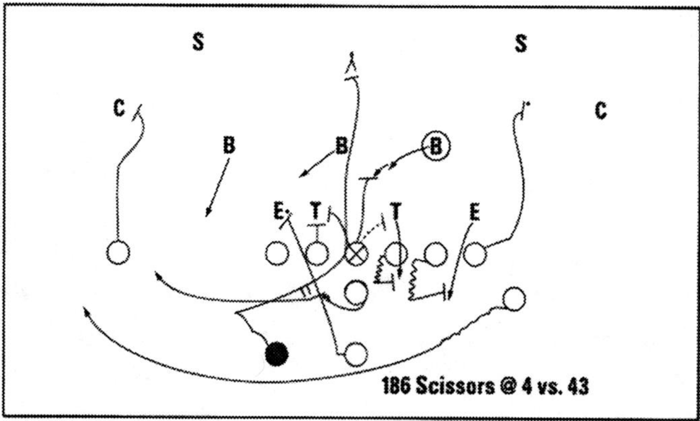

Diagram 5.37

You get into some tricky stuff against even defenses, so you must be sure about your rules. The right tackle and right guard are going to show pass and block the rushers where they see them. The center will block left, if the defensive tackle is an inside shade player. When the right guard shows pass, he must invite the tackle to rush up the field. If the tackle does not rush up the field and pinches inside, then your pulling tackle has to trap him. At least you'll get back to the line of scrimmage and won't have a minus-yardage play, although you probably won't gain much ground if you don't block the linebackers. The guard on the backside has his man on. If he can get his defender blocked without the center, then the center can block to the right, giving you an extra blocker to block playside. If the center can block to the right, the guard can block B gap or can leave and go to the linebacker level. Then you have an extra linebacker blocker. That possibility might be the optimum case. If you can get the right guard to block the outside linebacker in the 4-3, then you will have a really good play working.

You should get pretty good flow away from the play, as long as the right halfback fakes the option, the fullback comes inside-out and blocks the first defender who shows, the halfback goes cross-over-plant before he runs the scissors, and the quarterback reverse pivots and shows option action. You should get all the linebackers flowing. Hopefully, you will have a fairly good chance, no matter what happens up front, to get a good looking play run.

The left tackle pulls right up over the tail of the center and blocks the first backer he can find. Normally, you tell him to look for the backside linebacker because, once you've created flow, all those other backers are going to run out of the play. Team's running scissors have caused 4-3 middle linebackers to be all the way on the line of scrimmage away from the play, before they recognize the ball was handed off on the scissors play. The linebackers in the 4-3 want to run. Coaches recruit smaller people, faster people, and expect them to run like heck. Once they get them running, the misdirection can really work on them. The only real danger at linebacker is probably going to be the backside linebacker, once you've really created flow. You've got the tackle to block him. If you can get the offensive guard up the field to block him, then the tackle can look for either the safety or the middle backer.

186 Scissors at 4 vs. 4-4 Defense

If you call 186 scissors at 4 versus the 4-4 defense, the rules should hold up (Diagram 5.38). The left guard has to block a 2 technique on. If the defender is a one shade or A gap player, the guard will help on him and then go delayed to the backer. The center, then, has to block back on the inside shade. If the left gap is a problem, the center must go block it. Hopefully, you can get the guard to handle the defender by himself and let the center use his right assignment, which would be great. Then, the right guard and the right tackle, your playside linemen, can execute their outside technique, and you will block the C gap rusher with the tackle and the B gap rusher with the guard. If the defensive tackle does rush B gap and the guard blocks him, the center can go to the backside linebacker. If the defensive tackle over the right guard goes inside and the center blocks him, then the right guard is free to go to the backside linebacker. So, one of those two – either the center or the right guard – will block the tackle, while the other one blocks the backside linebacker. The tight end will release outside and cut off corner support. The left tackle is going to pull and gut. He pulls right up over the tail of the center and is probably going to block the backside inside linebacker, who's scraping fast. The fullback takes a little lead step, dives for the outside leg of the guard, and then blocks the first defender who shows off the tackle's tail. The spread end will get inside out on the corner.

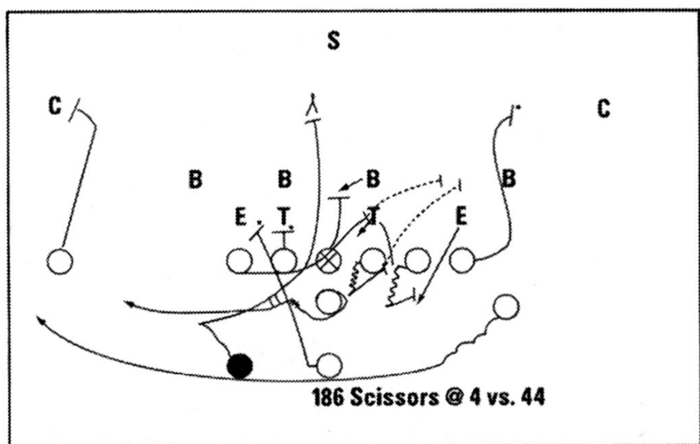

Diagram 5.38

The backfield action is unchanged on scissors. You can run this scissors play versus any kind of spacing you get. The rules will hold up. They will even holdup on the goal line defense, but you'll have to trap the backside A gap player. Anytime a pulling tackle who's assigned a gut has a problem penetrating, he traps it. You will get to the line of scrimmage, and the backers will make the play, but, at least, it's not a minus-yardage play. The players have to be coached that way. Theirs has to be a conditioned response.

189 Waggle vs. 50 Defense

The last play in the 80 series, or the quick-belly package, is the 81 and 89 waggle (Diagram 5.39). If you're going to show the same action as the quick belly, then you're going to want the wingback, the backside halfback, to come in three-step motion. You're going to want the fullback to take the quick-belly action. The word waggle means to attack opposite the hole called. The number called is 9, but waggle means you're going to attack the flank opposite the 9 hole. The backs, however, are going to go ahead, use the quick-belly footwork, and show option to the left.

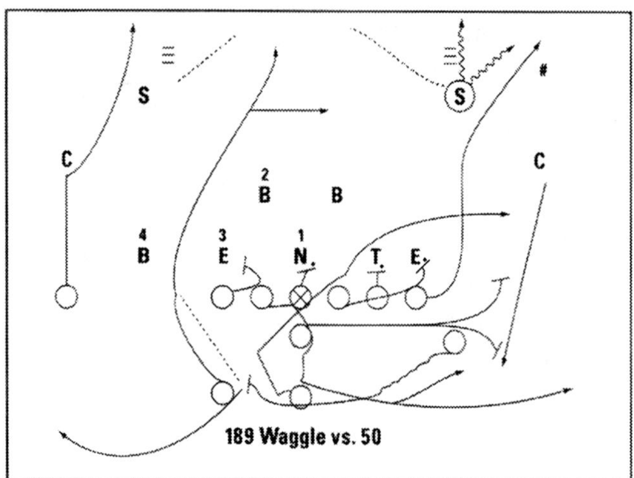

Diagram 5.39

Waggle tells the line exactly how to block. The blocking was explained in the 20 series package. The right tackle has gap-down-on. He's going to block the defensive tackle on him with his head to the outside and use aggressive technique. The right guard is going to pull and log the defensive end. The center is block 1 or cup left, so he blocks the nose with an aggressive technique. The backside guard is pull, cross over and lead the quarterback around the flank. He kicks out any penetration or blitz that might happen. The backside tackle is pull, check the second man, or he can block back on the third man.

You release the tight end outside to run his route. This route marries up with the rest of the 80 series, where he has been releasing outside. He can run his waggle route with an outside release. If you want to down release him, that choice is fine, too, and would help set up an easier log block. Both have a lot of merit. The spread end has the backside route. As the outside man, he runs a post and stays outside the hash mark. You want the tight end to run his waggle route deep on the numbers. The left halfback is going to run for a point one and a half yards outside the end man and right down the middle of the defense. If no safety exists, the halfback continues down the middle, splitting the two safeties. If a safety is somewhere between 10 and 15 yards, he will break it off and stay between the hash marks. If any safety rotates to the middle, he breaks it off. The fullback takes his quick-belly footwork and, on his way through the hole, is going to the backside flat (away from the number, but to the quarterback's waggle action), just as he does on 29 waggle.

The right half comes in three-step motion. When he passes the quarterback, he gears down, gets inside out, and blocks any defender who shows outside the left tackle's block. He is a blocker first. If no defender is there to block, he can go ahead and flare. At this point, the quarterback is going to come out and threaten the flank. He must step up inside any kick-out block. He looks for deep, short, or run. If the safety on the waggle side happens to rotate to the middle, you should have a touchdown to the tight end. If he backs up, it is still a good pass. You should be able to go deep, short, run, and be successful. If he rotates to the waggle side, then the quarterback knows he is going to be throwing back. When he throws back, the defense does not have enough people backside. The safety has rotated to the waggle side, but you have a post route to throw to and a crossing route to throw to. You always have the backside halfback possibly on the flare. You can run waggle to the split end side or to the tight end side; it doesn't matter.

189 Waggle vs. 4-3 Defense

Diagram 5.40 clearly illustrates no difference exists for the line or the receivers on 189 waggle or 29 waggle. The fullback is the guy who shows you the difference. He'll take his lead step and dive for the outside leg of the guard, just as in 86 quick belly. The quarterback is not reverse pivoting all the way around; he's taking two steps on the midline. The fullback's first step is the same as belly, so the defense will flow. Linebackers flow like crazy when this play is run – especially if they are assigned to key the fullback. This play is a great guard key breaker for the fullback. A lot of coaches do exactly that – key the guards and the fullback. The fullback, as he passes the quarterback, will come on out to the flat with the quarterback. This move is an important coaching point. The 89 waggle is not the kind of play you run if the inside backers like to blitz. In that case, you would go back and run 29 waggle or 29 waggle solid, because those plays pick up the blitzing very successfully.

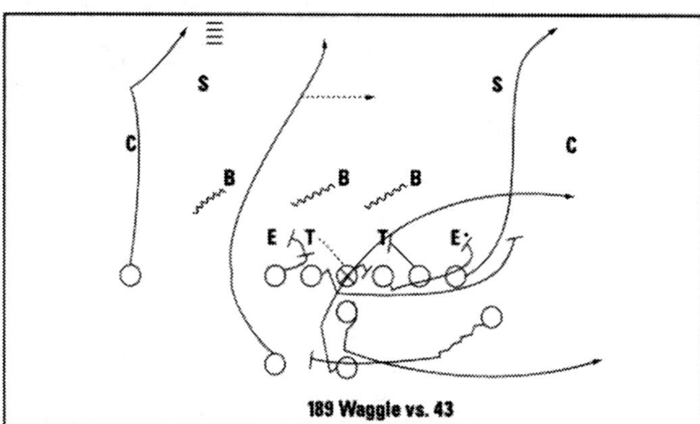

Diagram 5.40

189 Waggle vs. 4-4 Defense

Diagram 5.41 shows 189 waggle versus the 4-4 defense. A couple of key points of emphasis exist when attacking the eight-man front. If the tight end is assigned to use a down release or release inside on the pass, then the tight end can use a block release because of the inside shaded defender, before he runs his waggle route. If you are releasing him outside to make the play look like the other 80 series plays, then run his waggle route with the same outside release. Block release is a pretty good way to handle those 7 techniques. The release helps to slow the defensive end down and also helps the log block. But, in either case, run the waggle route and get deep on the numbers.

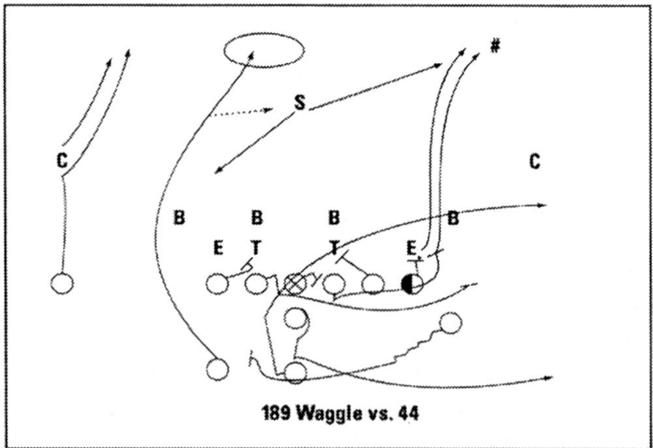

Diagram 5.41

The rest of the routes and the backfield action are identical to what has previously been discussed. The action of waggle pass protection versus the eight-man front doesn't change there, either.

Against the 4-4, if the middle safety rotates really hard to the action side, then the quarterback knows he is going to be throwing back. The corner is probably going to be covering the post, and, if the safety rotates to the waggle side, then no one is there for the halfback going right down through the seam. That danger exists for any rotating secondary.

186 Pass

One more concept exists in the quick-belly package, and that play is 86 pass (Diagram 5.42). The 86 pass is like 83 pass. This play is where you fake the quarterback-fullback action and then drop straight back. This play incorporates exactly the same blocking rules as in 87 pass. The rules are exactly the same for the linemen; they don't have to learn anything new.

It's up to you as a coach whether or not you want to throw play-action off the 83 and 87 footwork of the fullback or if you want to throw play-action off this 86 action. The only difference is the look of the backfield, especially the fullback's action.

The tight end is going to outside release and will get to about 14 yards of depth. You would like him to be very wide. If the ball is snapped from the hash mark, you

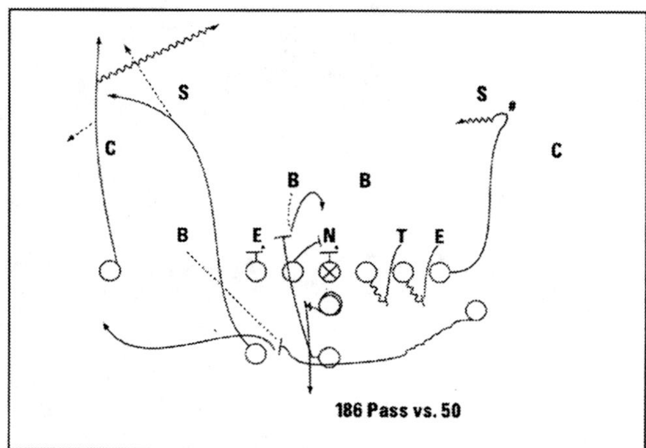

Diagram 5.42

want him out on the numbers. He will hook up at 14 and slide to the open area, wherever he can find it. The spread end runs a fly, and the left halfback runs a banana, the base route on 86 pass. If you decide to switch these routes up, then calling switch will bring the spread end on an out route and put the left halfback on a deep corner route. You can also add post, which puts the spread end on a post cut, while the halfback still stays on the banana cup.

The fullback is going to take his lead step, dive hard for the butt of the guard, and block the inside linebacker, if he comes. The wing is in three-step motion. When he passes the quarterback-fullback mesh, he will gear down and be responsible for the outside linebacker, if he comes. If neither backer blitzes, then the fullback hooks over the ball and the halfback flares wide. The quarterback will reverse pivot, ride the fullback, then drop five steps, and execute his pass reads. This blocking scheme is exactly the same as 87 pass, so the question is do you need it? It's up to you, the coach. If you want to use the whole quick-belly package, then this play is one more complement to the package. If not, you can get the same out of 87 pass, as the quarterback fakes 87 footwork. The quarterback and the fullback will be using 87 footwork rather than quick-belly footwork. The tight end releases outside in this entire package, because you have a hook route and the waggle route, you've widened the defensive end on the scissors, and you've cut off the corners on the 86 and the 89 option.

Summary

The quick-belly package completes the entire 80 series package. It is very comprehensive. The 80 series is a big part of the wing-T game, all the time, every year. You fullback will usually be close to 1,000 yards every year, if not over, and it may very well be the different blocking schemes you use in the 87 and the 83 that will constitute your number one play year in and year out.

6

Goal Line Attack

This chapter will review the wing-T goal line and short-yardage offense. Any book on the wing-T would be incomplete without a discussion of the goal line attack. Before putting together an effective goal line plan, a few questions should be discussed about the wing-T and about running it against various goal line defenses.

Goal Line Package Questions

First, when exactly should you go to goal line offense? Some important factors need to be considered. For example, do you go to goal line offense when you get to the three (or any) yard line? And, what about personnel changes? Do you need a goal line attack if the opponent does not go to a goal line defense? Most teams have a goal line defensive package inside the five yard line. They go to their goal line defense by substitution or to a different style of defense with the same personnel. The defense, at some point, will change its personality. But, is that when you go to goal line offense? You will have to answer those questions every week, and, sometimes, the answers are different from week to week.

The next questions to ask are: What personnel are you going to use? Are you going to keep the same personnel in the game? Or, are you going to substitute more big people? When you substitute big people, will the defense substitute more big people? Is it a fair trade-off? You also need to decide when to end goal line offense. For example, if you get the ball first down on the three yard line and get thrown for a two-yard loss on the first play, will you then get out of goal line? To answer that question, you will take the number of yards to the goal line and divide by the number of downs you have in which to score. If you start first-and-goal on the six yard line, then you need to make two yards per play on the first three plays, if you don't want to kick a field goal. If, on the first play, you make only one yard, then you are off schedule. Since it is now second-and-five, you have to make more than two yards per play. At this point, do you get out of goal line? You must make that determination on the basis of your players' abilities.

The final questions you must answer are as follows: What formation, or formations, do you use? How many formations are you going to use? What plays are in you goal line attack? How many plays are you going to run? What are the strengths and weaknesses of each team's goal line defense, and where should you attack that defense?

The following is a typical example of a goal line defense and a typical example of how to do game planning (Diagram 6.1). If you look at the defense in the diagram, you see a 6-2 defense. This team has probably made some kind of personnel change, unless they run eight-man fronts all the time and play only three defensive backs. Normally, you will not see two noseguards in the game, but you will see four defensive backs. Seeing a big guy coming in for a small guy is a good clue your opponent will be in some kind of goal line defense.

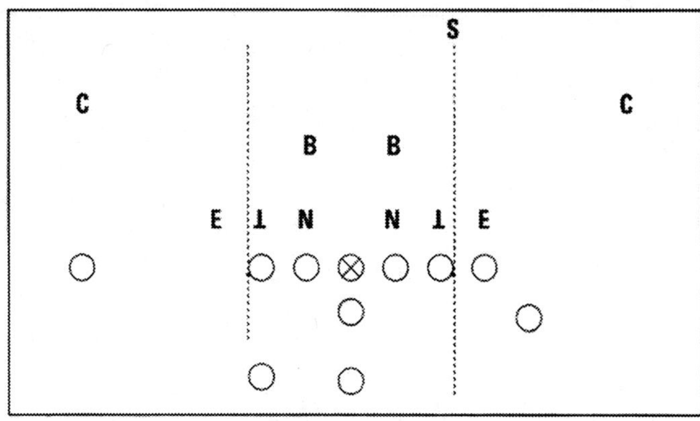

Diagram 6.1

Goal Line Game Planning Principles

Take the 6-2 defense and apply game-planning principles to this look. What are the game-planning principles? First, you draw an imaginary line through the outside foot of each of the tackles. Next, you count how many people are inside those imaginary lines.

The defensive backs will not be included for now; you will only count the front people. Anytime you get five or more people inside that box, you will decide to attack the flank. In this picture, four defensive linemen and two linebackers are in the box. If five people indicates attacking the flank, then what does six people indicate? The answer is to definitely attack the flank. In goal line situations, the defensive backs can crowd the line of scrimmage and play like linebackers, forcing you to account for them. You would definitely begin at the flank in these situations.

Some plays are run inside the tackles, even though you are facing a six-on-five numbering problem. Sometimes, going inside is worth the gamble because you might need only six inches. You will jam it up in there and knock the defense back to get six inches before linebackers and defensive backs can actually stop the play. You must have confidence the offensive line can do that. Otherwise, you will be relegated to a flank attack, even in one yard or less situations.

In this defense, as you see from the diagram, you should have flanking angles or one side of the defense outnumbered. You should be able to attack the flank and make good things happen, especially with run-pass options. This goal line attack works because you run the basic plays of the offense. You will make those base plays work against the goal line defense. If you have gone all the way down the field with a certain style of offense, then you should not have to change when in scoring territory.

As a rule, run-and-shoot offenses are able to move the ball effectively between the 20 yard lines. Yet, these offenses tend to stall when close to the goal line, where the field shrinks and fewer passing plays can be run. They cannot change their style and run the ball in from there. They are often unsuccessful because their emphasis is not on power running. The wing-T, on the contrary, will run the ball up and down the field with the base offense, and, when it gets to the goal line, you will continue to run those same plays. You might have to adjust the blocking slightly, but you will continue to run the same plays until you score. Against the 6-2 defense, you need to be able to attack the flank efficiently and save the inside plays for certain downs and distances where you feel the required yardage can be made for sure.

Goal Line Formations

In this section, the goal line attack will be illustrated from favorite formations. Two formations are used most in the goal line attack. The first formation is two tight ends, the fullback in his position, and either one of the halfbacks in the wing position with the other one in the diveback position, or double wing with both halfbacks in wingback positions. These formations give you good formation integrity in that you can go to either side with or without motion. The preferred formation is regular tight wing with two tight ends.

The second formation is an unbalanced formation. You put the wingback to the left, the diveback to the right, the tight end to the right, and the split end to the right in a four-yard split position. If a team is a corner blitz team or likes to blitz the safeties off the edge, then the extra man puts them in a dilemma. If they are going to blitz a strong safety or a corner, is he going to come from the outside? If he comes from the outside, you have widened him, and he is not as dangerous. If he comes from the inside, you have a flanking angle on him and can block him with the extra player.

If you have enough high-quality tight ends, you will substitute a tight end for the split end. The tight ends can go to either side and have mirrored assignments. If you keep the split end in the game and go with a tight formation, the split end should go to the pass and away from the run. The tight end then goes to the run and away from the pass. If you have two true tight ends, then you play the tight ends left and right, giving no tendencies to the defense.

When you go to the unbalanced formation, the split end will be either the normal split end or a second tight end substituted for the split end. When a second tight end comes in, he does not dictate any certain formation. You can be in tight 100, tight 500, or tight 900. These formations are favorites because all three give different advantages against different defenses.

Closed and Tight Calls

If you use two tight ends, you can call closed. If you are in 100 formation with two tight ends, you will call closed 100. Closed is the opposite of loose. If you call loose, you will have both ends spread out wide. If you call closed, you have both ends in tight end positions. You can also call tight 100. If you call tight 100, then both ends come into a tight end position, but this change also closes the splits in the offensive line. If you want two tight ends, but you want to keep normal splits in the offensive line, you will call closed 100. If you want two tight ends and also want to close down all the splits, then you will call tight 100. You can do that with any of your formations and use the terms closed or tight and do exactly what was just described. You either tighten down the splits or bring both ends into a tight end position. If you use the prefix tight, not only do the ends come into the tight end position, but you also change the offensive line spacing. The guards, the tackles, and the tight ends will move to one-foot splits. The defense is crowding the football, will try to penetrate, and try to get off before being blocked. The next thing tight does is get the offensive linemen up on the ball, so the offensive linemen put their feet even with the center's feet. Their helmets are about even with the center's helmet when you look at the line from the side. Normally, those linemen are back as far off the ball as they are legally allowed to be. Tight is the call used in this discussion of goal line offense.

Tight 944 Wedge

In this package, the first play run is for a six-inch gain. Two methods exist for gaining six inches, and both are blocked identically. The ballcarrier is a different person, and the backfield action is different, but the blocking scheme for both plays is wedge blocking. The diagram shows tight 900 formation (Diagram 6.2): two tight ends, closed-down splits, and the wingback to the left. If you want the opposite formation, the right half is in a wingback position and the left halfback is in a diveback position. That play is called tight 100.

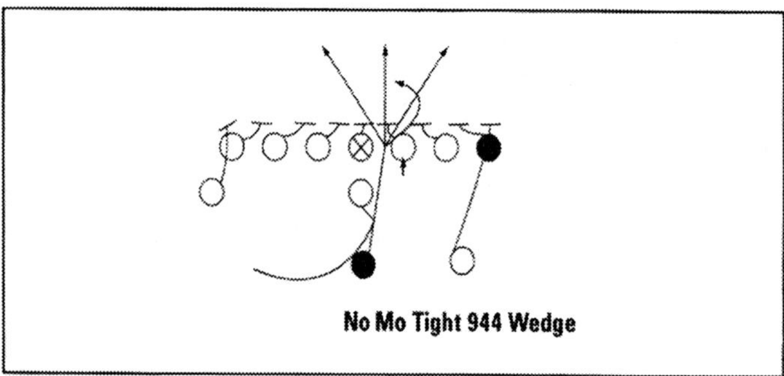

Diagram 6.2

The first play is tight 944 wedge. In tight 944 wedge, the line blocking will simply be wedge blocking. Wedge blocking is established as the center takes a fire step with his right foot. The right guard takes a fire step inside with his left foot. The center and the right guard form what is called the focal point of the wedge. This seam is the point of attack. It is also the initial aiming point for the backs, who will adjust from there. The left guard will fire step, but his job is to take his right shoulder and wedge it to the left shoulder of the center with no space between them. You cannot allow space, which is one reason why the splits are cut down to one foot. You must get the head across the front of any penetrators and get your playside shoulder wedged to the backside shoulder of the center. The left tackle and the left tight end are going to do the exact same thing. They will block inside and wedge their right shoulder to the left shoulder of the man adjacent to them on the inside. The right tackle and the right tight end will execute the same technique. The right tackle will wedge his inside shoulder to the right shoulder of the offensive guard, while the right tight end will wedge his left shoulder to the right shoulder of the offensive tackle.

Both halfbacks will be blockers. You will not use any motion and, therefore, will prefix the play with no mo, again, meaning no motion. The back in the diveback position will run as fast as possible for the tail of the offensive tackle and block off the end's tail. He must get his inside shoulder wedged next to the tight end and not allow any penetration inside. If he is in a wingback position, the same is done: run as fast as possible for the tackle's position off the tight end's tail and put the head to the inside of any penetration. He will wedge his inside shoulder to the outside shoulder of the man adjacent to him. The two backs will wedge their inside shoulders to the tight ends' outside shoulders.

The fullback will be the ballcarrier on 44 wedge, which is an open pivot dive play by him and the quarterback. The fullback will attack the center-guard seam on the right, but the quarterback will take the ball back as deep as possible for the handoff. The fullback can run through the called point of attack; jump over the pile; and break backside, if a seam exists, or break outside, if a seam is there. After the quarterback hands the ball off, he will fake a naked bootleg and, hopefully, pull a defensive player with him.

This play is quick hitting, and, many times, the fullback will jump over the pile to get into the end zone. If he is big enough, he can ram his way into the end zone. When you first practice goal line offense, the offensive line gets on the ball and the defensive players hold those big 100-pound blocking bags. Rather than having bodies on the ground, you will hold blocking bags in the same places where the goal line defense of your next opponent will be aligned. When facing the 6-2 spacing, you will put the backers and the defensive backs in their positions without any shields or big bags. You want the big bags up in the neutral zone. When you first practice the wedge play, you block the big bags.

By doing this, the offensive backs get a good feel for where the holes will be. You can do this with minimal danger or no danger at all to your offensive and defensive players because they are holding bags and no bodies piling up on each other. You can practice goal line without scrimmaging. The first few times you practice goal line, you practice against those big bags. After the backs and the linemen learn to feel where holes are, then you practice live situations.

The 44 wedge requires that everyone wedge his shoulder to the shoulder of the adjacent blocker, get off the ball, and allow no penetration. You will get those six inches if no offensive lineman allows penetration.

Tight 924 Quarterback Sneak

For the same required yardage, another play is designed to do the same thing. This play is also wedge blocking, except you also run quarterback sneak. The backs will show buck action. If you call tight 924 quarterback sneak, the line blocks wedge blocking (Diagram 6.3). The center will fire with his right foot, and the right guard will fire inside with his left foot. Those two get their shoulders together and form the focal point of the wedge. Everybody else wedges his inside shoulder to the outside shoulder of the man next to him.

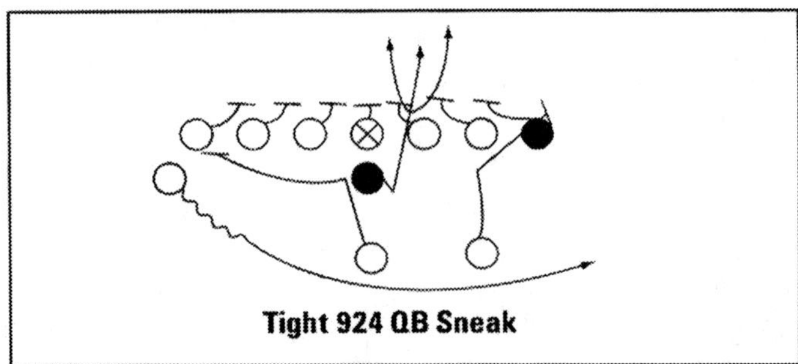

Diagram 6.3

The fullback is one of the wedge blockers. Normally, on 24, the fullback steps with his right foot for the left foot of center; the same is true on sneak, where his first step is the same as in any 24 guard trap. He will then veer tight off the tight end's tail and be a part of the wedge. The wingback will fake 21 sweep. The left halfback will go in three-step motion to take the sweep. The right halfback will dive for the tail of the right tackle and wedge his inside shoulder to the outside shoulder of the tight end. He will be one of the wedge blockers. The quarterback takes the snap and runs to the right center-guard seam, just as the fullback did on 44 wedge. He will run through the first opening he can find. He could try to jump over the pile. You simply tell your quarterbacks to get as much yardage in any bubble they can find. You are only looking for six inches here. You don't want a home run play. Wedge and sneak are the plays used for very short yardage – in other words, less than one yard.

Tight 187 On

For situations requiring one full yard, you will call tight 187 or tight 983 on. In Diagram 6.4, the play uses a tight 100 formation and runs tight 187 on. In this case, you will block gap-on-backer with the frontside of the offensive line and fire-on-backer with the backside of the offensive line. You will run this play with or without motion. If you

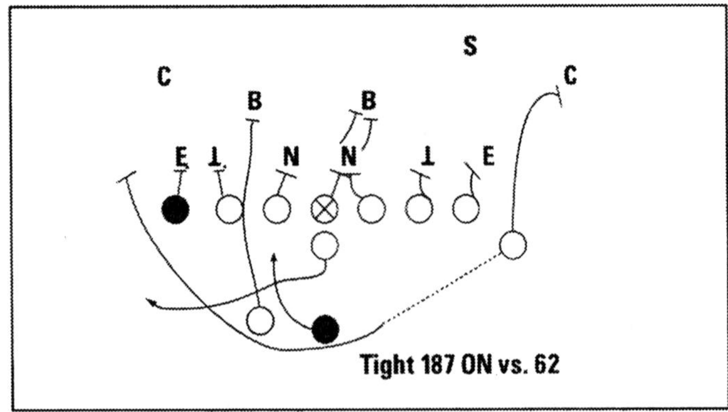

Diagram 6.4

decide not to have motion by the right halfback, you will prefix the call with no mo. The left tackle is the 7 man. He is the point of attack. He uses on technique with his head to the inside. If the defensive tackle pinches, then the left tackle must drive him down inside in the same direction he is pinching. The backs will read his block and adjust.

The left tight end comes off and also blocks on. He will put his head inside and use a left-shoulder block. The left guard will also block gap-on-backer. Against the 6-2, he has an inside defender, so he comes down and blocks gap. The center and the backside linemen, including the backside tight end, are all fire-on-backer. The center, the right guard, the right tackle, and the tight end will fire. What should happen is the center and the left guard both hit the noseguard in the A gap. Depending on the noseguard's reaction, you want the center or the right guard to come off for the backside backer. With one-foot splits, the center can get his head across the front and stop penetration by the A gap player. The left guard comes down to help by striking him before coming off. At this point, the left guard can come off and be the wall off blocker on the backside linebacker.

The left halfback and the fullback are running 87 on. They learned how to run this play early in training camp. The 87 and 83 is a basic play. It is one of the most consistent frequently used plays and is the best short-yardage play. For a full yard, less than a yard, and, sometimes, more than a yard, you will run this play. The left halfback will take off for the outside leg of the guard, while the fullback uses lead, crossover, square-up footwork. The quarterback will reverse pivot beyond the midline and mesh with the fullback on the second step. After he hands off, he will fake keep pass. The left halfback is reading the left tackle's block. If the defensive tackle is pinching down inside, then the left tackle should swing his tail and wash him down inside with his block. If this case exists, the left halfback will adjust to the outside and block the linebacker as he scrapes. If both the tackle and the defensive end are pinching inside, then the play will bounce all the way to the outside. If the left tackle has the defensive tackle blocked out, the halfback will stay on course to the linebacker. As the fullback takes his footwork, he will receive the ball and make the same reads the left halfback made. He will find the hole and accelerate through it. He must run with body lean and knock the pile back.

The wingback will go in motion, or you can call no mo. It depends on how the safeties react to motion. If the middle safety sees the motion and reacts to the flow, you hurt the play by bringing over an extra tackler. You would rather call no mo and let the right halfback be another fire blocker or go to cutoff. If the safety stays stationary, regardless of motion, then you will bring the halfback in motion. He will log the first free man at the flank to provide an extra blocker. The quarterback will fake the keep pass play. Keep pass solid will be one of the big plays on the goal line. The 83 and 87 on has been the most successful goal line play in all the years we have run the wing-

T, which dates back to 1979. We have great confidence in the play and have been fortunate to have talented fullbacks running the football.

Tight 189 Keep Pass (Solid)

The next play off the 87 on play is the tight 189 keep pass (Diagram 6.5). Keep pass solid has been used in the goal line offense. You do not want to bring the playside tackle down and have two extra defenders to block at the point of attack. The left tackle on solid will block on. He puts his head to the outside since this play is a 9 hole (flank). The left guard will pull and log the end man. The center must reach hard, and the right guard must also reach hard. You will have A gap penetration problems if they do not reach hard. They must get their heads across the front of the two A gap players. The right tackle and the right tight end will step and cup. They will account for the backside defensive tackle and defensive end. The fullback takes his footwork and, since you have called solid, has responsibility for the inside linebacker on his side of the formation. The wingback is in three-step motion. He must log the first free man at the flank. If you get a scraping linebacker from the inside to the outside, the motion halfback will block him. The pulling guard should be able to get the defensive end logged. The quarterback will reverse pivot slightly beyond the midline, mesh with the fullback, and, on the third step, get the ball up in the ready position to throw. He will attack the flank and have a run-pass option. Extremely important to goal line pass offense is goal line pass pattern distribution (Diagram 6.6).

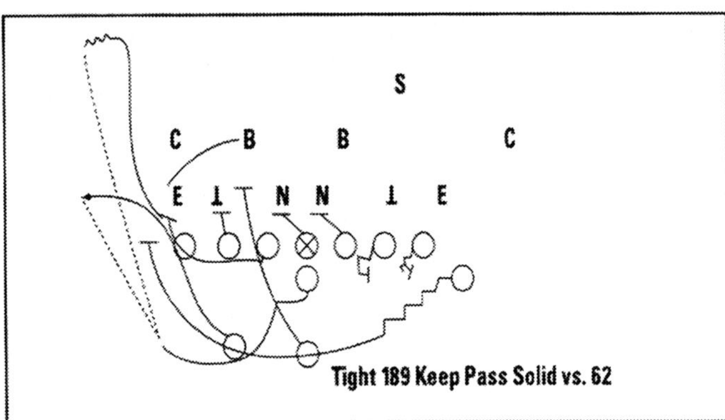

Diagram 6.5

If you look at the diagram of the end zone, the hash marks are 60 feet from the sideline. A pylon is at the back of the end zone on the end line, marking the width of the hash marks. Another pylon is on the end line at the corner of the end zone, and a pylon is on the sideline where the sideline meets the goal line on both sides of the field. These pylons are the orange markers at the end of the field. A set of goal posts is also there. The goal posts have the posts and the crossbar for field markings. All of these items provide markings for goal line pass patterns.

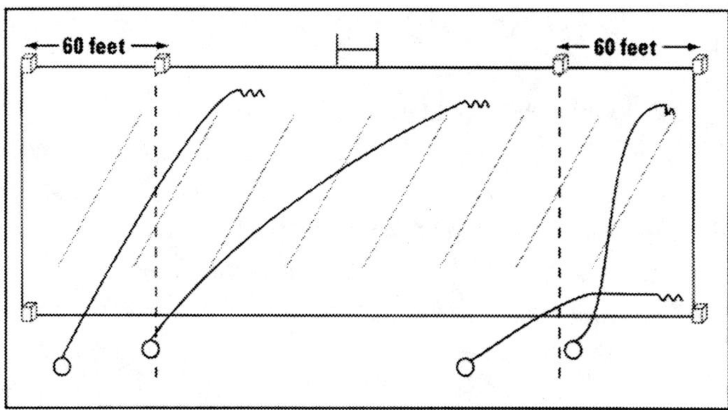

Diagram 6.6

Any receiver who runs a waggle route to the deep outside of the defensive secondary will be taught to take his release and run for the end zone corner toward the end zone pylon. When he gets about nine yards deep, he will hook up and gear down in an open area. Any receiver who will be running a flat route (whether a fullback in the flat running waggle or a halfback in the flat on keep pass) will get one yard across the goal line, run for the sideline, and gear down before he runs out of bounds. If using any crossing receivers, the inside crossing receiver will run for an open area between the far goal posts and the far hash mark. When they get to nine yards deep, they settle down and hook up in the open area. If a second backside crossing route is used, he will run for the near goal post and hook up between the goal post and the pylon at about nine yards deep in the end zone. It is very important to use the proper goal line pass-pattern distribution. This area does not have a lot of room, so you have to take advantage of every inch available.

Next, the goal line distribution to the keep pass play called tight 189 keep pass solid will be related. Here, the tight end will run for the corner of the end zone. He wants to be about nine yards deep when he hooks up in that corner. The left halfback has to get a yard deep in the end zone. He will run for a point 1.5 yards outside the tight man, get upfield one yard deep in the end zone, and then run for the sideline. He needs to find the goal line, using the pylon on his side of the field, get a yard across the goal line, and then run to the flat. The backside protection is step and cup. It is a two-man route with two backs and the backside tight end in the protection, so you can block any eight-man blitz. The quarterback will have a high-low stretch on the corner with a run-pass option.

Also from the 80 series, you will run the down option game. The first few plays diagrammed will be no mo tight 944 wedge, tight 924 quarterback sneak, tight 187 on, and tight 189 keep pass solid. Three of those plays are inside plays, and one is set up by an inside play. However, game-planning procedure dictates a flank attack for the 6-2 defense. The first few plays – 87 on, wedge, and quarterback sneak – are all used for gaining one yard or less. The rest of the attack is flank oriented. The first flank-oriented play is the keep pass.

Tight 182 Down Option

The next play is 182 down option (Diagram 6.7). The tight 182 down option will give the offense a chance to block all of the defenders up front. You will option the force player and the first man outside the defensive end. You want to clearly option him and not have some other defender at the line of scrimmage unblocked, which would allow him to stop the play. You will block everybody down and run to the flank. The blocking rules are the same as on any other down option. The tight end will block down on the defensive tackle. The tackle will rip through the defensive tackle to the linebacker. If the tackle cannot get to the frontside linebacker, then he will adjust to the backside linebacker. All other linemen block fire-on-backer. The center must reach hard to get his head across the front of any A gap penetrator. The left guard will do the same thing – reach hard to the right. The left tackle and the left tight end will also block with reach technique.

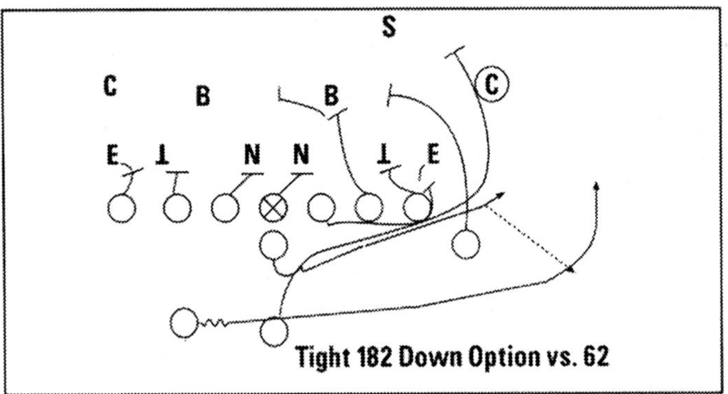

Diagram 6.7

The right guard, the right wingback, and the fullback will also be blockers against three of the four defenders remaining at the point of attack. You will block three of the four defenders and option the last one. As long as the defensive end is a seal player, you will log him with the offensive right guard. The right wingback will block the inside linebacker because he has a great angle on him. The fullback will cross over for the inside foot of the tight end, and the quarterback will reverse pivot flat down the line. The fullback and quarterback will mesh, and the quarterback will shuffle him into the line of scrimmage. The fullback will bend outside around the log block and will be the blocker for the free safety. The corner is the defender you will option. The quarterback executes a good mesh with the fullback, shuffles him into the line, and options the corner. The left halfback is in motion and is the pitch back. You have everybody blocked except the backside corner and will try to outrun him to the flank. Even if the backside corner gets there, the ballcarrier will have made the required yardage for either a touchdown or to stay on schedule.

Tight 181 Keep Pass (Solid)

You will also throw a pass off of 182 down option. The pass you want to throw is 181 keep pass solid, which is the same play you ran to the diveback side, except now, you run it to the tight end wingback side (Diagram 6.8). You will try to get the ball to the wingback in the flat quickly. He will get one yard across the goal line and run for the sideline a yard deep in the end zone. The tight end will run the seam route and look to hook up at a point nine yards deep in the end zone. Everybody else is blocking keep pass solid. The right tackle will block on. The right guard will pull to log the defensive end. The center and the left guard will reach hard across the front of the A gap penetrators. The left tackle and the left tight end will step and cup. The fullback will lead, cross over, square up, fake through the hole, and take the inside linebacker in protection. The left halfback is in motion across the backfield and will block the first free man at the flank. The quarterback meshes with the fullback and attacks the flank. His progression is deep, short, run.

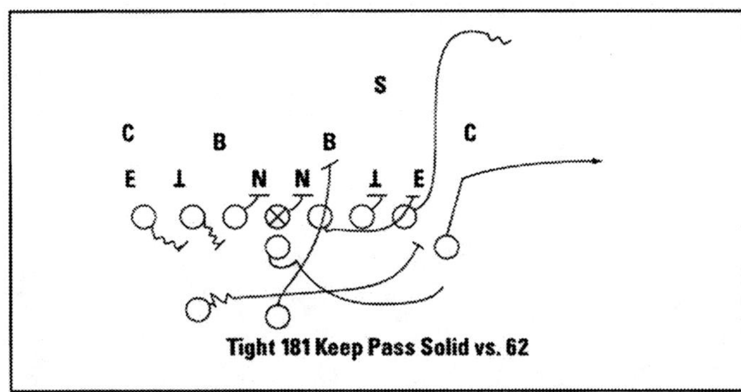

Diagram 6.8

A change-up to these routes is to cross both tight ends – send the halfback in the flat and run both tight ends on crossing routes. If you can get the defensive front blocked without the backside tight end, then you can run both tight ends on crossing routes. Most defensive teams are in man-to-man coverage near the goal line and end up running into each other, knocking each other off, and a receiver ends up standing wide open in the end zone. You will call keep pass solid and then add the word opposite. When you add opposite, then both tight ends will run crossing routes. This play is called tight 181 keep pass opposite.

Tight 134 Counter

You can also call tight 134 counter near the goal line. You run the tackle trap counter and pop it up inside with the halfback. The most important reason to run the counter is to set up counter bootleg. Counter bootleg will be a much better play on the goal line because it is flank oriented. You will not make a living running tackle trap counter against a 6-2 (Diagram 6.9).

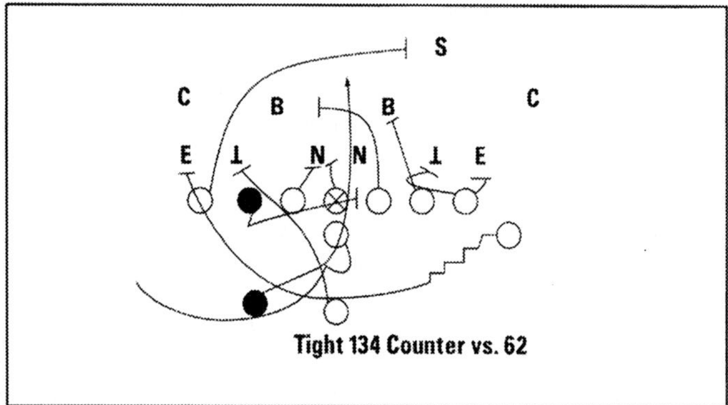

Diagram 6.9

If you decide you want to run counter, the tight end will either block backer-cutoff or block on. He will block either assignment, depending on what the problems are. The left tackle will pull and trap the first defensive lineman past the center. Against the 6-2, he will trap the noseguard in the A gap. If the noseguard is coming hard, he will not be a difficult trap. The left tackle should be able to get his head inside and execute a good trap block. The left guard's assignment is area-post, so he will come off and post the nose with his right shoulder. The center will block back and lead on him with his left shoulder, forming the post-lead or double-team. His rule is post-lead-backer.

The right guard's assignment is lead-backer-influence. If the noseguard is penetrating so fast the guard can escape around him, he will go across to block the linebacker. He can release right outside the nose to block the backer, and you should be able to trap the nose. The next alternative is to have the right guard use pass influence technique to get him upfield for the trap.

The right tackle will block the first backer from five, which means the first linebacker on his side of the line of scrimmage. The tight end will go to cut off. This hole is short for the backs. The fullback will cross over for the outside foot of the left guard and block the first defender who shows in that area. The fullback check blocks the defensive tackle with his left shoulder. The ballcarrier is the left halfback, who rocks his weight and then uses lead, crossover, square-up footwork with a short-hole landmark or aiming point.

The wingback will go in three-step motion and log block the first free man at the flank, setting up counter bootleg. The quarterback, since the left half is using short-hole footwork, will reverse pivot just beyond the midline. His second step wraps tight around the fullback. On his third step, he will give the ball and drag his arm as he attacks the flank to take the counter bootleg play.

You might ask yourself, "What happens to the defensive tackle and the defensive end on our right side? Will those players consistently stop the football play?" If you believe they will stop the play, then you should have the right tackle release to the linebacker and tell the tight end to pull flat down the line to execute a pull-check assignment on the defensive tackle and let the backside end run.

It is vital for this play to get blockers on the linebackers. For off-season research projects, the goal line offense has been studied and diagrams of why the goal line plays work have been tried. The most important factor in making goal line plays work is the blocking of the linebackers. Sometimes, you can get away without blocking a down lineman, but if you do not block those linebackers, then your goal line attack will rarely be successful.

Tight 134 Counter Bootleg (Solid)

Again, you will not run 34 counter (tackle trap) on the goal line very often because too many bodies are inside. You might run it once in a while, mostly to show people that you are willing to run it. You use it to set up the counter bootleg, which is a big play near the goal line. Many touchdowns have been scored with this play over the years, and this play should continue to be run as a staple of the goal line offense.

This play is called tight 134 counter bootleg solid (Diagram 6.10). You add the word solid to the call because you want the left tackle not to pull and allow the penetrating goal line defensive tackle to run into the backfield. You have the tackle either block on or block solid.

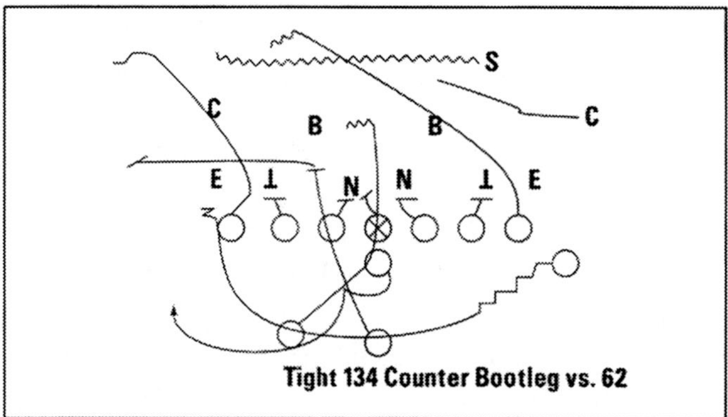

Diagram 6.10

The blocking rules for the play are as follows. The right tackle is gap-on-area-outside. He will block the man on him. He will put his head to the inside. The right guard's rule is gap-on-lead. He has a gap problem against a 6-2, so he will block down, but he must block the A gap. The center's rule is post lead. If he has nobody on him to post, he will lead with the left guard. Both blockers will post-lead the A gap player. The left guard is area-post. He will step out to post lead on the nose to the call side of the play. Since you will attack the flank to the left, you do not want the center and the left guard to drive the nose down the line. You want to show the post-lead action but hold the defender in the A gap. Since you call, "Solid," the left tackle will not pull to block chase. Since you are attacking the flank to the left, he will block on with his head to the outside.

The tight ends will both run patterns. The left tight end will use a down release, run for the end zone corner, and hook up nine yards deep. The backside tight end, your right tight end, knows that goal line pass pattern distribution requires him to run for the far upright. He will also hook up nine yards deep in the end zone between the upright and the pylon on that side.

The fullback, since you called solid, will change his aiming point to the outside leg of the guard. He will cross over to the outside leg of the guard, fake over an imaginary ball, and block the playside linebacker, if he is a threat to blitz, or else he will go through the line. The fullback will run his route in the flat one yard deep in the end zone, beyond the pylon at the goal line.

The wingback must go in three-step motion. When he passes the quarterback mesh, he must log block the defensive end and pin the flank down. The left halfback and the quarterback know that since you called 34 counter bootleg, they will both execute a short-hole technique. The left halfback rocks his weight and uses lead, crossover, square-up footwork, but he bends his path for the inside foot of the guard and will fake so well that he will get tackled by both linebackers. If not, he can hook outside toward the quarterback, attacking the flank.

The quarterback reverse pivots beyond the midline, because he uses footwork for a short hole. On his second step, he will wrap tight around the fullback's tail. On his third step, he will fake to the halfback and drag his hand as he attacks the flank. His read progression is deep, short, run. He will run the ball into the end zone uncontested unless the defense rotates hard with the action. The corner will play the flat, and the safety will have either tight end. Although the safety can cover either tight end, the other tight end will be open. If the backside corner tries to cover the backside end, he will be covering from behind and, at best, will only be able to make the tackle in the end zone.

Tight 129

Two basic plays remain to illustrate. Some of the 20 series plays are used at the goal line. You run the sweep, which is one of the basic plays in the offense. You run the sweep to the diveback side or the wingback side. You also run waggle quick off the sweep. Notice that the goal line plays are all the base plays in the offense. You use those plays on the goal line because they make up the base offense.

Looking at tight 129, you see it is sweep to the weakside, the diveback side (Diagram 6.11). You will start the wingback in motion to hand him the football. You will go to the weakside, especially if the safeties are in a position to come hard against the sweep when you run it to the wingback side.

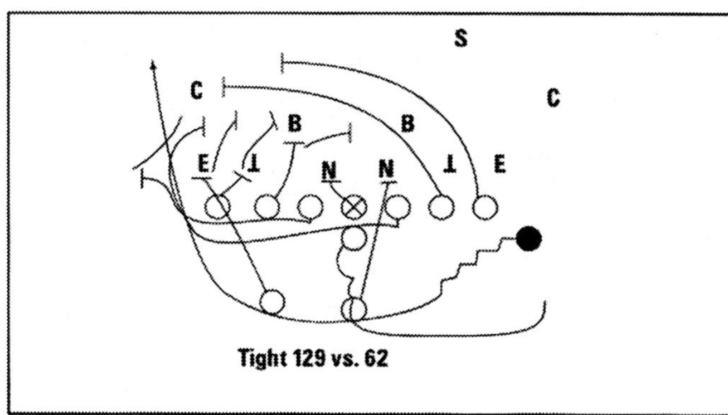

Diagram 6.11

If you examine the rules, the left tight end is gap-read-down. He will block down on the defensive tackle as he reads down. If that defensive tackle pinches inside and gets picked up by the tackle blocking down, the tight end can go to the backer. You want the tight end to think, "I'm going down on the defensive tackle and destroy him." He can use gapor down technique, but he will create movement on the defensive tackle. The left tackle also blocks gap-read-down and will block down, as well. Who does the left tackle block down on? The left tackle can block down on either the inside linebacker or the nose, depending on whether the center can reach the nose. With one-foot splits, the center can stop the noseguard in the A gap from penetrating and stopping the play. If the center can make that block, then the tackle will block the linebacker. A good center who you consider your best offensive lineman will be able to make the block with one-foot splits. The left tackle will release inside for the frontside backer, but probably will end up blocking the backside backer. All other blockers block normal sweep technique. The left guard pulls with two steps of depth, flattens out, and kicks out force tight to the left halfback's block. The backside guard will pull to the opposite guard, get depth, step around the trash, and then wall off on the frontside linebacker. The backside tackle and backside tight end are both going to cut off. You want to get cutoff blockers over to the point of attack.

The key to this play is the left halfback's block at the flank. The left halfback will take his first step for a point one yard outside the tight man. From there, he needs to react. If the defensive end is closing down hard, he makes himself vulnerable to the log block. If the defensive end is penetrating off the tight end's tail, the halfback will adjust his angle to stop the penetration and block him with his head across the front. You want the guard to get a deep path so he can kick out force outside the left halfback's block. If the left halfback has to block a defensive end who is skating outside, then he will let him go and continue to wall off on the inside linebacker, while the guard kicks the end out. If the end seals, then the guard pulls tight off of the left halfback's tail and kicks out the corner, who should be the force player. The right guard will wall off tight around the left halfback's block and will be looking for the frontside linebacker as he scrapes. The right tackle and the right tight end come across to the cutoff, with the right halfback running the ball.

The fullback must block the A gap to the right of the center, since the center has to reach. You tell the fullback, "Take off left foot for right foot of center, stay as tight as you can, and block him with your right shoulder." In college football, they are allowed to make that a cut block; in high school, they have to block at the hip.

The right halfback is in three-step motion, and the quarterback takes two steps on the midline. The quarterback will cross over as he gives him the ball. The right halfback is the ballcarrier and will get outside the left halfback's block to make a north-south cut. You tell the backs, especially if they are fast backs, that this one time is when they can outrun the defense (since they are only three to five yards away from the goal line). If they can make it by outrunning the defense, then they should go ahead and do it, but, before they try it, they must have confidence they will be successful. The quarterback will attack the flank to fake waggle. This play will set up a great play-action pass, which is the waggle.

Tight 129 Waggle Quick

The final play of the goal line attack is tight 129 waggle quick (Diagram 6.12). You set this up by running sweep to the tight end diveback side, which is the weakside. Now, you will show sweep action, but will attack away from the sweep fake.

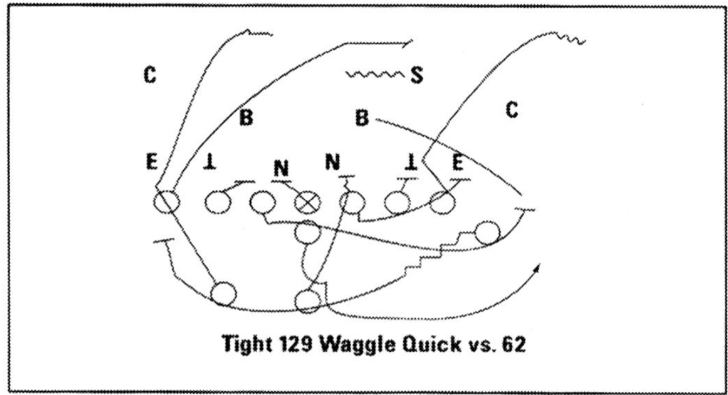

Diagram 6.12

What does waggle quick mean? Basically, it means the wingback will start in three-step motion and fake the sweep. The quarterback will fake the sweep and then attack the opposite flank on the waggle play.

Since the play is called waggle quick, the rules will be interpreted in the following way. The right tackle will block gap-down-on, so he will block on aggressively with his left shoulder. The right guard is still going to pull and log. The right tight end will use a down release to run for the end zone corner and hook up nine yards deep. Since the play is to the right, the right tight end is playside. Remember to use goal line pass distribution landmarks, because they will be crucial to the success of this play.

The right guard will pull to log the defensive end. He can pull with a man in his gap, because the fullback will step left foot for right foot of center and block the A gap player with his head to the outside. This block would be with the left shoulder for him. Since you have the fullback to execute this blocking assignment, the center can block using the away part of his rule. These blocking assignments go with the quick call. The backside guard will pull, cross over, and lead the quarterback to the flank. The backside tackle will pull to check two. The backside end has a crossing route. He will run for the far goal post and hook up nine yards deep in the end zone between the goal post and the pylon. The left halfback will fake the sweep block and aim for a point a yard and a half outside the tight man. He will also run a backside crossing route and will hook up at the near upright nine yards deep in the end zone. He will get open somewhere between the pylon on his side and the upright. The wingback fakes the sweep and gears down when he passes the quarterback. He will block any defender chasing the quarterback from behind.

The quarterback attacks the flank with the same progression. He can either throw or run the ball. If the defense is aligning the strong safety to the wing side and running across when the wing goes in motion, then the waggle play will serve as an effective 2-on-1, with the corner against the tight end and the quarterback. Normally, the corner will cover the tight end as the quarterback runs a flank. You will also see linebackers who try to run the quarterback down from inside out. The backside guard must pick up the scraping linebacker, if the quarterback decides to run the ball into the end zone. This block is possible if the offensive line stops all penetration, thus allowing the backside guard to pull. The alternative to waggle quick is waggle solid, which does not give the run option and is not usually used.

The quarterback can also decide to throw the crossing route to either the backside end or the backside halfback, both of whom are settling down in open areas. The quarterback will have the opportunity to throw many touchdowns on this play, if the receivers distribute themselves correctly.

Summary

As you can see, these goal line plays are also the base plays in the offense. They are the same plays you run all the way down the field. As you run these basic plays, you eventually find a way to make them work either by adjusting the blocking schemes or by adjusting the formations according to the particular goal line defense you are facing.

If you decide to run the sweep or the option into the unbalanced formation (i.e., right 900 or left 100), the extra end will block down. That change means he will block the first free man to his inside. You can also run keep pass from this formation. In that case, the outside end will run for the end zone corner, and the inside end will become an extra blocker. The unbalanced attack is especially effective if the defense does not shift with the unbalanced formation. This case is common, because the defensive players are vulnerable to the weakside if they shift over with the unbalanced line.

7

Wing-T Drills

Quarterback Release Drill

Objective: To teach quarterbacks to throw the ball with good height on the throwing release

Equipment Needed: One set of goal posts and one football for every two quarterbacks participating in the drill

Description: Partner up the quarterbacks into groups of two and line them up 15 yards apart facing each other on opposite sides of the crossbar on a goal post. All quarterbacks are participating in the drill at the same time. On the coach's command, the quarterbacks will throw the ball back and forth to each other over the crossbar. The height of the crossbar will force the quarterback to elevate his release. The drill will be repeated by the quarterbacks on the other side of the crossbar.

Coaching Points: In this drill, the quarterbacks should hold the ball in the proper passing grip, rotating the thumb down on the throwing hand. This grip will bring the throwing elbow out and give added yardage to the quarterback's range. The coach should emphasize throwing the ball in this drill with a high release giving the quarterback added distance to his throws.

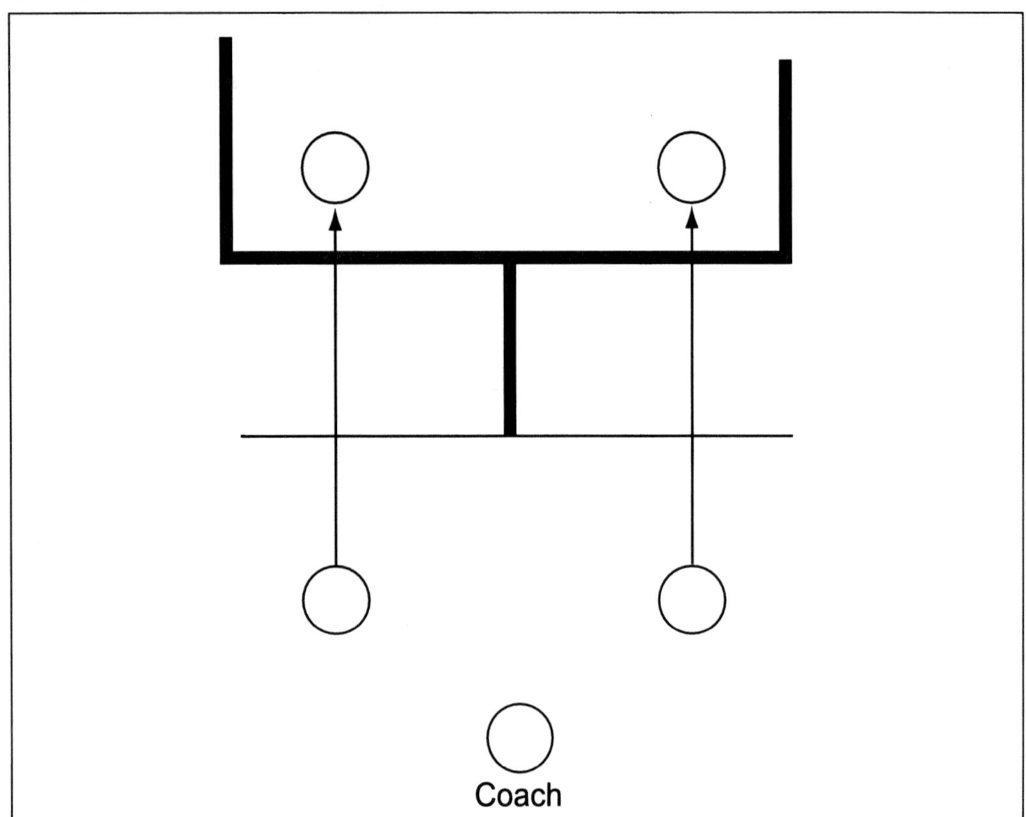

Team Thud Drill

Objective: To teach the offensive unit the assignments, techniques, and timing of the offense with live blocking

Equipment Needed: None

Description: Two offensive units will alternate running offensive plays against 11 defensive players. This full drill includes live blocking, but no tackling. The defensive players are instructed to react to the play, but not tackle the running backs. The defensive players should sprint to the ball and touch the backs with their nearest hand as they run past the backs. The offensive players will block full speed with live blocking techniques, and the running back will run the ball all the way into the end zone, so they learn the timing of the plays.

Coaching Points: This drill is great to use when practicing in full pads when your team is not scrimmaging live. The blockers are blocking live and at full speed tempo, but tackling isn't done on the backs. This drill does not include tackling. The defense is instructed to react to the play and pursue to the football, but not to tackle the backs; they will tag off the backs. The backs are instructed to run the ball into the end zone and finish the drill every time.

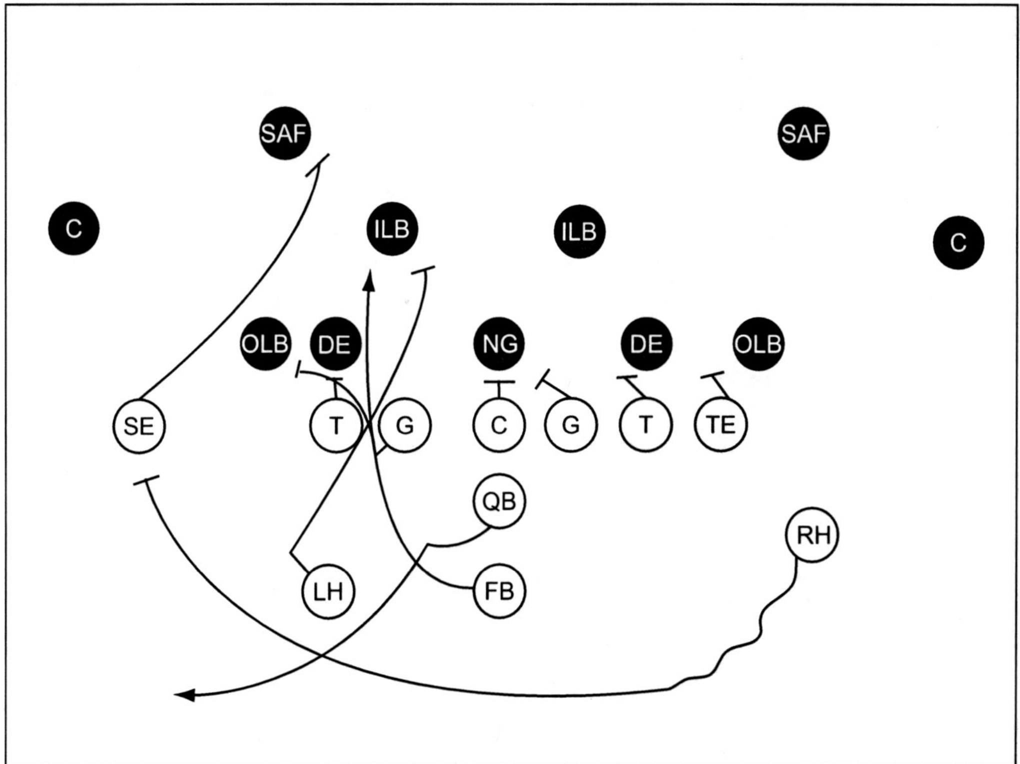

Team vs. Bags

Objective: To teach the offensive unit the assignments, techniques, and timing of the offense

Equipment Needed: Four or five 52-inch stand-up blocking dummies and six or seven hand shields

Description: Two offensive units will alternate running offensive plays against 11 defensive players, who will be holding blocking dummies or hand shields. The defensive players playing the defensive line positions will hold large 52-inch stand-up blocking dummies, and the players playing the linebacker positions will hold hand shields, so they are mobile. The defensive backs will hold hand shields or nothing at all. When practicing option or flank runs, the defensive backs should hold hand shields.

Coaching Points: This drill is great to use when practicing in helmets and T-shirts, when your team is not practicing in pads. The blockers can hit something without injuring themselves. This drill does not include tackling. The defense is instructed to react to the play and pursue to the football, but not to tackle the backs or even tag off on the backs. The backs are instructed to run the ball into the end zone and finish the drill every time.

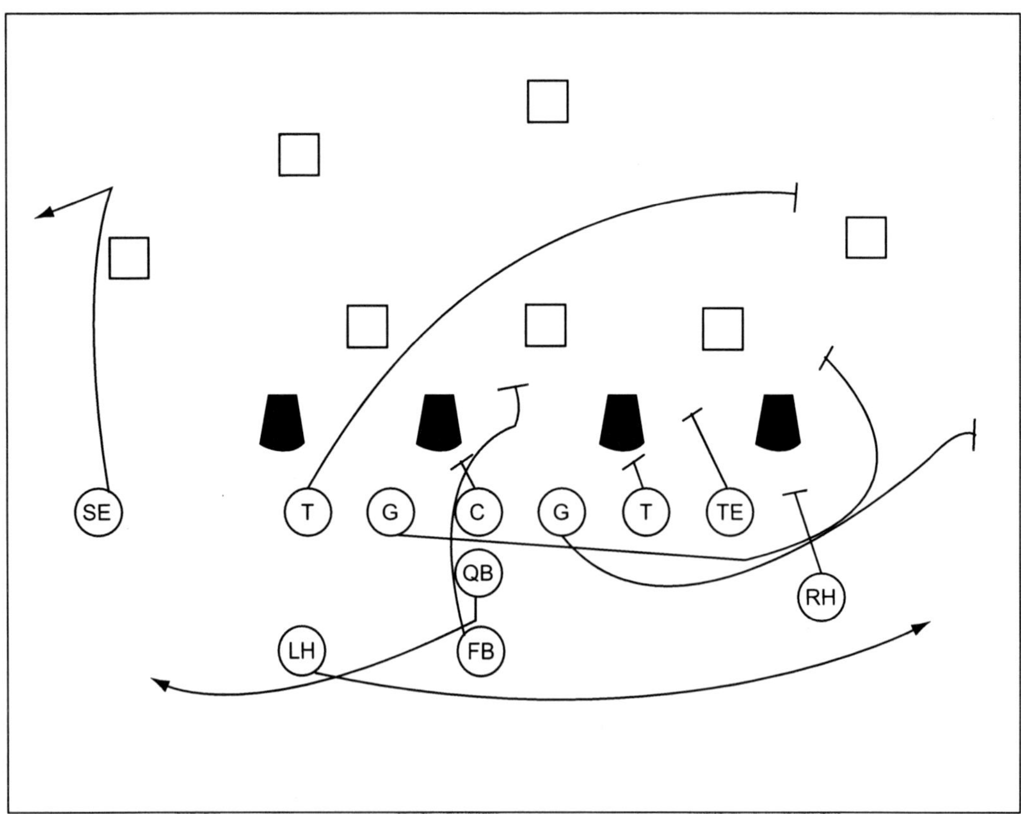

Blitz Pick up Drill

Objective: To teach the entire offensive unit to pass protect in a definite passing situation, when the defense will be bringing maximum pressure against the offense

Equipment Needed: None

Description: Two offensive huddles will alternate running pass plays against a defense instructed to run any blitz, stunt, or pressure they can use to put maximum heat on the offense. The offense must learn to protect the passer in the toughest environment you can possibly create for them. The offense is trying to simulate a third-and-long against a defense bringing maximum pressure. The defense should use the most pressure they can bring to create the toughest possible situation for the offense.

Coaching Points: The drill is designed to create confidence in the offense's ability to protect the quarterback, when the toughest possible situation exists for them. They develop the mentality that, if they can protect in this situation, they can protect in any situation. This drill is designed to make protecting in the game seem easy.

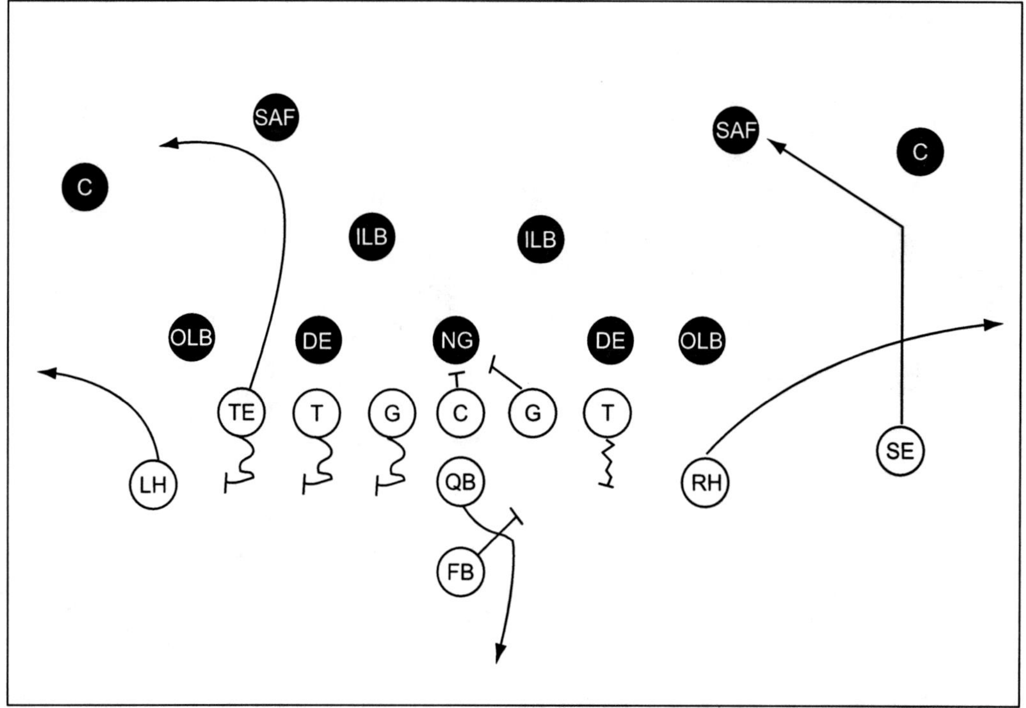

Outside Run Drill

Objective: To teach offensive guards, receivers, and backs to block perimeter run plays live against defensive backs and linebackers

Equipment Needed: None

Description: The offensive guards, receivers, and running backs will run outside running plays against the defensive backs and linebackers. Offensive tackles or defensive linemen will not be in the drill. The defense may or may not be allowed to tackle the backs to the ground. Draw plays or pass plays could be mixed into the drill to keep the defense honest, but the majority of the plays should be outside running plays. On the center's snap, the offense will run the play called in the huddle full speed and with live blocking techniques.

Coaching Points: Offensive blockers should concentrate on both their correct assignment and the correct technique. They should not lose focus on their techniques because they are competing against the defense.

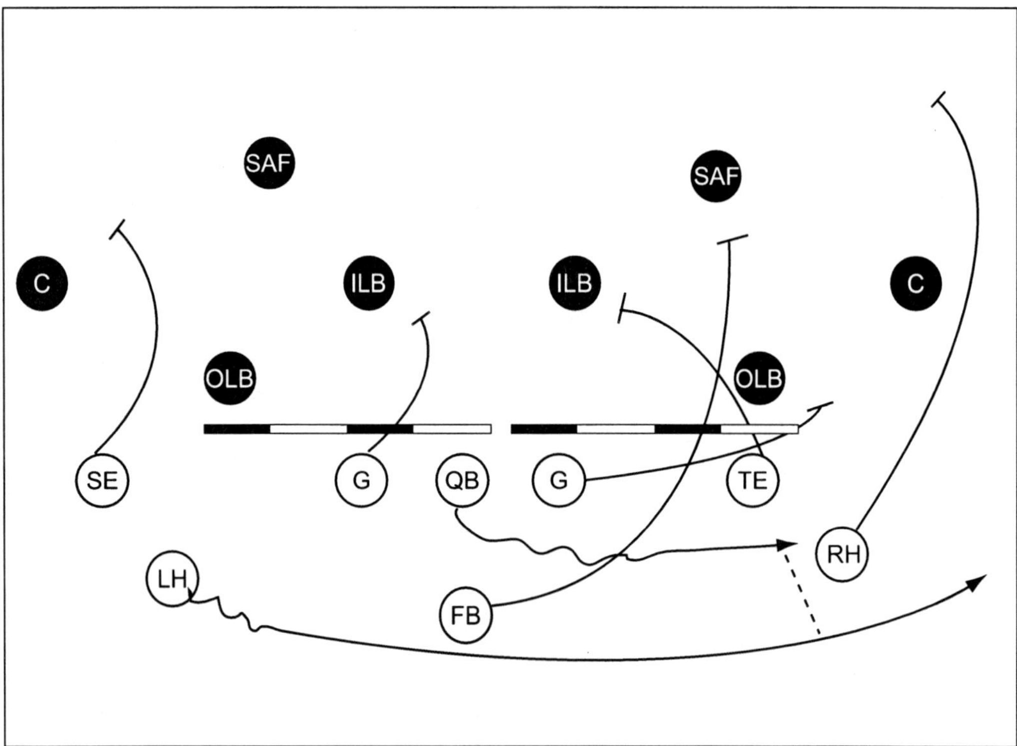

Inside Run Drill

Objective: To teach offensive linemen to block internal run plays live against defensive linemen and linebackers

Equipment Needed: None

Description: The offensive line, tight ends, and running backs will run inside running plays against a defensive line and linebackers. Wide receivers or defensive backs will not be in the drill. The defense may or may not be allowed to tackle the backs to the ground. Wide running plays or pass plays could be mixed into the drill to keep the defense honest, but the majority of the plays should be inside running plays. On the center's snap, the offense will run the play called in the huddle full speed and with live blocking techniques.

Coaching Points: Offensive blockers should concentrate on both their correct assignment and the correct technique. They should not lose focus on their techniques because they are competing against the defense.

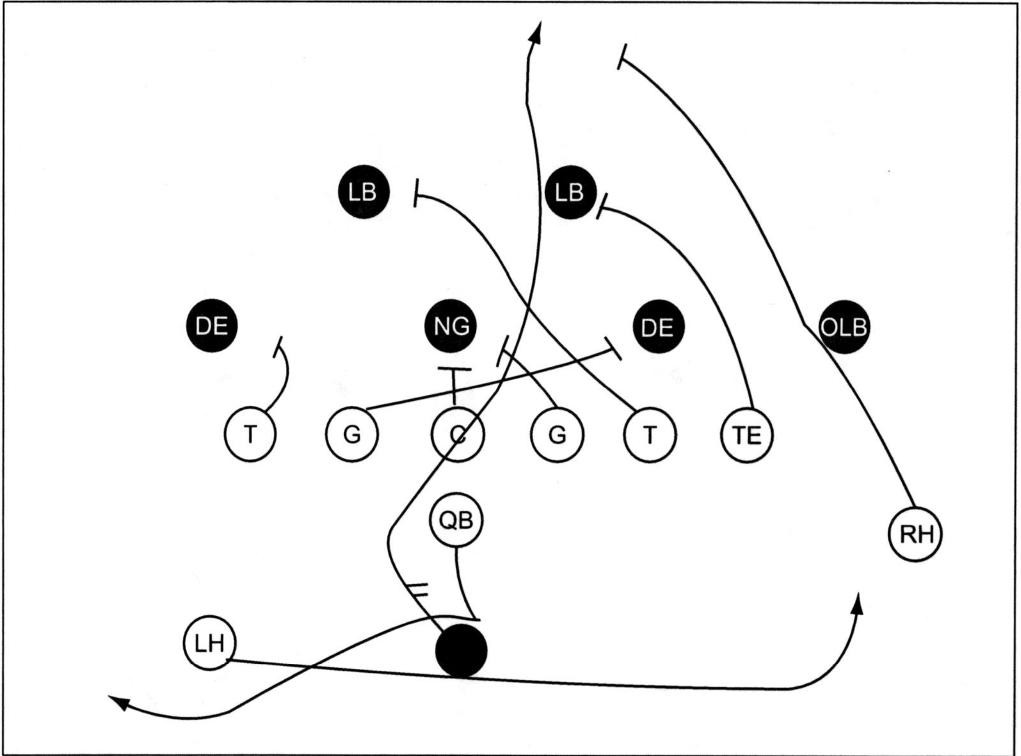

Double Team Drill

Objective: To teach tight ends and offensive linemen to double-team and trap block with a conditional post block

Equipment Needed: Two 52-inch stand-up blocking dummies and one hand shield for every six blockers participating in the drill

Description: Divide the blockers into groups of six. All tight ends are participating in the drill at the same time and will practice this drill with offensive linemen. Place stand-up dummies on the outside shoulders of the two outside blockers and the hand shield at linebacker level on the outside shoulder of the innermost blocker. On the coach's command, the middle blocker will post with his outside shoulder, the outermost blocker will lead (down block) with his inside shoulder, and the innermost blocker will pull to trap with his outside shoulder. The blockers switch places and practice all three techniques. Then, they practice the same three techniques to the other side. They will then switch places with the defenders and repeat the same sequence.

Coaching Points: The trapper takes a pull step and then adjusts to the post-lead block staying tight to the post-lead but not colliding with them. He is responsible for a smooth mesh and finishes his block back into the backfield. The post blocker steps with the inside foot and strikes with the outside shoulder in the numbers. The lead blocker uses down technique and strikes at the hip. The post-lead blockers swing their tails on contact by the lead blocker and finish the block down the line of scrimmage. The post blocker comes off the post to block the linebacker if he runs through making the post block conditional.

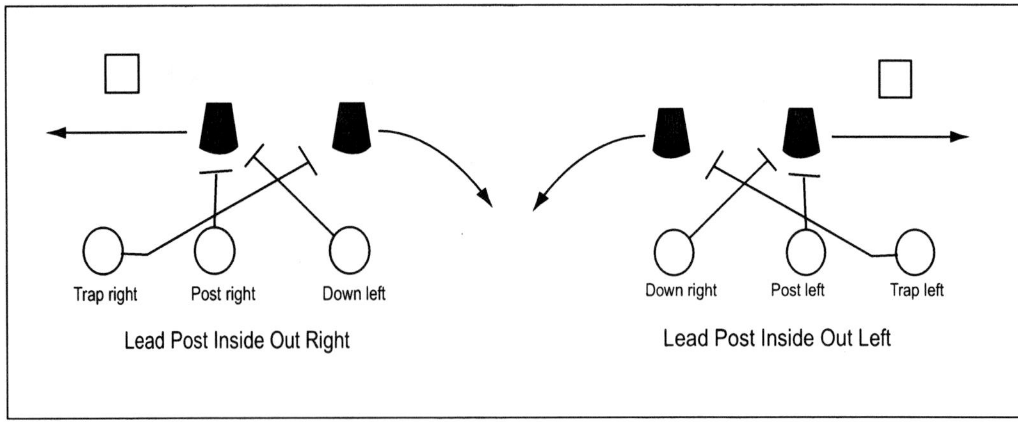

Guard Pull Drill for Waggle

Objective: To teach all offensive linemen to execute the offensive guard techniques for the waggle play

Equipment Needed: One set of spacing boards, two cones, and four hand shields for blocking dummies

Description: The blockers get into two lines at the guard positions. Two hand shields or dummies are placed at the defensive end positions. The other two hand shields or dummies are placed two yards from the end of the spacing boards and two yards deep in the backfield. (These shields can be moved around depending on the type of defense you are seeing.) The cones are placed one yard behind the offensive center's feet. The first two blockers execute the guard blocks for the waggle. They switch places with the two defenders, and the next two blockers jump up to the line to execute the guard blocks for the waggle to the other side. They also switch places with the defenders as the next two guards jump up.

Coaching Points: The frontside guard pulls flat down the line of scrimmage and executes log block technique on the defender lined up at the defensive end position. The backside guard takes a pull step, crosses over with his backside foot on his second step, and then kicks out the defender who has penetrated to two-by-two yards into the backfield or leads the quarterback up the field, if no penetration exists.

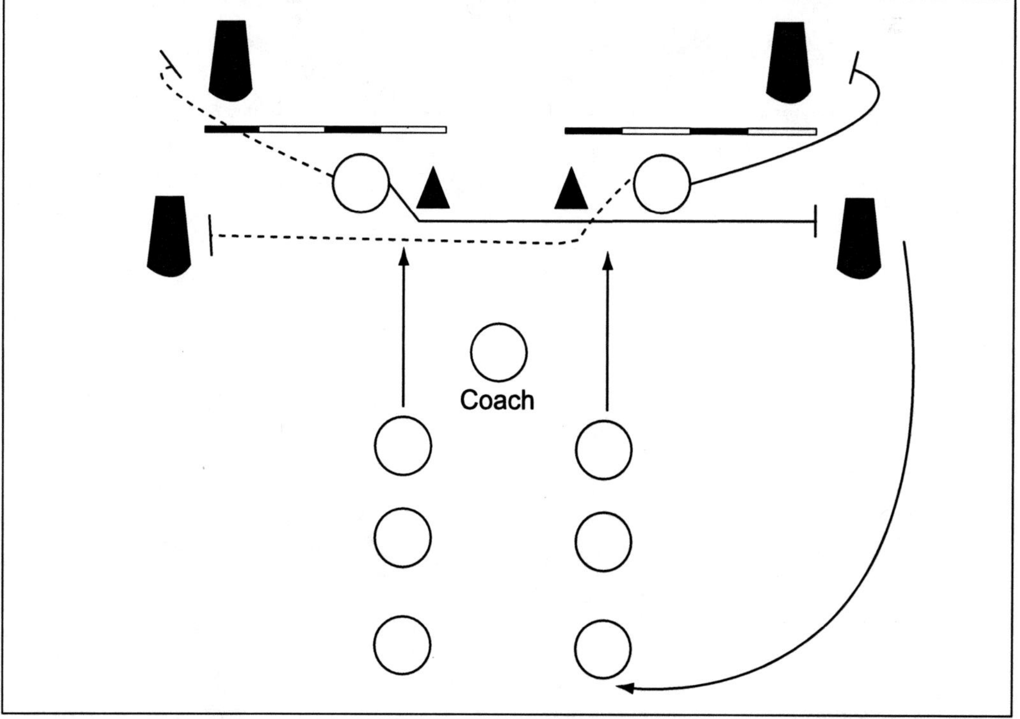

Guard Pull Drill for Sweep

Objective: To teach all offensive linemen to execute the offensive guard techniques for the buck sweep play

Equipment Needed: One set of spacing boards, two cones, and four hand shields or blocking dummies

Description: The blockers get into two lines at the guard positions. Two hand shields or dummies are placed at the inside linebacker positions. The other two hand shields or dummies are placed two yards from the end of the spacing boards and two yards deep in the backfield. (These shields can be moved around depending on the type of defense you are seeing.) The cones are placed two yards behind the offensive tackle's area. The first two blockers execute the guard blocks for the buck sweep. They switch places with the two defenders, and the next two blockers jump up to the line to execute the guard blocks for the sweep to the other side. They also switch places with the defenders as the next two guards jump up.

Coaching Points: The frontside guard takes two pull steps on a 45-degree angle away from the line of scrimmage, flattens out, starts downhill on his third step, and kicks out the defender who is two-by-two in the backfield. The backside guard pulls flat to the other guard's area, gets about one yard of depth, then walls off on the defender lined up in the linebacker position.

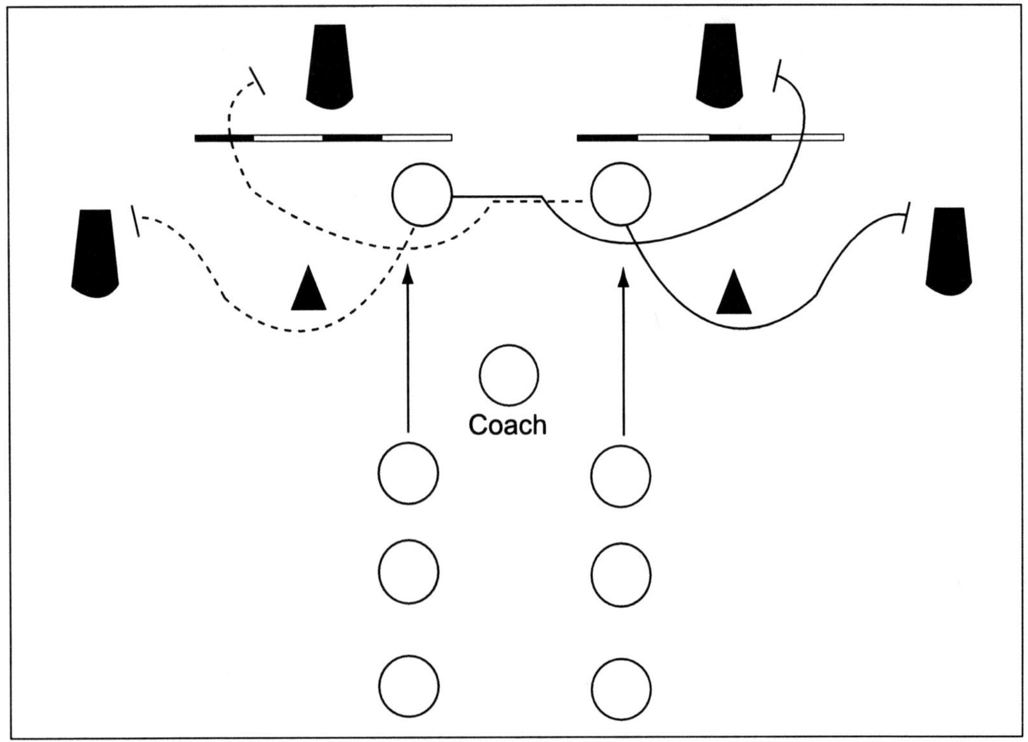

Receiver-Defensive Back Pass Skeleton Drill

Objective: To teach tight ends, wide receivers, running backs, and quarterbacks to execute their pass plays against defensive backs and linebackers running their pass coverages

Equipment Needed: One set of spacing boards and footballs

Description: Two offensive huddles will alternate running pass plays against defensive backs and linebackers. The offensive backs and receivers will align on a set of spacing boards. On the center's snap, all of the receivers take off down the field running a predetermined pass play, and the quarterback executes his coverage read to deliver the ball to the correct receiver. As the first offensive unit is finishing their play, the second unit should be breaking their huddle and hustling up to the line of scrimmage.

Coaching Points: The objective of this drill is to complete 75% of the passes attempted. Each receiver should be evaluated on the precision of his routes and his competitiveness against the defense. The quarterback should be evaluated on his timing, his strike points, his coverage reads, and his completion percentage.

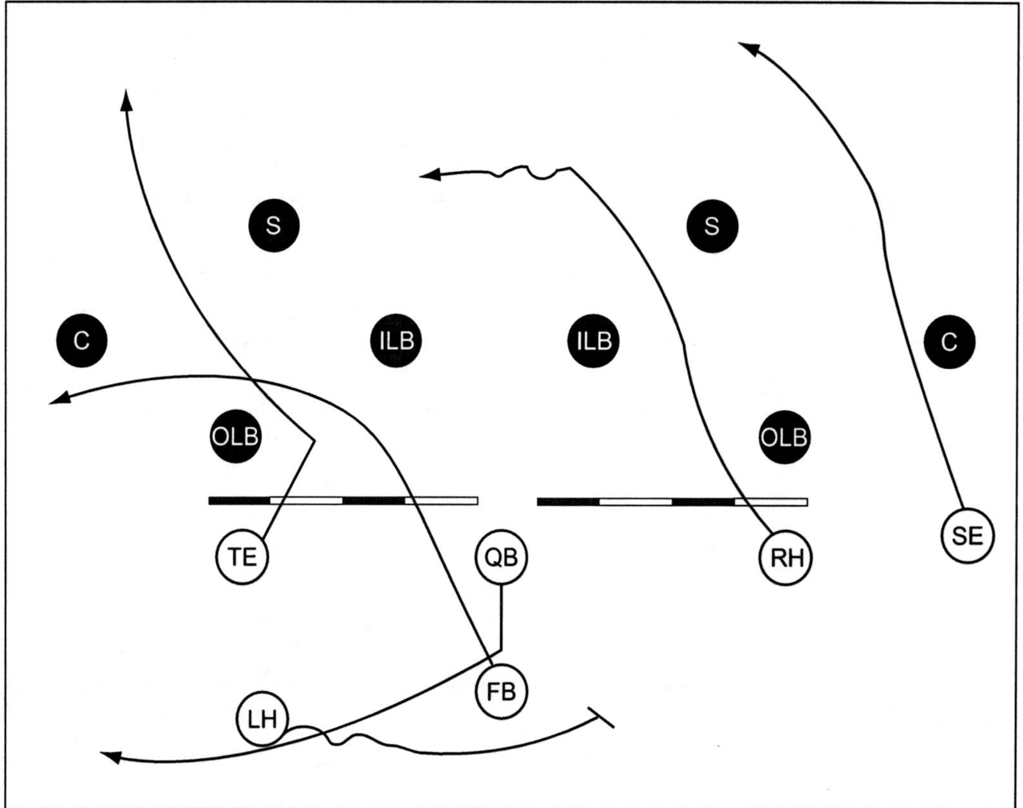

Receiver-Defensive Back 1-On-1 Drill

Objective: To teach backs and receivers to run individual 1-on-1 pass patterns against defenders

Equipment Needed: Four sets of spacing boards and footballs

Description: A set of spacing boards are placed on both hash marks on the 40-yard line going into the end zone. Two more sets of spacing boards are placed on the opposite 40-yard line going into the other end zone. Each set of spacing boards has a 1-on-1 match-up taking place on that section of the field. A different quarterback will also be at each of the four stations throwing to the receivers. On the quarterback's cadence, the ball will be snapped and the receiver will run a 1-on-1 pass pattern against a defensive back. Each quarterback is independent of the other. All tight ends will be at the same station. Spread ends and halfbacks will be working at the other three stations. The defensive backs will match up with corners against spread ends and safeties against tight ends and running backs.

Coaching Points: The objective of this drill is to complete 80% of the passes attempted. Each receiver should be evaluated on the precision of his routes and his competitiveness against the defender. The quarterback should be evaluated on his timing, his strike points, and his completion percentage.

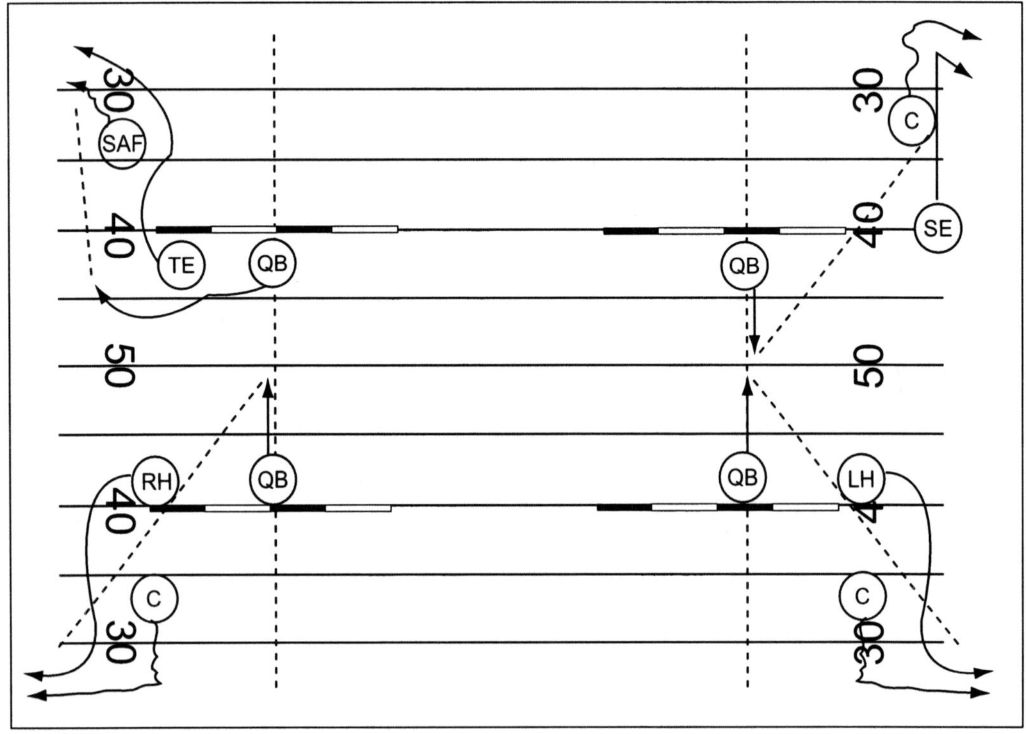

Receiver Strip Drill

Objective: To teach receivers to catch passes, turn up the field, and secure the ball against defenders trying to rip the ball out

Equipment Needed: Footballs and hand shields

Description: Align all but one of the receivers in two lines two yards apart from each other, which form the gauntlet. Every other receiver in the lines has a hand shield. The coach is the thrower in this drill and will stand 10 yards from the receiver. Only one receiver at a time will run this drill. On the coach's command, the receiver running the drill will start toward the gauntlet, catch the football, and turn up between the two lines. The receivers in the gauntlet will try to strip the ball or hit the receiver with the shield to disrupt his concentration. Each receiver takes his turn running through the gauntlet. When the drill is finished, the receivers will repeat the drill to the other side.

Coaching Points: The receiver must concentrate on securing the football with four points of pressure and explode through the gauntlet with good forward body lean.

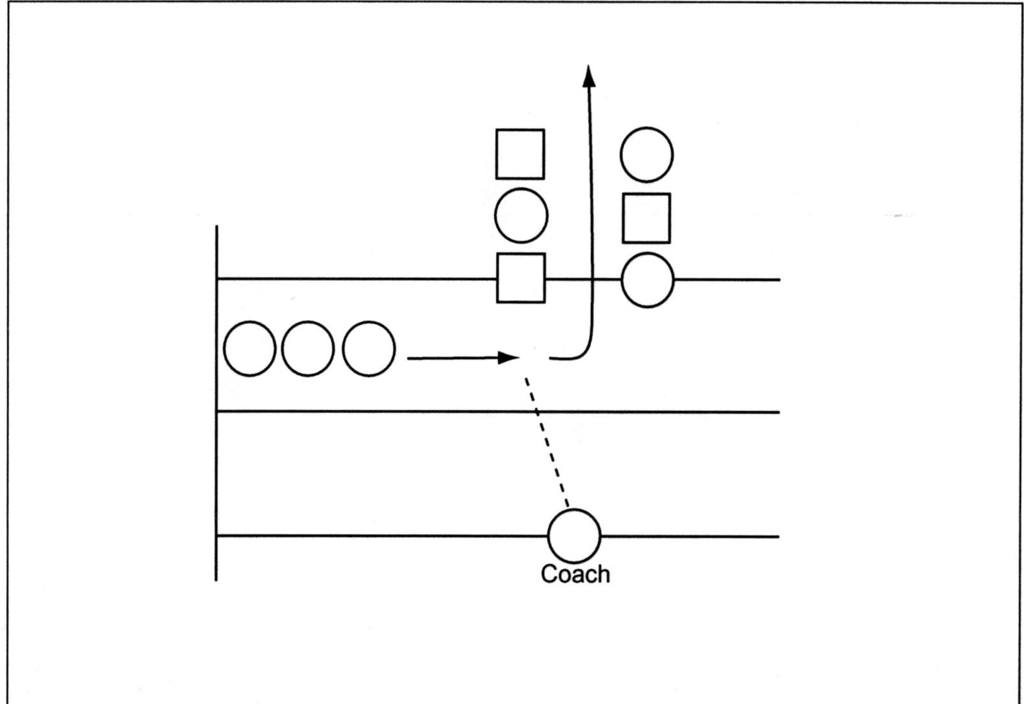

Receiver Distraction Drill

Objective: To teach receivers to catch passes when other players are around them putting hands in their vision.

Equipment Needed: Footballs

Description: Align the receivers on the hash mark facing the opposite sideline 10 yards away from the coach, who is in the middle of the field. The coach is the thrower in this drill. Two distracters are 10 yards away from the coach, also in the middle of the field. On the coach's command, a receiver will start across the field, running from one hash mark to the other. The coach will throw the ball between the two distracters, who wave their arms, but do not interfere with the ball. The receiver must concentrate on making the catch and not being distracted by the defenders. The receivers will then repeat the drill from the other hash mark.

Coaching Points: The distracters should show as much movement as possible without actually touching the ball. The receivers must concentrate on the football, ignoring the distracters, and concentrating on their catch, tuck, and cover fundamentals.

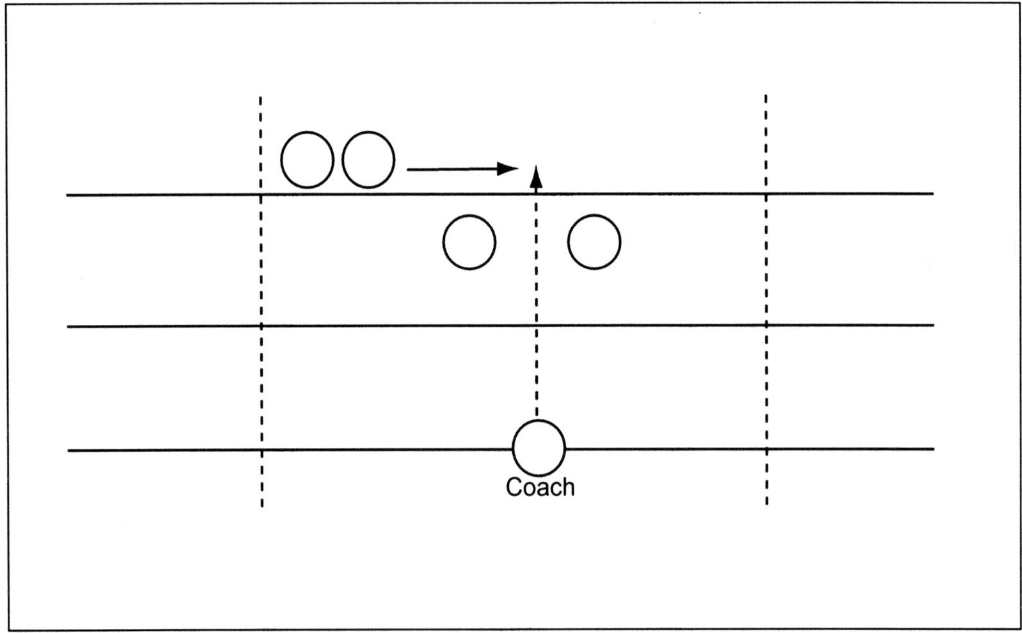

Quarterback Sprint-out Drill

Objective: To teach quarterbacks to throw the football while sprinting out

Equipment Needed: One football for every two quarterbacks participating in the drill and two cones

Description: Partner up the quarterbacks into groups of two and line them up 15 yards apart, with the thrower on the hash mark and the receiver on the opposite numbers. The ball is snapped from the hash mark, and the cone is placed four yards deep in the backfield behind the offensive tackle. On the coach's command, the quarterback takes the snap and sprints out or runs the waggle footwork around the cone. The drill is then repeated with the other quarterback throwing the ball. After a few reps, the cones will be moved to the other hash mark so that the quarterbacks get work on throwing to both the right and the left.

Coaching Points: In this drill, the quarterback should hold the ball in the proper passing grip, rotating the thumb down on the throwing hand. This grip will bring the throwing elbow out and give added yardage to the quarterback's range. The quarterback throwing the ball will wrench his throwing elbow to the middle of his back, which opens his hips to the throw. As the quarterback throws the ball, he should run after the ball as if he were chasing it; this action helps to insure accuracy.

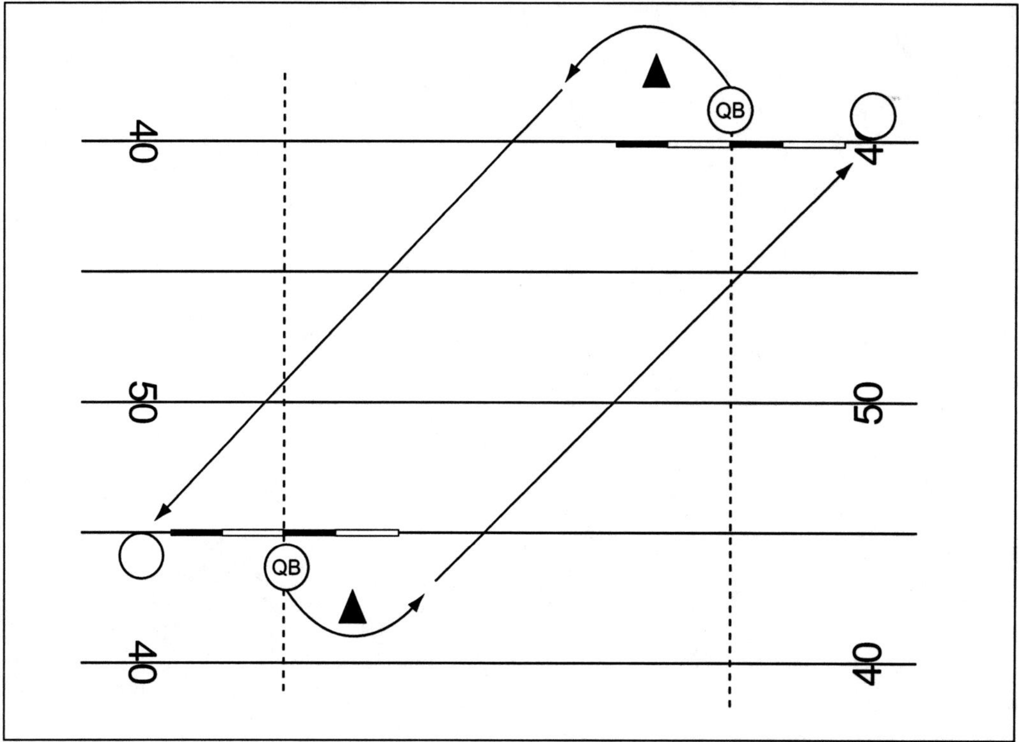

Running Back 90-Degree Cut Drill

Objective: To teach running backs to make the 90-degree cut simulating the sweep cut

Equipment Needed: Four cones

Description: All running backs are participating in the drill at the same time. The four cones are placed at the corners of a 10-yard square. All running backs start at one corner and, on the coach's command, run around the four cones. At each corner of the square, the running back will control his speed and execute a 90-degree cut to the next cone. After running in one direction, the backs will repeat the drill in the other direction.

Coaching Points: When making the 90-degree cut, the running back should plant and pivot his outside foot. When he pivots the outside foot, his shoulders will turn up the field as well. This technique makes the back more physical as a north-south runner.

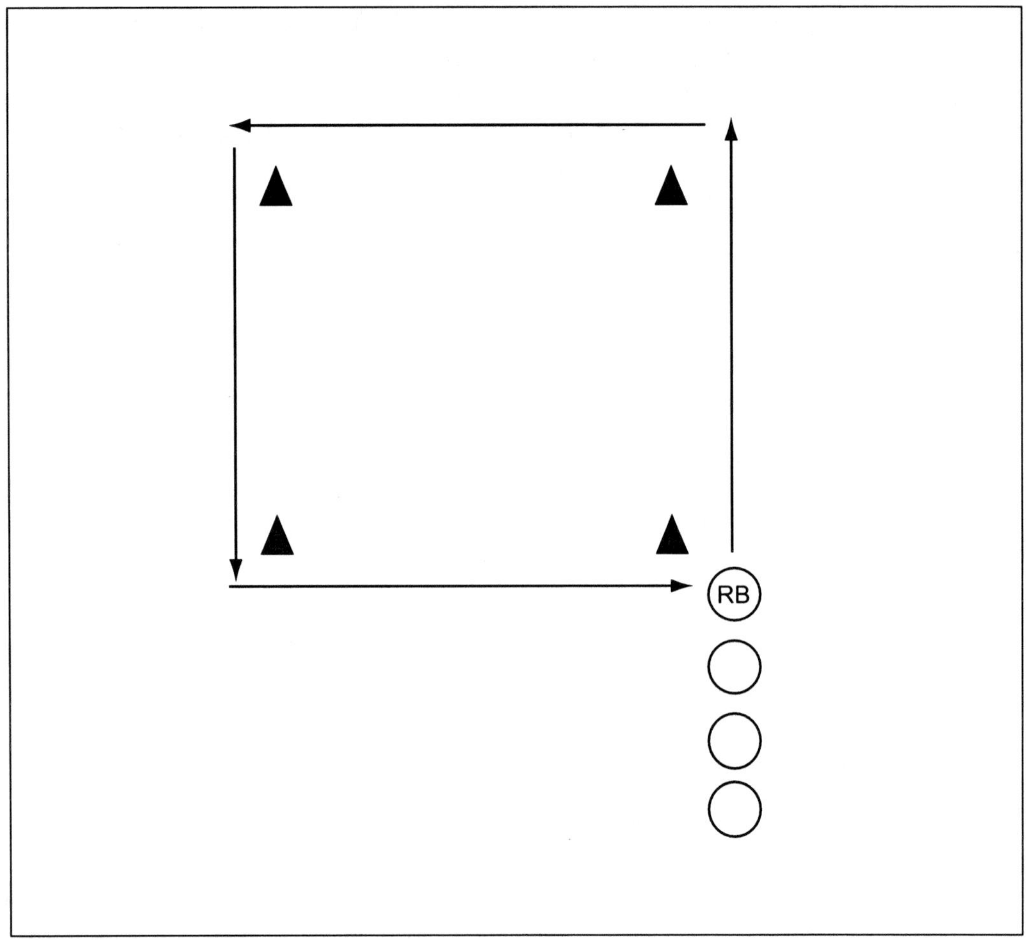

Quarterback-Running Back Option Pitch Drills

Objective: To teach running backs how to execute option plays, emphasizing the correct pitch mechanics

Equipment Needed: Two sets of spacing boards and two footballs

Description: One set of spacing boards is placed on the left hash mark and another set of spacing boards is placed on the right hash mark 15 yards up the field. On the set of spacing boards on the left hash mark are all of the left halfbacks, half of the quarterbacks, and half of the fullbacks. On the other set of spacing boards are all of the right halfbacks, as well as the remaining quarterbacks and fullbacks. The coach will call out an option play to one group and the mirror of that option play to the other group. After the first groups have run their play, the next group hustles up to the spacing boards and runs the same play. Halfway through the drill, the quarterbacks and fullbacks switch groups.

Coaching Points: The quarterbacks run the drills separately and on their own cadences, controlling the tempo of the drill. The extra quarterbacks will act as the pitch key and must challenge each other, making the drill tougher than the game.

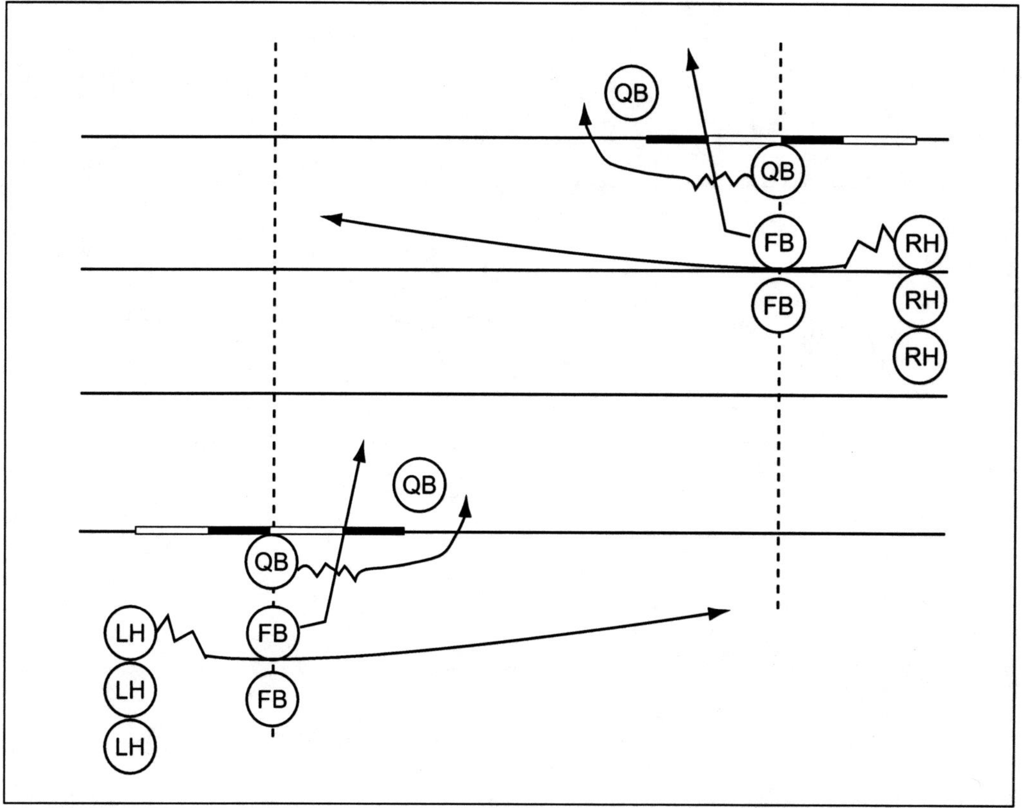

Running Back Technique Drill

Objective: To teach running backs and quarterbacks to perfect the plays in the wing-T requiring the most precision

Equipment Needed: One set of spacing boards, two 52-inch stand-up blocking dummies, and two hand shields

Description: A set of spacing boards is set up in the middle of the field. An entire backfield will run a play called out by the coach. The entire backfield will execute their assignment and technique. The quarterbacks control the tempo of the drill with their cadence. Each player in the backfield executes his technique against his backup who simulates the defense. If one of the backs is a blocker on the play, then he will block his backup holding a dummy or hand shield. If one of the backs is a ballcarrier, then his backup gives him a read for the correct running lane. The backup quarterback will be the read for options or passes. The same play is repeated until all of the groups run the play to both sides.

Coaching Points: This drill is not for drop back passing plays. The wing-T plays requiring the most precise execution should be practiced in this drill. All four backs should be executing their skills in this drill.

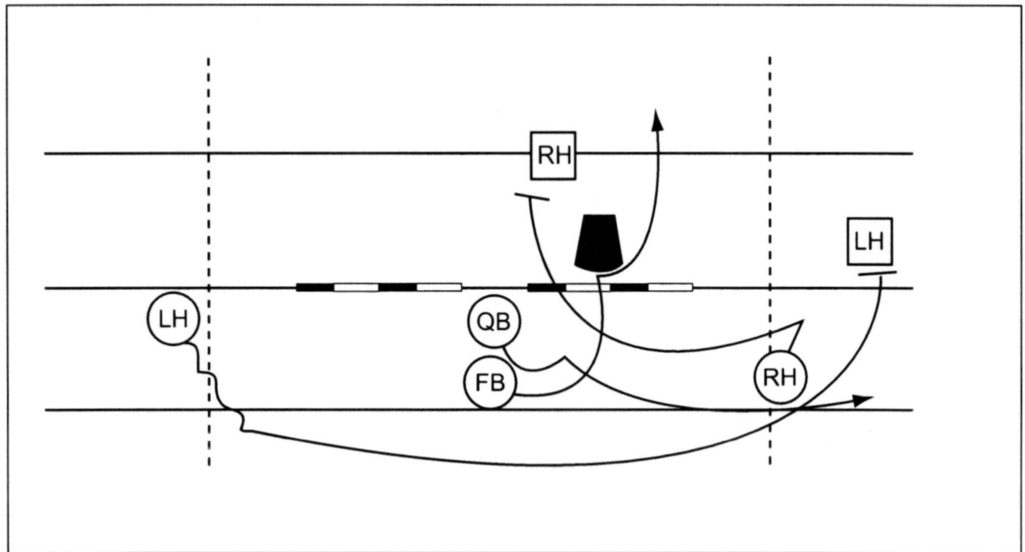

Running Back Pass Protection Drill

Objective: To teach running backs how to pass protect against a live pass rush by linebackers

Equipment Needed: None

Description: Two inside linebackers and two outside linebackers will align in a pass rush stance at their positions. The drill can be done with the fullbacks going against the inside linebackers and the halfbacks going against the outside linebackers or with the fullback practicing double reads. On the coach's command, one pass rusher will take off simulating a blitz against a back practicing pass protection techniques. If the halfbacks are in the drill, they will block the outside linebackers. If the halfbacks are not in the drill, the fullback will double read against both linebackers. Only one of the linebackers actually rushes against the fullback's double read. Repeat the drill to both sides.

Coaching Points: The pass protector must keep good knee bend and inside out position. He must also keep his head and shoulders back when making contact. Contact should be made with the hands striking the defender on the rise.

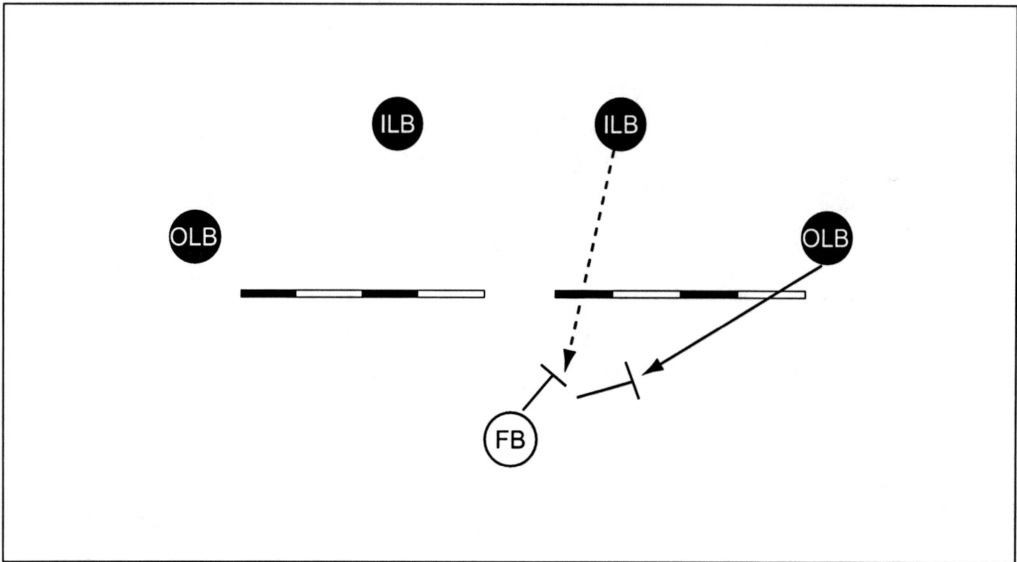

Running Back-Receiver Passing Against Air

Objective: To teach all backs and receivers to execute the timing and precision of the passing game against air with no defense on the field

Equipment Needed: One set of spacing boards and footballs

Description: A complete set of backs and receivers will line up on a set of spacing boards in a formation. On the center's snap or on the coach's command, the ball will be snapped and the offense will run a pass pattern against air. This drill can be done with one receiver running a route or the entire group running a complete pass pattern. The coach will direct the quarterback's direction orally or by acting as the defensive read. After the first group has finished running their pattern, a second group will sprint up to the ball and repeat the same play.

Coaching Points: The objective of this drill is to complete 100% of the passes attempted. Each receiver should be evaluated on the precision of his routes. The quarterback should be evaluated on his timing and his strike points.

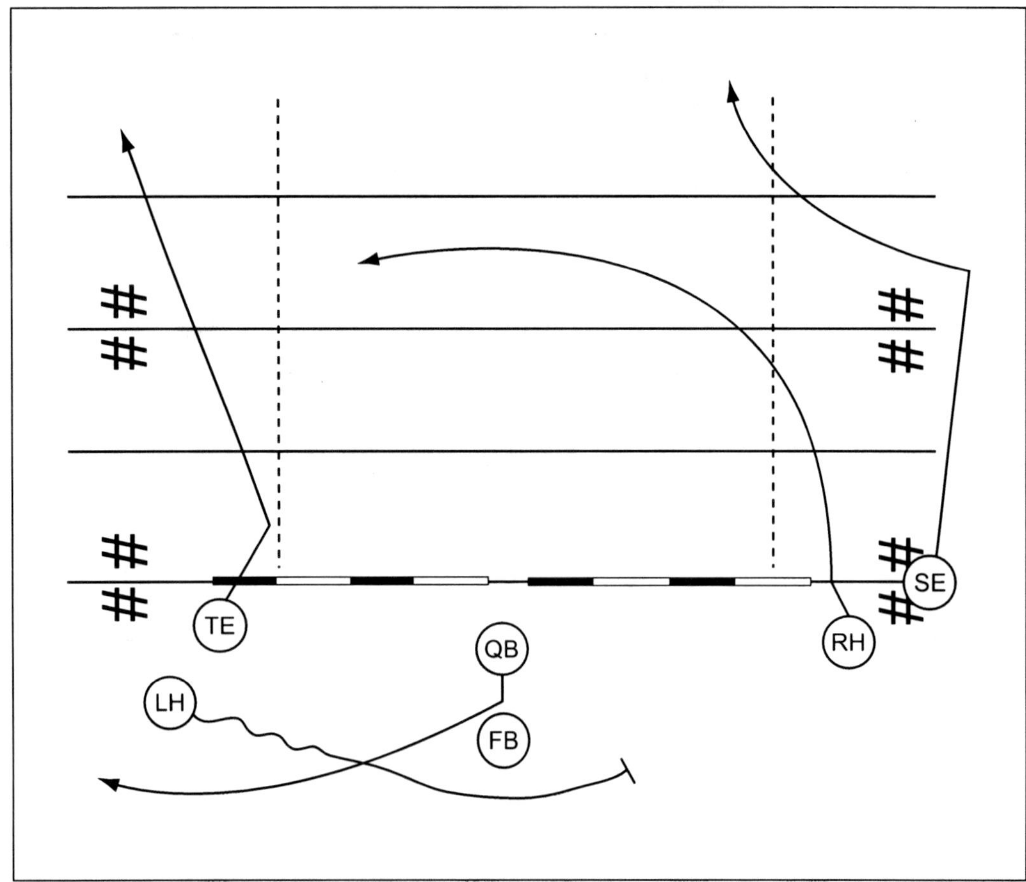

Goal Post Receiving Drill

Objective: To teach receivers to catch passes using only their hands and no other part of their body.

Equipment Needed: Footballs and a goal post

Description: Align all of the receivers in a single file line behind the goal post. The coach is the thrower in this drill and will stand on the goal line 10 yards from the receivers. Only one receiver at a time will run this drill. The receiver catching the ball walks up behind the goal post and puts his hands around the post, so the post is between his body and his hands. On the coach's command, the receiver running the drill will extend his hands and catch the ball without the use of any other part of his body.

Coaching Points: The receiver must concentrate on the fundamentals of the catch, but not the tuck and cover. He must hook the ball into the diamond formed by his thumbs and forefingers and secure the ball with hands only.

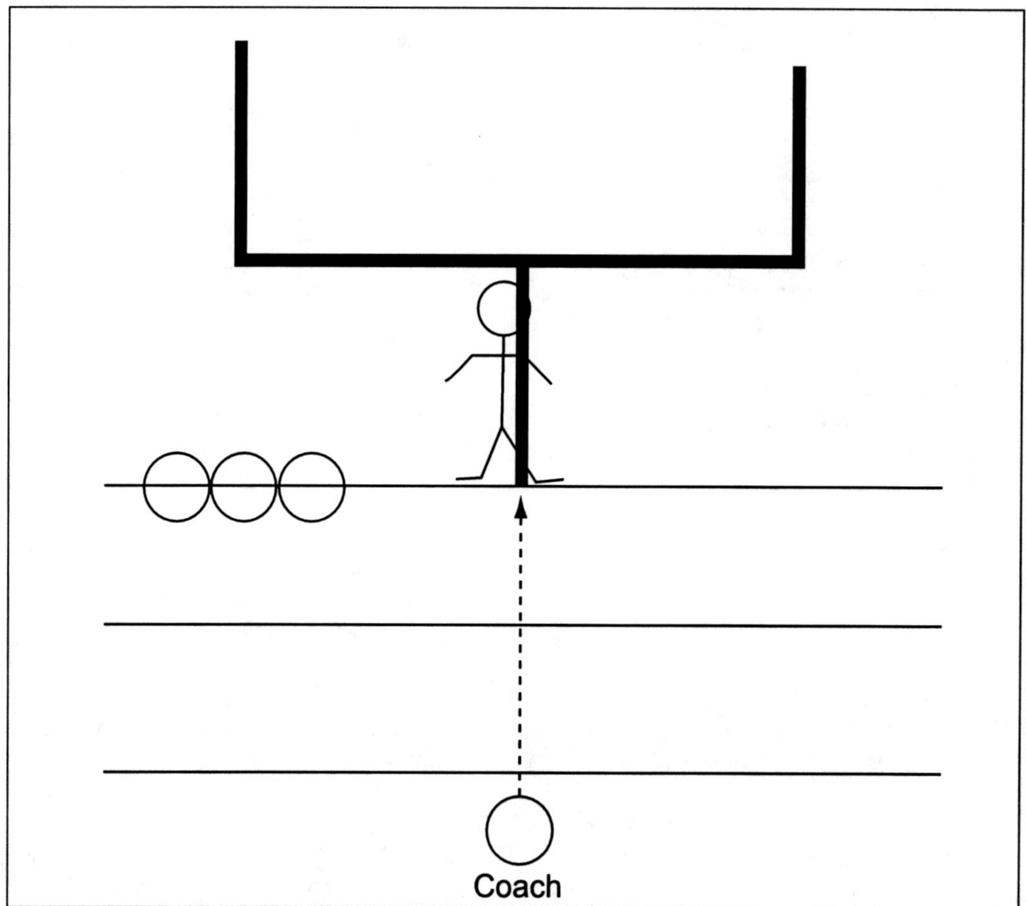

About the Author

Dennis Creehan is the defensive coordinator for the Calgary Stampeders of the Canadian Football League, a position he assumed in 2004. One of the most respected coaches in the game, his more than three decades of coaching experience includes successful stints at the high school, collegiate, and professional levels.

Creehan began his coaching career (1971-'74) at Keystone Oaks High School in Pittsburgh, Pennsylvania, after a stellar playing career as a strong safety at Edinboro University. A three-year starter for the Scots, Creehan served as team captain in his senior season, earned first-team all-ECAC accolades, and helped lead Edinboro to Lambert Bowl honors. At Keystone Oaks, he served as offensive coordinator and also coached wrestling and baseball.

In 1974, Creehan joined Johnny Majors' staff at the University of Pittsburgh, where he spent one year as a graduate assistant. He then served as the offensive coordinator at Carnegie-Mellon for a single season, before returning to his alma mater as defensive coordinator prior to the 1976 season. Three years later, in 1979, Creehan was elevated to the position of head football coach at Edinboro. During his six years at the helm of the Fighting Scots' gridiron program, his teams won two league titles and were nationally ranked four times. During his tenure at Edinboro, his teams posted a 39-20-1 record (.658)—a winning percentage that continues to rank as the highest in Edinboro football history. For his efforts with the Fighting Scots, he received three conference coach-of-the-year honors.

From 1985 to 1987 and 1991 to 1992, he served as the defensive line coach and special teams coordinator for the Edmonton Eskimos of the Canadian Football League. During his tenure with the Eskimos, Edmonton was 35-16, won two conference titles (1986 and 1991), and appeared in the Grey Cup (1986).

From 1987 to 1989, Creehan was the outside linebackers' coach at the University of California, Berkeley. He then moved to San Francisco State in 1990, where he served as the head football coach and assistant athletic director for the Gators for a year.

In 1992, Creehan was named head football coach at South Dakota. During his five years at the helm of the Coyotes, Creehan resuscitated a struggling program, leading his teams to 28 wins, including 26 in his last three years. In 1997, Creehan moved to Arkansas State, where he served as defensive coordinator for a season, before joining the staff at Rutgers University as the Scarlet Knights' defensive coordinator—a position he held for three years.

Creehan then served as the special teams coordinator at Duke University for two seasons (2001-2002), where he also worked with the Blue Devils' inside and outside linebackers. In 2003, he joined the staff at the United States Military Academy as the Black Knights' special teams coordinator.

Creehan is widely considered as one of the most knowledgeable coaches in the game on the Wing-T offense. He has written several books on the Wing-T and has been featured on more than a dozen well-received instructional videos on his popular offensive system.

A Hall of Fame member at both Bethel Park (PA) High School and Edinboro University, Creehan earned master's degrees from both Duquesne University in 1973 and Pittsburgh in 1977. He and his wife, Linda, have two sons: Kevin, a professor at Virginia Tech University, and Casey, an assistant football coach at James Madison University.